I0755066

SHAKESPEARE'S HOUSE AS IT NOW APPEARS.

WILLIAM
SHAKESPEARE
AS HE LIVED.

An Historical Tale.

BY CAPTAIN CURLING,

AUTHOR OF "JOHN OF ENGLAND." "SOLDIER OF FORTUNE."

"Sweet are the uses of adversity,
Which like the toad, ugly and venomous,
Wears yet a precious jewel in his head."
As you Like it.

WARWICK:

H. T. COOKE & SON, PUBLISHERS, HIGH STREET.

PREFACE.

THE nature of the following work is sufficiently indicated by the title. In it the most interesting portions of the career of Shakespeare, taken from the best accredited sources, are brought forward in a pleasing narrative, the dialogue being in the style of the Elizabethan period.

Throughout the work the writer has endeavoured, amidst a great deal of stirring incident, and a subordinate tale of much interest, to place the Poet constantly before the reader, whether on or off the scene. The story commences when he was about seventeen years of age, and carries him through some of the eventful "chances" of that glorious epoch which called forth his own "muse of fire," and caused him to ascend "the brightest heaven of invention;" and, after showing him the sharp "uses of adversity," leaves him at the moment of success, whilst Elizabeth and the entire Court-circle are turned to him whose matchless genius has just enchanted them.

CONTENTS.

CONTENTS.

WILLIAM SHAKESPEARE

AS HE LIVED,

STRATFORD-UPON-AVON, AND QUEEN ELIZABETH.

CHAPTER I.

A FOREST SCENE.

It was one morning, during the reign of Elizabeth, that a youth, clad in a grey cloth doublet and hose (the usual costume of the respectable country tradesman or apprentice in England), took his early morning stroll in the vicinity of a small town in Warwickshire.

Lovely as is the scenery in almost every part of this beautiful county, which exhibits, perhaps, the most park-like and truly English picture in our island, it was (at the period of our story) far more beautiful than in its present state of cultivated improvement.

The thick and massive foliage of its woods, in Elizabeth's day, were to be seen in all the luxuriance of their native wildness, unpruned, unthinned, untouched by the hand of man, representing in their bowery beauty the wild uncontrolled woodlands of Britain, when waste, and wold, and swamp, and thicket constituted all.

The fern-clad undulations and forest glades around, too, at this period, were peopled by the wild and herded deer—those "poor, dappled fools—the native burghers of the desert city"—which, couched in their own confines, their antlered heads alone seen in some sequestered spot amongst the long grass, gave an additional charm to the locality they haunted, in all the freedom of unmolested range, from park to forest, and from glade to thicket.

In these bosky bournes and sylvan retreats, unmolested then by the axe of an encroaching population; nay, almost untrodden, save by the occasional forester or the fierce outlaw; the gnarled oaks threw their broad arms over the mossy carpet, giving so deep a shade in many parts, that the rays of the mid-day sun were almost intercepted, and the silent forest seemed dark, shadowy, and massive, as when the stately tramp of the soldiery of Rome sounded beneath its boughs.

As the youth cleared the enclosures in the immediate vicinity of the town, and brushed the dew from the bladed grass on nearing the more sylvan scene, the deep tones of the clock, from the old dark tower of the church, struck the third hour. The sound arrested him; he paused, and turning, gazed for some moments upon the buildings now seen emerging from the mist of early morning. At this hour no sign of life —no stir was to be observed in the town.

> "The cricket sang, and man's o'er-labour'd sense
> Repaired itself by rest."

Although the youth looked upon a scene familiar to his eye (for it was the place of his birth, and from whence as yet his truant steps had scarcely measured a score of miles), his capable eye dwelt upon every point of interest and beauty in the surrounding picture.

He had reached the age when the poetry of life begins to be felt; when an incipient longing for society of the softer sex, and an anxiety to look well in the eyes of the fair; to deserve well of woman, and to be thought a sort of soldier-servant and defender of beauty, is mixed up with the sterner ambitions of manhood.

Perhaps few forms would have been more likely to captivate the fancy of the other sex than the figure and face of this youth, as he stood at gaze in the clear morning air, and contemplated the landscape around. In shape, he was slightly but elegantly formed, and his well-knit limbs were seen to advantage in the close-fitting but homely suit he wore. Added to this figure of a youthful Apollo, was a countenance of genius, intelligence, and beauty, peculiarly indicative of the mind of the owner. His costume, we have already said, was homely; it was, indeed, but one remove from the dress of the common man of the period. A gray doublet of coarse cloth, edged or guarded with black, and tight-fitting trunks and hose of the same material; to these were added a common felt hat with steeple crown, and shoes without rosettes. In his hand he carried a stout quarter-staff, shod with iron at either end. No costume, however, could disguise or alter the nobility of look and gallant bearing of that youth. After regarding the view presented to him in the clear morning air for some moments, he turned, leaped the last enclosure which pertained to the suburbs of the town, and pursued his way through a wild chase or park, avoiding the more thick woods on his right.

How slight and trivial are sometimes the accidents which control the fate of man!

On setting out from his own home, the stripling had intended to traverse the woodlands which lay between his native town and Warwick, in order to keep an appointment he had made with some youthful associates of the latter place—some wild and reckless young men with whom he had lately become acquainted. The church clock, however, whilst it informed him he had anticipated the hour, determined him to change his intention of going straight to the trysting-place, and he turned his steps in a different direction. He therefore left the deep woodlands on his right, and sought the enclosures of Clopton Hall.

This change of purpose, in all probability, saved the life of the handsome lad. As he turned from the woodlands on his right, and sought the fern-clad chase and plantations in which Clopton Hall is embosomed, a tall, fierce-looking man, clad in the well-worn suit of a ranger or forester, stepped from the thick cover. As he did so, the forester lowered a cross-bow, with which he had been taking a steady aim at the stripling, from his shoulder, and stood and watched him till he disappeared.

"Now the red pestilence strike him," said the man. "He has again escaped me. But an I give him not the death of a fat buck ere many days are over his head, may my bow-string be the halter that hangs me."

"Nay, comrade," said a second forester, at that moment coming forward, "believe me, 'tis better as it is; thou must e'en drop this business, and satisfy thy revenge by a less matter than murder. I half suspected thy intent, and, therefore, have I followed thee. Come," he continued, "thou must, I say, forgive the affront this lad has put upon thee."

"May the fiend take me then!" returned the ruffian.

"Nay, thou art most likely the property of St. Nicholas methinks. Whatsoever thou dost," said the other, "certainly he will catch thee by the back if thou should harm this youngster."

"Why, look ye," said his fellow. "Have I not reason for what I do? The varlet (who I shrewdly suspect hath an eye upon the deer) constantly haunts our woods. Not a nook, not a secluded corner, not a thicket but he knows of, and explores. At all hours of the day, and even at night, have I caught sight of him wandering alone. Sometimes I have seen him, lying along, book in hand, under a huge oak, in Fullbrook wood; at other times I have watched him as he stood in the twilight beside the brook, which flows through Charlecote Park. As often as I have tried to gain speech with and warn him from our haunts, he has been ware of me; plunging into the covert (nimble as a stag), so escaped.

"Once, however, I came warily behind him while he stood watching the deer as they swept along a glade in Fullbrook; and heard him repeating words which rivetted me to the spot, nay almost took from me the power of accosting him. Not, however, to be outworded by a boy, I pounced upon him."

"Go to!" said the other laughing, "then you collared him, I suppose, and took him off to the head-ranger to give an account of his trespass. Was't not so! Eh?"

"You shall hear," returned the ranger. "At first I felt too much respect to rebuke him. There was something in his look I could not away with. He seemed somewhat angered too at being molested and caught by surprise; and there was that in his eye which could look down a lion, methought. After awhile, however, I gave him some of my mind, threatened to report his trespass to the knight our master, and to give him a taste of the stocks, or the cage."

"Good," said his fellow, laughing. "You said well!"

"Nay, 'twas not so good either, as it turned out," said the ranger.

"How so?" inquired his comrade.

"Why, he took my rebuke mildly at first, merely saying he sought not to molest the game, but only to enjoy the liberty, freedom, and leisure of the wild woods."

"Well," interrupted the other, "between ourselves, that seems natural enough. But, an all the lads in the country were to do the same, they would soon drive the deer from their haunts, and render our trade a poor one."

"So I told him; and that I should not be so easy the next time I caught him straying in our woods. Nay, that I would then, indeed, cudgel him like a dog."

"Ha! ha! and how took he that threat?"

"Mass! I would you could have seen how he took it," said the irate ranger, "for I shall never forget the change it wrought. He looked at me with an eye of fire, reared himself up like a startled steed, and railed on me in such terms as I think never man either heard or spoke before. Nay, an I had not known he was the son of a trader here in Stratford, I had taken him for the heir of some grandee, for never heard I before such a tongue, or such words of fire."

"Go to!" said the other; "and how answered ye that?"

"At first I felt awed; but, when he dared me but to raise a finger in the way of assault, and stirred my wrath so, that I laid hands on him, he struck me to the earth; when I rose, and again attacked him, despite my skill at quarter-staff, he cudgelled me to his heart's content."

"What, yonder lad?"

"Ay, yonder boy! His strength and skill were so great that, had I not cried *peccavi*, I had died under his blows."

"And for this you are resolved to shoot him!"

"I am! I cannot forget the disgrace of his quarter-staff. My very bones ache now at the bare remembrance."

"Aye, but thou must forget it, comrade," said the other; "for to shoot him, look ye, might get the rangers all into trouble. He hath, you see, gone out of our bounds this morning; but let us follow, and if we find him we will both beat him. As far as that goes, I am your man. 'Tis allowable, and in the way of business. But for shooting the lad—fie on't! 'tis cowardly and dangerous. Ever while you live, forbear your bullet on a defenceless person."

"Well, be it so!" said his fellow. "I agree. He hath had the best of me, for once in his life. But, at least, will I be revenged:—blow for blow."

"Hath he good friends, said ye?"

"None of note."

"What then is his father?"

"The wool-comber who dwells in Henley Street."

"Enough! Now let us but catch him, and by 'r lady, we'll beat him so that he shall scarce disport his curiosity amongst our woods again."

"Nay, but if we kill him?" said the other, with a sneer.

"Then must our master bear us out; we are hired to keep off all lurking knaves. By fair means or foul, it must be done. An we kill him, we'll e'en knock over a buck, and lay it to's charge. Swear we caught him red-handed in the fact, and there an end."

CHAPTER II.

THE YOUTHFUL SHAKESPEARE.

About a couple of hours after the above conversation between the two rangers, the subject of it might have been seen lying along, "like a dropt acorn," book in hand, under cover of the thick belt of plantation skirting the grounds of Clopton Hall. Occasionally, his gaze would turn upon the huge twisted chimneys and casements of the building, just now beginning to show symptoms of life. The thin blue smoke mounted into the clear air, and the diamond panes of the windows glittered in the morning sun. At this period the sports of the field formed the almost daily avocation of the country gentlemen in England. Men rose with the sun, and with hawk and hound and steed commenced the day at once. Scarce was the substantial breakfast thought of till it had been earned in the free air, amidst the woods and glades. Accordingly, as our student lay perdue in the covert, he beheld the falconer of the household of Clopton with the ready hawk, the grooms with the caparisoned steeds, the coupled hounds, and all the paraphernalia of the field.

The family of the Cloptons were not altogether unknown to the youth, and the hall being only a mile from the town, Sir Hugh was a sort of patron of Stratford, and in constant intercourse with the inhabitants.

As his party had ofttimes ridden through the streets, our hero had scarce failed to remark amongst the cavalcade a beautiful female of some seventeen years of age. This fair vision, who with hawk on hand, looked some nymph or goddess of the chase, was, indeed, the only daughter of Sir Hugh Clopton.

To one of the ardent and poetic soul of our young friend, the mere passing glance of so exquisite a creature as Charlotte Clopton had suggested more than one sonnet descriptive of her beauty. Yes, the glance of the lowly poet from beneath the pent-house which constituted the shop of his father, had called forth verses which, even at this early period of his life, surpassed all that ever had been penned; and Charlotte Clopton first caused him to write a stanza in praise of beauty. At this early period of his life, too, his fine mind teemed with the germs of those thoughts which, in afterdays, brought forth. so many lovely flowers. The impression of his own passionate feelings in youth furnished him with the ideas from which to pourtray the exquisitely tender scenes of his after-life.

To a youth of spirit, the sight of preparation for the sports of the field was full of excitement. Most men love the chase, but mostly those of a bold determined courage.

Participation in the sports of people of condition was, however, denied to the lad, as his condition in life barred him from aught beside the sight of others so engaged. His capacious mind conceived, however, at a glance, all the mysteries of wood-craft, and his truant disposition leading him to become a frequent trespasser, the haunts and habits of the wild denizens of the woods were familiar to him.

If, therefore, he was debarred from following the chase himself, he loved to see the hunt sweep by—

> "When the skies, the fountains, every region near,
> Seemed all one mutual cry."

In addition to this, there was an insatiable craving after information of every kind. He had been educated at the Free School of his native town, and had far outstripped all competitors in such lore as the academy afforded, and he now perused every book he could procure, making himself master of the subjects they treated of with wonderful facility. He was drinking in knowledge (if we may so term it) wherever it could be reached; whilst, in his truant hours, no shrub, no herb, no plant in nature escaped his piercing ken.

His exquisite imagination, unfettered and free as the air he breathed in the lovely scenery of his native country, created worlds of fancy, and peopled them with beings which only himself could have conceived. In the solitude of the deep woods he loved to dream away the hours.

> "On hill or dale, forest or mead,
> By paved fountain, or by rushy brook,"

it was his wont to imagine the elfin crew, as they "danced their ringlets to the whistling wind."

It was observed, too, amongst his youthful associates, that he seemed to know things by intuition. Those who were brought up to the different mechanical trades in the town or neighbourhood found in him a master of the craft at which they had worked. "Whence comes this knowledge," they inquired of each other, "and where hath he found time to pick it up?" "Body o' me," his father would ofttimes say, "but where hath our William learnt all this lore? Thus worded too! Master Cramboy, of the Free School, albeit he comes here continually to supper, and uses monstrous learned words in his discourse, never tells us of such things as this lad discourses to us." Neither was all this superfluous knowledge, "ill inhabited like Jove in a thatched house." He was already a poet, turned things to shape, and gave to airy nothing

"A local habitation and a name."

CHAPTER III.

CHARLOTTE CLOPTON.

Clopton Hall was situated in a sort of wild chase, or park, in which hundreds of broad, short-stemmed oaks grew at distant intervals; and through this chase a deep trench had been cut in former days by the legions of Rome, the thick plantation which formed the belt immediately around the house being just in rear of the Roman ditch.

The hawking party, on this morning, as they gradually assembled and mounted their steeds in the court of the mansion, rode through the gatehouse, along the avenue and into the chase. Here they breathed their coursers and careered about till Sir Hugh had mustered the different servitors and attendants appertaining to a matter of so much moment as his morning diversion, and was ready to go forth.

As they did so, the youth noticed the lady he had before seen, and whose exquisite form had made some slight impression upon his imagination. Nothing could be more skilful than the way in which she managed her horse, he thought—nothing more lovely and graceful than she altogether appeared. The steed she rode was a magnificent animal, and one which none but a most perfect horsewoman could have backed; and as he plunged, and "yerked out his heels," he shewed his delight at being in the free air, and proved "the metal of his pasture."

It was a fair sight to behold one so delicately formed as that lady restrain the ferocity, and, by her noble horsemanship, reduce to subjection the wild spirit of that courser; and so thought the studious boy in the gray jerkin.

Well, however, as she had hitherto managed the animal, now that it was growing even more excited by the number of horses around, it seemed every instant becoming more and more unruly. It was in vain that a tall handsome cavalier, who had kept an anxious eye for some time upon the movements of her horse, now spurred his own steed beside the lady, and kept near her bridle-rein. The brute reared, and stood for a few moments, striking wildly with his fore feet. After a while, however, and whilst all sat in helpless alarm, the lady still keeping her seat, the steed recovered himself, plunged forwards, and bolted from the party.

Few situations could be more perilous than that which Charlotte Clopton now found herself in; few more distressing to the spectators to witness; since to attempt aid is ofttimes to hasten the catastrophe.

To follow a runaway steed, in the hope of overtaking it is, perhaps, one of the worst plans that can be adopted, as the very companionship of the pursuing horse is sure to urge on and accelerate the pace of the flyer.

Yet this course the tall dark cavalier (who seemed Charlotte Clopton's principal esquire) unhappily adopted.

As he beheld the maddened horse tearing across the park, swerving amongst the oak trees, and threatening every instant to dash out the brains of the rider amongst the branches, he set spurs to his own courser, and galloped after her. It was in vain that Sir Hugh shouted to him to return. In vain he roared and railed, and called to him that he would murder his child by such folly.

The lady, however, kept her seat. She managed even to guide her steed into the more open part of the chase. For (like the mariner in the storm) she well knew that whilst the tempest roars loudest, the open sea gives the vessel the better chance.

The sound of the horse following, however, totally ruined her plan, and rendered her own steed more determined. He flung aside, turned from the direction his rider had coaxed him into, and galloped towards the spot where our hero was standing amidst the trees. It was by no means difficult to conjecture that destruction to the beautiful creature, thus borne along as if on one of the "couriers of the air," was almost inevitable.

The next minute, as the youth of the grey doublet, in a state of breathless anxiety, stood and watched this race, himself concealed in the thick foliage, the horse (like some wild deer seeking cover) plunged headlong into the Roman ditch.

The entrenchment was of considerable depth, so that both steed and rider, for the moment, disappeared below the grassy ridge. It was, however, but for a moment: the next, the maddened steed sprung up the opposite bank.

The rider was, however, no longer on his back: she had been cast headlong from the saddle, and our hero saw, with terror, that her riding-gear was entangled on the saddle, and that she was being dragged along the ground by its side.

But few minutes of exposure to such a situation, and that sweet face had been spurned out of the form of humanity, and her delicate limbs broken, torn, and lacerated. But the youth (although he saw at once that it would be vain to attempt to arrest the powerful brute by seizing the bridle) in a moment resolved upon a bolder measure. As the horse neared him, he rushed from his concealment and (ere it could swerve from his reach), with the full swing of his heavy quarter-staff, struck the animal full upon its forehead, and with the iron at the extremity of his weapon, fractured its skull.

So truly and well was the blow delivered, that the steed fell as if struck by a butcher's pole-axe, and the next instant was a quivering carcase upon the grass,

In another moment the achiever of this deed had unsheathed the sharp dagger he wore at his waist-belt, cut away the entangled garment of the lady from the saddle, and was kneeling beside her insensible form. As he did so, he felt that he could have spent hours in gazing upon those lovely features.

Meanwhile, the cavalier who had followed (but who reined up his horse when he observed the steed of the lady dash down the slope, and then remained gazing on all that followed in a state of utter helplessness), so soon as he beheld the extraordinary manner in which she had been succoured, again set spurs to his horse.

Dashing recklessly across the Roman trench, he galloped to the spot, and throwing himself from the saddle, snatched the lady from the supporting arms of her rescuer.

There was a retiring diffidence, an innate modesty about the youth who had aided the lady, which kept him from intrusion. Nevertheless, he felt hurt at the manner in which the handsome cavalier had snatched her from his arms. His indomitable spirit prompted him almost to thrust back that officious friend, and like Valentine, exclaim—

"Thurio, give place, or else embrace thy death:
I dare thee but to look upon my love!"

The next moment, however, remembrance of his own condition, and the station in life of her he had saved, flashed across his brain. He drew a pace or two back, and recollected how far removed he was from her he had so promptly succoured. As for the attendant cavalier, he seemed to see nothing but the still insensible form he hung over. "Oh! thank heaven, Oh! thank heaven, she breathes," he said wildly, "she is not dead—speak to me, Charlotte—speak but one word to your poor cousin, if but to assure him of your safety."

"I think she is recovering, fair sir," said the youth, again approaching. "See, she opens her eyes."

"She does—she does!" said the cavalier, as he raised her in his arms. "I would we had a few drops of water to sprinkle in her face; 'twould do much towards hastening her recovery."

"That shall she soon have," said the youth; and darting off, he hastened towards a rivulet, which, brawling along on the other side of the plantation, ran through the marsh land beyond, and emptied itself into the Avon.

Taking off his high-crowned hat, he dipped it in the stream, and returned as speedily. As he did so he observed that Sir Hugh Clopton, and such of his party as were mounted, had now reached the spot; whilst the fair Charlotte, having regained her senses, was clasped in her fond father's arms.

Handing the water to one of the attendants, he again drew back, and leaning upon his quarter-staff, stood regarding the party unnoticed.

"Now praise be to heaven for this mercy," said Sir Hugh. "In my pride and joy of thee, my Charlotte, I bred yonder steed for thy especial use. I thought to see thee mounted as no other damsel in Warwickshire, and see the result. Ha, by my halidame, I swear to thee, that had not the brute perished in his own wilfulness I had killed him with this hand."

"Nay, blame not my poor Fairy," said the lady; "he did but follow the bent of his joyous spirit, when he found himself in the fresh pasture. 'Twas thy timely succour, coz," she said, turning to the tall cavalier beside her, "which I suspect saved me when I fell."

"By my troth then, nephew," said the old knight, grasping the youth's hand, "'twas well done of thee, and thou hast redeemed thy first fault in following the runaway horse."

"Alas, uncle," said the cavalier, "I fear me I have redeemed no fault, neither deserve I any praise. I saw my fair cousin cast headlong to the earth, and then dragged beneath the heels of yonder horse. No mortal help, it appeared, could avail her. I felt the blood rush to my brain; I was about to fall from my saddle, when lo, a lad stepped from beside the trunk of yonder oak, I heard a heavy crashing blow, I saw Fairy fall as if pierced by a bullet in the brain, and I found thee, Charlotte, saved. And that reminds me," continued the cavalier, looking round, "he who did this gallant deed was this moment by my side."

"Ha, say'st thou, Walter," said the burly knight, "where, then, be this lad whom we have not even thanked for his service? Stand back, my masters."

As Sir Hugh spoke the attendants fell back, and discovered the graceful figure of the youth in the grey doublet, as he leant beside the tree. The old knight immediately stepped up, and grasping the youth by the hand, led him into the circle, whilst the young cavalier was more fully describing to the lady the bold and instantaneous manner in which she had been rescued.

The youth sank on one knee, and taking the lady's hand, pressed it to his lips. "Believe me, lady," he said, "the delight I experience in serving one so fair and exquisite, a thousand times o'erpays the duty."

"Why, gad a mercy," said the old knight, "thou art a high-flown champion, methinks. Nevertheless, lad, we are indebted to thee in more than we can either dilate on, or thou listen to with patience fasting. Let us return to the house, my masters all.

"Come Sir Knight of the quarter-staff," he continued, "'fore gad, we'll not part with thee till we have learnt how to do thee good service.

"Yet stay," he said, as he was preparing to mount, and whilst steadily regarding the youth, "art not of the town here? Have I not seen thy goodly visage somewhere in Stratford? Troth have I. Why man, thou art the son of my respected neighbour, the wool-comber in Henley Street—John Shakespeare."

"His eldest son, an it so please ye," said the youth, blushing.

"'Fore Heaven, and so thou art!" said Sir Hugh. "And what, good Philip?—is not thy name Philip?"

"William," said the youth.

"And what good wind, then, good William Shakespeare, hath blown thee so opportunely this morning to our neighbourhood?"

"Marry, the same wind, good Sir Hugh," said a tall, dark-looking man, dressed in the habiliments of a forester, and accompanied by a companion quite as ill-favoured as himself, and who at this moment thrust himself into the circle: "the same ill wind, Sir Hugh, that makes him haunt every wood and dell in the county."

This interruption somewhat startled the party. Sir Hugh turned and looked at him with surprise, whilst the object of the remark of the forester in an instant confronted the man. "Thou art an insolent caitiff," he said, "thus to speak of one of whom thou knowest nothing."

"An I know nothing of thee," said the forester contemptuously, "'tis more than my comrade here can testify. By the same token, thou has stolen upon his forest-walk, 'will he, nill he,' and beaten him on his own beat, as it were, and so put him to shame."

"And I am as like to do the same by thee with the like provocation," returned young Shakespeare. "Thy comrade laid hands upon me, and dishonoured me by a blow. For the which," he continued, significantly, "*I beat him.*"

"And for which," returned the forester, "we have followed thee hither; and, time and opportunity serving, will return the beating with interest. Thou art warned, so look to thyself, and keep from our woods in future."

"Gramercy," said Sir Hugh, now interrupting the dispute, "but what saucy companions are these?"

"We are outlying keepers of Sir Thomas Lucy, of Charlecote, Sir Hugh," said the man, doffing his hat, and making a leg.

"Outlying, I think, by'r Lady," said Sir Hugh, "in every sense of the word. Thou hast railed on thyself, Sir Ranger, in accusing this youth of the offence of trespass, since thou art even now thyself trespassing here, and putting an affront upon a youth whom it is our pleasure to hold in good esteem. Begone, lest I give my people a hint to cudgel thee for thy presumption."

"Nay, then our master shall hear of it," said the keeper; "an thou encouragest those who lurch upon his grounds, the sword must settle it."

"'Tis with thy master I *will* settle it, thou arrant knave," said Sir Hugh; "I talk not with such caitiffs."

"And yet dost thou take up with yonder son of a trader in Stratford town," said the fellow, with a sneer. "'Want of company,' saith the proverb. Eh?"

"Hark ye, sirrah!" said young Shakespeare (like lightning seizing the keeper by the green frock, and forcing him up to the dead horse), "trader or noble, I warn thee to put no further affront upon me before this fair company; for, by the hand that brained yon steed, I can as easily teach thee as awful a lesson. Begone!" he continued. "I am alike ready to meet thee on thine own or other grounds, singly or together, with quarter-staff, or rapier and target."

The man looked cowed, he glanced towards his comrade, and both disappeared.

CHAPTER IV.

THE FAMILY OF THE CLOPTONS.

To Charlotte Clopton the introduction of the stranger youth, the relation her cousin gave of his opportune appearance, and the ready manner in which he had rescued her, seemed like some dream.

Indeed, under circumstances such as she now for the first time beheld the youthful poet, he was scarcely to be regarded, we opine, by a lady's eye with impunity.

Rendered insensible, as we have seen, by her severe fall, on recovery she found herself almost miraculously saved from a dreadful death. Whilst he who had rescued her, appeared to have come to her assistance "like some descended god."

"Who ever loved, that loved not at first sight?" The heart of Charlotte was from that moment hopelessly, irrecoverably, lost.

The family of the Cloptons was of ancient descent. Sir Hugh was a widower, having no other offspring but the daughter we have already introduced to our readers. Of suitors doubtless the fair Charlotte might have had plenty and to spare; for, when broad lands are coupled with exceeding beauty,

> "From the four corners of the earth they come
> To kiss the shrine."

Sir Hugh had, however, made election for his daughter, of one who had been her companion from childhood, a cousin of her own, Walter Arderne. This young man, who was now about two and twenty years of age, absolutely doated on his affianced bride. His fortune was ample, and the woods of Arderne could be seen from the grounds of Clopton. Added to this he was extremely handsome, of a most amiable and generous disposition, brave as the steel he wore, and "complete in all good grace to grace a gentleman."

And yet withal, although Charlotte loved him as a brother, esteemed him as a friend, and had been taught to regard him as her future husband, to entertain any more tender feelings towards him she found impossible.

Still, Walter Arderne being thus the constant companion, the affianced husband of Charlotte, although numerous other cavaliers saw, and seeing, admired, their brief bow was soon made. They saw—they were smitten by the blind bow-boy—but they felt that the prize was appropriated worthily and withdrew.

Few men, indeed, were more worthy of a lady's eye than Walter Arderne. Gentle, generous, and frank, as we have before described him—rich and handsome withal—it seems scarcely possible that his fair cousin could fail in returning the strong love he felt for her. Yet so it was, and whether this love "chosen by another's eye" was distasteful to her, or that she thought the near relationship any bar to a more tender feeling, it is certain the very thought of her betrothment was disagreeable. Still Walter had been her friend, her companion, and her champion from childhood's hour, and under his fostering care and tuition she had become a sort of Dian of the woods and groves. Dearly did she love the bounding steed and the chase: the wild, the wold, the hawk, and the free air.

Her father's wishes also were law to her, and as she found it would be a terrible disappointment to him were she to own her dislike to a marriage with her cousin, she had suffered the engagement to remain unchallenged.

For centuries the Cloptons had seemed a doomed race; as if some ban was upon them they had been strangely unlucky by flood and field. Gentle by birth, noble in spirit, and in the enjoyment of all the world could give, they seemed doomed to be unfortunate. There was even a melancholy about the old hall itself consequent upon the mishaps and disasters that appeared the hereditary portion of the family. The sons were brave, their banner ever in the van, but they fell early in the fight. The daughters were chaste as they were beautiful, but an early grave had almost always closed over them. Nay, the villagers called the old manor-house the house of mourning, so invariably had most of its numerous occupants been swept off. An old legend (they affirmed) proclaimed this near extinction of the line of Clopton, and that the hall would be unlucky whilst their race continued its owners.

The brave old knight, gentle and even-tempered as he was, and whom on ordinary provocation it was difficult to anger, was peculiarly sensitive on this subject. Any allusion to the wild legend from a servitor, or rustic on his estate, would be sure to be followed by displeasure or dismissal; whilst mention of it from one in his own rank would have been considered equivalent to an invitation to the dark walk at the end of the pleasance, armed with rapier and dagger.

Sir Hugh had beheld his children fade away, apparently of hereditary disease, one after another in their early youth; all except the beautiful Charlotte, the pledge of a second marriage, and whose mother had died soon after giving birth to this their only child, and he was in consequence tremblingly alive to the slightest alarm of accident or illness. It was under such circumstances that Sir Hugh, in accepting the guardianship of his nephew, had learned to look upon the well-favoured Walter almost with the eye of a parent, and had set his heart upon a marriage between him and his lovely child.

Under such circumstances, too, had young Shakespeare performed the piece of service we have described,—a service beyond reward (as the old knight worded it), beyond aught he had to bestow; and it was under such circumstances that the youth became an occasional visitor at Clopton Hall, where he was admitted on an equality with the inmates, and received in a manner perhaps no other circumstances would have been likely to lead to.

The line drawn between persons of different condition in life was then more strictly kept, and more accurately defined than in our own day. But the good sense of Sir Hugh led him to appreciate superior attainments wherever they were to be found. The ignorance of youth proceeded, he thought, from idleness; the continuance of ignorance in manhood from pride—the pride which is less ashamed of being ignorant than of seeking instruction. At Clopton, therefore, men of worth were received, even though of low estate.

CHAPTER V.

A DOMESTIC PARTY IN ELIZABETH'S DAY.

On the evening of the day on which the accident had happened to Charlotte Clopton, that lady, together with her father, her cousin Walter, and young Shakespeare, were assembled in an ample apartment at Clopton Hall, situate on the ground floor, the windows looking out upon the lovely pleasure-grounds in the rear of the building. The youth had spent the entire day at the hall, and in the society of those to whom he had rendered so great a service.

Indeed any person (albeit he might not so well deserve consideration by this good family) would still have been a cherished guest; nay, even an "unmannered churl," under the same circumstances, would have been tolerated and made much of; but in this lad, Sir Hugh and his family found something so extraordinary, so superior, and of so amiable a disposition, that it appeared a blessing and an honour to have him as an associate beneath their roof.

Those who can associate with persons above them in rank, it has been said, and yet neither disgust or affront them by over-familiarity, or disgrace themselves by servility, prove that they are as much gentlemen by nature as their companions are by rank and station. If our readers wish to picture the youthful Shakespeare's first introduction into "worshipful society," and amongst people of condition of his day, and where he received those first impressions from which some of his delicious scenes have been drawn, they must imagine to themselves a large and somewhat gloomy oak-pannelled room, whose principal ornament is the huge elaborately-carved chimney-piece, which, in truth, seems to occupy one entire side of the apartment, and appears inclined also to march into the very centre thereof. The apartment (albeit it was, as we have said, by no means stinted to space, and had an exceeding quiet, retired, and comfortable look withal) was by no means constructed or fashioned after the more approved style of modern architecture. The ceiling was somewhat low, traversed by an enormous beam, and cut and carved elaborately, displaying fruits and flowers, heraldic devices of the brave, and all those extraordinary and grotesque figures which the cunning architects of old were so fond of inventing. On the side of the apartment opposite the huge chimney-piece, and on which side hung several scowling and bearded portraits, stood a sort of spinnet or harpsichord, and beside that leant an instrument, fashioned somewhat like a bass viol of the present day, but of a more curious form, and elaborately inlaid with ivory, a viol-de-gamba, an instrument then much in vogue. Two ample casements which opened inwards, and which were festooned by creeping plants, the eglantine and sweet jessamine, and which casements, as we have before said, looked into the green and bowery garden, and through which the soft evening breeze of May breathed the most exquisite perfume, gave a sort of green and fairy light to the interior. A heavy oaken table with enormous legs was placed near the window. Upon it were to be seen a silver salver, with several bottles of antique and most exquisite pattern, containing liquors of comfortable appearance and delicious flavour. These were flanked by high glasses of Venetian workmanship. In addition to these articles, several high-backed cane-bottomed chairs and one or two stools formed the remaining furniture of the room, and which, in comparison with our own over-crowded style, would perhaps have been termed only half furnished.

Nic-nacs there were few or none. Two or three dull-faced miniature mirrors, looking all frame, hung heavily against the pannelling, and even a cross-bow, several rapiers, one or two matchlocks, and other weapons of ancient fashion, were to be observed; whilst, to complete the picture, on the ample hearth (although the room constituted what in the present day would have been called the withdrawing-room of the mansion) sprawled several of the smaller dogs then used in field sports, and an enormous hound, sufficiently large and powerful to pull down a stag; and in the enjoyment of the sight and flavour of the good wines placed before him, sat the portly form of the master of the house. Beside the open window stood the youthful cavalier Walter Arderne, and on one of the oaken lockers or benches in the embrazure of the casement, was seated Charlotte Clopton. As she leant her cheek upon her hand, one moment she gazed abstractedly into the bowery garden, the next her eyes wandered into the softened light of the interior of the apartment, and rested upon the features of her deliverer, young Shakespeare. This youth stood beside the spinnet, and (unconscious of the sensation his narrative produced upon the ears and hearts of his hearers, and of the beauty of the description) was giving them the plot of a tale in verse which he had that morning been perusing, when the lady's danger interrupted him.

He related the story briefly, but in such language that his listeners were wrapt by the recital. He even accompanied his description by some action, and where he wished to impress his hearers more especially he endeavoured to recollect and repeat the lines of the poem, piecing out the story, when memory failed him, with such verses as he made for the nonce.

In addition to these, the principal personages of our chapter, there was one other individual in the room, who (albeit he occupied the background of the scene, being crouched up in a corner) is also deserving of a description.

This was a sort of hanger-on, or appendage to the establishments of the old families of condition in England not then quite extinct—a sort of good familiar creature, attached to the master of the house principally, and indifferently familiar with all and sundry, in doors and out—a sort of humorist—a privileged, seeming half idiotic, though in reality extremely shrewd and clever companion, who used his folly "like a stalking-horse, under cover of which, he shot his wit;" but who was indeed more the friend than the fool of the family, and oft-times consulted on matters of moment by the good knight.

This individual, clad in somewhat fantastic costume, fashioned by himself, be it understood, and which it was his especial pleasure to wear, (for Sir Hugh would by no means have forced any one in his establishment to wear motley,) was seated in a huge high-backed armchair, in a corner of the apartment, where, with his legs drawn up under him on the cushion, his hands clasped together over his breast, and his thumbs in his mouth, he kept a shrewd eye upon the other occupants; the long ears of his cap every now and then, as they shook with a sort of nervous twitch of the head, alone proclaiming that he was not some stuffed ornament, occupying the position it was his wont usually to choose in the apartment.

The story Shakespeare had related seemed to have made an impression on his own youthful mind. It professed to pourtray that baneful passion jealousy—a passion which, when once indulged, is the inevitable destroyer of conjugal happiness. It formed one of the old romances then in vogue amongst such as delighted in reading of the sort; for in those days of leisure, sobriety, and lack of excitement amongst females in the country, reading, spinning, embroidery, and other ornamental needlework, principally occupied the hours of the elder; and out-door amusements and music the younger. Those females who were given to literature, however, would, in our times, have indeed been considered learned, since many (albeit they eschewed light reading) understood both the Greek and Latin tongues to perfection, and many were no less skilful in the Spanish, Italian, and French.

In the narration of this story, and whilst (as we have said) young Shakespeare gave his own version, might have been observed gleams of that mighty genius which was, in after-times, to astonish the world.

His relation had, indeed, much of the fire and descriptive beauty which he afterwards threw into every line of his writings. He called up before his hearers the fiery openness of the injured husband; boundless in confidence, ardent in affection. He touched upon the soft and gentle simplicity of the victim; her consciousness of innocence; and her slowness to suspect she could be suspected. And, lastly, he described the clever devil, the fiend-like and malignant accuser, with matchless power.

Indeed the enormity of the crime of adultery, and upon which this story touched so forcibly, was in after days (as our readers doubtless recollect) made by the great dramatic moralist the subject of not less than four of his finished productions.

Another thing remarkable, and which struck all present, was the facility with which, by a touch as it were, he ever and anon (and as if by some incomprehensible magic of description) impressed the climate and country, the manners and customs of the actors in this romance, upon the hearers.

The relation had, indeed, seemed to the auditors like a dramatic performance. The melody of the speaker's voice, and the lines he uttered, left his audience as we sometimes feel after the scenic hour. There was a want of some soother of the excitement produced.

The old knight felt this. He took his viol-de-gamba and drew his bow lightly across the strings, producing that silver and somewhat solemn sound which those who have heard the instrument so well remember—sounds suited to the hour, age, and scene, and which give their own impressions of days long passed away.

"Come, Charlotte," said Sir Hugh, after executing one of the pieces of music then in vogue, "now a madrigal in which all can join. This youth hath put a spell upon us with his sad story. Come, a madrigal; and after that our evening meal in the garden, beneath the mulberry-tree. Do thou take the first, whilst I and Walter chime in second and third, and Martin shall e'en do his best to help us."

"Nay, uncle," said Martin, jerking out his legs straight before him, then putting them to the ground gently, and then lightly executing a sort of somersault and coming forward, "I pr'ythee hold me excused. I shall but spoil your music: my voice is rugged. I am not gifted to sing squealingly with a lady. A psalm or so at church, or a quaver after supper I can execute; but my voice is like the howl of an Irish wolf when I sing a part with the lady Charlotte: blessings on her celestial throat."

"Nay, Martin," said Charlotte, as she seated herself, "thou wilt not refuse when I tell thee it is to pleasure our new friend, to whom we owe so much."

Martin glanced quickly upon Shakespeare, as she said this, and then slowly turned his eye upon the young lady.

He stroked his chin knowingly, and seemed to be considering them both very curiously. "Truly so," he said, "we do indeed owe much to this lad. May God requite the debt." So saying, the familiar walked to the window, and, looking affectionately in the handsome face of Walter, as he stood leaning against the casement and regarding Charlotte, he put his arm through that of the young cavalier, and remained beside him whilst the madrigal was sung; his own fine bass voice coming in with singular effect, and belying his modest assertion of incompetency.

To say that the voice of the lovely Charlotte delighted Shakespeare would be to say little; he felt ravished and enchanted, and it left an impression upon the young poet which he never forgot from that hour!

And oh! how calmly, how contentedly, and how quietly flowed the hours of private life even during such a reign of glory as that of the great and good Queen Bess!

In those days the whirl of events, the increasing villany of the world, the petty doings of the actors in this vale of tears, the very minutiæ of crime and sin, the most paltry acts "committed on this ball of earth," in town, city, village, and hamlet were not as now, printed and published and blown into every corner of the kingdom, a few hours after commission. Even the leading events of the day, the acts of the great amongst the nations of the earth, and all the stirring deeds going on in the world, and which shook and overturned thrones; even these travelled slowly, and though posts "came tiring on," still rumour, full of tongues, made oft-times many slanderous reports ere the true one was manifest.

To the country gentleman his domain was his little world, his court, wherein he received the homage of his neighbouring dependents and tenants.

The charm of life consisted in these pursuits, those associations—nay even those superstitions, and those antiquated customs which modern utilitarianism has driven from the world. Whilst, as we have said, mighty events shook the nation, men continued to pursue their even way in that station of life in which it had pleased Heaven to call them.

After the madrigal, the old knight, with the viol-de-gamba clutched between his legs, fell fast asleep, his wonted custom in the evening; and having gently relieved him from all care of the instrument by withdrawing it from his custody, Charlotte invited the trio to a stroll in the garden, where they held converse upon various matters, occasionally interrupted in their discourse by the quaint sayings and witticisms of the shrewd Martin.

CHAPTER VI.

A DISAGREEABLE VISITOR.

'Twas a pleasing picture, that old knight taking his evening nap in his oak pannelled room, so quiet and so retired, so undisturbed, except by the cooing of the wood-pigeon, or the distant bay of the hound in the kennel.

The evening breeze sighed drearily through the branches of the gigantic cedar-tree in the garden, and whispered softly through the luxuriant plants and shrubs which hung about the diamond-paned windows.

'Tis a sweet time that evening hour, in an old mansion far removed from the bustle of the world. The oak floor, too, in the centre of the apartment, was coloured faintly by the many tints reflected through the stained glass in the upper compartments of the windows, and where the arms and crest of the Cloptons were variously multiplied and emblazoned. The dark polished oak of the huge chimney-piece, as the shadows of evening descended, seemed framed of iron or ebony, the grotesque figures, here and there ornamenting the higher parts, with their demoniac faces and satyr-like bodies, seeming ready to pounce upon whoever came within their reach.

Whilst the old knight enjoyed his siesta, every now and then giving a sort of start in his deep sleep, or a prolonged snore, and then twitching his muscular face and changing his position, the door of the apartment was gently opened, and a tall shadowy figure, after hesitating for a few moments at the threshold, and looking round, entered cautiously, and approaching the sleeper stood and gazed long and fixedly at his countenance.

What a contrast might a looker-on have observed in those two faces! —the one round, ruddy, redolent of health, and shewing no traces of guilt or care; the other worn, pale, anxious, and cadaverous-looking. The broad brim of the stranger's hat was drawn down and pulled low over his forehead, his dark and grizzled hair looked thin and perished, matching well with the iron gray of his complexion, and his forked beard, presenting altogether a worn and haggard appearance, a man of dark passions, evil thoughts, and sinister disposition.

After gazing for some time at Sir Hugh, the stranger laid his heavy gauntlet upon his shoulder and suddenly awoke him.

The knight opened his eyes, stared at the dark countenance so suddenly presented to him for a few moments, and then starting up, stepped a pace or two back and laid his hand upon the hilt of his rapier.

The grim stranger smiled at the startled look of the old knight, "Fear me not, Sir Hugh," he said. "I come not with intent to do thee harm."

"Fear thee," said Sir Hugh contemptuously, "wherefore should I fear? But thou comest upon me in my secure hour here—and I know thee not. Stand off, lest I smite thee."

"That would be a poor reception for an old friend," said the other, smiling a grim smile.

"An old friend!" said Sir Hugh, in tones of surprise; "truly then thou art an old friend with a new face. May heaven protect me, if ever I looked upon that white-livered visage of thine before."

"Art thou quite sure of that, Sir Hugh Clopton?" said the stranger. "Look again; time and care and climate have written, I dare be sworn, strange defeatures in my face, but yet methinks twenty years ago the name of Parry was not altogether unknown at Clopton."

"Parry!" said Sir Hugh, starting; "art thou Gilbert Parry? and what doth the banished traitor Parry within my walls? Hence, sirrah; I wish for the companionship of no man polluted with crimes such as thine."

"Nay, soft, Sir Hugh," said the visitor, "I come with credentials from one thou darest not slight. Look ye, I am bearer of a letter from the Nuncio Campeggio, and I demand speech with Father Eustace, who dwells in thy house here."

Sir Hugh again started; he took the letter from the hand of his visitor, and read it attentively.

"Truly," he said, "the letter is as thou say'st. In it I find I am ordered to give thee shelter here for the space of one week; affording thee and those with whom thou consortest such secresy and seclusion as thou may'st desire. I dare not deny the hospitality so enjoined, but in good sooth I had as lief thou had'st sought it elsewhere, Gilbert Parry."

"'Tis well," said Parry, taking his riding-cloak from his shoulders; "Clopton hath secret chambers, I know, as well as that devoted servants of the Catholic Church dwell beneath its roof."

"May I not know," inquired Sir Hugh, "of the business which employs the talents of Gilbert Parry, and makes the Pope's Nuncio his introducer within my walls?"

"At more fitting opportunity perchance thou mayest," returned Parry, whose manner had become more assured after he observed the impression the letter he had delivered had made; "at the present moment I require rest and refreshment."

Sir Hugh said no more; he stepped to a concealed pannel beside the huge chimney-piece, and drawing it aside, ushered his guest into a small closet-like apartment, and then carefully closed the pannel again. A narrow winding staircase ascended from this small room into the chamber above, and which was only known or used by Sir Hugh himself, together with Martin and the priest, who occasionally visited at the Hall.

After entering, Sir Hugh signed to his guest to ascend the staircase.

"Thou wilt find every accommodation here in this chamber, he said, "and refreshment shall be served to thee by one I can trust. Father Eustace is at present absent from Clopton, but to-morrow I expect he will return."

"I would confer with him without delay," said Parry, "so soon as he returns."

"Be it so," said Sir Hugh, retiring from the apartment, and descending the stairs; seeming, as he did so, by his manner, not sorry to withdraw from the companionship of his new guest.

As soon as he had descended into the small apartment we have before described, he paused for a few moments, and then unlocked and opened a low postern door, which admitted into the garden, and, guided by the voices of his daughter and her party in the distance, immediately sought them.

It was by no means uncommon for the Catholics, during this reign, to hold secret intercourse with each other after the fashion we have just described, going from house to house with the utmost care; the more violent and remorseless making it their practice to seek refuge ofttimes amongst the quieter gentry, and, under cover of their respectability, carrying on their designs with greater security.

In pursuance of such custom, Sir Hugh's new visitor had now sought shelter at Clopton. He had, on that same evening, arrived at Stratford in company with others, and immediately on dismounting from his horse, had walked across the meadows, entered the grounds, and being well acquainted with the localities, introduced himself into the house without being seen by any one.

When Sir Hugh joined his daughter and her party, there was a something of anxiety upon his brow which was not usual with him. But so deeply interested were Charlotte and Walter Arderne with the conversation of their new formed acquaintance, that they observed it not. The quick eye, however, of the shrewd Martin (who so well knew his old master's habits) saw at a glance that something had puddled the clear spirit of the knight; and advancing towards him, they walked apart and held converse together.

"Is there ill news toward?" said Martin. "Something I perceive hath disturbed you, and broken in upon your slumbers."

"I have had a visitor, Martin," said Sir Hugh; "one with whom I had long closed the accounts of acquaintanceship as a dangerous companion."

"Know I the man?" inquired Martin.

"Like myself you did so," returned Sir Hugh; "but evil courses drove him from the country some years back. You remember Gilbert Parry?"

"What," said Martin, "he who was condemned to death as a traitor some five years ago, and to whom the Queen graciously granted a free pardon?"

"The same. He hath been with me just now."

"He was ever a restless dangerous knave," said Martin; "his visit might well have been spared. I trust it was a short one."

"Nay," said Sir Hugh, "he hath claimed the hospitality of Clopton on matters of moment connected with holy mother Church, and hath shewn me letters from the Nuncio Campeggio, and from Ragazoni at Paris."

"He comes from abroad, then, I dare be sworn," said Martin, "and on no good errand depend on't, and he makes Clopton his place of residence on his first arrival, in order to be in security whilst he spies into the localities, and sounds his instruments; ah, and by my fay, 'tis a crafty and a dangerous companion, whose designs may get us into trouble. But an I dive not into his contrivances I would I might never taste hippocras again."

"I would have thee do so, Martin, if it be possible," said Sir Hugh, "for I like not such guests; albeit, their visits are sanctioned and enjoined by the mighty in our Church. Nay, it was but last week I had a visit from Ralph Somerville, of Warwick, who held me in dangerous converse a whole hour, upon the necessity of smiting all heretics and persecutors. His discourses on religious matters shewed a distempered brain. Troth, I was glad to be rid of him."

"'Tis strange," said Martin, "to behold the spirit which everywhere actuates those who profess more religion than their neighbours, both Protestants and Catholics. By my faith, men will dispute upon the subject, cut a throat for religion, indite most learned matter appertaining,—anything but live for it."

"'Tis even so, Martin," said Sir Hugh with a sigh, "and therefore doth it behove us, and all those who are not of this bigoted and intolerant spirit, to guard our hearths from the danger of such association. A presentiment of evil is upon my mind since this man's coming, which I cannot shake off. Be it thy business to look to his wants this evening. To-morrow Father Eustace returns, and we shall then know more about his designs."

"Ah, that Eustace!" muttered Martin to himself. "Hath he ever seen this man?" he inquired aloud.

"I think not," said Sir Hugh; "they have never met to my knowledge."

"Enough," said Martin; "leave him to me. Now break we off, and let us join our party. See where the lady Charlotte leads her two attendant swains toward the house yonder. This new-found friend, Sir Hugh," continued Martin, "this youth, whose merits seem so far beyond his fortunes, is he likely to remain long at Clopton?"

"He tarries here to-night, Martin," said Sir Hugh, "and shall be ever welcome. We are deeply his debtor."

"Humph," said Martin significantly, "I supposed as much, and I suppose it must even be so,—*but*——"

CHAPTER VII.

PLOTS AND COUNTERPLOTS.

England, up to the period of Elizabeth's reign, at which our story has now arrived, had been blessed in the enjoyment of the most absolute security.

The scene, however, was now beginning to change, and multiplied dangers to threaten the maiden Queen from various quarters.

Scotland and its affairs gave Elizabeth continued uneasiness, and every new revolution amongst the wild and turbulent nobles of that rude land, caused her fresh anxiety, because that country alone being not separated from England by sea, and bordering on all the Catholic and malcontent countries, afforded her enemies an easy mode of annoying her.

Nothing could be more romantic, wild, and extravagant than the stories which those of the English who had penetrated far north brought back of the state of the nation, and the manners and disposition of the inhabitants; and which, if they were to be believed, described the chieftains in the hill countries as living amidst their wild and savage retainers in a singular style of feudal grandeur and semi-barbarism.

Nay, such was, in reality, the nature of the rude Highlanders in the remoter districts of Scotland, that, for an Englishman to attempt to penetrate into their fastnesses, would have been attended with the same difficulty and danger as at the present time a journey into the centre of Africa is exposed to. So that to the generality of the English nation the interior of Scotland was a *terra incognita;* whilst the dark and ominous rumours continually floating about, pictured the very court itself of that distracted country in a most strange and unnatural light. Murders, conspiracies, rebellions, and every sort of consequence upon misrule and headstrong passion, seemed the every-day occurrence there.

In Ireland, too, (where the inhabitants were equally wild, reckless, and opposite to England,) every invader found ready auxiliaries.

Alienated by religious prejudices, that nation hated the English with a peculiar and deadly animosity; an animosity which has rankled in their breasts up to the present time, and caused the shedding of rivulets of blood.

The anxiety of the Queen, on account of the attempts of the English Catholics, never ceased during the course of her reign, and was at this period greater than ever: whilst the continued revolutions happening to all the neighbouring kingdoms were the source of her continued apprehension. Plots after plots were concocted in all quarters against her life, and which were being as constantly brought to light by one extraordinary chance or another.

The Cloptons, as we have seen, were members ef the Church of Rome, though they were of the milder sort of Catholics, steering clear of all those intrigues and conspiracies which the more bigoted of their persuasion were so continually engaged in.

They were, indeed, well thought of and regarded by the government and the queen, and the good Sir Hugh was beloved and respected by all parties. Still the iron rule of the Church of Rome was upon him and his household, and held him under subjection. Many, therefore, were the narrow escapes he had experienced from being drawn into the violent and bloody plots and conspiracies the more dangerous and bigoted members of his creed had already been engaged in.

In a former chapter our readers have seen a person of this latter sort arrive stealthily at the Hall, and fasten himself upon the secret hospitality of Sir Hugh, in virtue of the powerful letters he produced.

What the designs of this man might be it was impossible to fathom, and Sir Hugh well knew that from the circumstance of his being himself considered but a mild and lukewarm Catholic by the more zealous and violent party, (although he might be made use of,) he would scarcely be initiated by them into their secrets.

Under such circumstances, the faithful Martin, (whose devotion towards the family of his old friend and patron amounted to a species of worship,) in taking upon himself the office of attendant upon the unwelcome guest, resolved to play the spy upon him at the same time, and, if possible, pluck out the heart of his mystery. The absence of the priest (who frequently resided at the Hall) favoured this design; and (on leaving Sir Hugh) Martin ascended to the apartment usually occupied by Father Eustace, where he doffed his motley coat, and induing the garments of the priest, suddenly presented himself before Parry.

The talent for humour possessed by this singular being made his design peculiarly agreeable to him, for to play a part (even under dangerous circumstances) was quite in accordance with his disposition.

On entering he found the object of his visit seated upon the small truckle bed with which the room was accommodated, and which (except two chairs) was all the furniture in it—the bed standing in a recess.

The room itself was one of those small, curious chambers peculiar to the buildings of the Catholic gentry during this and the subsequent reign. It seemed evidently to have been contrived for purposes of seclusion and concealment, and was more like the cell of a monastery than a chamber in a private dwelling. Cribbed, as it seemed to have been, out of some corner of the edifice, where an apartment would never have been thought of; the only light by which this closet-like room was illuminated in the day-time being from a small concealed window, so contrived as not to be visible from the grounds without.

So deep in his own contemplations was the occupant of this chamber, that, at first, he did not observe the entrance of the disguised Martin. When he did so, however, he quickly started to his feet, and the riding cloak which he had unfastened slipping from his shoulders shewed that he was armed (as the phrase goes) to the very teeth. Rapier and dagger were by his side, a pair of the huge, ill-contrived, petronels of the period at his waist, and in place of a shirt it was evident that he wore a sort of hauberk of linked steel beneath his upper garments; in fact, a more dangerous-looking and dishevelled companion the shrewd Martin had seldom beheld.

"The peace of Heaven be upon thee, my son," said Martin, as the visitor confronted him.

"Such peace as Heaven wills," returned the other.

"Those who have to do the work are not permitted peace of mind or body in this world. Art thou him to whom I am secretly commended at Clopton, the good Father Eustace?"

"Such is the name men usually give the wearer of these garments of the Church, my son," returned Martin. "I would they clove to the body of a more worthy representative."

"The business I have with thee, good father," said Parry, "is of that dangerous and imminent nature that I may not trust to thy word alone. I must be furnished with proof of thy identity. Sir Hugh Clopton affirmed but now that Father Eustace was at present absent from the Hall."

"I have but now returned," said Martin, "and immediately have sought thee out by Sir Hugh's desire. What you have to communicate can either be withheld or given freely, I seek not to know the secret of others. Letters of import, as I learn, hath procured thee a secret asylum here, without which, as thou art aware, thou could'st not have been received, neither can I hold converse with thee, unless thou canst shew such documents or explain the reasons of thy coming hither."

"Enough said, father," returned Parry, thrown off his guard, "those documents thou shalt have; meantime hear the reasons which have moved me to this visit, and my intent in seeking thee."

"Proceed," said Martin, seating himself, whilst the other walked restlessly up and down the small room, apparently carried away by the violence of his own thoughts.

"Thou knowest my early history," he said, "and how that after being an undutiful son, a sabbath-breaker, and a blasphemer, the devil lured me to the commission of crimes by which my life was forfeited to the laws?"

"I have heard these things," said Martin, "and such part of the story needs no repetition. The Queen granted you a free pardon, for which you are doubtless grateful, and resolved in making amends?"

"I had resolved on doing so," said Parry, "and hoped for days of repentance and happiness, but none came, as you shall hear. The fiend still held possession. I wandered about in woods and solitary places, for the sight of my fellow creatures was horrible to me. Nay, I thought every one seemed happy but myself, and the evil one constantly whispered that there was no mercy for Gilbert Parry. Again, therefore, I sought society, gave the reins to my evil desires, and myself up to evil ways, and again conscience troubled me. I had rest neither by night nor day. I feared the night, lest the enemy should take me before morning. I tried to pray, but could not. I passed whole days as if my body had been pricked down irrecoverably, persuaded the fiend was in my apartment. Nay, my very body was in flames. To cry for help was vain, no relief came, and I was ever filled with evil thoughts. Such, holy father, were the torments I endured for five years. At length it appeared to me that this state of persecution arose from some cause in which I was called upon to exert myself. Then considered I of the persecuted state of our religion, and that I was called upon to strike a blow for its welfare. In short I resolved to do a deed which (by destroying the great enemy of our Church) should obtain for me the crown of martyrdom."

"Proceed, my son," said Martin, who, seated with his chin upon his doubled fists, was listening to and contemplating the excited Parry with the utmost attention. "Proceed, my son, wherefore dost thou stop?"

The narrator of his own troubled thoughts regarded Martin with a deep and searching look. "Methought I saw a devilish smile upon thy face," he said sternly. "Is the relation of such things subject of ridicule?"

"Rather of pity," said Martin; "I smiled to think that a whip and a dark room might have dispelled such phantoms. The most absurd doctrines are not without such evidence as martyrdom can produce."

"You think, then," said Parry, "that penance and flagellation were required?"

"Call it so, an if you will," said Martin, "fasting is good for digestion, and real pain for imaginary suffering. Doubtless you lived well whilst this frenzy lasted. You was, you say, leading a wild life, perhaps drunk one-half of the twenty-four hours, and mad the other. A bad state of the stomach produces fumes upon the brain. I would have exorcised the fiend by blood-letting, blisters, purgation, and purification. But proceed, you was about to say what this continued spiritual ague wrought you to."

"The cutting off of one who is the bitter enemy of our creed, the usurper of the throne of these realms," said Parry, "the putting to death of Elizabeth Tudor."

"Ah, ah," said Martin, "methought 'twould tend that way. She to whom you are indebted for a life, is to pay the forfeit of life for her clemency."

"And you disapprove of my project, then?" inquired Parry.

"Nay, I said not so much, did I?" returned the shrewd Martin.

"But you inferred so much, did you not?" again inquired Parry.

"Mayhap I did, mayhap I did not," said Martin, who saw by the eye of Parry that his own situation, thus shut up with such a man, and under false colours, was somewhat perilous, especially as Parry in his excited state began to fumble with the poniard at his waist. Martin in short now saw that his companion was mad. Under such circumstances to shew fear or distrust is to perish.

"In trusting Father Eustace," said Parry, placing himself between Martin and the door, "I was led to expect I should find one ready in every way to forward and aid so great a design. Such was the assurance I received from Ragazoni. I brook no prevarication, priest; neither will I run the risk of betrayal." So saying, Parry drew his dagger from the sheath, looking at Martin at the same time with the ferocity of a tiger ready to spring.

"'Tis not often that ministers of the Holy Mother Church are threatened thus," said Martin coolly, and without altering his position.

"I will drive my dagger to the heart of every member of this household," said Parry, "rather than endanger the success of my project."

"That in itself would ruin the project, as far as you are its executor," returned Martin, "since you would be likely to be apprehended and suffer for your violence."

"Swear upon the hilt of my poniard not to divulge what I have just related," said Parry, becoming somewhat less excited, and thrusting his dagger close to the mouth of Martin. "Swear."

"I am ready to do so," said Martin, quietly moving the steel from its close proximity to his lips, "with one reservation however, that Sir Hugh Clopton is to be informed of it."

"Ah," said Parry, seeming to reflect, and as suddenly changing from his excited state to comparative calmness, "was I not told to take the advice of Father Eustace, as to the propriety of making Sir Hugh Clopton acquainted with this design? And you advise such measure, do you, father?"

"Most assuredly; for what other purpose have you sought his roof?"

"For the purpose," said Parry, "of being in the vicinity of others cognizant of my design in this country, and of conferring with yourself in security, since my steps and motions, until I took refuge in Warwickshire, have been closely watched."

"Good," returned Martin. "Now, wilt follow my advice since you have been sent to seek it?"

"I will," said Parry.

"Thus it is," said Martin; "dismiss all further thoughts connected with your design to-night: partake of the refreshments I have brought with me, and then seek the repose you so much need. *To-morrow* we will talk further, taking Sir Hugh into our counsels; and so I take my leave." As he said this Martin rose, and was about to pass Parry, carefully making a circuit so as to get between him and the door, the latter following him as he did so with a doubtful eye.

"You are a different man from the person I was led to expect in Father Eustace," said Parry, still dallying with his drawn dagger.

"I am as you see me," said Martin, "true to my word and to the master I serve."

"And you swear not to divulge?" said Parry.

"Except to Sir Hugh—I swear," said Martin.

"Be it so," said Parry, sheathing his dagger and stepping aside. "Good night, father."

"To-morrow early I will again be with you," said Martin. "Good night, and the next moment he was outside the small apartment.

CHAPTER VIII.

STRATFORD-UPON-AVON.

On the skirts of the county of Warwick (saith a modern author), situated on the low meadowy banks of a river, there is a little quiet country town, boasting nothing to attract the attention of the traveller but a fine church and one or two antique buildings with elaborately carved fronts of wood or stone, in the peaceful streets. There would seem to be little traffic in that place, and the passing traveller, ignorant of the locality, would scarcely cast a second look around. But whisper its name into his ear, and, hand in hand with his ignorance, his apathy will straightway depart. He will stop his horse; he will descend from the saddle; he will explore those quiet streets, he will enter more than one of the houses in that little town; he will visit that old church, he will pause reverentially before its monuments; he will carry away with him some notes—perhaps some sketches; and remember what he saw and what he felt that day to the very close of his life. Indeed you will seldom fail to see, even in that quiet little town, small groups of people on whose faces and in whose demeanour you will recognize the stranger stamp. There is something to see in those unfrequented streets; and they have come a long way to see it. What wonder! The town is Stratford-upon-Avon.

Such is indeed Stratford-upon-Avon at the present time. But in the sixteenth century it presented a somewhat different aspect.

The different towns in England, at this latter period, were just beginning to emerge from their state of primitive rudeness and irregularity, and the houses to be distinguished for a style of architectural beauty and comfort as dwellings, which has not since been improved or exceeded.

The various contentions and intestine jars which had, almost up to the reign of Elizabeth, drained the population, and kept men from all peaceful occupations and improvements, and in consequence of which the squalor of their dwellings and tenements were but one degree improved from the rudeness of the Norman period, was now to give place to a style which, if but one tenement remain to us in a town of the present age, we look at it with delight and admiration. Stratford-upon-Avon then, in the year 1584, might be said to partake largely of both these styles. In some parts were to be seen those irregular ill-built wooden tenements. little removed from the hut of the Norman citizen. These standing apart, and without regard to streets, formed the abode of the poorer sort of inhabitants, and chiefly constituted the suburbs; whilst several regular streets were to be found composed of handsome, strong-built, heavily-timbered, and substantial dwellings, having their shops encroaching into the streets; their beetling storeys above; their long passages running backwards, with ample yards and gardens in rear; and their low-roofed wide-chimneyed, secluded, and comfortable rooms, secured by massive iron-studded doors, and accommodated with heavy cumbrous articles of furniture.

Here and there too, in the midst, were to be seen the mouldering remains of some dark monastic building of a former day. The walls of edifices, built in the dark ages of monkish intolerance, whose grated windows and low-arched doors told of the Saxon and the Dane, when, save the splendour of religious architecture, there was nothing between the hut and the castle.

Nothing could be more rural and picturesque than Stratford-upon-Avon on a bright summer's day. Its streets, as we have before partially described, and (as was mostly the case in unwalled towns at this period) were, except in the very centre of the town, composed of houses detached at irregular intervals, many of the edifices being partially screened by the luxuriant trees which shadowed their fronts, and grew in the gardens in rear: added to this, in the suburban thoroughfares of this town, it was not uncommon to find a clump of tall elms or oaks growing in the very centre of the road, beneath whose boughs the rude bench, the horse-trough, and the creaking sign proclaimed the immediate vicinity of the smaller hostel.

If the traveller looked from the town, he beheld the high road he was to traverse on leaving it, o'ercanopied by the forest scene without, whilst on entering the suburbs, the sloping roof, gable ends, and heavy chimneys were only here and there to be caught sight of amongst the living verdure in which they were embosomed.

Besides this, as he proceeded, the picture was added to by the various signs of the several trades, which proclaimed the occupation of the indwellers, and before many of the houses were placed long benches on which, in fine weather, the townsfolk were to be found seated, conversing cozily together in their quaint-cut doublets and steeple-crowned hats. Large tubs of water also, by order of the chief magistrate, were placed beside each dwelling, as a precautionary preventative against the spread of fire amongst these stout-timbered edifices. The highways, however, even in the outskirts of the town, were by no means so well cared for as in our own times, and in foul weather, in place of a well-paved or Macadamized thoroughfare, the road was knee-deep in mud, and cut up fearfully with cart wheels and other traffic of the time.

In what would now be called a small and somewhat mean-looking dwelling, but which in the reign of Elizabeth constituted the habitation of a good substantial citizen, resided John Shakespeare, a dealer in wool in Stratford-upon-Avon. The house itself had nothing in its outward appearance to recommend it, except the strength of its build and the stoutness of its timbers.

It was neither "a goodly dwelling or a rich." Its rooms were both stinted to space and somewhat low in roof. But little did its inmates suspect that from the mere legend of one of its indwellers having first drawn breath beneath its roof, that house would create more interest in the world than the most magnificent palace the world contained, and that in after-ages the four corners of the earth would send forth votaries to see, to worship, and to offer adoration at its shrine. And still less did its occupants imagine that in the person of one of their own children they possessed a treasure, whose very name, unthought of and slightly regarded as he then was, would prove dearer than Pluto's mine, more rich than gold.

Let us for a moment take a glance at the interior of this hallowed residence, and view it at the precise period of time to which the minds of those who now visit it are wont to revert; and when he who was in after-times to throw so great an interest over every cupboard, corner, and cranny of its stout-timbered walls, was in life, and dwelling idly in its apartments.

In an inner apartment of the ground-floor was seated on a high-backed oaken chair, a female of some thirty years of age. If the reader has ever bestowed his attention upon the portrait Rubens has left us of his first wife, it will save much trouble in the description, since both in feature and figure this very handsome middle-aged female was the counterpart presentment of that portrait.

Opposite to her, and apparently engaged with books and accounts pertaining to his business, pen in hand, and inditing what, in the present day, would be called a cramped piece of penmanship, sits a very comely and respectable-looking man. Nay, if we look closely at him we shall pronounce him to be a splendid specimen of an Englishman, both in countenance and figure. His face is exceedingly handsome, the complexion of a rich brown, the features high and aquiline, hair of a dark auburn, slightly tinged with grey, whilst a close-clipped curly beard worn round the chin, and a thick moustachio on the upper lip, complete the picture of one of those true-born English yeomen whose ancestors drew their arrows to the ear in the fields of Cressey, Poictiers, and Agincourt. If our readers then look upon this pair they will behold the father and mother of England's pride and glory, John and Joan Shakespeare.

In the female there is a dignity of look and manner which seems somewhat out of keeping with so lowly a home as the one we find her in. She looks one whose presence would have better suited the hall than the cottage. One come of gentle blood, and born to fortune instead of being the wife of a tradesman in a country town, handsome and genteel-looking as nature hath made that husband.—Such is in truth the case, as John Shakespeare married one of the daughters and heirs of Arden of Wellingcote, in the county of Warwick.

This pair, however, were not the only occupants of the small inner apartment in which we have found them, as some half-a-dozen curly-headed varlets, male and female, of various ages, from three to ten, were sitting and sprawling about the floor, clambering upon chairs, exercising their lungs in concert, and ever and anon calling forth a short reproof or a caress from their handsome parents.

After a while, the wool-comber shuts up his books, places his pen in the inkstand, and folding his arms, remains wrapt in deep meditation.

There is something of care and anxiety in his countenance. His thoughts and cogitations, as he occasionally glances upon his good-looking spouse, and then watches the young fry upon the floor, become more troubled; and, apparently to hide the growing heaviness of his brow, he rises, walks into the shop in front, reaches down his steeple-crowned hat, and looks forth into the street,—the little curly brood breaking cover as he opens the door, and bounding joyously into the sunshine in the streets.

As they do so, they are met, caught up, and kissed, (at least the younger ones,) by their elder brother, just now returning to his home.

"Ah, Will, good Will," cries one, "where have you been tarrying so long?" "Naughty truant Willy," cries another, "you've been rambling over to Warwick with Dick, the tanner's wild son, duck-hunting, I dare be sworn." "Nay," cries a third, "I know he has been otter-hunting all night in the river; see his staff is red with blood. You have brought us some skins, good William, hast thou not?"

"Nay, in good sooth, you varlets," said the elder brother, entering the door with the whole fry clinging round him, "I have neither wild fowl from the marshes, nor otters from the river; for none have I been in search of. I come home empty-handed this afternoon, for which you must forgive me."

"And where, then, hast thou been, William?" said his father, somewhat gravely. "This idle wandering life of thine will, I fear me, lead to nothing. Master Pouncet Grasp has fairly given me warning that he will have no more to do with thee. He complains that you keep no regular hours; you heed no orders or directions he gives; that you set him at naught, in sooth, and make his other lads more idle than yourself. Nay, he says you spoil his parchments, spill his ink in waste, and that, in truth, he must either be ruined or be rid of thee."

"Out upon the miserable scrivener," returned William, laughing. "I did but pen a stanza in place of drawing a lease, and lo! he has never forgotten it. But, in good sooth, dear father," continued the youth, "I fear me I shall never thrive in the office of Pouncet Grasp. I find the dry work of a copying-clerk but an idle waste of the life Heaven hath blessed me with. I was not formed to draw leases, wills, and other tenures and tricks of lawcraft.

"Between two hawks, which flies the higher pitch,
Between two dogs, which hath the deeper mouth,
Between two girls, which hath the merrier eye—
I have, perchance, some shallow spirit of judgment;
But in the nice sharp quillets of the law,
Good faith, I am no wiser than a jackdaw."

"Thou canst rhapsodize at a good rate, my son," said the father, "that I well know. But in good truth thou must turn over a new leaf with Lawyer Grasp, or he will turn thee off, William!"

"Nay," urged the youth, "since we have entered upon this matter, I must tell thee, father, that never since the pupil age of Adam was there poor wight more unfitted for a lawyer than myself; my pen runs riot when I put it upon parchment; I cannot indite the undoing of the widow and the orphan, even when the *foul* copy lies before my nose. I turn a writ into a love-song, and when I should copy out an ejectment, lo! I find I have penned the words of a madrigal."

"The more the pity, William," said the father, "for to speak sooth to thee, I find myself by no means in so thriving a condition as I could wish. There be a many of us now in family, great and small. Business slackens with me, and in good sooth, lad, an I do not better in the next three months than I have done the last, I may e'en close my books, shut the house, and stick up bills to let the premises. Ruin, William, stares me in the face, if matters mend not anon. A bad time such for you to be thinking of changing from the vocation I have placed you in."

"Neither would I think of changing, father," returned the son, "did I think that, by remaining *in* the law, I could help you or advance myself. But believe me, so opposite is the dull routine of the desk, so abhorrent to my soul is the craft of a lawyer, that rather than follow such a calling I would take the sword my grandsire won at Bosworth, and seek a livelihood in any place where men cut throats in the way of profession. Those were sad times, father, but they were stirring times, those days of York and Lancaster, when—

"Trenching war channell'd our fields,
And bruised our flowrets with the armed hoofs
Of hostile paces."

As the youth uttered this with something of a theatrical air, and giving the words great force by his utterance, his father looked at him with considerable curiosity. "Now, by my halidame," he said, "I cannot half fathom thee, William. Truly thou art a riddle to make out. Seeming fit for nothing, and yet good at all things. I would I knew, in good sooth, what to put thee to."

The lad smiled. "Nay," he said, "I must not be undutiful towards one so good. I will then continue to try and please this godless lawyer till something better turns up. And now I must tell thee I have made a friend of one well known to thee, and who is willing to serve us in requital for some little service he hath received at my hands."

"Of whom dost thou speak, William?" inquired the father.

"Of Sir Hugh Clopton," returned the youth.

"Nay, and thou hast made friends of Sir Hugh and his family," said John Shakespeare, "thou hast done thyself good service, and, mayhap, he may advance thee in life: though what he will find thee fit for, William, I wot not."

"Truly, father," said William, "I confess myself but a tattered prodigal, only fitted to eat draff and husks. Nevertheless, an thou wilt but admit me, I would fain join these hungry varlets at their evening meal, and beg a blessing of my honoured mother, whose sweet face I have scarce looked at these two days past."

"Well, come thy ways in, thou scoffer," said John Shakespeare, good-naturedly. "I defy the evil one to be angry with such a madcap as thou art."

So saying, Master John Shakespeare turned and entered the house, his eldest son following with all his little brothers and sisters clinging to him—one upon his back, another in his arms, and the remainder pulling at the skirts of his coarse gray doublet.

To picture the private hours of the great is a difficult, as well as a thankless, task we opine, since ofttimes more is expected than is in reality to be found; and our readers will scarce be contented to find the youthful Shakespeare—in all the freedom, amiability, and kindness of his disposition—the great, the illustrious, the unmatchable—the mere playmate of his little brothers and sisters, and, whilst sitting beneath the huge chimney in that small dark room, as he watches the preparation for the evening meal, engaged in a joyous game of romps.

Yet such is the case. The gentle William, despite the greatness of his spirit and the waywardness of his disposition, which seems inclined to settle to nothing, is the darling of that home circle, the joy of his brothers and sisters, and, when at home, entering into all their little amusements and pastimes with heart and hand,—nay, their nurse when sick, and even assisting his mother ofttimes in her little attentions towards them,—ere he himself, in all "the unyoked humour of his idleness," sallies out to join his youthful associates of the town.

Our readers will, therefore, not be surprised to find that great mind, which in a single line could send a thrill through the soul of his readers, intent upon an infantine game in the "ingle neuk."

The pecuniary difficulties John Shakespeare had hinted at to his son were consequent upon his having maintained a somewhat "more swelling port than his faint means would grant continuance." No man in Stratford was better thought of or more respected than neighbour Shakespeare. There was something about him so well bred and so superior to his station in life, that he bore with him a degree of influence seldom granted except to rank and fortune.

The chief magistrate of the body corporate of Stratford was in the early charters called the high bailiff. This office Master John Shakespeare had filled some few years previous to the date of our story, and the execution of such office had led him into expenses which he had since in vain tried to abridge. "To some men, their virtues stand them but as enemies," and thus the good and companionable qualities of Master Shakespeare, notwithstanding his domestic habits, were so greatly esteemed that his hospitality was taxed accordingly, and his hearth seldom unhonoured by guests after business hours. Nay, at no hour was the little back parlour of his house entirely free from the gossiping neighbour who came down to talk over the politics of the town, or discuss the latest floating rumour of the stirring events of Elizabeth's reign.

Newspaper intelligence, we have said, there was none at this period, and, in the absence of such a vehicle for information, men's mouths were filled with any stirring tidings, and they donned their castors and hurried about in a country town, stuffing each other's ears with false reports, and frightening the place from its propriety when any event of particular import happened.

"From Rumour's tongues
They brought smooth comforts false, worse than true wrongs."

"Heard ye the news, neighbour Shakespeare?" said Master Doubletongue the mercer, entering the small parlour we have attempted to describe, and joining the family circle. "Heard ye the news to-night?"

"Good or bad be it?" said John Shakespeare smiling, "it would have been curious news an it had travelled hither before you brought it, neighbour Doubletongue. Come, sit, man, sit, fill your cup and give us your news. What! hath Dame Illwill been brought to bed of twins, or how goes the story?"

"Nay, neighbour," returned Doubletongue, who was one of the veriest scandal-mongers in Stratford, "Dame Illwill hath not produced twins, neither do I think she will produce the half of twins. By the same token, I heard the Leech say, 'twas after all but a dropsy that had caused all this scandal in her disfavour. But body o'me, heard ye not the news just now brought to town?"

"That Dame Illwill's affair is likely to end in a bottle of smoke? why, man, thou hast just told us as much."

"Ah," said Doubletongue, taking off his cup like one who found he had in him wherewithal to interest his auditor, "then I *see* you have not heard the news. Ergo, the news is mine to give."

"Then I take it, neighbour," said John Shakespeare, "there are but two ways, either to give or to retain it. Come, another cup will perhaps help its deliverance."

"Nay," said Doubletongue, who but half relished the lack of excitement his intended communication seemed to make, "you will scarce keep the native colour in your cheek, neighbour, when I do tell ye what's afloat to-night. The affair, then, gossips, is thus——"

"Whose affair?" interrupted John Shakespeare, "not the one you just now spoke of?"

"Did I hint anything?" inquired Doubletongue.

"About a certain female you did," said John Shakespeare.

"Of illustrious rank?" said Doubletongue. "Why, then you *have* heard?"

"We have heard what you have just told us," said John Shakespeare.

"The news?"

"The news."

"What! of Queen Elizabeth?"

"Nay, Heaven forbid we should sit to hear such words uttered about our gracious Queen," said John Shakespeare with much solemnity. "'Tis even dangerous to breathe such a scandal in such a quarter."

"Then of whom were we speaking?" said Doubletongue. "I gave no news. I have none to give but concerning our gracious——"

"Of Dame Illwill, I thought you spoke?" said John Shakespeare.

"Dame Illwill," said Doubletongue, contemptuously, "who cares about Dame Illwill? and who, think ye, neighbour, would trouble themselves to stab her?"

"Stab her!" said John Shakespeare, "who talked of stabbing?"

"I do," said Doubletongue; "its my own news, man. It's what I am come to propound, to expound, and to promulgate. Only you will not bear with me. The Queen is stabbed, killed, and murdered; our good and gracious Queen hath been murdered, I say; now, there is my news."

"Heaven forbid!" said John Shakespeare, starting to his feet. "That would bode ill luck to England at this moment. Heard you this report, Master Cramboy?" he continued, addressing another of the townsmen who entered at the moment.

"Which report, and whence derived, neighbour?" said Cramboy (who was master of the free-school at Stratford); "for there be many rumours just now come into town; the difficulty is to get the true one."

"That relating to the death of the Queen by the hand of an assassin," returned John Shakespeare, "and just now given us by neighbour Doubletongue here."

"Where gott'st thou *that* news, goodman Doubletongue?" said the schoolmaster, with considerable asperity in his manner, "and how came you to take upon yourself to promulgate, disseminate, and divulge such a fable?"

"Nay," said Doubletongue, who stood somewhat in awe of the pedant, "I know no harm in relating what I have just heard from neighbour Suddle of our town."

"Out upon the barbarmonger," said Cramboy, "he is ever inventing one lie or other; I advise thee to shut thy ears against all his monstrous conceptions, and thy door against his visits. Know'st thou not, simple mercer as thou art, that to imagine the Queen's death is treasonable as to attempt *her life*. Ergo, thou hast committed, or rather aided in spreading the contagion of matter containing treason, and art *particeps criminis* with that lying knave Suddle, who goeth about seeking whom he may deceive."

"Nay," said Doubletongue, "if such be the case, I will myself go about to retrace my steps, and gainsay all I have said."

"'Twere best you did so," said Cramboy, "with the addition, Master Doubletongue, that for the future the good folks are never to believe any rumours either you or Suddle may bring them. And harkee, neighbour, when you are asked the real state of the case, you can tell your friends that it is not the Queen who has been stabbed, but the Prince of Orange. For that is the actual verity."

"Body o'me, but that is it, then, is it?" said Doubletongue: "well then, there has been a royal personage murdered, after all. Grant that, my veracity; grant that, and God be praised, therefore, I am not then altogether a liar. But stay, an I obey your first injunctions, good Master Cramboy, who will believe this second report at my hands? I shall scarce be credited, methinks."

"So much the better, neighbour," said Cramboy; "the less men credit in these days of trouble, always excepting holy writ, and the more they keep to their own affairs, the better for them. And therefore go *not* about *at all;* but sit ye down and fill your tankard, whilst I expound what really hath happened."

"One way or other, we shall at last learn the rights of this matter," said John Shakespeare, laughing; "you said but now, Master Cramboy, that the Prince of Orange hath been murdered?"

"At Delft, by the hands of a misguided fanatic, such is the awful story, John Shakespeare. For what saith the book? 'Villany that is vigilant will be an overmatch for virtue, if she slumbereth.' One Balthazar Gerard, a Burgundian, it seems has long entertained this design against the Prince of Orange, and, in order to destroy that famous restorer of religious liberty, has, at the same time, sacrificed his own life. On my word," continued the pedant, "these Jesuits are fearful fellows, and will murder us all in the end. Nay, it is affirmed the Spanish arms are making rapid progress in the Netherlands, and that Antwerp is ta'en. Truly, the Prince of Parma carries all before him in those parts. Nay, 'tis further said the States are reduced to such extremity, that they have sent an ambassador to London to offer to acknowledge our blessed Queen for their sovereign, providing always she will grant them her protection and assistance."

"And there it is," said Master Doubletongue, "there hath not been so bloody a wild beast seen ravening, burning, and destroying us poor Protestants, as that terrible Spaniard Philip since the world began. Heaven keep us from his hot pincers, his thumb-screws, his iron boots, his hostile intrigues, and cruel enterprises!"

"Amen, neighbour, say I," returned Master Cramboy, "though I marvel much you will allow your tongue so much liberty, neighbour, seeing that, as I firmly believe, Philip of Spain hath a paid spy and intelligencer in every town of the kingdom. Nay, his wicked designs are said to be fully directed against England at this moment."

"I trust no paid spy is to be found within my house, neighbour Cramboy," said John Shakespeare, laughing, "so that my worthy friend Doubletongue is quite at liberty to rail upon the Spaniard to his heart's content here."

"I meant nothing but in the way of caution to our good neighbour," said the pedant, "and whose tongue would be much the better for an occasional bridle, whilst the unrighteous are in sight. By the same token there are at this moment some half-dozen strangers staying at the hostel of the Checquers, whom none of us can fathom. Master

Mumble, the headborough, talks of paying them a visit, and putting them to their purgation. Truly, we are in a dangerous condition, neighbour, and it behoves every one to look well to the main chance."

"I think with you," said John Shakespeare, "that our prospects seem not so fair as hitherto they have seemed. There is no question but that Philip of Spain, with all the power of his united empire, will fall upon England anon. His sole aim is the entire subjection of the Protestants. But come, since your news hath driven off my wife and all her children, let us even walk down to the Falcon and discuss these matters further. 'Tis now eight o'clock, and I dare be sworn the Dolphin parlour is well filled with guests. Heaven keep our blessed Queen in its own safety, for an these paid spies and jesuitical villains should hit her life, I fear me we shall be devoured by the wolf of Spain."

So saying, Master Shakespeare rose, and accompanied by his son and two fellow-townsmen, took their hats and sallied forth.

During the foregoing discussion so many bumpers had been tossed off by the two newsmongers, that Master Doubletongue was becoming a trifle double-sighted, whilst the pedant, who was sufficiently domineering over his neighbours on most occasions, was now rendered doubly important and overbearing.

"Methinks, Will," whispered the elder Shakespeare to his son, "you had better give Master Doubletongue the aid of your guidance, lest he measure his length in the gutter. He seems somewhat flustered, and inclined to quarrel with the road for not being of sufficient width."

"Thank ye, good William, thank ye," said the mercer, as he availed himself of the youth's assistance, "the causeway seems progressive to-night, the stones wherewith it is paved, ever and anon, do rise up to salute my nostrils, and there they come again."

"Now that's what I call a circumstance," said Cramboy, "neighbour Doubletongue has been fuddled every night before curfew, for the last twenty years of his life, and has not yet learnt to carry his liquor seemly. An the watch pass us they will be scandalized at his condition, and take us all up for being drunk at unseasonable hours in the streets. I pr'y-thee, good William, convey him to his own door, and deposit him in safety there."

CHAPTER IX.

THE TAVERN.

When the pair reached the Falcon, they found a goodly assemblage in the "Dolphin" parlour of that hostel. This apartment was appropriated to a certain clique of jolly companions in the town, who often met together after business hours,—a sapient and most self-important fraternity, which in our own times would have been designated a sort of club. They were indifferently ignorant upon all subjects unconnected with their respective trades and callings, and according to their ignorance was their importance and self-conceit.

Matters connected with their own town and county it was their especial privilege, they thought, to discuss, but affairs in general, and the politics of the world, were also brought under consideration. Their oracle, or as we should at present term him, president, was one Master Michael Teazle, the clothier, who, in his wisdom and his care, sought in his various harangues to "dress the threadbare state of the commonwealth and turn it, and set a new nap upon it,"—generally concluding, like Cade, that the Queen's council were no good workmen, and that he himself, being a working-man, could best understand the management of the State.

This man was, in fact, a somewhat extraordinary individual, and in possession of considerable talent; one who, in our own times, would have most likely been either a popular sectarian preacher, or a violent demagogue. But in Elizabeth's day, there being no proper vent for the effusion of such a spirit, he was merely the oracle of his gossiping society of his own town. Too indolent for real and useful work, he neglected his own business to spy into the affairs of his neighbours, and too dissipated for any profitable employment; except that he was kept from utter ruin by an industrious wife, he would, with all his wise saws, have starved.

The piece of news which had in the present instance reached Stratford, had called forth from Master Teazle a considerable harangue upon the state of the country, and the imminent danger Her Majesty's government, her own life, and the safety of themselves individually, were exposed to from the intrigues of the Catholics; and in taking upon him to expound what *had* already been done, he took upon him also to say what *should* be done.

"I maintain, my masters all," said he, "that these Jesuits should be pistolled like mad dogs wherever one can light upon them; for look ye, are they not educated, and brought up, and fed, and nourished, in superstition and bigotry? Are they not infused with a bitter hatred against our Queen, whom they treat as an usurper, a schismatic, a heretic, a persecutor of the orthodox, and one excommunicated and made horrible by the *ridiculous* Pope." Here he stopped and looked around with great importance. "Nay," he resumed, "look but upon this affair of the Prince of Orange! Sedition, rebellion, and assassination are the expedients by which they effect their purposes."

"For mine own part," said Master Lambe, the glover, "I know not precisely in what consists a Jesuit."

"Why, then, lament therefore," said Teazle, "since not to know *in what* consists a Jesuit, is not to know the danger to be apprehended *from* a Jesuit."

"Expound unto us, neighbour," said goodman Hyde, the tanner, "what is your version of such a wild beast?"

"Wild beast is a bad term to apply to a Jesuit," said Teazle, "as you will see by the story. To propound what is a Jesuit, we must e'en go back to the order of Jesuits founded at Douay by Philip of Spain; and thus it is:—he erected a seminary for Catholics to send their children to, in order that they might be brought up, and educated with a view to the crown of martyrdom. Neither to be deterred by danger nor fatigue from maintaining their principles. And into the breasts of these pupils is instilled the most inveterate hatred against Protestant England in general, and Stratford town in particular; and to our blessed Queen nothing but poison, steel, and perdition. Ahem!"

"There art thou wrong, brother," said Master Cramboy. "The order of Jesuits was erected when the Pope perceived that his lazy monks and beggarly friars sufficed no longer to defend the Church, and that the unquiet spirit of the age required something more keen, active, and erudite to defend it."

Well, neighbour, well," said Teazle, (who was generally somewhat in awe of the learning of the pedant), "I sit corrected. Be it, however, as it may, you will bear with me in holding that prevarication, and every stratagem which serves their ghostly purposes, are the especial privileges of the Order."

"Thereafter, as may be," said Cramboy; "we will discuss that point anon. Meanwhile, thou art right, insomuch that the seminary you have mentioned, and which the Cardinal of Lorraine has imitated at Rheims, and the Pope has also followed the example of at Rome, are all under the direction of Jesuits—violent, intolerant, and dangerous. And, therefore, may Heaven bless our glorious Queen, who put that caitiff Campion to the rack so lately, and broke his bones under the very nose of the Duke of Alencon, whilst he was making suit for her hand in marriage."

"A decent hint to him of the sort of martyrdom he might expect in case his suit was a successful one," said John Shakespeare, laughing.

"A grievous martyrdom had all England suffered, an the French duke had prospered," said Teazle.

"'Twere best not to pursue that theme, neighbour," said Master Lambe, "lest we run into dangerous ground, like Charles Arundel Stubbs, of Lincoln's Inn, who wrote a book, and called it 'The Gulph in which England was to be swallowed by the French marriage,' and lost his right hand, as a libeller, for his pains."

"A severe sentence upon a loyal subject," said Cramboy, "for look ye how Stubbs bore his punishment! I was there, and saw him suffer. He took his hat off with his left hand, and waving it over his head, cried, 'God save good Queen Elizabeth!' Methinks the right hand of such a man would have been better unlopped. It might have done good service hereafter."

"Go to, my masters, 'enough said is soonest mended,' as the old saw goes. An I were the Queen, after what has happened, I would take Spain by the beard," said Teazle; "for look ye, my masters all, how that king of red-hot ploughshares and burning pincers groweth more powerful daily. Already hath he made himself lord of Portugal, and gained settlements in the Indies; not only arrogating to himself the commerce of those regions, but all the princes of Italy, and even the Pope of Rome, are reduced to subjection beneath his sway. Austria and Germany, too, are connected with, and ready to supply him with troops at his beck. See, too, how the bloated toad sitteth upon his throne, swelling and sweltering in wealth as well as bigotry; with all the treasures of the Western Ind in his diadem."

"O' my word, neighbour," said Master Lambe, "an such be the case I should be chary, an I were the Queen, of chafing such a swollen reptile, lest he spit poison upon me, and burnt me up with the breath of his powerful nostrils; methinks, an I were Her Majesty, I should be careful how I gave my crown to the chance of battle with such an enemy."

"Go to, neighbour," returned Teazle, "thou lookest but along thy nose, and no farther. See'st thou not that what *must* come *will* come; and *will* come, may come when most *unwelcome*. Now, an I were the Queen, I would take Philip of Spain by the nose at once, ere the Netherlands relapse again into servitude, assailed as they are by those veteran armies employed against them. By my manhood, I say Elizabeth should at once trust to her people, and assault the whole force of the Catholic monarch ere it grow so great that it will swallow up the world. Nay, an I were appointed general-in-chief, I would conduct an army over to Holland, and deliver the country from the danger at once."

"Perhaps, neighbour," said John Shakespeare, "you have heard a rumour that some such measure has in truth been thought of. A power of dauntless spirits are, it is said, at this moment assembling under the Earl of Leicester."

"A fico for the Earl of Leicester," said Teazle; "pr'ythee what sort of a soldier is he to oppose against the experienced captains and sturdy infantry of Spain? Now, an I had been called to name the man fit for such command I should have named——"

"Thyself," said Cramboy. "Ah, ah! a very pretty piece of soldiership we should have in thee."

"Thou hast said it, not I, neighbour," returned Teazle. "*But*, an I had said myself, I had at least named one quite as equal to the emergency of the case as the man of rings and carcanets, of broaches and feathers, thou hast just named."

"Methinks 'twere wise not to pursue such comparison further," said Master Lambe; "'twere best for those to speak civily of the bear who are such near neighbours to his hold, lest the ragged staff reach our coxcombs."

"What gentlemen of note are engaged in this expedition?" inquired Cramboy.

"I hear," said John Shakespeare, "that he carries with him a glorious retinue, being accompanied by the young Earl of Essex, Lords Audley and North, Sir William Russell, Sir Thomas Shirly, Sir Arthur Basset, Sir Walter Waller, and Sir Gervase Clifton, added to which five hundred gentlemen ride in his select troop."

"Still do I maintain," said Teazle, "that the selection of my Lord of Leicester is not a good one; he possesses neither courage nor capacity equal to the task, and were I in presence of the Queen, with the Earl leaning at the back of her chair, I would say the same."

"And how would you speak of those in commission with him?" inquired Cramboy, "To begin with Essex, what think you of him?"

"As of one better to be led than to lead. Essex is a brave boy doubtless, and a clever, but then he is rash, headstrong, and unweighing. Curb him never so little and he flings up in your teeth. Give him his head and he knocks out his own brains."

"What of Lords Audley and North?"

"Put into the scale against the other one and their weight will about weigh against his lightness. Ergo, the three together are as naught."

"And how say ye to Sir William Russell?"

"But so so. Marry a good blade and a stout man, a proper fellow of his hands. But for brains the accompt is very minute indeed."

"How of Sir Arthur Basset?"

"As of one fitter to feat in a couranto, at court, than trail a pike in the Low Countries."

"Nay, then, 'tis vain to say more," said Cramboy, "since of the whole five hundred in my Lord of Leicester's troops I dare be sworn, in thy opinion, there is not one fit to wield a rapier or poise a caliver."

"Thou hast again said it, neighbour, and not I," returned Teazle. "Though in sooth, an I had, I had not been far out."

"'Tis well then," said Cramboy, "that in maritime affairs a better selection hath been made. Heard ye, my masters all, that Sir Francis Drake hath been appointed Admiral, with a fleet of twenty sail and two thousand three hundred volunteers, besides seamen to serve in it? They have already sailed for the West Indies against the Spaniards. How like ye that piece of news?"

"That likes me somewhat better," said Teazle, "and I can venture to predict some good to accrue therefrom. Drake is the man to make the settlements smoke for it. He will burn, sack, and destroy all along the Spanish main, whilst the other will but make a sort of harnessed masque through the Low Countries. Such is my poor opinion, and time will prove in how much it is correct. So fill a cup to Sir Francis Drake, another for our gracious Queen, and one more for Stratford town. Huzza! huzza! huzza!"

After this loyal outbreak there was a short pause. This was at last broken by neighbour Dismal, who (albeit he drank his quantum at these meetings) seldom spoke much, and when he did so generally threw a gloom over the whole assemblage. He always had, however, his *one say*, which was a sort of concentration of the worst piece of news he could collect for the nonce. And as he was a man of undoubted veracity, unless he was pretty well assured of the truth of what he uttered, he never uttered it at all.

This usually gave his *one wisdom* a most startling air of gloom and horror, and when he rose to speak, or even coughed his preliminary ahem, he was honoured by the most startling silence. On the present occasion he prepared to broach the subject matter with peculiar solemnity, actually rising from his seat, and, as he steadied himself with both hands upon the table, delivering himself, somewhat after the following lively fashion.

"Neighbours all," he said, "I have listened to the discussion of the foregoing matter with considerable interest. Our good neighbour, Teazle, hath handled the subject of the proposed expedition in very able style. He hath been replied to quite as cleverly by my learned and worthy fellow-townsman, Cramboy. Such discussions are, however, at the present moment, methinks, better left to those whom they most concern, inasmuch as subjects of nearer interest to *ourselves*, it doth appear to me, more nearly concern *ourselves*. Neighbours, I know I have been accused of being a kill joy, a melancholy man. Some call me Goodman Death: and the little boys hoot at me, as I walk at night, and say, 'There goeth Goodman Bones.' Nevertheless, I have been merry twice or once ere now. I was merry on the day I married Mistress Dismal, and I was merry the day I buried her. I was also merry when my father died, and left me in possession of his business. But I cannot say I am merry just at this time. Neighbours and jovial friends, I will conclude my speech briefly and heartily. By the same token, I wish you all your healths, and, at the same time, hope we may some of us meet here again next week *well* and *happy*. How far we are likely to do so is another matter, and of that you will be better able to judge when I tell you that **The Plague** is in Stratford-upon-Avon at the present moment!"

CHAPTER X.

THE CHURCHYARD OF STRATFORD-UPON-AVON.

After young Shakespeare had safely deposited Goodman Doubletongue at his own door, and left him in charge of the good housewife, he turned his steps towards the Falcon, with the intent of rejoining his father there, and hearing the news of the town; for the son and sire were upon the delightful terms we sometimes, though not often, may observe between parent and child.

In both the elements of high character were so mixed that there could be no drawback to their love: they were more like companions of the same age than father and son. The same tastes, the same pursuits, the same high spirit and honourable feelings pervaded both.

Certes, the mind of one was of a far more extraordinary character than that of the other, but that in no degree lessened the feeling of respect and love young Shakespeare felt for his father, and that father's example and influence helped to form the man.

Always the creature of impulse, the youth, after conveying Master Doubletongue home, as he neared the Falcon, suddenly resolved to turn his steps in another direction; and, in place of listening, in the hot sanded parlour of the hostel, to the discussions of the Stratford wise-acres, whilst he felt the influence of the balmy breeze of night upon his cheek, he passed the hostel and strolled towards the outskirts of the town. He felt indeed that the hour was more fitted for communion with his own thoughts than listening to the ridiculous dogmas and politics of the goodly fellowship of the Falcon.

Since his visit to Clopton a new scene had opened to him, and his feelings had become somewhat changed. He had beheld, nay, become intimately acquainted with a being of a superior order to any he had yet met with, and in the lovely and amiable Charlotte Clopton he had found that perfect specimen of female excellence which his imagination had, even at this early period of his life, loved to picture. Nay, perhaps, had he not in youth thus beheld some such bright excellence—some such reality of his conceptions—we might have wanted those delineations of grace and purity, those fairest flowers of perfect excellence—the Viola, Miranda, Desdemona, Juliet, and the sweetest Imogene of his maturer years.

To see and to feel the influence of companionship even for a couple of days with the fair Charlotte, so soft in manner, so fair in form and feature, so anxious to express her feelings of gratitude for service rendered, and not to love her, was impossible. And during his visit the bright face of the young lad might have been observed beaming with admiration and affectionate regard upon Charlotte as she sang and accompanied herself upon the spinnet, and which, had it been noticed by her betrothed, might have perhaps caused some sparks of jealousy and uneasiness.

It was lucky, however, in young Shakespeare's case, that the great mind of the youth came to his aid in this situation, and whilst in company with her of whom even a previous glance had called forth his admiration. During his visit he had also comprehended the politics of the family he was introduced amongst. He beheld the thorough gentleman, the confiding honourable old cavalier, the knight *sans peur et sans reproche*, in Sir Hugh Clopton. He saw the youthful esquire, the lusty bachelor, the free open-hearted, brave, and devoted servant, the lover, whose whole soul and every thought were upon his fair mistress, in Walter Arderne; whilst in that cunningest pattern of excelling nature, the lovely Charlotte, he saw one far removed from his own sphere of life. So much so, indeed, that "it were all one, that he should love some bright particular star," "and think to wed it," she was so much above him. So thought the modest youth. And yet again it was easy for him also to observe that the strong affection of the lady's suitor was unrequited, and his feelings unreturned, save by those of esteem and friendship. Under these circumstances, we say, the strong sense of the youth came to his aid, and, if it did not hinder him from falling desperately in love, it somewhat curbed his feelings, and hindered him from discovering them to the object of his admiration. He felt the barb of the arrow rankle in his heart; but his pride and proper feeling helped him to subdue, and conceal the smart. So true it is that—

"As in the sweetest bud
The eating canker dwells, so eating love
Inhabits in the finest wits of all."

We fear it must be acknowledged that the youthful poet, at this period of his life, was of a most untamed and wandering disposition; that his life and his employments were rather desultory; and that when once his steps turned towards the wild scenery which so abounded around his native town, all was forgotten of home duties, and engagements pertaining thereto.

This must, however, be excused in one whose mind was of so extraordinary a character.

Amongst other haunts which young Shakespeare loved to frequent at times, and even when the shadows of night gave a more solemn feeling to its precincts, was the churchyard of his native town. And perhaps those who have lingered, and looked upon that sweet scene during night's silent reign, whilst the moon has silvered the tops of the surrounding trees, and the waters of the Avon mirrored the beautiful structure on its banks, will better understand the feelings of young Shakespeare in such a place. Things more than mortal seem to steal upon the heart, and thoughts of early and shadowy recollection to haunt the mind.

Let those who have not visited this locality at "the witching hour," take a stroll into the ancient churchyard of Stratford. Let them feel the influence of the man everywhere around them, and imagine him at such a time. Let them look up at those demoniac heads which the cunning architects of the Norman period have carved on every coigne of vantage, together with the shadowy grandeur of the walls and buttresses.

Let them glance over the verdant mounds and the mossy tombstones of the silent tenants around, and then ask themselves what were the thoughts engendered in such locality? Have they not some dark and shadowy conceptions of Elsineur? Doth not the postern of the old churchyard wall open to admit the Monkish procession for the obsequies of the fair Ophelia, with all the pomp and circumstance of the times?

Do they not see before them the whole scene, and hear the words of the distracted Laertes as he stands beside the open grave of his sister :—

"Lay her i' the earth,
And from her fair and unpolluted flesh
May violets spring! I tell thee, churlish priest,
A minist'ring angel shall my sister be,
When thou liest howling."

Or, in that moonlight scene of beauty, and whilst the reverential awe it engenders steals upon the heart, doth not some remembrance of Juliet's tomb, the hour, and the deeds therein performed, float over the mind, and the words of him who sleeps so near recur?

Those, we say, who can feel this impression, can best imagine the influence the hour, and the hallowed spot, had upon the youthful mind of him who in after-life was to draw upon such feelings in order to produce the scenes we have mentioned. At the present time, and whilst young Shakespeare took his way through the churchyard, the feeling of awe which is sure to pervade the mind, more or less, in such a place, was peculiarly impressed upon him. It seemed a presentiment of some evil to come, which he could not shake off. He stopped and gazed around, and a chaos of wild thoughts and imaginings coursed one another through his brain as he did so. Within that sacred pile the knightly and the noble, the soldier of the cross, the fierce Norman, and the proud Churchman were entombed,—"*hearsed in death*,"—the very men who had lived in the days he was so fond of dwelling on; those fierce times of contention and civil butchery.

The associations connected with such a scene are indeed peculiar; the beings of a former age in all the panoply of war re-appear, and (as we gaze upon the architectural beauty of the holy edifices they have left behind them) we love to imagine their steel-clad forms,—their deep devotion; whilst remembrance of their heroic acts in the field is mixed up with the superstition and feelings of their day.

Whilst the youthful Shakespeare gazed upon the mounds, and the mossy tombstones, and the soft flowing river; as he listened to the dreary whisper of the breeze through the trees, a feeling of awe crept over him, and his imagination reverted to the world of spirits—

"When churchyards yawned and graves stood tenantless."

The living stood alone amongst the dead. Slowly he took his way, that extraordinary youth: his thoughts and conceptions seemed a wonder to himself; at one moment he gazed upwards at the o'erhanging firmament, "that majestical roof, fretted with golden fire;" then he stood upon the margin of the flowing river, and watched its waves, as they passed onwards and were lost in the distance, like the hours passing into eternity, and mingling with those before the flood. *What were those thoughts* at that hour and period of his life? who could write them, or could he himself have described them? *We think not*—perhaps he may have himself given us something nearly akin. He may *have* then thought with his own Prospero—

> "The cloud capp'd towers, the gorgeous palaces,
> The solemn temples, the great globe itself,
> Yea, all which it inherit, shall dissolve;
> And like this unsubstantial pageant faded,
> Leave not a rack behind. We are such stuff
> As dreams are made of, and our little life
> Is rounded with a sleep."

Man holds strange communion with himself in such a sanctuary. "The present horror of the time suits with it." There is even a sort of fascination to the spot, and a longing, a yearning after something supernatural. Even the hoot of the owl, or the cloistered flight of the bat, hath a charm in character.

Such, perhaps, were the thoughts of this youth, for he lingered long in the churchyard wrapt in his own imaginings. At length, as he heard an approaching footstep along the path, he slowly turned from the sacred edifice, leaped the wall, and sought the woods of Charlecote.

As young Shakespeare left the churchyard, the person whose approach had interrupted his meditations slowly walked up to the porch of the church.

As the new comer turned, on reaching the porch, the clock from the tower sounded the first hour after midnight; a deep and clanking note which swam over the adjoining fields and was lost in fainter replications. "'Tis the hour," said he, "and now for the man."

The midnight visitor was apparently a tall figure, wearing the long riding cloak of the period, and which completely enveloped his form, whilst his broad-brimmed hat, and the sable plumes with which it was ornamented, as effectually shadowed his features.

"'Tis the hour," he said, as the iron tongue sounded from the tower. "And now for this unsafe partisan." A low whistle (as if from some person lying perdue without the wall of the churchyard) was almost immediately heard, and in a few minutes another footstep was also to be distinguished as if from the town.

The figure in the cloak immediately advanced towards the approaching sounds, and as he did so he freed his right arm from his cloak, and, pulling it more completely over the left shoulder, felt that his rapier was easy in the sheath, that his other weapons were free to his hand, and also that the dagger in his girdle was handy to his grasp.

Readiness in the use of the various weapons (at that time a part of the costume of a completely dressed cavalier) was one of the accomplishments of a gentleman, and the steps and bearing of the person we have described (although but partially distinguishable in the shade of the tall trees of the churchyard) proclaimed that he was a person of some condition.

He walked slowly and deliberately down the path towards the gate, so that by the time he had traversed half its length, the swinging sound of its opening and closing proclaimed that the person advancing had passed into the churchyard. The moon at this moment had become hidden behind one of the dark clouds which seemed to threaten a coming storm, so that (in the deepened gloom of the avenue) the tall cavalier (although the closing gate and approaching footsteps proclaimed the proximity of the new comer) could not at the moment distinguish him.

There seemed no desire for concealment on the part of either, as they walked boldly past each other. Only a close observer might have observed in the motions of each considerable caution and distrust. The hand closed over the hilt of the half-drawn dagger, and each gave the other what sailors term a wide berth in passing.

The gloom of the place, as this moment indeed, completely hindered the features of either party from being distinguished even in passing; nevertheless, as they moved by, each stared the other in the face with a sharp and piercing eye, and after having passed a few paces, both simultaneously wheeled round and retraced their steps. As they did so, the first comer repeated in a low tone a single word, as if to himself, which was immediately answered by the other, and both turned; a sign then passed between them; some mysterious signal, perhaps, like the words they had uttered, only known to the parties themselves.

"Gilbert Charnock!" said the first comer. "Is't not he?"

"The same," returned the other; "and dost not thou answer to-night to the name of Gifford?"

"Right," said the first; "you have come at the hour named."

"I am sworn to do so," replied Charnock.

"And are you armed to do as sworn to do?" inquired Gifford.

"I am, if on trial the object of our meeting here is found to be dangerous to the cause."

"He has been found so," said Gifford.

"And yet our friend. One joined heart and hand in that cause. And yet to die by our hands."

"Either he or ourselves, besides others implicated in the plot: nay, the cause itself demands the sacrifice."

"And he will be here to meet us?" inquired Charnock.

"He has sworn it."

"Which of us is to deal with him?"

"Why this question? The lot was drawn by you."

"Enough: and he is even now in concealment at Sir Hugh Clopton's. Is't not so?"

"So far I traced him by the mad acts he hath committed since leaving France, and by which conduct our faction is placed in jeopardy."

"But come; it still wants several minutes of the appointed time. Walk aside here, and I will tell you in how much the man is unfortunate in his position. You know the circumstance of his coming amongst us, and how he undertook to be the instrument, the steel, the dagger, as it were, by which our arch enemy was to be reached."

"I do, and how he refused to share the glory of the enterprise with others, and resolving to take the whole upon himself, suddenly and secretly set off, without further circumstance."

"There shone out the dangerous madness of the man," returned the other, "and by-and-by comes a reaction, by which we are all endangered, as thus: it appears that on his arrival in England this Parry was as suddenly seized with scruples, and under influence thereof he goes about to certain gentlemen, to advise with them as to the propriety of his undertaking this pious act. Luckily, it seems, he hath, as yet, consulted with men who are deemed at least safe, or we ourselves had scarce been here to-night. By some he was told that the enterprise was criminal and impious; whilst others, again, applauded it. Nay, even Ragazoni, the Nuncio, and the Pope himself (to whom he wrote a letter), desired him to persist in his resolution."

"Methinks that such authority might have satisfied his scruples."

"Not a whit as you shall hear; for so deeply did the fiend palter with him in favour of the heretic Elizabeth, that even when he had opportunity twice, thrice, nay, a dozen times repeated, he could not strike the blow."

"The evil one surely mounts guard over that iron-hearted woman," said Gifford, "or she could never have escaped the many designs set on foot to cut her off."

"One would think it," returned Charnock, "and in the instance I am speaking of, she seems to have been specially guarded by some familiar; inasmuch as although Parry, albeit he managed matters so well that he gained an introduction and a private audience of the Queen, no sooner did he find himself in the presence, than his scruples returned with so much force, that he commenced an exhortation in place of driving his dagger to her heart; and after praying of her to tender her life, and grant us Catholics more indulgence in the exercise of our religion, he actually informed her there were numerous conspiracies at that moment formed against her."

"And how escaped he being apprehended and examined?" inquired Gifford.

"Ah, there consists the marvel," returned Charnock; "but it seems the Queen looked upon him as a harmless maniac, and took little account of what he uttered. She trusted for safety to God and to her people's love, she said, and so dismissed him."

"Indeed," continued Charnock, "it seems then, that the interview for the time completely prostrated all Parry's energies; and lest he should be tempted, as he owned, by the opportunities he found of approaching her ere his words could have effect, he always came to court unprovided with any offensive weapon."

"And then he afterwards relapsed into his former violence; was't not so?"

"It was. He returned to France, saw the Nuncio and Ragazoni, became again confirmed in his first intent, and has again recrossed to England, where his madness and his extravagant conduct are likely to compromise all his friends. Nay, an he is not speedily silenced, we shall assuredly perish by the gibbet."

During the foregoing conversation of the conspirators, thus met in the seclusion of the churchyard of Stratford, (a trysting place they had fixed on as more likely than any other to be unmolested by the prying eyes and ears of the curious,) they had slowly traversed round the sacred edifice; and now, as the taller stranger finished his discourse, they arrived at the north porch, and stood concealed in its shadow.

"We seek an edifice dedicated to the service of religion for a strange and awful purpose," said Gifford, as he gazed along the footpath leading from the church.

"Since it is to serve the purposes of the true religion," said Charnock, "let us trust to the greatness of the cause to sanctify our doings. Hast thou any scruples?"

"None," said Gifford. "But time passes. How, if our man fail?"

"That would bode us ill," said Charnock; "though I think it unlikely that he will do so. Between the hours of one and two was the time I appointed him to be here, and he swore to me that he would not fail."

"And how didst thou get opportunity of speech with him?" inquired Gifford.

"By following him to Clopton soon after his arrival; where I gained an interview, and bade him hither in the name of our leader. Hark, the signal; 'tis he!" and the two conspirators advanced along the path, whilst at the same time footsteps were heard.

CHAPTER XI.

THE STRATFORD LAWYER.

The arrival of strangers to take up their abode for any length of time in such a town as Stratford-upon-Avon, always furnished matter of curiosity and speculation amongst the inhabitants. The neighbours were known to each other so well, and there was comparatively so little travel, that a certain degree of suspicion attached to all new-comers in those dangerous days. When any of the townsmen had business, even a few miles off, it was usual for them to arrange matters so that two or three might travel in company. Neighbour Fustian, the hosier, having business in Warwick, agreed to travel the road in company with neighbour Lambe, the glover, whose trade made him a visitor to Coventry, whilst the latter stayed the convenience of mine host of the Falcon, who was, peradventure, bound for the latter town, and all three, mounted and armed, went and returned in company, rather than trust purse and person singly to the chances of the road.

Robbing on the highway, although by no means so common as in the preceding reign, was still frequent. The woods were thick in this part of Warwickshire, and the gentlemen of the shade found it easy to elude pursuit after a highway robbery. Nay, but a few short years before, and during the York and Lancaster feuds, which had deluged the land with blood; what with disbanded men-at-arms, thieves, and caitiffs of one sort or other, the roads were but cut-throat defiles, and the country round a continued battle-field.

So that during the troublous reign of Henry VI. it had been especially ordered, that between the towns of Coventry, Warwick, and Stratford-upon-Avon, the highways should be widened, by cutting down trees on either hand, in order that travellers and wayfarers might have more room to defend themselves against the numerous robbers and caitiffs infesting those parts.

On the morning following the transactions we have recorded in the foregoing chapter, there were several subjects of interest commented upon and discussed in the little back room which constituted the office of one Pouncet Grasp, the head-lawyer of the town. One was the sojourn of several strangers, whom no one knew anything about, at one of the hostels: another was a dark and alarming rumour of a suspicious sort of illness having broken out in the suburbs: and another was the circumstance of a man, having all the appearance of a person of condition, having been found, stabbed in several places, and lying, with the pockets of his doublet rifled, a stiffened and unhandsome corse, in the road leading to the ferry beyond the church.

Master Pouncet Grasp himself was seated upon a high stool near the window of his office, which looked into a green and bowery garden, having at its further extremity a most pleasant bowling-green; the river just to be distinguished in the distance beyond, amongst the marshy meadows.

Some two or three clerks were seated in different parts of the apartment, all busily engaged, pen in hand, scrawling strange hieroglyphics upon certain sheets of parchment before them, making a dreadful sound of incessant scribbling with their pens.

Master Grasp himself, the monarch of all he surveyed, and an especial tyrant over the unfortunate clerks he presided over, was the only personage in that small apartment who seemed to have freedom of thought and motion, and license to take his attention from the crackling parchments beneath his nose.

If our readers have ever taken the trouble to picture to themselves the clerk of Chatham, with his pen and ink-horn hung round his neck, they will have some idea of the figure of our Stratford lawyer in his own office. Only that, whereas we imagine the clerk of Chatham to have been a sort of dreamy, drawling person, Master Pouncet was rather more swift, sententious, and mercurial. Law had sharpened his wit, irritated his temper, levelled his honesty, and urged his avarice.

Any one to have watched him when alone in his glory, and only seen by his clerks, would have taken him to be half insane. The moment, however, a client or a stranger appeared, he put on a new face and a demeanour suited to the occasion; appearing wise in council, amiable in disposition, and staid and sober in manners, whereas before he had been like a chattering ape irritated with a hot chestnut.

"Now do I wonder who these strangers may be," he said, leaving off his writing and jumping round in his seat; "truly I must run down to goodman Doubletongue and confer with him on the subject. Will Shakespeare," he said, jumping back again, "get thee down to——Ah, I forgot that pestilent Shakespeare hath not been to the office for a whole week. Ah, the caitiff! Oh, the villain! See, too," he said, opening his desk and searching amongst his papers, "the vile rubbish he inditeth when he *is* here in place of copying what is set before him. What! you grin there, do ye? driving wights that ye are. Grin, my masters, *whilst ye work*, an ye list. But, an ye *leave off* to grin, see an I brain ye not with this ruler. Shakespeare—ah, a pretty name that, and a precious hounding scamp is the fellow that owns it. Here's goodly stuff toward! Here's loves of the gods and goddesses for you! Here's Venus, Adonis, Cytherea, hid in the rushes; Proserpina and Pluto, besides half a dozen heathen deities, devils, satyrs, and demigods, all dancing the hays in a lump!" So saying, Pouncet Grasp turned over the leaves of a sort of manuscript poem, written upon a quantity of backs of letters and dirty sheets of paper, and, after glancing through the contents, sent them fluttering and flying at the head of one of his clerks.

"There," said he, "that's the way my ink is spoiled, and my documents destroyed. I suppose now, that your friend and crony there," he continued, addressing himself to the young man at whose head he had thrown the manuscript, "I suppose your unintelligible friend calls that incomprehensible and unaccountable rubbish a sort of rough draught of a poem. I'm not learned in such productions, but methinks he that wrote of such lewd doings ought to be whipped at the cart's tail, or put in the stocks at least."

"I was not aware," said the youth addressed, (and who under cover of his industry had been laughing all the time Master Grasp was reading the poem), "I was not aware William Shakespeare has ever written a poem about the gods."

"*Si—lence*," cried Grasp, sticking his pen behind his ear and looking fierce, as he wheeled round and faced about, first to one and then to another of his clerks. *Si—lence*, ye scoundrel scribblers, or by the Lord Harry——"

The clerk, who knew from experience the irritable nature of his taskmaster, took the hint and redoubled his exertions with the pen and parchment before him, only occasionally, as he stole a furtive glance at his companions and observed the lawyer's attention in another direction, lolling out his tongue or executing a hideous grimace at him.

"I pr'ythee, sirs, inform me," said Grasp, again interrupting the silence he had commanded, "when was that mad-headed ape last in this office?"

"Of whom was it your pleasure to speak?" inquired the youth who had received the compliment of the poem at his head.

"Of whom should I speak, sinner that I am, but of him of whom I *last spoke*—that incomprehensible, uncontrollable varlet—that scribbler of bad verse—that idle companion of thine?"

"He was here but yesterday," said the lad.

"Yesterday!" said Grasp, "why I *saw* him not; I *heard* him not; neither did he indite a line of that I left for him to work at."

"He was fetched away almost as soon as he came," said the lad.

"Fetched away! who should fetch William Shakespeare away I trow, and from my house, without leave, licence, and permission granted *from* and *by* me to take the person of the said Shakespeare?"

"Master Walter Arderne, from the Hall, called for him, and they went away together," said the lad.

"Master Arderne, an called for one of my lads here! why what's in the wind now I trow, and why sent ye not to the Falcon for me, ye sinner?"

"He asked not for you, sir," returned the lad, "he asked for William Shakespeare."

"Now the fiend take thee for a stupid dolt," said Grasp; "what an if he did ask for William Shakespeare, of course it was me he wished to confer with; only, as he found I was out, he inquired for the first idiot who had sense enough to take his message, and the chance fell upon the greatest scrape-grace and the most consummate ape in the whole lot.

"Miserable sinner that I am! That varlet hath forgotten to deliver the message he received from Master Arderne. Who knoweth the import of such message, so entrusted, and confided, and given, and—and—lost perhaps for ever? ——Ah! and——Peradventure Sir Hugh Clopton hath been seized with apoplexy, and I have been sent for to confer about his will, or mayhap Master Arderne hath wished for my advice, anent drawing up the articles of marriage betwixt himself and that most beautified of young ladies his cousin.——Or, peradventure the match may have been broken off, and he may wish for my advice on the let and hindrance thereof. Nay, it is impossible to say in how much I am deteriorated and damaged, both in purse, person, and reputation by the mistakes, misconduct, and mismanagement of that pestilent conglomeration of vices, idleness, and villany—that scurvy companion, that ill favoured——"

"William Shakespeare, I suppose you mean," said that youth himself, who at the moment entered unperceived, and stood smiling at the door whilst he listened to the scurrility of Grasp. "Nay, finish your sentence, and fill up the measure of your abuse, master-mine," said Shakespeare, advancing towards Grasp, who seemed struck all of a heap by his presence. "I have heard it is your pleasure to rail upon me behind my back, and, as I well know I deserve some slight portion of your anger, I am as well content to receive it myself, in place of its being put upon these lads, my fellows."

"Nay, good William," said the lawyer (whose excitement seemed to have vanished in a most unaccountable manner, in the presence of his clerk); "I named you not, I meant you not, I spoke not your name, that I am aware of. At least not at this precise moment. Did I name our good William lads? Did I couple his name—?"

"If you did, I care not," said the youth, "since (as I have before said) I feel myself in some sort deserving of your censure. The law suiteth not my disposition, neither can I give my mind up to its dry study. I wrong thee, Master Grasp, when I attempt to serve thee, and I should use oceans of ink and reams of paper ere I learnt even how to serve a writ properly. It is easier to pretend to be what we are not, than hide what we really are, Master Grasp, and I will be content to be under imputation of those ill names you have given me, provided you add not lawyer to the number; only, in as much as you have favoured me with those terms, we must be content to part. I do not *beat thee*, Master Grasp, because thou art weak in body, and somewhat old; but I do warn thee not to couple my name in future, when you speak of me, with those opprobrious epithets you have just used. I am no villain at least, and so farewell for ever, Master Grasp." And Shakespeare turned abruptly and left the office.

"Now that's what I call a circumstance," said the lawyer; "here's a large mouth, here's a goodly gentleman: a stipendiary, a stripling, a mere school-boy, who hath scarce been two months in my office, and to rebel, and take himself off thus. Well, be it so. I am well rid of the rebel, but an I have him not on the hip ere long, my name is not Grasp. And now I forgot to demand of him the message sent to me from Clopton Hall. My boots! my boots!" he called to the serving-wench, "and tell Davey to clap saddle upon Sorrel. Troth I will ride to Clopton, and inquire me of the steward what's amiss there."

When the serving-man brought the lawyer his boots, he announced a client in waiting. "One to advise with your worship," said the man, "upon matters of import, as he saith."

"Ah," said Grasp, "what manner of man, Davey man, and where from,——what's his name too?

"A would not give his name, but a said he were from Warwick," said Davey.

"From Warwick, Davey? eh? Right, good Davey. I do expect one from Warwick to-day,—I had forgotten as much—and so you shewed him into the front chamber?"

"I did, master," said Davey.

"And is all in order in that apartment, Davey?"

"It be so," said Davey.

"Papers, parchments, deeds, and strong boxes, all in their places, Davey?" inquired Grasp.

"Yes, master, like nest-eggs. He! he! he!"

"And you told him I was engaged with another client on business of import,—of immense import,—eh, Davey?"

"Trust I for that!" said Davey.

"Good, then, take him a cup of wine, Davey. Tell him I will see him the moment I am disengaged, and then bring me hither my capon and tankard. And d'ye hear,—after you have done that, mount Sorrel yourself, and ride over to Clopton; make some excuse to introduce yourself into the servants' hall, and just take a look, and observe if there be anything out of the common there. You understand?"

"He! he! hap I do," said Davey, with a knowing wink, as he hurried out to execute his several commissions.

When the important little lawyer condescended to give audience to the particular client his serving-man David had announced, he found himself in company with a tall aristocratic-looking person, dressed in the somewhat faded appointments of a military man of the period: that is to say, he wore the leathern doublet usually covered by the breastplate and backpiece, the stains upon it shewing it had seen much service in the field as well as the table, whilst the scarf and jingling spur still farther denoted the profession of arms.

"Master Algernon Neville!" said the man of parchment, as soon as the striking figure of the visitor saluted his eye on entering the room. "I would your honour had sent in your name. I should hardly have kept you so long in waiting here. Body o' me, I had no idea it was your honourable self."

"Nor much desire so to find it, I dare be sworn, Grasp," said the visitor. "But, sooth to say, I am come to thee again, and upon the same errand as when I last was here."

"Advice, eh?" said Grasp; "truly your honour shall have it,—the best I can give."

"I am bounden to thee, good Grasp," said the visitor, "for thy advice; but there was, as thou knowest, something else I required of thee besides thy advice, good as it doubtless was."

"Moneys?" said Grasp. "Truly I am not likely to forget I did also advance certain moneys,—moneys you required to take you over to Scotland."

"And now, if I require more moneys," said the visitor, "can you accommodate me again?"

"Marry can I," said Grasp; "what sum does your honour require?"

The visitor hesitated. He looked shrewdly at Grasp, and taking the pen from the inkstand marked on a piece of paper several figures.

"I want that," he said, handing the paper to Grasp.

"Mass, a round sum!" said Grasp; "but upon such security as you can give you shall have it, honoured sir. Nay, double an you want it."

"Why, gad a-mercy!" said the visitor, in some surprise, "hast thou been the Virginian voyage since I saw thee last? Rich thou hast always been since I knew thee, but so ready to part with thy moneys I never knew thee before."

"Your honour will pardon me for the simile," said Grasp; but there are a sort of men who are fortune's favourites, and who like cats ever light upon their legs. Your honour hath surely heard a piece of news which nearly concerns you?"

"I know of no news likely to effect my fortunes," said the visitor, "having but lately arrived in England. Hast thou anything of import to communicate?"

"Body o' me," said Grasp, "why, I concluded you *had heard*, or I had communicated it immediately I saw you! Know you not the Earl of Westmoreland is dead!"

"Nay, is this true?" said Neville, starting.

"True as that your honour is his next heir," said Grasp.

"And where died he?" inquired the visitor.

"In Italy, where he hath been long in exile, as thou know'st."

"Ah!" said Neville, "this is somewhat unlucky!"

"Unlucky?" said Grasp. "Heard ye ever the like o' that! What can be unlucky that bodes your honour so much good? You are in fact and in right, *de facto et de jure*, next heir to the earldom of Westmoreland."

"Would that I had known of this but yesterday!" said Neville, abstractedly; "'twould have spared me from participating in this last business."

"Did your honour observe anything?" said Grasp, staring at his visitor, who seemed wrapped in the thought and cogitations consequent upon the news he had just heard.

"'Tis no matter," he muttered at length to himself, "I will betray them all. Harkee, good Grasp," he continued, after a considerable pause, "'tis quite true, that which thou say'st. I am next heir to the title and estate of Westmoreland. But it follows not, therefore, that I shall succeed to them, as I am in disgrace and under suspicion. Could I indeed do some acceptable service to the Queen, I might recover those estates and honours forfeited by the rebellion of the earl just now deceased."

"That were, indeed, a way to recover," said Grasp; "but does your honour know of any acceptable service that might do yourself honour and her majesty pleasure?"

"I do," said Neville, "and you can aid me in it; but I warn you, it is attended with danger."

"In aiding you I serve the Queen, it seems," said Grasp, "Is't not so?"

"It is so," said Neville.

"Ergo, it is profitable," said Grasp.

"It is so," said Neville.

"Then am I content to encounter the danger," said Grasp, "since I am well aware that titles, honours, and profit are not to be gained without some sort of risk; and now tell us, honoured sir, what is to be done."

"To discover a plot and arrest the traitors," said Neville.

"Ah," said Grasp, with alacrity, "that were indeed a circumstance. An you could find such a matter as a ready-made plot, and light upon a nest of traitors, I should say you were in luck's way, as usual, good Master Neville."

"I can do both, good Grasp," said Neville, "and that not a thousand miles from this town; nay, not a thousand yards from this house."

"Ah, say'st thou," said Grasp, "not a thousand yards from this house? As sure as my name is Grasp, your words point at the strangers who have been for the last two days playing at hide-and-seek at the Checquers. Am I right, good sir?"

"You are," said Neville.

"Now, praise be to my sagacity," said Grasp, "I all along suspected those mysterious men of being evil-doers. There is treason and concealed villany in their very shadows as they glide about. What is the nature of their designs and their intent, good Master Neville? are they emissaries of the Spaniard? or are they——"

"Let it suffice, their intentions are dangerous to the safety of the Queen, and they are secretly drawing into their conspiracy many Catholic gentlemen in this county who are discontented with the present government. Nay, five of them are sworn by the most binding oaths to sacrifice themselves to the service of taking the life of the Queen."

"Oh, the villains!" said Grasp, rubbing his hands with delight at the prospect of being accessory to the discovery of a conspiracy of so much magnitude. "Oh, the caitiffs! a plot to destroy our blessed Queen, and ruin the nation! now that's what I call worth living to hear of. I'm a made man, that's clear."

"Nay, but," said Neville, "we must go warily to work, good Grasp; and I must damp the exuberance of thy glee a trifle, inasmuch as this business is likely to implicate and deprive thee perhaps of a client of thine."

"Ah," said Grasp, his countenance falling a little, "that's rather bad, who is the man?"

"Sir Hugh Clopton."

"Thou hast taken my breath away," said Grasp, recoiling a pace or two. "Sir Hugh Clopton, whom men call the good Sir Hugh, engaged in such a bloodthirsty and jesuitical plot as this? Are you quite sure, honoured sir, of the correctness of what you utter?"

"I am quite sure that some of those engaged and deeply pledged to assassinate the Queen have been in hiding at Clopton Hall within the last two days. Nay, I shall be able to identify several of the best Catholic families in this county, as having been in correspondence with emissaries in Scotland, not only to assassinate Elizabeth, but to set the Queen of Scots at liberty, and place the crown upon her head."

"Nay, this is glorious," said Grasp; "the plot does indeed thicken, as the saying is. The fiend take the good Sir Hugh; I would sacrifice fifty such clients, and see them hanged, drawn, and quartered into the bargain, for such a chance as this. And now let us lay our heads together, and consult how to capture these bloody-minded conspirators with most advantage to our own proper selves. How shall we proceed, honoured sir? Shall we rouse the whole *posse comitatus*, and attack the house in which these miscreants are engendering, and hatching, and concocting these horrors; or, shall we go incontinent, and give secret intelligence to Sir Thomas Lucy at Charlecote?"

"That I must leave to your discretion, good Grasp," said Neville. "Your part must be to secure them ere twenty-four hours have elapsed. Meantime, I must ride post haste to London, and give information to the Queen or her ministers of the whole affair."

"I would your worship would remain here, and capture the caitiffs, whilst I proceed up to town with information," said Grasp. "Methinks, as you are a man of *war*, and I am a man of *law*, that would be the most proper arrangement."

"By no means," said Neville. "Manage the matter as I have told thee. Do it well and effectually, and reward is sure to follow to us both. It is essential that I should myself gain favour by the discovery, and if I should succeed to the estates and title of Westmoreland, I shall not forget the service you have rendered. Be wary, and prosper. Farewell." So saying, the visitor hastily took his leave, and a few minutes afterwards was riding furiously towards Warwick, on his way to London.

"Now, there's a bloody-minded and dangerous Jesuit for you," said Grasp to himself. "He thinks I know not that he's a Catholic, I suppose, and that I cannot guess he has been as deep in this vile plot as the rest of them. But I do bear a brain, and I can perceive that the death of his relation hath completely turned his conscience, and now, in place of helping to murder the Queen, he's going to hang up all his associates, by turning evidence. A bad world, my masters, and bad folks in it! But then it's by the bad I gain and thrive; bickerings, quarrellings, evil-speaking, lying, and slander, plots, counterplots, conspiracies, hangings, and headings, are my especial good. So now to consider and contrive this matter. Let me see—I instantly hasten off to the high bailiff, get together a sufficient body of his men, and then, my masters, look to yourselves! A plot to kill the Queen, subvert the Government, and burn the whole kingdom in an *auto-da-fé!* By all that's good, the business will not be effected without blood-letting on both sides! Let me see, who have we of approved valour and conduct to aid us in this capture? There's Master John Shakespeare; he's a good man and a true one, that will thrust in, and smite hard. His grandsire did good service at Bosworth Field. Then there's Goodman Rivett, the armourer; he hath an arm of might, and a heart of steel,—him will I also look up, an we need special men. Then there's— Yet," continued Grasp, pausing, and considering the matter, "methinks, after all, it would be better to put the affair at once into the management of Sir Thomas Lucy. Yes, I will incontinently and instantaneously proceed to Charlecote, and do so. Let me see; 'tis now about one hour after noon. I shall catch the proud knight just before he takes his post-prandium ride."

So saying, Grasp donned his hat, and prepared for his visit to Charlecote.

CHAPTER XII.

THE SONNET.

When Shakespeare took leave of his newly-found friends at Clopton, he left a deep impression behind him.

There was a feeling amongst the trio, which two of them at least could not understand; so greatly had the youth's manners struck them, so forcible was the interest he had created; whilst the third and most interesting of the party found that the handsome lad had unconsciously robbed her of her heart.

"By 'r Lady," said the old knight, "yonder stripling is one of the most singular companions I ever met; without being in the least forward in manners, he somehow impresses one with a feeling of inferiority I cannot understand. He's an extraordinary youth, my masters; and, an he turn not out something beyond the common, I am not a Clopton."

"How well he talks on all subjects!" said Arderne; "and yet how modest doth he seem!"

"How beautiful were those verses he wrote this morning!" said Charlotte.

"If he did write them," said Martin, "lady mine; *for mark ye*, they may be the offspring of another brain."

"*If* he wrote them! Martin," said Charlotte: "why, who else could have written them, think ye?"

"Why not another as well as he, lady mine?" said Martin, archly; "what one man can do, another might effect. Methinks one older and more learned must have indited those lines."

"Nay," said Charlotte, "I know not wherefore, but sure I feel that none but he could have penned that sonnet."

"Gramercy," said Martin, "this is to have an opinion of merit, indeed! Doth that stripling, that hero of the quarter-staff, seem to you, Master Walter," he continued, shrewdly glancing at Arderne, "to have so much merit that none other can come up to him?"

"I confess the lad hath made a singular impression upon me," said Arderne, "an impression I cannot shake off or understand. I never was in company with so amiable a youth before."

"Let us hear his verse again," said Sir Hugh. "Come, Martin, thou hast a voice, thou shalt read it."

"Ahem," said Martin. "I am no hand at a stanza; I shall mar the good verse, I fear me. Nevertheless, I will essay it."

THE SONNET.

Who will believe my verse in time to come,
  If it were filled with your most high deserts?
Though yet, Heaven knows, it is but as a tomb
  Which hides your life, and shews not half your parts.
If I could write the beauty of your eyes,
  And in fresh numbers, number all your graces,
The age to come would say, this poet lies,
  Such heavenly touches ne'er touched earthly faces.
So should my papers, yellow'd with their age,
  Be scorn'd like old men of less truth than tongue;
And your true rights be termed a poet's rage,
  And stretched metre of an antique song:
But where some child of yours alive that time,
You should live twice,—in it, and in my rhyme.

Sir Hugh was a man of parts. He was a man, too, of strong sense, and, for the age in which he lived, might have been esteemed and accounted a learned man withal.

Had he chosen to be more of a courtier, and his creed been different, he might have risen to some eminence as a statesman.

He felt considerable astonishment, and expressed no less admiration, at the beauty of the verses just recited.

"Now, by my fay, good Martin," said he, "I do somewhat lean to thy opinion in the matter, inasmuch as it seemeth scarce possible so young a lad could have penned such stanzas. Nay, by our Lady, I know not where to look amongst our old poets in order to find aught to equal those lines."

"Then where hath the lad gotten them from?" said Arderne. "Peradventure he hath fetched them from some recent book of songs and sonnets; they say young Spencer hath lately written."

"'Tis not in Spencer's vein," said Charlotte; "and since we have so far discussed the matter, I must needs say that I can almost vouch for his having written them."

"Ho! ho!" said Martin, with a shrewd look. "La! you there now. Come, tell us the when, the where, and the how, Lady Charlotte. Let us have the circumstances under which this sonnet was written, since you confess to so much knowledge of the matter."

"Nay, Martin," said Charlotte, blushing; "it was by accident I discovered so much. Walter and myself had been walking under the shade of the tall trees at the end of the garden, when I observed the youth standing, with arms folded, and gazing upon us in the arbour at its extremity. As we leisurely approached him, I saw him tear a leaf from a small book he held in his hand, and write something in it. When we entered the arbour and joined him, in putting up his book, he dropped the stray leaf, upon which he had been writing, and I own I was wicked enough to let it lie, and secure it after he had left us."

"Well," said Sir Hugh, "the lad is certainly a youth of merit, and I feel bound to befriend him in what I can. We must bethink us, Walter, in what way we can serve him materially."

"He is at present, as he tells me," said Arderne, "a clerk or writer in the service of Lawyer Grasp; albeit he liketh not the drudgery and confinement of such a life."

"I wonder not thereat," said Sir Hugh; "since to sentence a lad of so much genius to be a scrivener's clerk, is like putting my best bred palfrey into a mill, or shutting up a soaring falcon in a thrush's cage. We must do something for him, Walter, for we owe much to him."

Such were the kind intentions of the good Sir Hugh towards one to whom he felt under considerable obligations, and doubtless he who had caused those grateful feelings would have felt the benefit of them from one so well off in the world. "Wishing well, however, hath not a body in it;" and our intents of to-day are oft-times marred by the events of to-morrow.

The promises of the powerful are oft-times a sort of "satire upon the softness of prosperity;" and in a few days the good Sir Hugh was himself involved in difficulties which made him oblivious of all, save honourable extrication from their labyrinth.

The conversation which had taken place regarding the sonnet, occurred on the day following that on which young Shakespeare had left the Hall: a day made more memorable to two of the inmates, from the circumstance of the unwelcome visit of Gilbert Parry, and which it is our purpose now again to refer to, in order to explain certain other matters appertaining.

It will doubtless be remembered by our readers that the shrewd Martin had played the spy upon the insane conspirator, and succeeded in making himself complete master of his horrid and perilous intentions. Intentions, the more dangerous to all who were in the slightest degree implicated, as the bloody designs and desperate projects which were suspected to be in existence against the Queen on all sides, had determined Elizabeth's council to make terrible examples of all whom they might discover. To the good Sir Hugh, however, the danger likely to accrue to his own person was the least consideration; and when the faithful Martin, accordingly, on the following morning, informed him of the intentions of the visitor and his own suspicions of his sanity, the good knight was struck with consternation. It was early morning when Martin told his tale to his patron, and when the old knight having just descended, was making the round of his kennel and falconry, and the relation at once filled him with terror, pity, and indignation.

"I will incontinently visit this dangerous caitiff," he said, "and if I find matters as bad as you say, I will take means to secure him and prevent mischief. If he be indeed mad, it is my duty, as a Christian man, to lay him under restraint; but if he be sane and resolved on such attempt, I swear to thee I will arrest him with my own hand, and deliver him over to justice."

"Beware!" said Martin, stopping him as he was hastening off in search of his visitor. "Beware, good master mine, how you introduce yourself alone into the den of a tiger. This fellow is dangerous in the extreme; and on the slightest hint of your knowledge and disapproval of his designs, will fly upon you and attempt your life. A madman I have heard say, in his furious fits, hath twice the strength of one in possession of reason."

"I value not his madness a maravedi," said Sir Hugh, whose anger was predominant at the moment. "A murderous caitiff and condemned felon thus to introduce himself into my house! By our Lady's grace, an he draw weapon or lift hand against me, I will smite him in the teeth with my dagger, and kill him like the reptile at my foot."

"At least, let me accompany you," said Martin, who saw that the angry spirit so seldom aroused was now predominant, and therefore the more resistless.

"Follow an ye list," said Sir Hugh, "but I tell thee I am quite able to cope with such a fellow, and equal to arrest him if I find his purpose treasonable;" so saying, and followed by the faithful Martin, Sir Hugh re-entered the house, and the pair, introducing themselves into the secret wing of the mansion, immediately ascended into the chamber in which Parry had been shewn the night before.

Sir Hugh was the first to enter, and, with the angry spot upon his brow, after hastily glancing round the small room advanced to the bed and pulled open the curtain with no very gentle hand.

The bed, however, was unoccupied, aud the room tenantless, although the crumpled state of the coverlid of the couch and pillows shewed that the occupant had thrown himself upon it during some part of the night at least.

" There is the form," said Sir Hugh, " but the game is off."

" There is no saying where such a customer may have crept to," said Martin, peeping under the bed, then getting up on one of the chairs and looking out of the small window upon the roof. " The man I am sure is as mad as a March hare; let us descend and see if he is any where secreted in the small apartment below."

Sir Hugh accordingly descended, and (both together) searched in every closet and hiding hole with which the place was accommodated, but the bird had certainly flown, having, without doubt, passed into the garden by the small postern door which opened on the inside.

Proceeding into the garden they searched through its walks and alleys, but the object of their search was no where to be found, and the small door which opened in the thick high wall at its extremity, and admitted into the thick plantations beyond, being wide open, they naturally concluded their visitor had fairly decamped in his insane mood as unceremoniously as he had entered. Sir Hugh, however (although he could not but feel relieved at the absence of the dangerous intruder), felt considerable annoyance at the whole circumstance. He was oppressed with the knowledge of the maniac's treason, and which, notwithstanding the powerful letter brought to him from the Nuncio Campeggio, he was resolved to divulge to the Queen's council. At the same time he also determined to do nothing rashly. Father Eustace was expected in a few hours, and must be consulted, whilst Martin, meanwhile, undertook to endeavour to trace the madman and observe his motions if possible.

In such a case delays are dangerous, as the good Sir Hugh found, for Parry, whose vagaries had alarmed some of those connected with the dangerous plot, having been met with in Stratford, and then followed to Clopton, was lured into a secret appointment and put to silence with at least half a dozen wounds; and the whole affair in a few short hours after was in progress of being fully divulged. Of this, however, Sir Hugh was not likely to become acquainted, till the news reached him in an unpleasant shape. The circumstance of a man having been killed just without the town was by no means an uncommon event; and as Martin had failed in tracing Parry, and Father Eustace's return was delayed, except that there was a degree of mystery attached to the appearance and disappearance of the visitor, in a few days the circumstance was almost forgotten.

Meantime, whilst, with swift passage, events were hastening onwards, and which were to involve some of the *dramatis personæ* of our story in the perils and miseries of life, how calmly and how treacherously flowed on the even tenor of their hours. Mischief, as we have seen, was afoot; a secret society, consisting of one or two dangerous fanatics, resident in the county of Warwick, an Irish gentleman of rank, and several other desperadoes, had met, as we have before hinted, at one of the low hostels in the town of Stratford, and which locality they had chosen for some reason best known to themselves.

These men, involved in a desperate enterprise, and sworn to devote themselves to death one by one, till they had achieved it, whilst they sought to increase the number of their associates, found danger even in the over zeal—the frenzied enthusiasm—of one of their own instruments, whilst another was about to prove false and betray them; nay, at the very moment when, like the alchemist of old, their toils were to be rewarded with progression, the vessel containing the elixir was to burst, and destroy all within its influence.

These emissaries were at work in various directions,—secretly, stealthily. They had friends in France, in Spain, in Italy, in Flanders even; the day and the hour at which the first attempt was to be made was fixed; the very hooftreads of the horse which carried the unscrupulous Neville towards his design, in imagination, were counted by them; whilst he who was then, as his associates supposed, hastening towards this purpose, from a sudden change having taken place in his before desperate fortunes, was indeed posting to London; not, as he had sworn, in order to make essay upon the life of Elizabeth, but to betray the whole plot to the council, to aggrandize himself, and give to the gibbet and the executioner's knife, his sometime friends.

And such are the inscrutable ways by which Providence works out His ends: such is the wisdom of the Great Director of events, and such are the vain designs of man. Ever driving headlong onwards, hastened by evil passions, obstinacy, wickedness, and pride, to inevitable destruction;—destroyed by their own villanous devices, thirsting for blood, grasping at riches, feeding absolutely on each other, the wicked perish miserably.

CHAPTER XIII.

MOTHER AND SON.

Those of our readers who have visited Stratford-upon-Avon, and looked upon the house in Henley Street, that house which has caused so great an interest in the world, will remember the lattice-windowed room in its upper floor, that room in which (as their eyes have glanced around its walls) their feelings have perhaps been excited almost unto the shedding of tears;—that room in which some portion of the early youth of him whose idea is enshrined in the hearts of all who speak our English tongue, was passed.

It is mid-day, and seated in that room are a mother and an elder son. The mother is employed in some sort of curious work, whilst her baby is cradled, and asleep at her side. Spinning perhaps, like "the spinsters and the knitters of the sun,"—

"Weaving her threads with bones,"

lace-making; and as she works, she chants some old ditty,—some song, "that dallies with the innocence of love, like the old age."

"Come away, come away, death,
And in sad cypress let me be laid;
Fly away, fly away, breath,
I am slain by a fair cruel maid:
My shroud of white, stuck all with yew,
O, prepare it—
My part of death no one so true
Did share it.

Not a flower, not a flower, sweet,
On my black coffin let there be strewn;
Not a friend, not a friend, greet
My poor corpse, where my bones shall be thrown;
A thousand, thousand sighs to save,
Lay me, O where
Sad true lover ne'er find my grave,
To weep there." *

And whilst she sings, the youth, her son, seated upon a stool at her feet, is deeply engaged in perusing the goodly-sized volume he holds upon his knees.

Such is the picture. The sun streams through the diamond panes of that ample window, and gives a glowing tint to the red curtains of the old square-topped bedstead, and other cumbrous articles of furniture; the high-backed chairs, and the heavy oaken table in the background. What would the illustrious of the world,—what would the most honoured in the world's esteem, of our own day, for arts, for arms, or for learning,—what would they give for *one* glance into "the dark backwaıd and abysm of time,"—but *one* glance, so to see that mother and her son;—that mother who implanted grace in her child; that child whose high spirit had been tamed and cultivated by her influence? And what, indeed, should we all be, saith a great writer, but for the influence of women in our youth?

They give us life, and they also give us the life of the soul. How many things do we learn of them as sons, lovers, or friends?

The youthful Shakespeare loved to hold sweet converse with his handsome mother, and whom he loved so well. From her conversation in his boyhood he had taken his first impressions of things: from her

* "Twelfth Night."

legendary stories, (so sweetly related,) he had gathered many facts of history. In winter's tedious nights, how oft had she pictured to him all she had heard from her own parents, of the York and Lancastrian wars, and the horrors to which England had been reduced—"Discord in every state, discord in every family!" From her's, and from his father's relations, over the winter's fire, were gathered the boy's first impressions of those fierce English, whose characteristics (according to their foes) were force of pride, and obstinacy—those doggedly resolute, those invincibly cool islanders, who, in all their splendour of their feudal pride, had so often walked through the vasty fields of France, as if in some harnessed masque, eating up the lands on all sides, and still fighting onwards in their own joyless way: burning, slaying, and destroying for so many centuries, till they made captive at Agincourt, not only of the French king, but the very realm.

'Twas thus the boy had learnt his first lesson in the history of his country, not either exactly as a lesson, but in the homely popular form of a winter night's tale, as the simple story, or faith of a mother.

And what we thus inbibe with the milk we suck, and with our growing blood, is a living thing as it were, and what the boy loved to listen to as a simple story, the youth loved to follow out as a study. He reads of the events his mother has told him of, and given him a taste for, in the chronicled history of the wars of the time; whilst the little of life and splendour he has already seen, in the brilliant era in which he lives, has given him, even now, an impression of the pride, pomp, and circumstance of the Norman period.

Yes, the mind of the boy had been moulded by his mother, and a great deal of his just appreciation of women, and his delineations of the exquisite females he has drawn, are derived from the impressions she has given him.

As he reads from the thick volume, in which he learnt more accurately the facts, and date, of the history of his own country, he occasionally pauses to listen to his mother's song, to gaze up in her face, and to question her upon some point hė has arrived at, and which he remembers to have heard her relate before.

Music and singing were much more cultivated (even amongst the humble classes) than in our own times, in England, and where indeed they are now scarcely cultivated at all. The sweet old songs "of the old age," are for the most part lost to us, they have departed with the quainter dwellings in which they were warbled.

In those days the strains which floated through the halls of the great, and the notes which were heard in the low-roofed apartments of the citizen, were calculated to soothe and quiet the passions of man. In our own times they are meant to arouse and excite—they are a whirl, a discordant noise. The lullabys which the mother chanted as she worked, were scraps of songs, great favourites at the time, and afterwards adapted from the recollection of the hearer in some of his works:

> "Take, oh, take those lips away,
> That so sweetly were forsworn,—
> And those eyes, the break of day,
> Lights that do mislead the morn.
> But my kisses bring again,—bring again,
> Seals of love, but seal'd in vain,- -seal'd in vain." *

Not only the history of his own land, and which all ranks at this period were lamentably ignorant in, did the youthful Shakespeare receive the rudiments of from his mother; but she loved to amuse him with those stories of romance she had learned from her own parents, and which had been handed down from the chivalric ages, when the female of high degree was the teacher of youth. The great lady—"of exalted rank and inaccessible,"—who cultivates the mind of the youthful page—a mother, a sister, a guardian angel, and yet of such high degree, that she seems (in the austerity of her counsels, and the difficulties to be overcome, ere her favour can be gained) to great even to receive the adoration of him whose service costs so many sighs. Till in the end, as the accomplished knight is produced, the incarnation of merit and grace all fades away before the powerful god.

The youth achieves greatness, and becomes lord of that beautiful lady, her dark castle, and her broad domain, "with shadowy forests, and with champions rich."

CHAPTER XIV.

THE LOVERS.

But three days had intervened since young Shakespeare's introduction to Clopton Hall, and again he was a visitor there.

Although his own desire for the society of its amiable inmates might reasonably have led the youth to repeat his visit, his better judgment would have hindered him from so soon returning to Clopton, had he not been led to do so by Walter Arderne.

That young man felt so great a desire to renew his acquaintance with the youthful poet, that he had sought him out on the day following his visit; and had, indeed, been with him every succeeding day in the interval.

To one so amiable in disposition and so generous in sentiment as Walter Arderne, the difference in station between himself and friend was no bar to intimacy. Indeed, he felt so much in every way his own

* This song, which, no doubt, was a favourite in its day, in inserted in Beaumont and Fletcher's "Bloody Brother."

inferiority, whilst in company with this singular new acquaintance, that it seemed when in his society as if the condescension was on the other side. At the same time the joyous spirit of the youthful Shakespeare, and a spice of reckless daring in his disposition, gave an additional charm to his companionship. So that intimacy, which (amongst many) has been the source of the deadliest enmity, in this case led to the firmest friendship.

"I know not wherefore, good William," said Arderne, as they slowly wended their way towards Clopton, "but towards thee my feelings of friendship and attachment are greater than is ordinarily experienced between men not connected by blood. I am by birth thy superior, my prospects in life are more brilliant than thine, I mix with the choice spirits of the country here, and yet (albeit I am looked on as a wit, a setter of exploits, a leader of diversions, a good blade, and a sportsman), yet, somehow, my genius seems rebuked when in thy presence; I feel myself as it were naught. Nay, despite thy sober suit of homely cut and fashion, there is a superiority in every look, tone, and movement of thine, which I feel and wonder at."

"Nay," said Shakespeare, "this is something too much, good sir. 'Tis your love and friendship which makes you think thus. Be assured, the gay and gallant Walter Arderne can never be outshone by so quiet, so unobtrusive a wight as myself,"

"Ah, so thou say'st," returned Arderne; "but why is it that I feel this veneration on so short an acquaintance with a mere boy? Thy converse is different from that of men even of learning and great attainments. There is a force, a feeling in every word thou utterest, which makes its impression. Yes, there is a manner about thee, William Shakespeare, which is inexplicable; whilst thy slightest remark upon the most trivial flowret in the hedgerow seems to me worth all the uttered wisdom of the schools."

"Nay, then," said Shakespeare, laughing, "thou art but flouting me, good Master Walter."

"Truly, thou art an extraordinary youth, good William, and the way thou hast drawn out the different characters we have met with as we walked the streets even to-day, and made them display their peculiarities and their follies, is as singular as all else pertaining to thee."

Whilst they held converse thus, Walter Arderne and his new friend drew near to the garden and pleasure-grounds of the Hall. As they did so, the eyes of the lover detected his mistress in the distance. She was slowly pacing along one of the walks, and perusing some verses written upon a small scrap of paper. Arderne stopped as soon as he saw Charlotte Clopton, and as he watched her graceful form amidst the trees, he seemed for the moment wrapped in his own thoughts.

"Were it not," he said, after a pause, and turning to his youthful friend, "were it not that I so entirely love thee, good William, were it not that even in our short acquaintance I so highly esteem thee, I should hesitate to bring one so superior to myself in contact with her I adore;

and were it not that thy superiority is so great, I should scorn to own such a feeling to thee, William Shakespeare, lest I compromised my own station by such thoughts. 'Tis strange, but so it is; and to any one but thee, I should have shamed to give my thoughts tongue on such a subject."

Arderne sighed as he said this, and again looked towards the object of his ardent affection. "She loves me not," he said, "'tis vain for me to suppose she does. Her manner, despite her willingness to oblige her father, and even to persuade herself she feels inclination to wed with me, too plainly shews I have little or no real interest in her heart. Had I but thy winning tongue and gift of speech, good William, I might do much. Nay, it were good that thou shouldst plead for me, and tell her of the violence of my passion; and thou shalt do it too."

"Nay," said his friend, "that would be somewhat out of the usual course of wooing. I pray you hold me excused in this Master Arderne."

"Not a whit," said Arderne, "the thought is a good one. Women oft-times are led to prize that which those they think well of value,—to open their eyes and see clearly the hugeness of an affection they have not before appreciated."

"But I know not how to woo a maid for myself," said his friend, "since I have never yet made suit to one, how, then, am I to play the suitor for so accomplished a cavalier; I who hath not ever seen the court?"

"Tush, tush, man," said Arderne, "there's ne'er a courtier of them all could match thee, I dare be sworn."

And thus did the boy poet—the lover under circumstances so peculiar, spend another day at Clopton Hall, and where all he saw gave him a second impression of life in a different sphere to that in which he had hitherto moved. True to the whimsical project which had suddenly seized him, Walter Arderne left his friend with a fair opportunity of pleading for him to the fair Charlotte.

"When thou art tired of examining those worm-eaten volumes," he said to Shakespeare, "I dare be sworn thou wilt find Mistress Charlotte in her favourite arbour in the garden. Sir Hugh and myself are promised forth this morning. Farewell, therefore, for the present."

Our readers will readily imagine that the renewal of acquaintance between this youthful pair would be likely to ripen the growing affection they felt for each other. Concealment, however, seemed to both a matter of necessity. Neither dared to own, even to themselves, that they loved. Pride came to the aid of each. In one it was the pride which fears even the shadow of suspicion; in the other it was the pride of birth. The pride of ancestry, however, is soonest subdued in such cases; that of conscience is more difficult for the blind god to overcome.

And the youthful poet and the exquisite Charlotte found themselves thrown together, where every scene of beauty around them was conducive to the growth of their passion.

The locality has oft-times much to do with love.

The lady, in all her glowing beauty, seemed even more lovely amidst her own shadowy groves, with the time-honoured towers of her ancestors looking majestic in the distance. The perfume from the sweetly-scented shrubs and flowrets, the whisper of the soft breeze through the luxuriant trees, the cooing of the wood-pigeons in the distant plantation, the hum of the bees, and the plash of the fountain, each and all were felt by one who was so prone to feel.

And he himself who walked beside that beautiful girl, thus surrounded by all the appliances of rank and station, how did he appear in her eyes in his lowly suit? Had he nothing to recommend him, and did he seem unfitted for the companionship of one so much more elevated in station? Did he appear to feel himself out of place or abashed by all he saw? We think not. The lady looked upon that face of youthful beauty; the soft curly hair even then thin upon the high forehead, the features so beautifully formed and so expressive; that eye so soft, and yet at times so full of fire, and whose glance was like the lightning's flash; the small beautifully-formed and downy moustache upon the upper lip; and all this, added to a figure which for grace and symmetry might have vied with a Grecian statue. And as she looked and listened to his sweet and honied sentences, she felt that all around would darken down to naked waste without his society. The conversation of him who but a few days before she would have passed without perhaps deigning to look upon, seemed to have opened a new world to her. Such is love,—that most fantastic of passions, which is said to be but once felt, and once felt never forgotten.

The affections of women are perhaps easier won than those of men. They are commonly more disinterested, and "prize not quality of dirty lands." Seldom do we find that women display such open heartlessness, such acts of infidelity, as men.

"For however we do praise ourselves,
Our fancies are more giddy and infirm,
More longing, wavering, sooner lost and won,
Than woman's are."

That the fair Charlotte should, on better knowledge, more fully appreciate the merits of her companion, we of latter days, who imagine the man from his works alone, can hardly wonder at; and the peculiarities of the position of the lovers made her, falling desperately in love, the less extraordinary. Had the youth of inferior degree presumed upon the favourable impression he could not help seeing he had made, the pride of the lady might have better befriended her. But there was ever a certain reserve about him, when matters seemed verging towards their issue, which perplexed and somewhat piqued her.

The expression of his eyes, when occasionally she detected him gazing upon her, was hardly to be mistaken, but then his respectful reserve would as suddenly return.

This was, however, a state of things which could not last, and perhaps, of all men, the ardent, the impassioned Shakespeare, in his early youth, was the most unlikely person to withstand such a strife as he was exposed to, and come off victorious, however honour, and friendship, and pride, might come to his aid. The knowledge that he was beloved by the fair creature beside him, the locality, the opportunity afforded him of expressing his own feelings, altogether, even in this his second visit, nearly made shipwreck of all his good intentions, and once or twice he was about to seize the hand of the fair Charlotte, and after owning the ardour of his affection, fly from the spot for ever.

He, however, during this visit did manage to contain and conceal his passion; nay, he even performed the office of friendship which had been entrusted to him, and as he spoke of the fair lady's betrothed husband, he praised him for those good qualities he had already found him to possess, and spoke of him as one worthy the love and regard of any woman, however excellent and high in station. This was a theme, however, which he perceived was somewhat unwelcome, and the beauty grew wayward as he pursued it. With girlish tact she beat him from his theme, as often as he renewed it, and sought to lure him to other subjects more congenial to her thoughts whilst in his society. Nay, perhaps had he studied how best to advance his own suit to her he could not have hit upon a way more likely to succeed.

The fair Charlotte was piqued at what she considered his insensibility, and without considering what she did, she almost let him understand that it would have been much more grateful to her to have heard the speaker's own merits extolled than those of Master Arderne.

"And yet," she said, with a sigh, as she glanced archly from her fringed lids, whilst her eyes were cast down in mock solemnity, "and yet I should be ungrateful were I not to join in your praises towards my bold coz, for in good sooth I am indebted to him for many of the accomplishments I possess. He hath taught me to fly my hawk with e'er a cavalier in Warwickshire. Nay, I think I could even shoe my palfrey as well as ride him, if necessary. I am sure I could train a hound as well as himself, and, as for the treatment of the poor brutes in all their ailments, that I am confident I understand quite as much as old Hubert, the head huntsman, or any of his underlings. Now, all these matters I have been fairly taught and perfected in by my cousin, therefore see an I be not under obligation indeed."

"And is such the praise that one so true of heart and hand deserves?" said Shakespeare. "Methinks, in this world, where so much silliness, selfishness, vanity, and falsehood exists, a perfect cavalier, without fault and honest, open and free too as he is brave and handsome, deserves more praise from the lips of beauty than for paltry knowledge you have ascribed to him."

"Paltry knowledge!" said Charlotte, laughing, "what call ye paltry? Why, these accomplishments I have enumerated to thee are the essentials of a country gentleman, as necessary for the woods and fields as dancing, dicing, and swearing are for the town. But methinks 'tis somewhat early for you to have taken note of the silliness and falsehood existing in the world; one so young can scarce have observed such matters, I should have thought."

"Pardon me, good lady," said Shakespeare, "what may be in the world at large I am, indeed, for the most part ignorant in. But our good town of Stratford hath in itself some fair specimens of the human mortal, which he who hath eyes to mark, and brains to consider, may easily profit by, and lay up in his memory."

"Methinks so shrewd an observer, and so keen withal, may chance to find us all fair mark for the shafts of his wit," returned Charlotte; "we shall learn to fear you, young sir, an ye prove so hard upon your neighbours."

"Nay, fair lady," said Shakespeare, "my observations hath only had to do with those in my own sphere of life. The little I have seen as yet in a higher grade, hath been glanced at during my boyhood at the Free School of my native town. Nay, if I may venture to judge, I should say that the same vices, the same ambitions, the same petty feelings, jealousies, and envious heart-burnings, are to be observed in the smaller circle of a charity-school and its rulers, as are to be observed in the great and universal theatre of the world. Amongst those who rule, we do not always find examples of unerring goodliness, grace, and virtue, but rather intolerance and pride, and in most others ill-will, conceit, envy, hatred, and uncharitableness; large promise; much of puritanism, but a plentiful lack of true merit."

During this visit, the fair Charlotte, who was all joyous anxiety to contribute to the amusement of her guest, made the round of the kennel and the falconry, in order to initiate him into the mysteries of the management of some of her pets.

In those days, as we have before hinted, men of all ranks took delight in out-door sports and diversions. Their amusements were, for the most part, in the open air, and the chase, and the terms of wood-craft were ever mixed up in their conversation. The veriest lout in his holiday excursion loved to see his mongrel cur hunt the meadows and marshes for game, or catch the cony in the extensive warrens which then existed around. The youthful Shakespeare, it may therefore be well imagined, was passionately fond of seeking the haunts of the game, abundant as it was in the neighbourhood of his native town. Under these circumstances the sporting establishment at Clopton was looked over with considerable interest by him, and as the fair Charlotte petted the favourite hawk which usually graced her wrist, she taught him the several terms of falconry, and even explained how the various grades of men in the old time were recognized by their hawks. "An eagle," she said, "is for an emperor; a gerfalcon is due to a king; a falcon-gentle and a tercel-gentle, these be for a prince; a falcon of the rock is for a duke; the falcon peregrine for a belted earl; your bustard is for a baron; a sacret for a knight, and a lanair is for a squire; and then," said Charlotte, as she continued to count up further varieties, "we have the goshawk for the yeoman, the spave hawk for Sir Priest, a muskyte for a holy-water clerk, and a kestrel for a knave or varlet."

Whilst thus situated and employed, how swift is the growth of love between two beings of disposition and character such as we have described. As the youthful poet watched the expressive face of the beautiful girl beside him, whilst she spoke so eloquently upon a subject of interest to her, and as she gave herself up to the management of her falcon, or played with and fondled her favourite dogs, he became more fascinated with her artlessness and beauty. He marked the natural grace of her movements, as, in all the freedom of unchecked enjoyment, she entered into the excitement of the hour. He observed the nymph-like figure, the glowing face, the luxuriant tresses uncontrolled in the soft breeze, and he listened with delight to the joyous and ringing laugh; and as he beheld her thus, his admiration was touched with sadness, for he thought that all this elegance and beauty was far removed from his hopes. "One fading moment's mirth" perchance was bought "with twenty watchful, weary, tedious nights."

Attended by the head falconer and one or two of his men, as they followed the flight of Charlotte's hawk, they had extended their ramble to some considerable distance beyond the chace, and the mid-day sun was so oppressive, that they returned through the thick and shadowy woods, which on one side extended to within a short distance of the Hall. And here too—as the grasshopper uttered his peculiar chirp in the prickling gorse and thorn, and as the sweet scent of the fern pervaded the air—these unfrequented glades gave rise to thoughts only incident to fresh and stainless youth ere the blunter feelings of riper years rob us of their verdant freshness.

Images of vernal brightness floated before the poet's mind, and feelings of youth, and hope, and joy were blended with the thoughts of her he loved: images such as Shakespeare could alone have conceived. And she who was the object of that love, as she listened to the sportive gaiety of his words, during this ramble, and as he called forth the elves and fairies of his brilliant imagination, she felt as if wandering in a magic grove and breathing the sweet odours of an elfin bower: and then, again, he peopled the glades with bright forms, fresh and lusty as in the first ages of the world. And when he himself parted from his fair companion on reaching the Hall, and he returned again through the plantations of Clopton, he sought out each spot which Charlotte had seemed most interested in, and dwelt upon each look, and tone, and word, she had uttered. 'Twas indeed a midsummer day's dream, a situation in which he was carried from the reality of the present, to the realms of fancy, a dream that haunted him in after years. The thoughts and imaginings which pervaded the mind of the youthful Shakespeare, during these moments, were what perhaps he himself would have failed in describing.

Few of us can convey in words the heavenly images which float in celestial ether, as it were, through the brain. We feel in the feeble attempt the unsufficing medium of language. Words are but the clayed embodiment of the swift thought. The thought itself is the essence of the soul—poetry unspeakable. We cannot word that which is divine. Language has no power to render again the shadowy dream—the musing reverie.

Whilst under the influence of feelings such as these, the society and the haunts of men were uncongenial to the poetic youth, and he usually sought out the wildest scenes of his native country. Over park, over pale, he bounded, and the keepers, who caught sight of him occasionally in their forest walks, failed in arresting him in his rambles.

CHAPTER XV.

CHARLECOTE.

In a former chapter we have seen the sharp and sententious Lawyer Grasp, in the act of girding up his loins and preparing to set forth upon a somewhat important mission: a matter, indeed, not likely to be effected without some little danger to all concerned in its execution. The shrewd lawyer, however, to say the least of him, was not altogether devoid of courage, and, albeit his valour was modified by a certain degree of discretion, he loved to be first when anything was to be gained by leading the van.

In the present instance he thought he spied a good chance of promotion, both as regarding his instrumentality in apprehending or gaining notice of a dangerous plot, but he also hoped to make a profitable intimacy with the proud owner of Charlecote: and, as he spurred his palfry onwards, visions of suits, and testaments, and title deeds, and strong boxes, pertaining to the domain he was entering, floated through his brain in rapid succession.

Plots and complots, conspiracies, and secret meetings to kill a queen, were, indeed, in his eye, as nothing, unless pertaining to the advancement of one small person who wrote himself attorney in the town of Stratford: and who hoped, one day, to be the richest and greatest man there. The world around was nothing: the covering sky was nothing; England was nothing, except as pertaining to Master Pouncet Grasp; nay, so long as the small circle of air around his own proper person was wholesome and fit for the purposes of respiration, it would have been all the same to him if the atmosphere in general were infected with the plague. He was, indeed, without question, the most selfish little caitiff that ever drove a quill upon parchment.

Charlecote, the residence of Sir Thomas Lucy, was one of those vast, irregularly built, but picturesque looking mansions, which gives impression, at first sight, of the architectural style of the Tudors. Redolent of red brick picked out with white, full of large bay windows, beetling balconies, twisted chimneys, gable ends, and gate-houses. A magnificent structure looking like a brick-built palace, situate in the midst of the most luxuriant foliage; which partially concealed its multitudinous offices, its falconries, its dog-kennels, and its thick-walled gardens.

As Grasp, therefore, approached this curious building, he beheld its embattled towers and massive chimneys embosomed in ancient trees of vast size, and most soft and lovely foliage. Nothing, perhaps, could be more impressive than the whole scene. The vast park studded with mossed trees, and the herded deer couched in the fern, beneath the shade. The gigantic avenue, flourishing in all the grandeur of its undecayed age, and each particular tree throwing its deep shadow upon the grassy carpet beneath, with the lordly mansion only partially seen at its extremity.

As Grasp entered this gloomy, but majestic avenue, he drew bridle, and paused for a few moments to reassure himself, and consider matters over, and as he did so, he became impressed with the deep and solemn silence reigning around, a silence only occasionally interrupted by the baying howl from the kennel, an occasional winding note from the huntsman's bugle, or the clear ringing sound of the old clock from the tower of the red brick gate-house.

As the little lawyer gazed around, a sort of awe crept over his paltry soul, he became at each step more deeply impressed with the greatness of the man he was about to approach, and from the wealth he saw around him, he began to consider whether he himself was worthy of coming into the presence of one so mighty. For Grasp's idol was money, the only Providence he believed in or worshipped.

Added to this he knew from report the aristocratic and exclusive disposition of Sir Thomas, his haughty bearing towards his inferiors, and his dislike of intrusion, and he began to doubt whether the knight might take it well, that he had come thus in person to communicate with him, more especially as he himself had very lately been engaged in a suit against Sir Thomas, instituted by one of the tradesmen of Stratford, and in which Grasp, by trickery, had managed to get a verdict against the great man.

In short, as Grasp approached the house, he began to feel that he would almost rather have demanded an interview with Queen Elizabeth herself, than with the owner of the domain of Charlecote. He even began to doubt, whether (if Sir Thomas should happen to catch sight of him before an opportunity offered for introducing his important mission) the proud knight would not either order his attendants to whip him out of the park-gates, or perhaps even set his hounds upon him and hunt him through the grounds. These thoughts and apprehensions the more forcibly impressed themselves upon his mind, as the caitiff was well aware he fully deserved as much at Sir Thomas's hands.

However, the business he was upon at length outweighed all other considerations, and setting spurs to his sorry nag, he hastened onwards and neared the house.

As he did so he found that he had timed his visit exactly as he had anticipated, and that Sir Thomas and his family were about to take their afternoon excursion. For (amongst his other peculiarities) the old knight was exceedingly punctual and precise in all his doing, keeping the even tenor of his way, and timing his different movements as exactly as the clock in the tower of his gate-house was true to the dial in the pleasaunce. As Grasp therefore approached he beheld the palfreys and attendants of the family party, mustering in front of the mansion, —a goodly sight to look on, and which made Grasp open his eyes as he beheld it.

Sir Thomas, like most others in the country at this period, was one of those proud men who like to do every thing with circumstance and parade, and accordingly if he only rode across the park to shoot a buck, he usually was attended by a round dozen of his keepers and servants.

At the present time, as he was about to take his afternoon ride, and perhaps pay a formal visit to one or two of his immediate neighbours, his party, including his own family and the attendant serving-men, amounted to about a score. The sight was a gallant one,—such as in our own times we may behold represented upon the artist's canvass, or during the scenic hour, but never again with all its circumstance in real life. There were assembled the serving men and attendants, with the three white Lucys embroidered in silver upon their green hunting-frocks. The head falconer, clad in a sort of loose frock of scarlet cloth; the keepers carrying the hawks upon a stand, and several attendant grooms with the knight's favourite dogs in their charge. For, as with men of this sort the sports of the field was the chief occupation of life, so the companionship of their dogs and hounds seemed almost necessary to their enjoyment; they seldom made a journey without the favourite hawk or hound, and they as seldom rode to take the air on the most ordinary occasions, without being provided with the means of striking any game they might put up in their route. The hawk upon the wrist was as necessary also to the lady, as the spur upon the heel to the knight. The most interesting part of the present display, however, and that which struck the little lawyer with a sort of dread, was the sporting old knight himself, and his three daughters, as they came forth and mounted their steeds.

There was, indeed, something about Sir Thomas Lucy, that, to a man of Grasp's sort, seemed unapproachable, incomprehensible, and even awful. His tall gaunt figure, clad in his hunting-frock of scarlet cloth embroidered with gold, with all the tasselled appointments to match—the long leather gauntlets upon his hands—and the high russet boots upon his legs, were well matched by the grey hair and peaked beard, the aquiline features, and the pale complexion of the stern-looking old knight. In fact, there was a something inexpressibly noble in the appearance of that grey old man. He looked one of the Norman knights of the crusading times returned to his halls,—so pale, so wan, so antique, and yet withal so knightly in his bearing. The hand seemed formed for the rapier, the head for the helm, the heel for the spur. If the little lawyer felt at the moment somewhat impressed with the appearance of the old knight, now that he was about to approach him, he was no less struck with the grace and beauty of his daughters. They seemed to his eye, at that moment (and as he regarded them, seated upon their palfreys), creatures of a superior race to the generality of human mortals; celestial beings, with "beauty too rich for use, for earth too dear."

In fact, Grasp was so feelingly impressed with a sense of inferiority as he approached the presence of the Knight of Charlecote, that once or twice he was about to wheel his steed, and return as he had come.

Indeed he certainly had done so, had not the old knight suddenly caught sight of him, just as he came into the open space in which the party was assembled, and fixed him like a basilisk.

It happened unluckily for Grasp, that the avenue was not often made a thoroughfare for any but visitors to the Hall, and accordingly, the apparition of the meagre-looking lawyer, clad in a sad-coloured suit, carrying a little bag in his hand, and bowing to the pommel of his saddle every step he took, rather struck Sir Thomas Lucy with astonishment. The knight had just at that precise moment thrown his leg over his palfrey, and settled his gaunt person fairly in the demipique, or war-saddle, it was his usual wont to use, when he espied the lawyer; and the effect upon both was like the boa-constrictor suddenly coming in sight of its prey. The lawyer seemed transfixed for the moment, whilst the magnifico, with his movements arrested, regarded him with a stern and curious eye.

At length Sir Thomas signed to one of his attendants to approach, and, pointing to the lawyer, desired him to inquire into the meaning of the intrusion.

"Inquire me of yonder man," said the knight, "wherefore he hath approached the house on this side, and which it is our desire to keep secluded from public resort, and the eyes of the common and popular."

"He hath business of great import, and craves an immediate and private audience with your worship," said the serving-man, after communicating with Grasp.

"Hath he a name?" said Sir Thomas.

"He had rather your worship heard his business first and his name afterwards," said the serving-man, "so much did he inform me when I made inquiry; but I rather think it is Master Grasp, the lawyer of Stratford."

Sir Thomas winced. "And what doth Master Grasp, the lawyer of Stratford, require with Sir Thomas Lucy, of Charlecote?" dryly he said. "Inquire me out his business; and if he tell it not, convey him round to the proper entrance for people of his sort; and, d'ye hear? wait on him out."

During this colloquy, the lawyer had gained somewhat of his self-sufficiency, and, dismounting, approached Sir Thomas, and ventured to accost him.

"Will your honourable worship," he said, "favour me with a hearing at this unseasonable moment, upon matters of high import, connected with the safety of our gracious Sovereign the Queen and the welfare of the whole realm?"

"If thy communication be of so much importance as that," said the knight, "it behoves me, as a true subject, to give attention to it. The body public and the safety of the realm demand so much of us."

"'Tis a matter of so much importance," said Grasp, "that it concerns all who wish not to be burned, racked, whipped, beaten, and otherwise tormented to death by the Spaniard. 'Tis no less a matter, Sir Thomas Lucy, than a discovery I have made of a nest of traitors, who are, at this moment, assembled together, at Stratford, for the purpose of contriving the murder of our Queen and the delivery of the kingdom into the hands of Philip of Spain."

Grasp delivered this piece of intelligence with so much eagerness and vehemence, that he had approached quite close to Sir Thomas, in his anxiety that his news should not be overheard, and the old knight was in something impressed with its importance. He, however, drew back from too close contact with the Stratford lawyer, warning him to remove a little further from his person.

"Your communication is doubtless of the utmost importance," he said coolly, as he prepared to dismount; "we will instantly hear all you have to say. Nevertheless, confine your eagerness to serve Her Majesty within proper bounds." So saying, Sir Thomas dismounted from his palfry, and coolly desiring his daughters to continue their ride, led the way into the house, and, followed by Grasp, entered his private study.

The loyalty of the man would not permit him to pause a moment, as soon as he fully comprehended the nature of the business. He took two turns up and down the apartment; and then ordered the head-keeper to be summoned into his presence. "I will arrest these miscreants with my own proper hand and with my own people," he said, "instantly, without a moment's delay. Meantime, I will send over to my good neighbour, Sir Hugh Clopton, and inform him of it, so that he may meet me at Stratford on my arrival there, and aid me in this capture. Not so much," he continued to himself, "that I require his assistance, as that he may partake with me in the honour of cutting the throats of such vile wretches, an they resist lawful authority."

"May it please your worship," said Grasp, "there is a thing, I omitted to say, and which I had said, only that I feared its knowledge would most heartily grieve, astonish, and dismay your worship."

"You have already both astonished and somewhat grieved us," said Sir Thomas, "in delivering the piece of intelligence you came here charged withal. In how far you may be further able to dismay us, we may be perhaps permitted to doubt: nevertheless, we would fain be made acquainted with the nature of this omitted circumstance."

"Sir Hugh Clopton," said Grasp, "your worship spoke of him as aiding and assisting in the capture of these bloody-minded conspirators."

"I did so," said Sir Thomas. "Said I not well, good Master Grasp?"

"Your worship hath the gift of saying well," returned Grasp, who found himself gaining ground, he thought, in Sir Thomas's good graces. "But I grieve to say that Sir Hugh lieth under the imputation of being deeply implicated in this plot."

"How!" said Sir Thomas, losing something of austerity in his surprise. "Sir Hugh Clopton implicated in such a hellish conspiracy as this you have named? Had any man holding rank equal or superior to mine own, said so much, Master Pouncet Grasp, he had lied under the imputation of a liar and a caitiff at my hands."

"Nay," said Grasp, "I ask your worship's pardon, I had it from him who gave me the clue to the whole matter,—the honourable gentleman I told you of,—the right honourable Master Walter Neville."

"Say, rather, the arch traitor—the doubly dishonourable villain Neville, who goeth about to purchase benefit for himself by the blood of his party. An such a man be your informant? Credit me, the information is incorrect. I listen not therefore to it, it is naught."

Meantime, whilst Sir Thomas held converse thus with Grasp, he had at the same time, in the most quiet and business-like way, been encasing himself in one or two pieces of defensive armour which had hung at hand, behind the great chair on which he usually sat. Taking down a richly inlaid breast-plate, and which he had worn in his youth in the wars of the Low Countries, he fitted it on with care and precision, as one to whom the business of arming was a habit of easiness. He then indued a cumbrous back-piece to match, buckled the shoulder-straps without assistance, and girded the whole tightly together with an embroidered belt round his waist. After which (laying aside the light rapier he usually wore), he adopted a stout, heavy-hilted, and somewhat ponderous blade, and thrusting a pair of enormous petronels and his dagger into his girdle, stept forth into the centre of the apartment completely equipped for the business on hand, and looking, what our readers of the present day would have termed, as perfect a specimen of Don Quixote de la Mancha as they could have wished to behold.

Those who looked upon his tall gaunt form and sinewy limbs, however, might see that, eccentric as was his appearance, he would be rather an awkward customer to engage with or offer an affront to; and so thought Grasp, when he beheld the knight's military toilette completed.

Nay, a sort of unpleasant feeling began to creep over him; a presentiment of hard knocks, bullets, and grievous wounds suddenly pervaded his mind, as he looked upon this military figure clattering about in his cuirass, and coolly selecting his ponderous weapons for the nonce. For Grasp, it must be remembered, (albeit he lived in stirring times,) was a man of peace, and whose whole life nearly had been passed in a small dark back office in the town of Warwick, where he had been brought up and initiated in all the tricks of his craft.

However, as he had been the exciting cause of Sir Thomas's taking the affair upon his hands, and as he knew the knight would be likely to make a clean business of it, he felt that now to hold back would be to lose all the advantage he had previously promised himself.

Could he but manage to be exceedingly prominent and useful in this capture, he felt certain that it would lead on to fortune.

"I have never yet fought," he said to himself, "except with my pen. Now I am going to wield a weapon which, if it be only half as deadly and destructive in my hands, I shall make unpleasant work withal. But, in good sooth, I feel as though I had rather *prepare* the writ than *serve* it in the present case."

So eager was Sir Thomas to pursue the adventure, and make capture of the conspirators with his own hand, that he tarried not for any of the customary formalities.

He resolved to take all responsibility upon himself, and "standing to no repairs," swoop upon the culprits. Accordingly, having mustered the serving-men he had warned for this service, and seen to their efficiency in regard to weapons with a military eye, the whole party wheeled out of the gate-house of Charlecote and took their way towards Stratford.

CHAPTER XVI.

THE ATTACK.

Many of our readers, who have searched with curious eye through the various localities and peculiar points of interest at Stratford, will doubtless recollect a small antiquated-looking inn, situated on the Avon's bank,—a building whose outward favour and stout-timbered walls, together with its massive chimneys and general appearance, would proclaim it to have been a house of some mark in its day.

At the period of our story this building had degenerated from a goodly farm-house to a hostel called the Checquers, and was the house of entertainment generally used by the commoner sort of wayfarers. It was a house altogether of no very good repute, in which the brawl and the night-shriek might be occasionally heard by the more respectable dwellers in the town,—a house often visited too by the watch, and carefully looked after by the authorities.

It was a dwelling also often changing owners, and had been lately taken by a stranger, a dark, taciturn, evil-looking host, whose appearance nobody liked, consequently he was but ill supported.

In short, since the present landlord had been its occupant, save and except an occasional guest who appeared to have arrived from foreign parts, and departed as quickly and silently as he had come, the Checquers was almost without guests. So that, albeit its former dissolute repute might be said to have departed from it, the inn had now assumed a mysterious sort of note, and was as celebrated for closed doors and quietude, as it had before been for riot and open debauchery. Some said the landlord was a Jesuit; others, that he was an emissary of the Spaniard; whilst others again affirmed he was both the one and the other, and all agreed that he was an ill-favoured, unneighbourly, and exceedingly disagreeable person.

It was at this hostel, Master Neville and his associates had previously taken up their quarters, and here they had been frequently visited during the dark hours by certain cavaliers who hitherto had seldom remained till dawn.

Master Muddlework, the head constable of the town, had considered it consistent with his duty twice to visit the Checquers, in order to observe these suspicious-looking strangers, but each time he had done so he had failed in finding anything to fasten his suspicions upon; so that whether a good look-out was kept, and the major portion of the strangers had concealed themselves, or that they were really absent at the moment of his visit, the functionary had, as we have said, quite failed in observing anything unusual or particular; except it was the mysterious quietude and closed-up doors and shutters of the sometime rollicking hostel.

In short, nothing could exceed the degree of interest with which this inn and its occupants were at this moment regarded,—an interest which had become general throughout the town, all on a sudden apparently, and it was towards this hostel, as our readers doubtless are aware, that Sir Thomas Lucy and his party were now advancing.

To the suggestion of Grasp, that it would be better, he thought, to wait till the shadows of evening had descended before they approached the town, Sir Thomas gave a decided negative. All dark doings, he said, were foreign to his nature. He had proceeded by the shortest and most expeditious route towards his design, as in duty bound, the moment he heard of this vile assemblage, and, Heaven willing, he would proceed as straight to the capture of the caitiffs.

With military precision and precaution, however, he gave directions so as to ensure the more sure success of his undertaking, and halting for a few moments in the road, he divided his party in twain, sending one portion full trot forwards, with orders to make a slight detour, and enter the town on the further side, whilst he so timed his own movements as to come within hail of the suspicious hostel at the precise moment his other party approached it.

This done, according to previous concert, the two portions extending from the right and left, in a moment completed a very pretty cordon around the hostel; so that not a mouse could shew its nose outside the walls without being seen. Quickly as this movement had been executed, it had been as quickly seen by the inmates apparently; for the door in the rear, which had been open the moment before, was immediately closed and secured.

This proceeding convinced Sir Thomas in a moment that the inmates of the hostel kept a good look-out, and at the same time led him to suspect what he indeed quickly found, namely, a desperate resistance. Such indeed might reasonably be expected, for the vigilance of the Queen's council was at this time so keen, and the various plots of the day so continually being discovered by one chance or other, that there was small hope of success, unless the utmost secresy was maintained.

Ordering his party instantly to dismount, (whilst the horses were put in charge of a small reserve,) Sir Thomas drew back and desired Grasp to advance to the fore door of the Checquers, and demand admittance in form.

"An it so please yonr worship," said Grasp, "I had rather not take upon myself so much of the responsibility of the action as that would amount to. Your honour is a justice of the peace, and may therefore reasonably take the lead. I will follow and bear witness to the lawfulness of whatsoever it may please your valour to perform; but I had rather not strike the first blow."

"Or receive it either, I believe," said Sir Thomas, *sotto voce*. "'Tis well," he added aloud, and immediately setting spurs to his palfrey, he was, the next moment, beside the strong iron-studded front-door of the hostel, which he struck forcibly with the butt-end of his riding-whip.

As he expected, the door was fastened, and to his repeated summons no answer was returned. At length he uplifted his voice, and in a loud tone, demanded instant admittance in the Queen's name. Upon this the lattice-window was thrown open, and a man's head appeared at it, —a pale, cadaverous-looking wretch, with long lank hair, and glassy and excited eye.

"What seek you here?" he said. "There is death in the house, and the doors are closed against visitors to-day."

"Let them open to those who come in the Queen's name," said Sir Thomas. "I come to seize the persons of all within this house. Dead or alive, it matters not, I will arrest the bodies of all here consorting and assembling."

"Ah," said the man, "and who then art thou, thus commissioned, and from whom hast thou such anthority?"

"I am Sir Thomas Lucy, of Charlecote," returned the knight, "and if I mistake not, thou art Ralph Somerville, of Warwick."

"And how if we refuse you admittance?" said Somerville. "How then, Sir Thomas Lucy, of Charlecote?"

"Then I will make forcible entry," said Sir Thomas, "and those who oppose me must be content with the mishaps that attend such procedure."

"Of what are we accused, that we are thus molested in our retirement?" said Somerville.

"Of high treason, in conspiring to take the life of our blessed and gracious Queen Elizabeth," said Sir Thomas.

"Then receive the wages of your service, heretic," said Somerville, at the same moment discharging the contents of a petronel full in Sir Thomas's visage.

The weapon was thrust so near to the face of the knight that the powder blackened his features, but the ball, luckily, just missed his head, and passing downwards on his cuirass, glanced off harmless.

"'Tis well," he said, with his usual coolness, as Somerville immediately closed the window. "Forwards, men, and force the doors instantly."

The house had, apparently, been prepared in anticipation of such an assault; for, as the party advanced to the attack, several calivers were discharged from loop-holes, which had been made in the walls at the upper part, and two of Sir Thomas's men were shot dead ere they could reach the doors.

As the remainder, however, did so, they found the entrance so strongly barricaded that their efforts to get in were fruitless; whilst at the same time they were exposed to the bullets of those within during the attempt. Sir Thomas saw this in a moment, as he rode about superintending the affair, and indeed drawing several discharges from the besieged upon his own person.

With military quickness and decision he immediately dismounted, and rallying some half-a-dozen of his men who were bearing back from the hot fire of the besieged, he seized upon a ladder which he espied lying near a sort of out-house in the rear. This he ordered his people to man on either side, and leading them on, sword in hand, they rushed with terrible force against the back door of the hostel, giving it such a shock, that door and lintels together were nearly unshipped.

"Another rush," cried Sir Thomas; "one more, and we have them!"

Accordingly on dashed the men with this novel battering-ram, and again and again they assailed the door. Any one who could have observed Grasp at this moment, would have doubtless considered that he had suddenly gone mad, since what between his anxiety to be amongst the first, and near Sir Thomas Lucy, and his mortal fear of the whistling balls, he cut a most ridiculous figure. One moment he rushed forward with the party who were using the ladder as a battering-ram; the next, as the sharp report of a well-loaded caliver jarred his ears, he fairly bolted off, turning again when he had gained a few paces to the rear, flourishing his blue bag, and shouting at the assailants with all his might, to break in and take the rebels.

"Serve the warrant, take the body, seize the person!—Take them dead or alive!" he cried, as he jumped about. Meantime the ladder, being well and chivalrously managed, at about the fourth rush carried in the door, and Sir Thomas, with portentous strength, carried his body along with it into the kitchen of the inn, a petronel in one hand and his heavy rapier in the other, closely followed by his men. Contrary to his expectations, however, the apartment was empty; "Guard the entrance!" he cried, as he dashed into the next apartment. "The villains will escape us yet! Kill whoever attempts to get out!"

Rapidly, and followed by his men, Sir Thomas made search through the lower portion of the hostel, without, however, finding a soul, although it was evident they had but the moment before escaped, the rooms being filled with the smoke of their discharged fire-arms.

Glancing round upon his followers, who were now for the most part within the hostel, he directed them instantly to search the upper flooring, whilst he kept guard below.

This was, however, more easily said than done. The staircase was found to be impracticable, being barricaded by a large quantity of faggots, which had been drawn up and jammed tightly together.

"Ah," said Grasp, whose ferret eyes were everywhere at once, "may I never draw an inference again, if I do not think the rogues have ascended by a ladder through yonder trap, and then drawn the ladder up after them."

At this moment, and whilst all paused to consider the next move, the barrels of several calivers were thrust through as many holes which had been perforated through the ceiling, and a very lively discharge was kept up upon Sir Thomas and his party, which killing one of the men, quickly sent Grasp and the rest out of the doors; Grasp, who in his hurry and agitation being the last, closing the door behind him, and actually shutting Sir Thomas up alone amongst his foes.

"Heaven bless and preserve us all from conspirators," said the lawyer, jumping about and wringing his hands, as he hastily glanced amongst the scared domestics, "they have shot, killed, and destroyed the knight of Charlecote, as sure as I am a sinner! Sir Thomas Lucy is certainly murdered outright by this nest of vipers, for I see him not amongst us here?"

Confusion and dismay, indeed, sufficiently pervaded the attacking party. They readily imagined their lord and master was slain, and to the horror of such a catastrophe was added their doubts as to what was next to be done; so that whilst some drew off from the near vicinity of the house, others mounted their horses, and set off full cry to the town to get assistance.

In short, the assaulters felt the want of a second in command. They were struck with dread at the supposed death of their leader, and the head falconer being killed also, there was no one to lead them to the recovery even of the old knight's body, if he was indeed shot, or his rescue, if only wounded.

Grasp, however, did all he could to exhort some half-a-dozen who remained to make another attempt, to gain the interior. But the men very wisely demurred.

"Who think ye is to enter yonder dark place, to be killed like a fox in a hole?" said one.

"Nay," said another, "the matter is now none of ours to meddle with. If our master be killed by these villains, some one else must take it up, we have no further warranty to go forward; all we can do is to wait till assistance comes from the town."

In the midst of this colloquy, (and which had hardly taken as many moments as words used,) to the astonishment of the speakers, the sound of firing again commenced within the dwelling,—quick, short, and rapid, sounded the shots; whilst the old inn, as the gazers regarded it, although it seemed convulsed with internal discord, remained closed up, and its exterior undisturbed as if nothing extraordinary was going on. At the same moment, too, shouts and sounds from the town proclaimed that the townsfolk were coming to the scene of action.

"Gad he here," said Grasp, "what may this portend? The miscreants surely cannot be contending against each other, and cutting their own throats from sheer disappointment at being discovered in their villany!"

At this moment, and in the midst of these speculations upon the matter, the door opened, and enveloped in a volume of smoke, which burst out with him, begrimed too with soot and dirt, appeared Sir Thomas himself, who instantly closing the door after him, and coughing violently from the effects of the fumigation he had endured, waved his sword for his people again to advance.

CHAPTER XVII.

THE CAPTURE.

To account for this appearance we must return to the knight after he had been shut up within the hostel.

As he had never for a moment intended to give ground, he was in no wise daunted at being thus left alone, aud as the closing of the door shut out the glare of light, it most probably was the means of saving his life, for could those above have distinctly seen and levelled their pieces at him, they would have shot him like a wolf in a trap. For the moment all was quiet, and casting his eyes round the gloomy kitchen Sir Thomas spied the remains of a fire in the grate, whilst fearful and hurried whispers, gradually growing louder and more vehement above his head, proclaimed that the conspirators were in earnest consultation.

Without a moment's delay, Sir Thomas (by aid of the fire on the hearth, and such combustibles as he could hastily collect) set to work with might and main, and lighted up a blazing bonfire in the very middle of the apartment.

The rushes with which the floor was partially strewed, materially assisted the blaze, and heaping chairs and other less cumbrous articles upon it, whilst the astonished conspirators fired at him through the loopholes, he soon effected a very alarming conflagration.

It was lucky for the knight that the construction of such a measure of defence, as that of perforating an upper floor to fire through, necessarily precludes any precision in taking aim, as it is almost impossible in a small opening of the sort, to get a good sight whilst levelling downwards, and consequently, although a continued discharge took place, whilst the knight busied himself in getting up the conflagration, although the balls flew about his ears and buried themselves in the floor at his feet, not one struck him.

Under these circumstances, and whilst the conspirators were ignorant that the combustion which already became disagreeably apparent to them was being effected by one person, their persevering foe completed his arrangements, and jerking his powder flask into the flames, quickly opened the door, and as he could no longer remain safely within, coolly walked out.

Reassured by his appearance, those of his followers who were at hand hastened to the support of the knight, who instantly directed Grasp to proceed round to the door on the other side, with several of the men, and make instant capture of any of the conspirators who attempted to escape on that side.

"I have smoked the traitors in their den," said he, "and anon we shall have them swarming out. Make prisoners of all you can secure. Hurt none who yield, but suffer none to escape. If they resist, kill."

The anxiety of Grasp to see these mysterious plotters almost overcame his personal apprehensions. He therefore hastened round with the men under his charge, and in a few minutes the conflagration within forced the besieged to attempt a sortie. The door before which Sir Thomas had posted himself was thrown open, and (as smoke and flame gushed out) forth rushed half a dozen men so completely begrimed in soot that their features were scarcely distinguishable.

The conspirators evidently had made up their minds to a desperate effort at escape, for they dashed to the right and left sword in hand, cutting at all who opposed them.

"Yield thee, caitiff," cried Sir Thomas, flinging himself upon the foremost, and seizing him by the collar of his doublet with an iron grip, before he could strike a blow. "Yield thee, miscreant, in the Queen's name!"

The man accosted attempted to stab Sir Thomas with his dagger, but the knight dragged him headlong down, and stepping a pace or two back, at the same time absolutely flinging him to his men, rushed upon the next in the same manner, and, in this way, capturing three with his own hand, whilst his followers kept them in play.

The scene we have described fully exemplified the nature of a period in which deeds of violence and bloodshed, consequent upon the seditious and superstitious bigotry of both religions, were by no means uncommon, breaking out too, as they oft-times did, in the midst of apparent tranquility.

Close upon the doors, in rear of the hostel, and at which the conspirators made their principal efforts at escape, stood Sir Thomas himself backed up by several of his men, conspicuous from his tall form and his activity in cutting down all who refused to yield.

Somewhat removed, and at a safer distance, were to be seen a crowd of the townsfolk, with a portion of the town guard and the head bailiff, who had hastened to the scene upon the alarm of the encounter, accompanied by a legion of old women and idle boys. These, as they learned the nature of the business in hand, became proportionably excited against the conspirators, whom they seemed inclined to tear in pieces so soon as they could fairly get at them with safety to themselves.

"Oh! the miserable sinners," said Dame Patch. "I thought no good was going on down yonder, with all their silence, secret meetings, and keeping us women from amongst them."

"I always said there was a plot hatching to blow up the town and kill every Protestant in it," cried Doubletongue. "God save Sir Thomas. See, there's the last of the rogues down and being bound hand and foot!"

Such was indeed the case, and, except Somerville and another of the conspirators who escaped Grasp and his party, the whole (amounting to seven individuals) were down or captured, and, being bound, were delivered into the hands of the bailiff for safe custody.

No sooner was the business done, and the capture fairly effected, than the eccentric character of the knight of Charlecote again displayed itself. He had borne himself manfully during the fight, and as one worthy of his crusading ancestors, but his hauteur and reserve immediately succeeded to the violence of action.

Drawing together his people, he gave directions for the removal of the wounded into the town, where their hurts could be looked to. After which he mounted his horse, and calling for a cup of wine, he lifted his hat, and drank to the health of the Queen, the discomfit of the Spaniards, and the confusion of all Jesuits. After which he turned his horse's head from the Checquers, now filled with the idle and the curious, who had managed to extinguish the fire, and rode off towards Charlecote.

"Nay, but how am I to dispose of these prisoners, Sir Thomas?" said the head bailiff, stopping him as he passed. "I should also like to learn the exact nature of the matter which hath led to this capture and the death of these people around us here."

"Of that you will better learn," said Sir Thomas, dryly, "by applying to your townsman there—Lawyer Grasp; and all further circumstances connected with them, I opine you will speedily be made acquainted with by the Queen's council, as I am myself led to believe by what Master Grasp hath informed me."

So saying, Sir Thomas bowed to the head bailiff, and rode away from the scene of his achievements.

CHAPTER XVIII.

A REVEL AT CLOPTON.

On the night which followed the action we have described, and which the inhabitants of Stratford long afterwards called the fray of the Checquers, Sir Hugh Clopton held an old accustomed feast at his house. The entertainment was given in honour of his daughter's birthday, the maiden having just completed her seventeenth year; and on this interesting occasion most of the old knightly families of the county of Warwickshire graced the scene. There came the Astleys of Hill Moreton, the De la Wards of Newton, the Clintons of Badsley, the Walshes of Mereden, the Blenknaps of Knoll, the Wellesbourns of Hastang, the Comptons of Compton Winyate, the Sheldons of Beoley, the Attwoods, and many other nobles, whose names now, like those once owning them, in all the pride of ancestral honours, are obliterated from the muster-roll of the living, and long forgotten in the very domains which owned them as lords; and last, though by no means least, came the knight of Charlecote and his lady, and their two lovely daughters.

It was indeed a goodly assemblage of the rank, youth, and beauty of the county of Warwick of that period. The old folks stately in manner and formal in costume; the men, looking in their starch ruffs, short cloaks and trunks, quaint cut doublets and peaked beards; and the women, in their jewelled stomachers and farthingales, like so many old portraits stepping forth from their frames; whilst the youth of both sexes, in all the bravery of that age of brave attire, glittered in silks and satins, gold and embroidery, bright jewels and richly mounted weapons. Nothing, indeed, could exceed the gallant look of the cavaliers who trod a measure in the dance, except it were the loveliness of their bright partners. Those youthful and fresh female buds of England, so celebrated for their native beauty; fair, and blooming, and swan-like in their graceful carriage—"earth-treading stars, that make dark heaven bright."

The music rang out from a sort of a temporary orchestra, formed at one end of the hall, arched over and festooned with sweet flowers and green shrubs. It consisted mostly of stringed instruments, which gave forth a silver sound, accompanied by the deep tones of the bassoon and the occasional flourish of the horn, and whilst the dancers trod a measure, and the different guests, in all the freedom of unchecked enjoyment, wandered about, how sweetly the strains floated through those oak-panelled rooms, reverberating in the long corridors and passages, and, mellowed by distance, thrummed in the upper rooms.

It mingled with the whispered softness of the lover's tongue, sounding doubly sweet by night. It added to the charm of beauty, as she listened to the flattering tale, till the coyness of the half-won maiden seemed to relax in music; and the glittering cavalier, with renewed hope, led her to the dance.

How inferior is the fussy and excited style of our own days compared with such a scene as this, where all was open-hearted gaiety and enjoyment, where, without effort, all was dignified, and brilliant, and picturesque.

The very serving-men and maids, ranged in a long row at the lower end of the hall, seemed to add to the effect of the picture. The men in their rich liveries with heraldic badge upon the sleeve; the maids, all in one sort of costume, fitting and becoming for their station in life; nay, the orchestra itself was a picture, composed as it was of respectable personages from the town of Stratford, grave-looking, bearded, and staid, working away at their different instruments, as if it was a matter of national pride and import,—the celebration of the fair Charlotte's natal day. Each in his quaint-cut doublet and scarlet hose. How they clutched at the bass-viol, those fat citizens, and glowed with the strains they produced; how the fiddlers jerked and worked at their bows, with heads going, and feet keeping time: how the puffed cheek of the horn-blowers seemed to grow distended to the degree of exploding; and how the eyes of the whole party seemed to roll about in agony, and follow the dancers as their strains excited them to fresh efforts; and how resolutely, ever and anon, they paused to take a long pull at the huge flagons placed within their reach; returning to their instruments with renewed vigour, and stamping to keep time, as if sitting still was almost too great an effort, and they longed to jump up, and fling out amongst the best there; urging one another to quicker movements and louder strains as the liquor mounted and the evening wore on.

Amongst that gay and brilliant throng there was one whose whole soul seemed wrapped in melody. The soft tones of the floating minstrelsy seemed to steal upon his heart. He stood apart from all: aloof in person as in mind, leaning against one of the quaint-cut ornaments of the room. As his eye wandered amongst the gay dancers, his countenance was at times lighted up by an expression which seemed divine. The greatness of his soul shone out in his glorious countenance, and yet, save by two persons, he was all unmarked.

It was the boy poet, the youthful Shakespeare.

Walter Arderne, who felt that no assemblage could be complete which wanted the presence of his friend, no hour enjoyed but in his company, had brought him again to Clopton, where he mingled in the scene, not so much a guest as a spectator. And yet unknown as unmarked, or, if regarded, perhaps but calling forth a passing remark upon his good looks, how greatly did that youth feel himself the superior of all there, elevated as some of them were in station. The fineness and acuteness of organic sensibility made him alive to all the mighty world of ear and eye. Nothing escaped him; and yet feeling this within himself, and in strength of mind a demigod, in profundity of view a prophet,* he moved amongst the throng, as if unconscious of being more than the most unassuming servitor in attendance. Gentle and open in manner as a child.

* Schegel's estimate of Shakespeare.

The good Sir Hugh welcomed him to his house, and presented him to two of his oldest friends, as one to whom he owed much. "A goodly lad," he said, "and of exceeding promise; a ripe and ready wit, sirs. By 'r Lady, but he hath the knack of making me laugh till my face is like a wet napkin. Nay, and he inditeth rhymes, too, it would do you good to hear. A poet, I'll assure ye, sirs, already, and a rare one, too. Go thy ways, lad; go thy ways. 'Fore Heaven we owe thee much, and hope to requite it."

"A young friend," said Arderne, to one of the ladies with whom he danced, and as he pointed the unconscious poet out to her, whilst standing at the lower end of the hall. "A young friend who, though in humble life, seems to me of somewhat extraordinary character, and in whom I am greatly interested. He unites in his genius the utmost elevation and the utmost depth; and the most foreign, and even irreconcilable properties subsist in him together. I cannot describe to you the delight I experience in the companionship of that youth." The lady glanced her eye towards the part of the hall indicated by Walter Arderne, as he mentioned his friend. It was but a glance, and she observed the person indicated. The words humble life was, however, quite sufficient to destroy all interest in the bosom of the beauty, for Clara de Mowbray (albeit she was both lovely and amiable) partook, in some sort, of the pride of her race. Added to this, she was the victim of an unrequited passion, and save for the tall handsome form and expressive features of her partner, she had no eyes.

"I should have imagined, from all I have this night beheld," she said, "there was but one in this room, nay, in this world, who could take up even a moment of your care or thoughts, fair sir. This new-found friend must, indeed, be a rare specimen, if he can wean your eyes for a moment from Charlotte Clopton. But that, indeed," she added, with a sigh, "is as it should be; she is, I think, to-night more beautiful than ever!"

Walter sighed, and unconsciously his glance wandered in search of his betrothed. "You are a shrewd observer, lady," he said, looking full in her expressive face,—and indeed, except Charlotte Clopton, whose beauty was of a different character, Clara de Mowbray was one of the most beautiful women in the county. "You are a great observer, lady," he said, "and yet you have failed to observe how much your own beauty excites admiration from all present to-night. Nay, I am not blind myself, however much I may lie under the imputation with which you have charged me."

"To love is no such heavy sin, Sir Arderne," said the lady, "an if it were so, you would indeed require sufficing penance and absolution, since you are a very votary to the blind god."

"And she to whom my vows are given," he said, "is she not worthy of an emperor's love?"

"She is worthy of the love of him who seeks her hand," said Clara, somewhat sadly. "She is my dear and early friend, and I could not wish greater happiness to her than in that store. Unless the emperor were Walter Arderne, and the empire he inherited here in Warwickshire, I conclude Charlotte would scarce become an empress."

"You speak not this as you think," said Arderne, doubtfully, yet delighted at so much confirmation from one of the intimate friends of his beloved Charlotte.

"I speak as I feel," said Clara; "I know the worth of both, and how well both deserve; and yet methinks youth and valour should not altogether succumb to Cupid. Were I a man, I should seek for action and to be worthy in *deed*."

The youth gazed with increasing admiration upon the radiant face of the lady. He almost doubted whether its exceeding loveliness did not equal that of his betrothed.

"Ah," he said, gaily, turning towards his new friend, who at the moment approached, "give us assurance, gentle Shakespeare, we that are in love; and teach this lady to respect the passion."

Shakespeare looked full at the lady; he seemed struck with the beauty of her face and form. "Love, first learned in a lady's eyes," he said, gaily,

"Lives not alone immured in the brain;
But with the motion of all elements,
Courses as swift as thought in every power;
And gives to every power a double power,
Above their functions and their offices,
Never durst poet touch a pen to write,
Until his ink were temper'd with love's sighs."

"That is indeed a singular being!" said the lady, gazing after the youth as he passed through the crowd and quitted the room. "Who and what is he?"

"'Tis him of whom I just now spoke," said Arderne; "but come, let us seek Charlotte Clopton; I thought I saw her leave the room but now to seek the purer air of the gardens. I will tell thee more of our acquaintance with this youth as we go."

It was a bright and lovely night, and, with all the freedom and licence of the age, many of the younger guests had sought the pleasure-grounds and gardens of the Hall, whilst their more staid guardians and parents held converse within doors.

Here and there was to be seen a group seated or reclined upon the velvet turf, whilst others paced up and down the terrace, or disappeared and were lost in the dark walks, till the joyous strains of the orchestra within again recalled them to the dance.

If the quick eyes of love had enabled the lady Clara to observe the object to which Walter Arderne's thoughts were that night fixed, the same observation had failed in shewing her on whom the affections of her rival was centred.

Indeed, although Charlotte Clopton, both from her beauty and her position as the heroine of the night, was necessarily the observed of all observers, and her hand sought for by every cavalier in the room, those who looked closely at her might have observed a tinge of melancholy in her countenance, and a restlessness about her which shewed she was not in the enjoyment of her own content. To herself hardly dared she own it, as her restless glance traversed the room, but she felt that one minute's conversation with her romantic friend,—nay, one word, or but an exchanged glance,—would be worth all the gallant speeches she endured from the gayer cavaliers by whom she was surrounded.

This new friend, however, had not once approached her on that night. He had studiously kept in the background, and although he had, unobserved, caught sight of her, he had even carefully avoided those parts of the room in which she was engaged with her various partners and friends. Nay, the pleasure he experienced in the gay and festive scene, like that of the fair Charlotte, was tinged with an occasional melancholy; a soft and dreamy sadness mingled with the brighter thoughts called into play by the sight of beauty and the strains of music.

With such feelings he quitted the house, and passed into the gardens of the Hall, those lovely grounds looking, as they did, so fair and soft, in the bright moonlight. And how often do we find it thus in life! How oft do we see the most worthy wending his way unnoticed, unobserved, unappreciated, and unknown, whilst the giddy, the frivolous, the vain, and even the vile, are sunning themselves in the smiles of patronage and favour, playing their fantastic tricks, and swollen with the success their cringing falsehood has attained, whilst patient merit, scorning the rout, passes on unsought.

The night, as Lorenzo words it, was but the daylight sick, "it looked a little paler." The youthful poet threw himself upon a grassy bank, shadowed by trees, and as the sounds of music crept upon his ears,

> " Soft stillness, and the night,
> Became the touches of sweet harmony."

And what indeed were the thoughts and imaginings the scene and hour gave rise to?—Thoughts softened by the sweet breath of a summer's night, loaded with perfume, and bearing harmony from the distance. At such moment the mind reverts to days long past, or even revels in the fabled ages of the early world. In such a night as this,

> " When the sweet wind did gently kiss the trees
> And they did make no noise; in such a night,
> Troilus, methinks, mounted the Trojan walls
> And sighed his soul toward the Grecian tents
> Where Cressid lay."

And,

> "In such a night,
> Stood Dido with a willow in her hand,
> Upon the wild sea-banks, and waved her love
> To come again to Carthage."

It was whilst Shakespeare remained thus sequestered and alone, and in the indulgence of the thoughts produced by such a situation, that the company had sought the gardens; and the walks, and alleys, the green slopes, and mossed banks, became suddenly peopled with bright forms, and which in a moment gave another and gayer aspect, and a totally different turn to the entire scene. The stillness, and the sweet touches of distant music, and which had so stolen upon his heart, was now changed to the sounds of laughter and loud conversation. In the shaded walks were now to be seen some tall form, clad in brave attire; his jewelled hat and gay plume bent down as he conversed with the lady at his side, and, in the open space before him, the different groups lent a lustre to the gardens which only gay costume and forms of beauty can give. As he remarked the scene before him, the joyous and sportive throng thus revelling in happiness,—the very heavens "thick inlaid with patines of bright gold," he presently observed a dark and ominous cloud slowly and stealthily mounting, as it were, from the south. It seemed to emerge from the distant woods like a pall, and—as if emblematic of the short-lived days of mortals—gradually stole over one side of the heavens.

Yes, that flaunting throng was like the pleasures of the world. "Those clouds were like its coming cares." Whilst he watched their slow development, a light footstep approached, and Charlotte Clopton stood before him.

Was it his fancy, or was it that the silver brightness falling on the spot on which she stood, gave an ethereal appearance to the beautiful girl, a ghost-like and shadowy look, which, for the moment, struck him with a sort of awe? He arose from his recumbent posture, and, as he did so, he observed she was unusually pale. Nay, as he gazed upon that sweet face and form, he could not help seeing that it was with difficulty she kept herself from falling.

"I fear me, lady," he said, (struck with sudden alarm,) "you are not well?"

"A feeling of illness has indeed come over me," said Charlotte, "and which I cannot entirely shake off. I thought the air of the gardens would have taken it away, but it has not done so."

"Suffer me to lead you in," said Shakespeare, taking her hand, "perhaps some cordial will restore you?"

"Not so," said Charlotte; "I have sought this spot as I knew it was a favourite one with you. I felt you would be here, and that I must see you. I know not wherefore, but a presentiment of evil is upon me. I feel as if I spoke to thee this night for the last time."

There was a wildness in the manner of Charlotte Clopton, as she said this, which increased the anxiety of her admirer, and, as he saw that she was really suffering from some sudden feeling of illness, he again entreated her to seek the house. She, however, again refused. "I have sought this opportunity to speak to you," she said, "for I felt I must do so; nay, I feel as if I should die unless I unburthened myself to one I so highly esteem, one to whom I owe so much, one so noble and so good; nay, were it to any but to thee, (generous and sweet in disposition as thou art, William Shakespeare,) I should shame to say so much. But well I know that none can know thee and refrain from loving; can trust thee and repent."

To say that the youthful poet could hear this from a being so beautiful, and not forget all the resolutions he had previously made to subdue and conceal his passion, would be to describe one of those over-perfect mortals existing only in the imagination of the prudish.

William Shakespeare was no such perfection of a hero; he had sought to quench his love's hot fire,

"Lest it should burn above the bounds of reason."

The intense feelings of youth, however, and which in after-life led him so forcibly to pourtray the passion he felt, now completely overcame all his prudential resolves.

The being he had thought so much above him, and in secret loved, had confessed her feelings. He was instantly lost to every thing but his love for her. Its hopelessness, its seeming treachery towards his new and generous friend, all were forgotten as he gazed upon Charlotte and returned her vows. And yet, what was this love, so pure, so unselfish, so unlikely ever to meet with reward? It rather lacked, even at its commencement, the rapturous intoxication of hope, and seemed, even at the moment of its mutual confidence, to partake of the bitterness of certain disappointment.

Whilst the various groups had been enjoying themselves in the grounds, the heavens had become gradually overcast, till one entire portion was mantled with the darksome veil now rapidly extending; distant rumbling peals, too, like the sound of heavy ordnance from afar, and large heavy drops of rain, gave notice of the coming storm. This, together with the renewed sound of music, warned the revellers around again to seek the shelter of the Hall, and, as Charlotte Clopton heard her name called, the lovers too felt that they must part. Yet still they lingered, and had more to say.

The voice of Martin, however, calling upon Charlotte, who had now been suddenly missed from amongst the guests, and sought for in the house, recalled them to the necessity of separating. Their parting seemed a sad one, and although the feeling of illness Charlotte had previously felt had now partially left her, she still felt a sensation of langour and a weight upon her spirits she could not account for.

Her lover observed this, and that her cheek, ordinarily so full of bloom, was deadly pale, giving her dark brown tresses a still darker shade, and he parted from her with an ill divining soul.

In his present frame of mind Shakespeare felt no longer any desire to witness the gaieties within doors, and yet he found it impossible to tear himself away from the gardens. He loved to breathe the neighbouring air, and as he listened to the music, he tried to fancy her he loved still adding to the grace and beauty of the assemblage.

Whilst he thus remained lost in his own thoughts, the threatened storm suddenly burst forth. The thunder crashed over head, and the lightning darted along the walks and alleys of the gardens, and then came the rain, rushing upon the earth like a cataract, suddenly bursting bounds.

These sounds were mingled with the tread of horses' hoofs as they clattered into the stable-yard, and then came a short and rapid word of command. A few minutes more and the music ceased; rapid and hurried footsteps were heard, as of guests suddenly departing, coupled with lamentations and sounds of alarm. The mirth of the assemblage seemed suddenly to have been marred, and their good cheer spoiled, and such indeed was the case.

In the very midst of the revel, and whilst the festive cup was drained around to the health of Sir Hugh and his fair child, that child had again been seized with illness and fainted.

Attributing it to the heat and excitement she had undergone, Sir Hugh bore her to her couch, and as she soon recovered from her swoon he again sought his guests.

When he did so, he observed that during his absence the party had been increased by the addition of some half a dozen cavaliers completely armed, and as he entered the room the chief of the party stepped up to him, and laid his hand upon his shoulder.

"Sir Hugh Clopton, of Clopton," he said, in a loud voice, "I arrest thee of high treason, in the name of our most sovereign lady the Queen."

CHAPTER XIX.

THE PLAGUE AT STRATFORD.

The swift passage of events, and which it has taken some little time to record, has necessarily obliged us to omit mention of several minor characters of our story, but who, nevertheless, have been playing their parts upon the stage as well as those of greater note and import. Amongst others, Master Dismal, whose cue it seemed to ferret out all sorts of disagreeables and who seemed to batton upon horrors, had not failed to follow up the hint promulgated at the Falcon regarding the sickness which had appeared in the town.

At the period of our story the plague was no uncommon visitor in the different towns in England, and awful were the consequences of such visitation when it appeared.

In cases of this sort when some dire disease breaks out amongst the poor and ignorant, they generally at first conceal it. Struck with dismay, they yet resolve to doubt the suspicious appearance till confirmation of its reality drives them to disclosure.

The plague was indeed so much dreaded at this time, that those first infected were looked upon with as much horror and dislike as if they were absolutely guilty of its production.

The very suspicion of its appearance was sufficient to frighten the town from its propriety. The inhabitants withdrew from the businesses and pleasures of life like snails within their shells. Each feared his neighbour, and all around was distrust and dread. It was this fear, together with the unclean state of the town, and most of the houses in it, which made the pestilence so quick and so fatal in its effects. Evils, it has been said, are more to be dreaded from the suddenness of their attack than from their magnitude or duration. In the storms of life those that are foreseen are half overcome.

This disease, however, was in general as formidable and as difficult to get rid of in a town, as its coming was sudden and unexpected. It was like the wind which sailors term the tiffoon, pouncing upon the vessel like an eagle upon the prey, and paralyzing the victim at once.

Master Dismal had received intelligence of this visitation by an anonymous communication, written upon a dirty scrap of paper, and which had been one night thrown in at his window.

The scrawl was in such strange hieroglyphics, and so vaguely worded, that any other person beside himself would have failed in hitting upon its hidden meaning; but the busy-body had a peculiar facility in deciphering and discovering horrors. Nay, his visitations amongst his neighbours and townsfolk were generally looked upon by them as a sure harbinger of evil in one shape or other. He was a sort of stormy petrel in the town, a forerunner of danger and despair. He even loved to watch the progress of misery and disease, contemplating the ills mankind are subject to, with a philosophic eye.

If a whole family were to be swept off, his visits continued as long as the disease lasted amongst them; and he made his entrance and took his leave with the doctor.

In fact, it was his recreation to study the maladies and miseries "the poor compounded clay, man, is heir to." Accidents and wounds, and indeed every sort of infliction his neighbours were subject to, it was his humour to watch curiously,—nay, he was even interested in the sight of a felon's ear, nailed to the cart wheel, whilst a knave set in the stocks, or a vagabond whipped through the town, was a matter of reflection, and a spectacle to be hunted after: and when Dame Patch was placed upon the cuckin stool, and then ducked in the Avon for lying and slander, he was observed next day to pay her a visit of condolence, whilst some affirmed that he had even remained a whole week in her dwelling to offer her consolation in her distress.

In addition to these peculiarities, we need hardly mention that the funeral bell was at any time a grateful sound to his ears, seldom failing to call him forth from his home, whatever his employment might happen to be.

Then again he loved to contemplate a batch of dirty urchins, in all the enjoyment of mud and mire, freedom and mischief, revelling in undisturbed possession of the kennel or the road, and to speculate upon the chances against one-third of them reaching maturity, or their probable fate if they did so.

Following the clue given him by the anonymous communication, and which he had received a few hours before he announced the news it contained at the Falcon, he had made a search through the locality hinted at. The note, which was vaguely and mysteriously worded, had pointed to some house in the suburbs; and, after duly calling over the different persons whom he considered likely to have been the writer of the billet, he fixed it upon a crazy, half insane fellow, living in a lone house in Henley Street.

Accordingly, when the shadows of evening descended, he went prying about, and peeping into all the windows, and listening at all the doors on either side that street. "Wat Murdake," he said to himself, "is a maniac,—a dangerous fellow at times, having fits of violence quite awful to look on. He killed his wife with a shoemaker's awl, pierced her ear when she was asleep,—at least, so it is said, and he confesses it even now in his ravings,—but that's nought. Many an old host that I know would be glad to do the same, if they dared, for the women do drive men to desperate deeds with that unruly member, the tongue. Wat Murdake is a dangerous fellow at times, and exceedingly mad always, but then he is pretty cunning, and keepeth a sure eye upon his neighbour. An I cannot find these plague spots, I will seek him and make inquiry, for 'tis good I saw into the matter at once.

"Ah! what's that I hear? A scream? No, it's only a child squalling, and the mother singing it to sleep with a merry song. There's no misery there. So pass we on to the next. What's that, a groan? No, it's a fellow practising on the bass-viol. All right I trow there; where music *is*, contentment rests, and no plague. What's this?" he continued, listening at the next house, "lamentations and words of woe? No, it's man and wife quarrelling. Ah! and there they go to blows. There is no real misery there, but what they make for themselves; they've plague enough, but not the plague I seek. Pass we on again. What's here? the bones rattling? Yes, dicing, drinking, and brawl. It's not there. It *may* come to that, but they don't begin *so*. There'll be death, perhaps, in the house, but it will be by violence, *not disease*—to-night, to-morrow, perhaps; who knows? And so Master Dismal passed on from door to door, taking his cue of good or ill from the employment of the inmates of the different houses. At length he came to a lone, squalid-looking hut, the last but one in the street, standing in its own untrimmed and neglected garden; a ruin with walls so rent as to shew one-half of its heavy-beamed rooms in a skeleton state; the remainder being patched up to expel the wind and rain, and reclaimed, as it were, in a slovenly manner, from the general state of decay.

The toad sat and croaked in the long damp grass, and the lizard crawled over the muddy pathway to the door, as Dismal stopped and listened.

"This looks like business," he said, "I quite forgot this house of ill-omen. Ah! what a dirty-mantled pond in the garden! Here we have it, sure enough! there's no mistaking these sounds! Let me see, this is the residence of Smite Drear and his family, the most drunken, ill-conducted, dirty, evil-minded lot in all Warwickshire—the man a vile caitiff, a puritan whose tongue is ruin; the woman a slanderer also, and a termagant; the children thieves, liars, and imps of ill. *I'm sure it's here; I know it's here;* it *must* be here; it *ought* to be here; it *is* here. Yes, and here it *is*, sure enough! If I could only get a peep into the interior, I should know in a minute. Let me see; where's my pouncet-box? Ah! there's another groan, and the sob of a female! I hear some one praying too; rather unusual *that*, I trow. I must go in. *But no*, I cannot *get* in, the door is fastened; I'll knock."

It was some time before the summons of Master Dismal was answered. But at last the owner of the hovel removed a broken shutter from an upper window, and thrusting out his head, growled a malediction upon the person disturbing him.

"Pass on," he said, "and trouble us not."

"I would crave permission," said Dismal, "to pay a visit on matters ——"

"*Crave* nothing here," said Drear, "*Seek* nothing here. Sickness and death are within our doors: we are accursed."

"I would fain offer consolation, and observe the nature of your illness," said Dismal. "I would inform the leech, or even summon *other* aid in your need."

"Who is it speaks?" said Drear, thrusting his head further out. Ah, I see! Hence, screech-owl—bird of ill; hence, wretch, lest I come down and beat thee! Hence, hound, whose bark never boded aught but death to the sick man. We wanted but thy visit to make us certain of our fate."

So saying, Drear violently put up his shutter and withdrew.

"Ah," said Dismal, "you may talk, my master, till you've tired yourself. But I know all about it now. If I cannot get *in*, by my troth I'll take care to put a sign which shall hinder you from getting *out*. Plague or no plague, I'll cause them to look in upon you who have authority to do so." So saying, Master Dismal took a large lump of red ochre from his pocket, and with considerable care marked up a broad red cross upon the door. He then, as he knew it was about the hour the watch passed, quietly withdrew to the opposite side of the street, and ensconsing himself behind the buttress of a wall, waited the event.

In a short time the watch came up; they passed Master Dismal where he stood without discovering him, and then proceeded to the very end of the street. According to their custom (in making the rounds at night) they then halted, ordered their pikes, trimmed their lights, and stood at ease for a few minutes, ere they returned down the other side of the street; examining each door they passed by holding up the light they carried.

At the first tenement they found nothing extraordinary, the fellow who carried the light, which was a sort of cresset at the end of a bar of iron, held it aloft, and as its lurid glare fell upon the house, it displayed its walls clear as in open daylight. "All right, pass," said the head constable, and so they passed on to the next.

Here the constable carrying the cresset was merely about to raise it and pass on, when, as he did so, the whole party were arrested in speechless alarm by a sign they knew too well from former visitation. "The plague!" said the first, in a voice modulated almost to a whisper. "The plague!" said the second, "why I heard not of it before." "The searcher's mark," said the second, "I knew not that he had been sent out." "Advance your light again, Diccon," said a third, "and observe if the house be padlocked up." "I see no fastening," said Diccon, "and yet, 'tis the searcher's mark, sure enough; pass on, in heaven's name, comrades;" and on passed the watch, no longer with measured tread, but with accelerated and fearful steps, to inform the headborough of what they had seen: Master Dismal stealing after them in a state of the most exuberant glee at his own conceit and its success.

The spread of the disease, as was usual at this period, was extremely rapid. Indeed, it had risen to some height in the town before the authorities would consent to believe it really existed. In such cases, and in former days, precautionary measures were seldom thought of. Men drove off all thought of the evil; when they found it was really amongst them, or what they feared, they kept to themselves. At first they turned sulky under the infliction, if we may so term it, barring up their doors and deserting the streets; they avoided each other as much as possible, seeking air and recreation and forgetfulness by taking to the wastes and commons around. Leaving their homes by the back doors, they almost deserted the streets in search of the necessaries of life. As it grew worse the town seemed depopulated, even before the disease had time to work, so empty were its streets.

But a few days had passed since all the out-door sports and diversions of the age and the season had been in full play. Those gay and jovial May-day games, in the quaint mazes of the wanton green; those rural fêtes and diversions—the wakes and revels—the May-pole dances—the parties of pleasure into the shadowy desert unfrequented woods, and which the peasantry of old were so fond of, all had ceased as it were on the instant. The human mortals feared each other, a secret dread—however each member of a family kept the native colour of his cheek—was in the heart of each. The very air seemed infected, and the aspect of the town took a ghastly hue. It smelt of death, men thought. Business stopped in it. No markets were attended. No strangers passed through it. It was a place infected, avoided, accursed.

CHAPTER XX.

MORE TROUBLE AT CLOPTON.

MEANWHILE, as misfortunes seldom come but in battalions, Sir Hugh Clopton (even before he had heard of the appearance of the disease) had been arrested of high treason, and carried off to London with several other gentlemen of condition in the county, and who had likewise been mixed up in the confession of Master Walter Neville.

It is indeed hardly possible to describe the dire confusion which ensued upon this unexpected event taking place on the night of the feast at Clopton Hall. Sir Hugh himself was the only person of his household and family who seemed to retain his self-command. Walter Arderne would, at first, have fain struck down the Queen's officer and expelled his men. The faithful Martin was almost distraught. The serving men and retainers were scared and indignant at the same time; and the guests in a state of astonishment and dismay.

"Heed it not, my masters all," said Sir Hugh, "'tis a mistake altogether. I a traitor to our blessed Queen! pah. I would she had but such traitors in all her foes; methinks I know where this matter originates, and shall set it right upon examination."

"I hope so," said the officer; "Nevertheless, there is one other I am to secure within your household, but my people have just learnt he hath fled on our approach."

"In the name of Heaven," said Sir Hugh, "who else lays under this strange misconception?"

"A priest but lately come from over sea, commonly called Father Eustace," said the officer.

"Eustace!" said Sir Hugh, "why he was here but now. Is he too accused?"

"He is," said the officer, "and must, if possible, be apprehended; some of my party have followed on his trail."

"Any more of my family, household, or personal friends implicated?" said Sir Hugh, somewhat bitterly. "I trust I shall set my accuser, whoever he be, before my rapier's point, when I promise him such mercy as it affords *no more*."

"I feel sorry to put any force upon you, Sir Hugh," said the officer, "especially before this goodly company, but my orders are peremptory, and I must convey you to Warwick to-night; to-morrow with all speed towards London."

"Nay," said Sir Hugh, "good sir, you but express my own wishes in this matter. To the Tower with me at once. An there be any limb or member o' my body found guilty of this sin—torture it: an the Queen find that my head hath entertained a thought against her—off with it: an my heart hath conceived treason—tear it out. To horse then in God's name, and let us put on without delay."

And truly did the good Sir Hugh bespeak himself, whilst most of the guests standing in amaze around, and, with tears in their eyes, beheld him made prisoner, and conveyed from his own domain. Under the circumstances in which he found himself, it was a great relief to the good knight that his daughter was saved from the grief and misery of seeing and taking leave of him.

The coming of the officers and the arrest of her father it was hastily arranged should be carefully concealed, and her attendants were enjoined to say that a sudden summons from the Queen had obliged Sir Hugh instantly to depart.

Meantime the faithful Martin undertook to remain in watchful attendance upon her, whilst Arderne, whose feelings would not permit him to stay behind, accompanied the party in charge of the old knight, and whom he swore never to leave till he was again at liberty.

"I will gain audience of the Queen," he said, "instantly, and not leave the Court until I know the vile traducer who hath thus denounced thee, uncle. Thou a traitor, indeed! Thou soul of honour, loyalty and truth! Treason hath no existence—no place to hide in aught where thou abidest."

And thus (as is oft the case in life) the scene became on the sudden overcast. At the moment of its brightness—the gaiety, the splendour, and the happiness of the party were dashed; whilst those who had met together with light hearts and fantastic spirits, dispersed with evil foreboding and slow and heavy footsteps.

In a party of this sort, in Warwickshire, it was customary ofttimes to keep up the revel till dawn, whilst every nook and corner of the dwelling was made available for those of the guests who chose to remain afterwards.

With the good old English hospitality which despised form, Sir Hugh had previously arranged for many of his most intimate friends to stay a few days at Clopton and partake in the sport his preserves afforded. The dogs and falcons were to have been put in requisition, and the heronry and the thick covers around beat for game.

Indeed two or three did remain at Clopton the next day; not for the purpose of recreating themselves with the old knight's hawks, but from their anxiety about the illness of the fair Charlotte, and in the hope of seeing her re-appear from her room with renewed health.

Such, however, was not to be the case, as she grew rapidly worse, and it was found necessary to summon the leech from Stratford. Soon after his arrival, the faithful Martin, with a face of alarm, took upon himself to dismiss the guests. His charge, he said, was extremely ill. Her complaint was pronounced by the leech to be both infectious and dangerous, and under such circumstances, it was advisable for them to shorten their visit. "Neither should I be acting rightly," he added, "if I concealed it, although the rumour may possibly be without foundation, but I have just heard the plague hath broken out in Stratford."

Thus were the halls of Clopton—and which but a few short hours before had displayed such a scene of gaiety and revelling,—as suddenly changed to gloom and melancholy.

The domestics seemed to glide about with noiseless step, hardly having heart to arrange the different rooms, so that many of them were left in the confusion and disarray they had been in when the mirth of the party was so suddenly interrupted; and, if the succeeding day was fraught with melancholy, the night was filled with terrors. Strange and awful sounds were heard in some of the rooms. Sounds which none could account for or discover the meaning of, although, at first attributing them to natural causes, the domestics made search through those parts of the house where they had been heard.

Coming thus at a time of grief and misfortune, and following sickness and the rumours of so dire a disease as the plague, these sounds had an ominous and awful appearance. The domestics, much as they loved their employers, and commiserated them in their present distress, were so much scared, that several fled from the Hall to their own homes; and, as the mysterious sounds continued night after night growing more violent, and even extending from the part of the house to which they had at first been confined; with the exception of two or three of the upper servants, the numerous domestics of the establishment had almost all deserted it.

The faithful Martin was sorely troubled. Living in an age when men's minds were easily affected by superstitious terrors, and a general belief existed in supernatural agency, he however possessed an uncommon degree of firmness and mental energy. At first he tried to laugh at the terrors and complaints of the different servants, as they brought continued reports of dreadful sounds existing in the western wing of the Hall, and where the secret hiding-places existed. Then, as his own ears confirmed their reports, he shut himself up, well armed, for a whole night in the apartments where the spirit was said to be most troublesome.

On this night, which was the third after the departure of Sir Hugh, the sounds were most terrific and awful. As if the evil genius of the house of Clopton was either rejoicing over the present state of the family, or impatient for their utter destruction, it seemed inclined to drive the inmates to despair by its violence.

Martin, having thrown himself upon the bed in the apartment we have before seen tenanted by the maniac Parry, was reclining in a half-dozing state, a couple of huge petronels in his belt and a drawn rapier upon the table, when he was suddenly conscious of some one entering the room, and sitting down beside the bed.

As he had carefully locked the door he was in something surprised at this visitation: but suspecting that some influence from without was at work, and distrusting the Jesuitical priest Eustace, after a while he quietly and cautiously rose, and then leaping suddenly from the bed, confronted the supposed visitant petronel in hand.

To his astonishment, however, no person was there,—"He looked but on a stool." The door, which had been violently burst in, was still wide open, but no one was in the room besides himself. This was the more extraordinary as Martin was confident he had distinctly heard the person enter, and with swift step passing into the apartment, seat itself by his bedside. Nay, so quick and sudden seemed the visit, that although a bold and determined man, Martin had felt paralyzed and unable to move for the first minute or two. His heart beat violently; he was certain some one was within a few inches of him as he lay, and yet he could not move a limb; till at length, shaking off the feeling, he rose to confront the intruder. Pistol in hand, he looked in every part of the small room, "searching impossible places" in his anxiety. He then descended the narrow staircase, and looked into every nook and corner of the apartment beneath, but found not even a cobweb amiss.

Returning to his couch he re-fastened the door, trimmed his lamp, placed it in the chair beside his bed, examined his petronel, and again lay down with the weapon firmly grasped in his hand. "If there be any deceit in this," he said to himself, "and which I feel inclined to believe is the case, I will make sure work of it with the practiser. A bullet through his heart or lungs, will lay his ghostship in the Red Sea."

There had never been much good feeling in existence between the shrewd Martin and the priest Eustace. At the present moment the former held the Jesuit in especial dislike. He had a suspicion that the difficulties in which Sir Hugh was now placed, arose from some intrigues of the priest, whom he knew to be of an unscrupulous and designing nature. The present noises he conceived to be some contrivance of this iron-hearted bigot, in order to scare the servants of the establishment from that wing of the building, and he accordingly resolved to make a severe example of whoever he detected. This idea nerved him to so great a degree, that the extraordinary sounds he heard at first failed in completely frightening him. The situation, however, was not altogether a pleasant one. The silence, the loneliness, the dangerous illness of his favourite Charlotte, the peril in which the old knight was placed, all crowded themselves upon his imagination as he lay and watched.

For some time nothing occurred to disturb his melancholy reflections, reflections which at length took him from the present horror of the time; and led on to other thoughts, till, at length, the heavy summons of sleep began to weigh upon his eyelids.

At this moment the clock from the old tower in the stabling struck two. Scarcely had it done so when a distant whirling sound was heard; it seemed at first like a rushing wind stirring the trees in the shrubbery without, and steadily advancing towards the house. It increased in sound as it did so, till it appeared to enter the house, and rushing up the staircase with fearful violence the door again was dashed open with a tremendous burst, the lamp was extinguished at the same moment, and the room seemed filled with some strange and unnatural visitants.

Starting up at the moment of the door being burst in, Martin discharged his pistol full at the entrance, and at the very instant the light was extinguished. He then jumped, sword in hand, into the middle of the room, whilst a rushing sound, as of persons moving about, was all around him.

The darkness, added to the horrors of his situation, almost unmanned the bold Martin, and spite of his determined character his heart now beat violently and his hair bristled on his head. Nay, so impressed was he with the idea that some spectral beings were in the apartment, and even in his own vicinity,—nay, perhaps, that the enemy of mankind was at his very elbow and about to clutch him, that, as he uttered a hasty prayer for the protection of Heaven, he executed several furious backstrokes round the apartment, cutting a huge gash in the bed furniture, demolishing the back of an elaborately carved oaken chair, and bringing down a cumbrous mirror, smashed into a dozen pieces with as many blows. Indeed, the natural sounds of this ruin in some measure did away with the awe the supernatural noises had created. There is always some relief in action in such cases. The coward, for instance, makes use of his legs, in the midst of apprehension, the brave man takes to his arms, and as the strange sounds gradually subsided, seeming to traverse through the rooms below in their progress, Martin ceased from his exertions.

He was, however, now completely converted to the opinion of the domestics that there was something most strange and most unnatural in this visitation. He felt awed and struck with dread, and, lowering the point of his weapon, he stood in the centre of the apartment listening attentively as the noise passed through the lower rooms. "There is surely something in all this," he said to himself, "which is beyond my comprehension. 'Tis a sound of warning. I fear me some dire misfortune is in store. Peradventure Sir Hugh is dead: great Heaven, perhaps executed on the scaffold! Alas, my poor Charlotte! But no, it cannot be so. Heaven help us in our need, for we seem a doomed people here."

A deep sigh sounded close to his ears as he finished his soliloquy, so heavy, so long drawn, and so startling, that his blood curdled in his veins. He felt that he could no longer remain in the apartment, and hastily leaving it he descended the stairs, and opening the sliding pannel, passed into the rooms usually habited when Sir Hugh was at home.

Here he felt in something reassured, and groping his way to the door which admitted to the garden, he threw it open and sought relief in the free air.

The night was dark and a drizzling rain descended; he stepped on to the grass-plat and looked up at the apartment of his sick charge. A light was in the room, a pale and sickly gleam, which seemed to speak of watching and woe at that dead hour. As he passed beneath the window he thought he perceived a figure gliding away, but the night was too dark for him to be quite certain; still he felt sure that he had seen the outline of a form which, gloomy as was the night, he recognized.

"'Tis he, I feel assured," said Martin. "I cannot mistake that form, even so indistinctly seen, for there is none other like him. Alas! alas! 'tis even so. He watches her window even in such a night as this. I saw they loved each other from the first. Well, we are in the hands of heaven, and 'tis wrong to murmur. If our ills are reparable, to complain is ungrateful; if irremediable, 'tis vain. Whatever happens must have first pleased God, and most pleased him; or it had not happened. There is no affliction which resignation cannot conquer or death cure."

As Martin resigned himself to this comfortable doctrine he turned and re-entered the house.

The dawn was now beginning to break, and he resolved to knock at the chamber door of the invalid and make some inquiry after her.

The first grey tint of morning began to render objects in the room visible as he passed through it. There stood the spinnet upon which Charlotte had so lately played, the music-book open. There was her lute lying beside the music, and where it had been laid on the night of the party, and beside that lay the hood and jesses of her favourite hawk.

Whilst Martin regarded these remembrances of one now unable to use or enjoy them, a pang of grief shot through his heart, that sorrowful feeling with which we look upon the relics of the dead, and whom we have loved dearly when in life; and with that feeling came the conviction that she who once played so sweetly on that instrument, and so bravely wore those trappings of her gallant bird,—she, the young, the beautiful, was already parted perhaps for ever from the pleasures of the earth,—sick, prostrate, dying,—nay, even at that moment perhaps dead.

With heavy heart and evil foreboding he ascended the great staircase and sought Charlotte's room. His step was heard by the nurse who attended on the invalid, and gently opening the door she came forth to meet him.

The nurse was one of the old servants of the family; she was pale as death Martin observed as he advanced along the corridor. "We have had a fearful night," she said.

"But your charge?" said Martin, "I trust in Heaven she is better."

"Worse, Martin, worse," she replied; "worse than I can bring myself to tell thee. She is now asleep, but hath been delirious all the night."

"Now the gods help us," said Martin.

"Amen," said the nurse; "she hath raved much and talked wildly. To thee, Martin, I will confess it, she hath spoken much of one she loves."

"I dare to say so," said Martin, musing.

"But not of *him* of whom she should so speak," said the nurse.

"Not of him our good old master would like to have heard her speak in such loving terms. Mayhap I should surprise you were I to say on whom her affections seem fixed."

"I think not," said Martin, significantly.

"You think not?" said the nurse, "and wherefore?"

"Because I know her secret as well as if she had told it me," said Martin. "I have seen it from the first."

"Hark!" said the nurse, "she is again in one of those fits. Hear you that name, and thus called on."

"I do," said Martin; "'tis as I thought. May I see her? Methinks I cannot be satisfied till I look upon her sweet face, if but for a moment."

"Remain here whilst I go in, and I will then summon you," said the nurse. "Ah me, 'tis very sad!" and the nurse passed into the room, closing the door behind her.

Martin seated himself on the bench beneath the window at the end of the corridor, and as he gazed upon the portraits of the Clopton family hanging on either hand, his reflections became even more saddened. In that array of beautiful females and noble-looking cavaliers, how many died early! Amongst those scowling and bearded men of middle age, arrayed in all the panoply of war, how many had perished in their harness! There was Hugo de Clopton, the crusader, the fiercest of a brave race, who had smote even a crowned king in Palestine rather than brook dishonour. There was the templar, who had died at the stake in France, true to his vow; and Blanche Clopton, whom the lascivious John had solicited in vain, and who had been celebrated at tilt and tourney throughout Christendom as "La belle des belles."

Each and all of these portraits, it seemed to him, had a curious history attached to them—a sad and stern tale in life's romance—and as he sat and regarded them he thought upon their descendant now lying sick in their close vicinity—her father accused of treason and a prisoner, at a time so inopportune.

"Strange," he thought to himself, "that this family, so noble in disposition, so high in their sense of honour, should seem thus marked out and pursued by fate.

"'Tis true the good Sir Hugh hath been called, by the clergy of his own persuasion, but a luke-warm member of the true Church; an irreligious man.

"Nay, Eustace hath upbraided him with leaning towards heresy; and the Protestant churchmen at Stratford, again, hath accused him of being neither of the one religion or the other—altogether a heathen.

"These churchmen are both men, however, who wrangle and fight so much about religion, vice and virtue, that they have no time to practise either the one or the other; whilst the good Sir Hugh hath, during life, been so fully engaged in acts of benevolence, that saving the hours he hath spent amongst his horses and dogs, he hath indeed little leisure to think about such controversies."

Whilst Martin sat thus chewing the cud of bitter fancy, the old attendant returned to him. "She again sleeps," she said, weeping, and you may look upon her sweet face once more. But oh, Martin, I fear me we are indeed in trouble; you will scarce behold that countenance, even yet so beautiful, without terror."

"Is she already so changed?" said Martin. "In the name of Heaven, what can be her complaint?"

"No noise," said the attendant, "but go in, and judge for yourself."

In a few moments Martin returned. Horror was in his countenance. "Her face is filled with livid spots!" he said. "We are indeed unhappy; she has caught——"

"The plague," said the nurse, as Martin hesitated, apparently unable to repeat the words. "The plague; 'tis even so, and she will not outlive this day."

"I will hasten to Stratford, and bid the leech again visit her instantly," said Martin.

"'Twere best," said the attendant, "be quick; but I fear me it is of little avail." And Martin, with fearful and hasty steps, left the corridor, and descended to the stabling of the Hall.

Besides Martin and the attending nurse, there was one other who watched with anxiety over the fate of the poor invalid, and who, albeit circumstances made it unpleasing to him openly to display the interest he felt, yet who sought in every way to gather some tidings of her state of health.

Amidst the general trouble in which the town was now involved, private griefs were less thought of, and consequently, although the inhabitants of the Hall were, by the good folks of Stratford-upon-Avon, known to be in some strait, whilst everybody was in apprehension for himself, commiseration there was little of, and intercourse there was none. Nay, the small remaining portion of domestics at Clopton had become so greatly alarmed by the visitation of the previous night, that they neglected their duties on this day, and remaining huddled together in the servants' hall, meditated altogether deserting the locality.

In addition to the supernatural sounds, they were now scared by a suspicion of the nature of the disease which had seized their young lady.

It was under such circumstances that, when Martin descended to the stables in order to dispatch a messenger for the doctor, he could at first find no one willing to undertake the message.

"I would willingly do anything I could to benefit the young lady," said one, "but I am about to leave the Hall."

"I cannot go into the town," said another, "for it is said that death is rife in its streets; and the folks are stricken as they walk. It would be a tempting of the disease an I were to run into it."

"Nay! we have had warning enough here," said another; "and albeit I respect Sir Hugh, I fear to remain, after what we have heard last night. Besides, if the truth must out, I believe the sickness hath come to Clopton; and folks must look to themselves. I have friends at Kenilworth, and I must seek them. They say too, that Sir Hugh hath been found guilty of a conspiracy against the life of the Queen, and I like it not."

"Hounds!" said Martin—"unworthy even to tend upon the generous animals you are hired to feed. Begone! pack—seek another roof, where you can batten on cold bits, and return kindness with base ingratitude." So saying, Martin saddled one of the steeds, and mounting himself, galloped into the town.

CHAPTER XXI.

DOMESTIC AFFLICTIONS.

It is evening—damp, dreary, and heavy, like the day which has preceded it.

An unwholesome closeness pervades the air; a heavy drizzling rain descends from the clouds upon the earth, enveloping all around in a dense mist, which hides the surrounding scenery.

Leaving his home, the youthful Shakespeare takes his way across the meadows, in which our readers may remember to have first seen him in the opening chapter of this story. His step, however, is less buoyant, and his heart is heavier than on that occasion. The clouds, which drive steadily on, are not less gloomy than his presentiments. Sickness and misery are amongst the neighbours he leaves; sickness and sorrow are amongst those he seeks.

Yet still as that youth wends onwards, now crossing through the fern (laden and heavy with moisture,) now diving into the thick plantations which lead into the chase of Clopton, nothing escapes his notice. The crow, "as it wings to the rocky wood," in the thickening light,—the coney, as it flashes into the cover,—the darting lizard, as it disappears in the thick fern,—the stoat and weasel, as they pounce upon their prey in the brake, all are noted by him.

His mind was oppressed and desponding, but it was a mind which no circumstances could entirely destroy the elasticity of, even for a moment. "There is a pleasure in the pathless woods," it hath been said by a modern poet; and there is society where none intrudes. But perhaps the feeling of pleasure experienced amidst solitude and sylvan scenery is only really and intensely felt by men of extraordinary parts and poetical imagination.

The fairest glade, and the wildest haunts of the untamed denizens of the woods, it was young Shakespeare's great delight to seek out and ponder amidst.

At the present moment he felt that no locality would soothe the sadness of his thoughts so well as the leafy covert he was in.

Even whilst the heavy rain was pattering amidst the foliage, and dropping from the surcharged boughs; the air misty and moist; and the darksome glade rendered more gloomy by the murky atmosphere, there was indeed to his eye and mind, something fresh to be remarked around in the changeful hue of the herbs, plants, and thick foliage, as the driving clouds constantly varied them; nay (as we have said,) the gloomy and dull aspect of the wood at that moment better suited his troubled thoughts than a more bright and splendid scene.

Some slight intimation of the troubles of his friends at the Hall had reached him; he had received a hint of the arrest of Sir Hugh, and the absence of his friend Arderne. He also knew that the fair Charlotte was unwell; and naturally attributing her illness to the shock she had received at the arrest of her father, he hoped that a few days would restore her to health. Still a presentiment of evil, and which he conceived was consequent upon the unhappy state of the town in which he had lived, pervaded his mind.

He had occasionally visited the neighbourhood of the Hall, and made some inquiry after the inmates; but in the absence of the good knight, and his friend Arderne, he had not considered it consistent with propriety to introduce himself into the house, coming as he did from a place infected with the plague.

On this evening, however, he resolved to gain some more assured tidings of those he felt so much interested in; and after pondering upon the matter, he resolved to approach the hall.

There was a solitude and silence about the house, as he gazed at it from the belt of plantation by which he approached, that he could not account for. No smoke ascended from those huge twisted chimneys; no sound (save an occasional dismal and long-drawn howl) came from the kennel. No person was to be seen, as of yore, flitting about, engaged in the numerous avocations of their daily duties. All looked dull and deserted.

He entered the court in rear, and proceeded to the stabling. The stables were for the most part empty, the steeds had been turned into the chase, and deserted by their attendants. He looked into the falconry; the hawks were upon the perch, and apparently well fed and attended to, for at that period a falconer would have as soon deserted his children as his hawks, but the attendants were at the moment absent; they had fled from the Hall, and located themselves in some out-buildings in the woods. As he entered the house, the same appearance of desertion struck his eye. He passed through a long passage, and gained the hall. There hung the old tattered banners, the unscoured armour, and the antlered heads of several large stags,—stags of ten,—all spoke of recent occupation and use. The cross-bow lay where it had been thrown a few days before; the thick hawking gauntlets and the dog-couples were mingled with whips and spurs, bits and bridles, and all the *mélange* of the chase and the country gentleman's occupation, but of servants or inhabitants there was no sign. He passed into the oak-pannelled room where he had first enjoyed the society of the family, and learned to love them for their worth. All looked desolate. The solitude and silence around made his presence seem an intrusion. The innate modesty of his disposition overcame his anxiety to hear tidings of the invalid. He felt as if prying into the secret sorrows of the owner of the mansion, and was about to withdraw, when the door opened, and Martin entered the room.

Martin started as he recognised the visitor, and a slight frown seemed to cross his brow. He was a curious compound, that man. He half disliked the youth for the virtues he at the same time admired in him, and which he saw had also won the love of the daughter of his patron, and which under no circumstance he considered could lead to a happy result,—now, however, all was at an end.

"Ah," he said, "art *thou* here? Art thou come to Clopton when all else desert it?"

"My anxiety to learn tidings of the family hath made me an intruder on your privacy," said Shakespeare. "I hope——"

"We have no hope," said Martin; "and you are not wise in coming hither. You have surely heard of our misery. Charlotte Clopton is dying. Dying of the plague. The nurse has just caught it of her and sickens too. All have fled from the Hall."

A few moments more, and Shakespeare had sprung up the great staircase, and sought the chamber of the invalid, Martin hastening after him, and in vain urging him not to enter her room. "The disease is of the most malignant character," he said. "The leech hath left the house unable to do us any good. 'Tis but a tempting of Providence to enter the room. I pr'ythee have thought upon your own safety."

"Perish all thoughts of self and safety!" said Shakespeare, dashing his hat upon the floor as he entered the chamber. "O fairest flower," he said, "cut down and blighted in thy budding beauty, do I indeed behold thee again thus—so soon to part with thee for ever?"

He knelt down beside her bed, took her hand, and carried it to his lips.

Her long luxuriant tresses, which had escaped from the ribbon that bound them, covered the white pillow like a cloud, and half-concealed her face. She raised herself as she recognised the voice, and, parting her hair, gazes eagerly in his face. "Thou art come then," she said; "once more come? Oh, blessings on thee for it. I have wished for thee; dreamt of thee; called for thee; and thou art come at last to set mine eye. What happiness to look upon thy face once more—even in death! And yet," she said, as she held him from her, "there is danger in your being here, I heard them whisper to each other of the plague."

"Oh, believe it not!" said Shakespeare; "there is no sign of such disease about thee. Thou wilt live, dearest lady. Cast but from your mind these sad thoughts, and you will yet recover."

"Not so," said Charlotte; "I feel as if I had not many moments on earth, and yet I know I shall not harm thee, for I have beheld the story of thy life in my troubled dreams. I have seen thee unknown, unthought of, unhonoured in the world. And then I saw thee enshrined in such a blaze of glory as no mortal ever before attained on earth:—the wonder of ages to come. Thy very name alone, whispered in thy lowly home, William Shakespeare, will make bearded men weep. Yes," she continued, vehemently, "I beheld thy figure standing upon an eminence so high above thy fellow-mortals, that, though all were striving to ascend towards thee, none could come beyond the plain on which that mountain stood."

The tears fell from the youth's eyes as he buried his face upon the coverlid of the couch, and listened to what he considered the prophetic ravings of delirium; and then he again raised his head and gazed upon her. There were no traces of disease to be observed in that bright form as he did so. The subdued light of the chamber gave her the appearance of a marble monument. In the abandonment of her grief, she had raised herself on one arm, and her beauty seemed even more dazzling.

"'Twas beauty
Too rich for use, for earth too dear."

The livid spots, which had so alarmed the nurse and Martin, had disappeared from her face. Her rounded shoulder and bosom were like the sculptured alabaster—rendered yet more white and polished by the soft, dark tresses, by which they were partially covered.

"I would have lived for thee," she said, "to have but served thee; to have made the paltry riches I own, available to thy genius."

As she uttered this, she sank down sobbing upon the couch. Shakespeare, in an agony of grief, tried to raise and recover her, but she sank quickly into insensibility: and when he laid her down again upon her pillow, as he looked upon her, he saw she was dead!

Dead! but without the ghastly appearance which the grisly tyrant stamps upon his prey.

"Death, that had sucked the honey of her breath,
Had yet no power upon her beauty.
Beauty's ensign yet
Was crimson on her lips and in her cheeks,
And Death's pale flag was not advanced there."

CHAPTER XXII.

BEREAVEMENT.

One week has elasped since the events narrated in the last chapter. The house of Clopton is shut up, empty, deserted. The good Sir Hugh is again at liberty; but the seas flow between him and Britain. After having been examined by Lord Hunsden, Sir Christopher Hatton, and Sir Francis Walsingham, three members of the Privy Council, he was released from confinement. The conspirators, all excepting the priest Eustace, who had escaped, and through whose intrigues the good knight had become an object of suspicion to the Council, were condemned to death and executed in Old Palace Yard two days after. With eager haste, and tarrying at each post but to obtain fresh horses, Sir Hugh and Walter Arderne had (immediately on the release of the former) galloped as hard as spur and bridle could urge on their steeds towards Clopton. Unluckily they passed Martin in the night on the road near Oxford, as he was hastening towards London with the intention of breaking the news of Charlotte's death to them.

One letter had, in a measure, prepared the good knight to find his daughter dangerously ill; but, as in those days, both the inditing and conveying a packet was a matter of considerable time and toil, letters were by no means so sure of coming to hand, or so speedily delivered as in latter times.

So that the unhappy knight arrived at the Hall to find desolation where he had left plenty. His house was shut up—his daughter dead. She had died of the plague, it was said; and with fearful haste, by order of the authorities of the neighbouring town, had been buried.

It far exceeds the descriptive power of our pen to paint the grief, horror, and despair of the good Sir Hugh and his nephew. For the moment they seemed stupified with excess of misery. They then threw themselves into each other's arms, and wept in their desolation, till the very violence of their grief in some sort relieved them.

'Tis extraordinary how the human mind, after a time, accommodates itself to the dispensations of Providence, however hard to bear. It was greatly in favour of the mourners that they had in each other subjects of anxiety. Each felt the hard lot of the other; and as each watched the deep sorrow of his companion, the very feelings and disposition to afford comfort, and urge patience and resignation, in some sort took from them the poignancy of their own feelings.

The old knight, after wandering about the house in a state of bewilderment for the first twenty-four hours after his arrival, became calmer, and seemed inclined to force himself to take an interest in his old occupations.

He visited, on the evening of the second day, the kennel and the falconry, accompanied by Arderne, and made the rounds of the different buildings and offices. Neither of them spoke much to each other, except an occasional word as they came upon some object of deep interest in connexion with her who was gone. "Look!" said Sir Hugh, as with quivering lips and tears rolling down his muscular cheeks and grey beard, he pointed to Charlotte's favourite hawk—a gallant bird, which sat and plumed itself upon its perch, "look!" said he, in tremulous accents—he could say no more; but in the utterance of that word what an agony of grief was expressed. Arderne, too, felt his chest heave, and the tears course each other down his cheeks, as he regarded the hawk. But the sight of the brave old knight struggling to master his grief for his sake, relieved the poignancy of his own sorrow. "Come, uncle," said he, "we must to the stables. Tarry not here. There is much to be looked after, and which wants your care. The attendants seem to have deserted their charge, and the stalls are for the most part empty;" and so they pursued their search around. When they came to the stable, if objects were wanting to produce the sharp pang of grief, here again they were to be found—objects peculiarly adapted to give the most intense feelings of sorrow, as they were associated with those accomplishments in his daughter, which the knight had held in the most estimation. There hung the gay trappings of her favourite steed, and there stood the steed itself, which the falconer had kept in its stall—a milk-white and perfect courser; and in the stable beside the manger, lay Charlotte's favourite hound—the dog, in her absence having apparently sought consolation in the companionship of the horse he had so often accompanied to the field.

The horse turned and neighed inquiringly, it appeared, to the old knight; and the dog shook himself clear of the straw, and bounding out of the stall, put his fore-legs upon Sir Hugh's breast, and seemed to ask for his mistress, and then it stood down, as if conscious of the fruitlessness of the query; and throwing up its great head, uttered a long melancholy howl.

The good knight regarded the dog for a moment in silence. He stepped up to the white steed; and as it put its nose affectionately in his face, he kissed it again and again. He then sought for his own saddle; and saddling and bridling the horse, he led it forth into the yard, followed by the hound.

As Walter observed the knight's movements, he quietly saddled his own steed, and they both set out together, and without a word took the road to Stratford. There was no necessity for Walter to inquire of his uncle their destination. He felt assured that the knight was about to visit his daughter's grave.

Although Sir Hugh had however endeavoured to resign himself to the decrees of Providence, and bear with fortitude the dire affliction which had visited his house, he found it impossible to pursue the usual tenor of his former life; the charm of existence seemed fled for ever—"life was as tedious as a twice-told tale." It seemed to him, that in the listless way in which he was pursuing his daily avocations, he was beginning over again. He rode forth without purpose, and pursued his route as chance or his steed directed.

Luckily this had been foreseen by a true industrious friend, one who, since the return of Sir Hugh to Clopton, had been sorely missed in his need by the good knight.

The faithful Martin, on his arrival in London, on finding that Sir Hugh had been liberated, and had returned to Clopton, was struck with dismay, inasmuch as he immediately surmised the shock the knight would be likely to receive on so immediately returning to his desolate home.

Sudden and quick in all his resolves, he sought out a friend at Court, and one who was under some little obligation to him for former services rendered. This was no less a person than Sir Christopher Hatton, a distinguished personal favourite of the Queen; a gentleman who owed his rise absolutely to his exceeding good gifts in the elegant accomplishment of dancing, and who walking into favour by a corranto, gradually gained ground in her Majesty's further affections by his activity in the galliard, capering higher and higher into the Royal estimation at each subsequent demivolt, till he successively attained the posts of Gentleman Pensioner, Captain of the Guard, Vice-Chamberlain, and Lord Chancellor. This gentleman, who (notwithstanding the oddness of his rise) was in reality a man of most amiable disposition, possessed a mind less biassed by the prejudices of his age than most of his contemporaries; and this most estimable man the faithful Martin sought out.

"Sir Hugh Clopton," said Martin, "hath been badly used in this matter; and inasmuch as his arrest and absence hath in some measure, by removing him from the government of his house at a time of sickness and distress, caused him much misery, the which his presence and management might have possibly obviated, I think the Queen is bound to shew him some sort of assistance in his great grief."

"Doubtless," said Sir Christopher, who was at that moment engaged in arranging a quick measure for the viol-de-gamba, and which he meant to adapt some exceeding curious steps to at the masque given by the Templars to Her Majesty on that very night, "doubtless, good Martin. Only shew me in what way I can serve the good knight Sir Hugh, and look upon it as done."

"Why look ye," said Martin, Sir Hugh is a man having as great excellence is his arms as you, Sir Christopher, are so celebrated for in the legs. Now if you could intercede for him with Her Majesty, so that the good knight might be appointed to some command in the Low Countries, the violence of action might do away with the poignancy of his grief, and force him from his home."

"I fear me this is rather a delicate matter to broach unto Her Majesty," said Sir Christopher.

"And yet," said Martin, "consider the miserable condition of this poor gentleman: make it your own case. Think, Sir Christopher, if you was to be bereft of all—of favour, fortune, influence at Court."

"Sir Hugh hath lost nothing of all this," interrupted Sir Christopher. "He hath lost no fortune and favour and influence at Court: he never had or sought for either the one or the other."

"But he hath lost his child," said Martin, "which is all these to him."

"In my case," said Sir Christopher, "I should *not* consider myself so utterly miserable were I to lose all you have mentioned. As long as I am lord of this presence," he continued, looking at the reflection of his exceeding handsome face in the mirror, and then regarding his well-turned leg and small foot, "I should not lack advancement. There are other Courts besides the Court of Elizabeth—other lands besides Britain—where a man's good gifts might be properly estimated;" and as Sir Christopher said this, he threw out his right foot, and pointed his toe with grace and effect.

"And there it is," said Martin; "bereft of favour and fortune, you would still have something to fall back upon, Sir Christopher. But how if a sudden twist were to dislocate that slim ancle, and the joint were ever after to be like the callous hock of a foundered steed? How then would you push your fortune?"

"Nay, then I should be utterly discomfited," said Sir Christopher, laughing; "foundered in good earnest—toe and heel—hip and thigh."

"And such is the condition of Sir Hugh," said Martin, "unless we can give a fresh fillip to his depressed spirits, and teach him to forget his griefs; he will despair, and despairing, die."

"I see the urgency of the matter," said Sir Christopher; "Her Majesty may lose a good blade in the stout knight, were he to die of grief. He hath received wrong, but he shall have speedy redress. Come to me to-morrow, good Martin—early, good Martin—my life upon it, I will in some sort content you."

Accordingly, a few days after Sir Hugh had returned to his desolate home, and when he was beginning, even more than at first, to feel the sense of his utter loneliness, and the heaviness of his irreparable loss, Martin unexpectedly returned, and, full of apparent haste and the urgency and importance of his business, presented a sealed commission from Sir Christopher Hatton.

The good knight was seated in the old oak-pannelled room, where we have first introduced him to our readers. His viol-de-gamba was in his hand, and he was listlessly executing an air which was a favourite with his daughter.

Those who have heard the tones of this obsolete instrument will readily remember its silver sweetness—tones which seemed peculiar to the age, floating with a delicious softness through those old apartments, and seeming, as they filled hall and corridor, to die away in echoing vibration; so soothing and so melancholy; so well adapted to soften the poignancy of the old man's grief, that, as he finished the measure, the tears coursed one another down his cheeks. Martin (who had stopped to listen to the strains for a moment) as the old knight laid down his bow, immediately stepped up to him and presented his packet.

The first meeting of the friends, as Martin had surmised, caused considerable emotion to both; but Martin concealed his own feelings under an affectation of despatch, and dashing the tear from his eye, bade the knight peruse the packet with which he had been entrusted, without delay.

"From whom and whence?" said Sir Hugh. "Methinks I had rather defer matters of business till another opportunity. There be many sealed letters I have received the last two days now lying in the hall, and which I have no heart to open or peruse; for what have I to do with affairs of the world? what interest have I in life or its businesses?"

"Nevertheless," said Martin, "this commission must be read, inasmuch as it cometh from one whose behests are to be obeyed. 'Tis from the Queen; and if I mistake not, Her Majesty requires your instant employment in her service. There is work to be done with spur and rapier, and you must undertake it."

"Nay then," said the knight, whose ardour was in a moment aroused at the prospect of military duty, "there never yet was a Clopton found wanting when he should serve his sovereign in the field: mine eyes are somewhat dim, good Martin, peruse the letter, and give me the substance of its contents."

"In how long a time," said Martin, after glancing at the letter, the contents of which he well knew, "can you be ready to set forth from hence, good master mine?"

"As soon as steed is saddled and led forth, and weapon girded on, I am prepared to mount," said Sir Hugh, "what other preparation doth a soldier want, good Martin?" "Alas!" he continued, looking round, "I have now nothing here to take leave of; nothing to care for. In the world I am nothing, and unless Her Majesty's services require continuance of my life, 'twere better I were gathered to my forefathers." Thus then was Sir Hugh, through the instrumentality of Martin, dispatched forthwith to join the expedition under the Earl of Leicester against the Spaniards. He came up with the Earl just as he had sat down before Zutphen, where the circumstance of war and the bustle of the camp, in a great measure alleviated the sorrows of the good old man.

With Walter Arderne, however, Martin had a more difficult part to play. He thought it wise to separate the uncle and nephew, because the constant sight of each other only served to remind them of their loss. He therefore, after the knight's departure, urged upon Walter the necessity there was for his not wearing out his youth in shapeless idleness. "There be many ways for a man to rise to distinction in the world at the present moment," said Martin, "and let ambition be now your mistress, good Walter."

"Alas!" said Arderne, "thou canst not feel for me, good friend, because thou hast never felt the desolation I feel. Ambition and all other passions are dead within me."

"Go to," said Martin. "Men that live *in* the world must be *of* the world. The health of the mind is of far more consequence to us than the health of the body. The Ardernes were never yet drivellers. Go forth, man, like your forefathers. I in some sort feel anguish of mind, as well as thou; but I give not way to it. Afflictions are sent by Providence. Let your head contrive and your hand execute, and you will forget your particular griefs in blows given and taken; nay, the time is coming when we shall all have to belt on the brand—that I foresee plainly enough. The Spaniard despises all other nations except the English; we have the honour of his hate because he cannot despise us; and we shall shortly feel the weight of his whole force against us. Of that you may rely."

"And whither, then, would you have me go?" said Arderne. "You objected to my accompanying my uncle; what course do you point out for me, so poor in spirit?"

"Why, look ye," said Martin, "there is an expedition now about to set sail for the purpose of attacking the Spaniards in the Indies. Men's mouths were full of it when I was near the Court. Two thousand three hundred volunteers, besides seamen, are enrolled under Sir Francis Drake. The success of the Spaniards and Portuguese in both Indies, and the wonders seen in these islands, have influenced the imagination of all men of spirit; an I were you, I would join this expedition,—see this new world and its strange inhabitants, and witness the matters said to exist there."

"And when would you have me to depart?" inquired Arderne.

"What time is better than the present?" said Martin. "How long doth the soldier require to get under arms, when he receives the order to fall in?"

"Methinks," said Arderne, "I have many places to visit and take leave of, ere I can quit them perhaps for ever."

"Take no leave of them at all," said Martin. "When you return, they will be fresh and fairer in your eyes."

"I have one friend, amongst the many I care not to see again, whom I must see and take leave of," said Arderne; "one whom I would fain spend some time with ere we part."

"Know I him?" inquired Martin.

"You have seen him often," said Arderne, "but you know him not. She who is gone knew him and valued him. 'Tis of her I would speak with him."

"'Twere best not," said Martin; "but (sith I do know the friend you speak of,) I cannot object. There is a kind of character in him I never found in other men. To part with such a one without seeing again is, I grant ye, hard. I give ye one day to spend with your friend, and then you must promise to depart for London."

"I promise it," said Arderne, who already felt relief from being, as it were, driven into action,—"I promise it, good friend, and the day after to-morrow I will depart from Clopton,—depart, perhaps, never to return."

"Good!" said Martin; "well-resolved and resolutely! I expect great things of this expedition, and thy conduct in it. You are just the age to adventure. In youth, we are apt to trust ourselves over-much; and others too little when old. At thy time of life thou art just between the two extremes. The proper season for action; *ergo*, thou wilt thrive."

It was evening when this conversation took place at Clopton, and gloom and melancholy still reigned supreme there. Perhaps the feelings of Martin and his young friend were even more depressed, inasmuch as they had a melancholy task to perform ere they left the place.

The good old servant, who we have before seen in attendance upon Charlotte, either from over-exertion or want of rest, had fallen sick just before her charge died. It was supposed at the time that she had taken the plague; such, however, was not the case, as she lingered on for some days after the young lady's death, and died at last, apparently of grief for the loss of her favourite mistress.

Before the death of this old domestic, she had requested of Martin that she might be buried in the vault with her beloved young mistress; and the request having been acceded to, this very evening was fixed on for the funeral. Arderne paced up and down the room (after the conversation we have just recorded) for some time in silence. He then turned to Martin. "I have been thinking deeply of what you just now urged to me," he said. "The force of it is so impressed upon my mind, that I am resolved at once to take my departure from Clopton. The place seems, since my resolve, to be hateful to me. To-night I will go forth; for since this matter has gone so far, I cannot bear again to sleep at Clopton."

"'Tis well," said Martin; "just as I would advise."

"And this friend?" said Arderne, "in whom I am so much interested. Thou likest him not, or I would bid thee tell him in how much I feel desirous of serving him; and that I commend him to thy especial favour."

"How know you I like not that youth?" said Martin. "I never said so, did I?"

"I surmised it from your manner," said Arderne. "You seemed to look askance upon him, as it were."

"Perhaps I had my own reasons for such seeming," said Martin; "and if I had so, those reasons are now naught. There is no farther cause for them. Believe me, he you call your friend, is one who, if I mistake not, will some day rise to great eminence. An he live to any age, the world will hear something of him, for he hath the brains of half a score of us common mortals, with all his modest look, and beardless cheek."

"Then to you I will intrust the task of saying farewell to him," said Arderne, "for, methinks, on reflection, it will but aggravate my feelings to see him again, since I am so suddenly to depart."

"Be it so," said Martin; "I accept the office."

"In one hour, then, we will say adieu, good friend," said Arderne, wringing Martin's hand. "This night I would fain dedicate to her we both loved; to-morrow shall find me far from Clopton."

CHAPTER XXIII.

THE VAULT.

It is night, and the moon sheds a pale and sickly light over the silent streets of Stratford-upon-Avon, and the surrounding meadows and woodlands.

Is it that the idea of pestilence and death being rife in that silent town gives its streets so sickly and melancholy a look—a sort of unnatural and unwholesome glare—or is the surrounding air, impregnated as it seems with disease, of a more rarified and peculiar character?

The square, thick-ribbed, and embattled tower of the guild of the Holy Cross, with its Norman windows and grotesque ornaments, alone looks dark in shadow. The streets and windows of the various houses seem to glance white and spectral. The tower of the distant church hath a ghastly look, and the very tombstones of the dead seem also more white and ghostly; whilst a thick mist from the river rises like a cloud in the back-ground.

Silence reigns supreme. Not a breath of wind stirs the foliage of the trees upon the margin of the river, or bends the long dank grass growing amongst the graves.

Suddenly the distant sound of a horse's hoof-tread disturbs the deep silence, and a solitary horseman, riding through the deserted streets of the town, approached the church-yard, and dismounting, after fastening his steed, entered it.

He takes his way slowly and with measured tread towards a vault attached to the church. His cheek is pale and haggard, and the large round tears course one another down it. It is Walter Arderne; he has come to spend the last hours he intends remaining in the vicinity of Stratford, beside the vault containing the remains of his beloved Charlotte.

The plague which raged in Stratford this year was now at its height. Already one-fifth of the inhabitants had fallen victims; and it was the custom, as much as possible, to bury the dead unobserved at night.

The remains of the domestic who had died at Clopton Hall were to be buried on this night after midnight; and as Walter Arderne knew the hour, he had preceded the corpse, intending to descend into the vault and gaze upon the remains of her he had so loved in life.

His feelings were, indeed, at the moment, wrought to a pitch of intensity. He felt that he could scarcely wait with patience for the coming of the body and the opening of the vault, so eager was he to descend.

"O Time," he said, as with folded arms, he stood gazing at the dark grating of the vault, "thy wings are of lightning in our pleasures; but thou creepest with feet of lead to the sorrowful and weary. And yet thou, who dost constantly move onwards, overcoming all things in thy flight, wilt at last conquer even death itself; thou, most subtle and insatiable of depredators, wilt at last take all."

A heavy rumbling sound interrupted the meditation of the mourner. It was the vehicle containing the body of the domestic from Clopton, and which, in its progress, had gathered up other bodies in the town on that night to be interred.

The ceremony was performed without the usual formalities, and in all haste. Walter drew aside as the buriers, preceded by the sexton, approached and opened the vault. They ignited their torches previous to descending the flight of steps, and when they did so a cry of horror and alarm proceeded from the sexton, who had first entered the vault, and he rushed out, whilst those who had followed seemed equally horror-stricken. They threw down the corpse, after a glance at the interior, and fled.

Walter, who had quietly followed, was struck with dread. He stopped, and taking up one of the torches, descended into the vault; when a dreadful sight presented itself,—a sight which, as long as memory held a seat in his brain, remained there.

The vault was situate deep below the surface. On hastening down the steps Walter held his torch on high, and when about half-way its rays fell upon a figure, which, like some sheeted ghost, leant against the damp walls.

Arderne was brave as the steel he wore, but at first he stopped and hesitated, whilst the door of the vault closing behind him added to the horror of the situation.

As he continued to regard this startling object, the light becoming more steady, he recognised the features of the figure.

"Oh!" he said, "do I behold aright, or do mine eyes play false?"

With horror in his features he approached nearer, and became confirmed in his first suspicion. It was Charlotte Clopton. She was dressed in her grave-clothes, as she had been consigned to the tomb. She appeared to have been but a short time dead, and in the agonies of despair, hunger, or, perhaps, madness, consequent upon the dreadful situation, she had bitten a large piece from her round white shoulder.

When the buriers of the dead returned, somewhat reassured by collecting all their number together, they found Walter in a swoon, with the body of Charlotte fast locked in his embrace. Separating them, they replaced the body in the coffin, and conveying Walter to upper air, closed up the vault for ever.

As the day broke, a tall cavalier rode slowly out of Stratford. The raven plumes of his hat almost shadowed his pale face, and his ample riding-cloak completely enveloped his form.

He reined up his steed as soon as he had cleared the suburbs, and gazed long and fixedly for some time at the handsome spire of the church. He then turned his steed, dashed the spurs into its flanks, and galloped like a madman along the Warwick road.

CHAPTER XXIV.

THE VILLAGE FETE.—ANNE HATHAWAY.

It is extraordinary how speedily the human mind recovers its elasticity after being bent down to the earth, as it were, with the weight of care.

Let the reader glide over some four or five months from the date of the transactions we have first narrated, and again look upon Stratford-upon-Avon. No trace remains of the deadly scourge which had so recently raged in the town; nay, even but small remembrance is to be observed in the visages or trappings and suits of the surviving citizens (now again mixing in the business of life and the pleasures of the world) of those relations and friends *put to bed with a shovel*. The fact was, that the plague was a constant visitor at this period, and fear of infection the bugbear of the time.* The visitation, however, being over, the inhabitants came forth again with renewed zest. They fluttered about like "summer flies i' the shambles," and sunned themselves in the anticipation of brighter days to come. It seemed quite a delight to walk the streets, where all looked so happy and contented. And yet how small indeed is the portion of life really and truly enjoyed by the poor compounded clay, man! Youth refuses to be happy in the present moment, and looks forward to future joys, never perhaps to be realized. Old age, again, takes a backward glance, and sighs over what has passed; whilst manhood (which appears to be occupied with the present moment) in reality is ofttimes forming vague determinations for happiness at some future period when time shall serve.

Master Dismal had experienced a perfect state of contemplative contentment during the recent visitation; he might now sit himself down and retire for a space, he thought; his researches had been most incessant, and his attendance upon his neighbours most praiseworthy; he could almost have written a treatise upon all he had beheld and studied; he had seen out no less than three sapient doctors during the progress of the plague, and could indeed, from his gathered experience, have himself practised the healing art as well as the remaining one. Now, however, that his vocation was over, for the present at least, and the inhabitants full of enjoyment, he determined to enjoy himself amongst them. It was exactly the twelfth day after Christmas-day that the thread of our story is resumed. A sort of village festival was held at the hamlet of Shottery, about a mile distant from Stratford-upon-Avon, and as several of Master Dismal's neighbours were hieing thither with light hearts and joyous spirits, thither he bent his steps also. "Who knows what sports may be toward?" he said, as he called for Lawyer Grasp and Master Doubletongue, on his way. "Peradventure I may be of some service; for albeit I do not wish to anticipate accidents or offences, the last wake I was present at, which was at the shearing-feast at Kenilworth Green, there were more heads broken by the lads of Coventry and Warwick than I can tell you. Nay, Dick, the smith, got such a fall at the wrestling, that he never joyed after. Yes, he died in three weeks. Aye, and Ralph Roughhead had his spine wrenched by the back trick."

In Elizabeth's day, when the bold peasantry of England did recreate themselves, their sports and pastimes were most joyous. Except in such a case as we have just described, and in which the hand of sickness bore them hard, their hearths were for the most part free from the withering cares of our own improving times. Light-hearted and jovial, they kept up the old world sports and pastimes which had been handed down from their forefathers. Those quaint games and rural diversions so frequently carried on in the green fields and bosky woods. Those cozy fire-side diversions which extended alike from the cottage ingle neuk to the manorial hall and the castle court.

* See Correspondence of Sir Christopher Hatton.

Many of the popular customs then in use had their origin in remote antiquity. The well-known custom of making presents upon New-Year's-day in England is as old, for instance, as the period in which the Romans sojourned in Britain, and by whom it was introduced amongst us. Amongst the Saxons the first of the new year was observed with great ceremony and hilarity, and in the reign of Alfred a law was made that the twelve days following Christmas-day should be kept as festivals. This is the original of our twelfth-day feast, and which, in Elizabeth's reign, and long afterwards, was kept with something more of jovial circumstance than is now customary. For what says Herrick—

"For sports, for pagentrie and plays,
Thou hast thy eves and holy days.
Thy wakes, thy quintels, here thou hast:
Thy May-pole, too, with garlands vast.
Thy morrice dance, thy Whitsun ale,
Thy shearing feasts which never fail;
Thy harvest home, thy wassaile bowle
That's tost up after fox-i'th-hole;
Thy mummeries, thy twelfe-tide kings,
And queens; thy Christmas revellings."

When Master Dismal reached Shottery, he found a goodly assemblage collected together enjoying themselves in various ways upon the green. A whole sheep, which had been given to the inhabitants of the hamlet by Sir Thomas Lucy, who possessed property there, was roasting before a huge fire. A company of morris-dancers, dressed in a sort of eastern or Moorish costume, and covered with bells, were capering away, toeing and heeling, and keeping time, their truncheons also bedecked with hawks' bells, and making a tremendous jingling.

Then the May-pole, decked with evergreens and berries, and surmounted with misletoe, had its joyous party dancing, and running, and threading, and laughing, till the green rang again. The lads were all in holiday trim, their short becoming jackets belted tightly round the waist, their trunks and well-fitting hose forming part of their picturesque costume. The lasses were also dressed for the most part in one style—the neat made boddice and the short stuff petticoat, so becoming to the female figure, and in which they looked handsomer even than if bedizened with lace and silk, and tricked out with jewellery. The glow of exercise was in their cheeks, and the forms of many there, as they sported in all the unchecked freedom of innocent enjoyment, would have been worthy studies for the artist's pencil.

The children of the village, who are seldom behindhand when diversions are in full force, had also their part in the performance. Tricked out in all sorts of scraps of frippery, and costumed for the nonce, they revived, in their own way, the Christmas-day pastimes, and bringing out the hobby-horse, the green dragon, and all the paraphernalia which had done service on the former occasion, they renewed (in small) the sports they had then and there beheld. The dragon flapped his wings, the knight engaged him, the merryman and the old pantaloon took equal numbers of adherents, and "fought on part and part." The snow-balls flew fast and furious, and loud and dire were the shouts and hallooing of the combatants. Then came the feast in the open air, for in those days men and women shrank not from the winter blast during their holiday sports, and after that the cup went round, the dance was renewed, and the twelfth-tide kings and queens were introduced in all their grandeur.

The village of Shottery was a lovely specimen of a rural hamlet in the days of Elizabeth. It consisted then but of some half-a-dozen houses or hamlets, which, sequestered amongst the deep woodlands, and each with its little orchard in rear, and its pretty flower-garden, formed a delicious picture.

Except, indeed, that the homesteads were of a more recent build, (having superseded the ruder sort of huts, one or two of which, however, yet remained,) Shottery seemed as sequestered and out of the way of the busy world as when, many hundred years back, Offa, King of the Mercians, granted its meadow to the church of Worcester.

Besides the actors in the different games, there were also many spectators, who stood about and occasionally mingled amongst the lads and lasses of the village; and amongst these visitors were several foresters or keepers belonging to the domains of the gentry around.

These men, as was generally the case when they met together at the different wakes, fairs, and country diversions, got up a shooting-match at the edge of the green. Warwickshire was always famous for its bowmen, and the caliver had not so entirely superseded the cloth-yard shaft but that it was yet a dear diversion amongst the peasantry. The cross-bow, it is true, was mostly in use, but the longbow was still much practised. The remembrance of its destructive powers, and the battles it had won in the "vasty fields of France," was yet ripe in the mouths and memories of the old host, when he told his winter tale; nay, even yet we shall find in this delightful province some remnant of the long-bow in almost every hamlet: there are indeed more archery meetings in Warwickshire alone than in all the other counties of England put together.

Amongst the many specimens of rural beauty enjoying themselves in the dance, there was one female who especially attracted the gaze of all assembled.

Pouncet Grasp (who had wandered over with Master Dismal and others to enjoy the scene, and, at the same time, see a client he had in the hamlet) seemed especially struck with her. Nay, even Master Dismal pronounced her of exceeding good proportions, and most comely features. He had never seen a fairer form, he affirmed, chiselled upon a tomb. "What a lovely corpse she would make!" he said, with professional enthusiasm; "an it please Heaven to take her early, and before age withered up her rounded limbs, and whitened her glossy black hair."

"Out upon it," said Master Doubletongue; "thy voice is like a screech owl's! Yonder lass will live to make wild work with the hearts of some of the village swains before she dies, for all her cherubim looks. I shall make shrewd inquiry about her. I'll wager a flagon there's some scandal to be heard. I never knew a well-favoured maiden yet, but her neighbours said something of her;" and here Master Doubletongue whispered in Grasp's ear, at which the lawyer laughed and winked his eye, as much as to say, "Ah, Master Doubletongue, you're a wag, but you're not far out either."

"An I might get yonder sweet-faced lass for a partner," said Grasp, who was a trifle roguish when out of his office; "methinks I could like to shake a toe amongst the circle."

"Nay," said Doubletongue, "I'm clearly with you there, neighbour; what a trim ancle she hath! By the mass, the keen wind which blows me into an ague here, shews her figure off to advantage. Accost her, Grasp, accost her! Methinks I should like to hear the voice which issues from so pretty a mouth."

"Go to," said Grasp, "I am somewhat diffident at speaking to a young lass where so many of her companions are around her. Do thou accost her, Master Doubletongue, and I'll be near to back you. See, the dance is finished, and she comes this way."

"You trip it featly, fair Mistress," said Doubletongue, as the damsel, whose appearance had so struck them, approached with two other maidens. "Will you join hands with me? Methinks I should like to join issue in the dance, and tread a measure with so fair a partner."

"Thanks, gentle sir," said the maid, laughing; "but I do not use to dance with any save those I know."

"Right," said a tall athletic-looking forester. "What do lawyers want dancing with village girls—Eh? Go to, Master Grasp, mate with your own degree. Fair mistress Anne," said he to the maiden, "you must be mine for the next dance."

The maiden shrank back with a look of dislike at the tall forester, which Grasp observing, interpreted it as a preference for himself as a partner.

"Thou art but a rude companion," said he; "and I would fain have the maiden's answer without thy counsel; she'll have none of thy partnership any how, I trow."

"No," said Doubletongue; "she wisheth not to have the scandal of such a partner. Go, fellow—go."

"Pshaw!" said the forester, "what a brace of old crones thou art—go, get thee down to the hostel yonder, and warm thee with a cup of wine, or an extra flannel shirt! Dance, quotha, and with such a lass as Anne Hathaway—Ha! Ha! Why, there's not a caper left in the pair of ye. Go, ye gray beards, go, or by my faith I'll make ye both dance to some other tune."

"Come, neighbour," said Doubletongue, who liked not the athletic make and savage look of the forester, "let us budge and exchange no more words with this scurvy companion. For, look ye there, the girl and he understand each other, depend on't. They are well matched. I know the fellow. He's a keeper of Sir Thomas Lucy's, and one of the greatest ruffians in the country."

But the village maiden evidently did not relish the companionship of the tall forester. She turned and would have tripped off with her two female companions without more controversy. The forester, however, who seemed somewhat flushed with good liquor, seized her by the hand, and insisted upon her being his partner.

"If I must dance with thee, Diccon, why I must," she said, as she was led by the rude keeper to another party; "but it is ungentle of thee to force me to do so against my free inclination."

"Thou art ever thus coy with me, Anne," said the forester, "and ever avoidest my company. Why dost use me thus, when I have sworn an hundred times I would die to serve thee?"

"I like thee not, and would have no further words with thee," said the maiden. "Thy presence poisons my delight. I have told thee so I know not how oft. I pr'ythee prove the love thou dost profess, by leaving me."

"Beware I shew thee not how love can turn to hate," said the dark forester, bitterly. "Thou shalt not spurn me thus for nothing. Come, thou shalt dance," and forthwith the forester led the maiden out to join the dancers.

Gazing upon the revellers, and at no great distance from the spot where the forester and his unwilling partner danced, stood a youth, apparently about seventeen years of age. He leaned upon a stout staff, and regarded the dancers with a countenance so melancholy, that it was evident (although he listened to the pipe and tabor, and watched the glee of the revellers) he had no part in their enjoyment. It was young Shakespeare: he had been absent some time from his native town—no one knew where he had sojourned, or what part of the world he had visited during this sequestration of himself from a neighbourhood recent events had rendered so full of melancholy associations. He had occasionally given his parents intimation by a few lines, or some message, of his welfare, and had but a few days before returned to Stratford.

It is not to be supposed, that one so full of observation would fail in remarking the very handsome female we have described. "The prettiest low-born lass that ever ran on the green sward."

With a melancholy mind he had bent his steps that day towards Shottery. Such revels as the present he had before ofttimes taken part in, and now (albeit he was in no mood for joviality), with the feeling and desire to observe the happiness of others, he had remained to look upon the sports.

His thoughts, indeed, were sad enough. He had lost his good friends from Clopton, after the terrible affliction of their house. He had been left alone after having tasted the sweets of their society, and this too in the midst of misery and disease. 'Tis true, that owing to the good management of his parents, and their being of more careful habits than the generality of the neighbours in their condition of life, they had kept the disease from their hearth, and for that he had reason to be thankful. But, added to the feeling of melancholy which the events we have before narrated had caused, was the knowledge that his father's circumstances were daily growing worse, and he felt too that he himself, although he had reached a time of life when he ought to be doing something, was without purse, profession, or prospect.

These thoughts, however, gradually gave place to interest in the surrounding scene. His was a mind and disposition which could scarcely witness the happiness of others without partaking of their joy, and gradually he became more and more interested. As he continued to observe the beautiful villager (for she was in the full blossom of her charms), he noticed that she seemed uneasy with her partner, and averse to his rough attentions. Watching more closely, he observed the overbearing style of the forester, and the increasing timidity of the maiden. That was enough for him. He moved nearer to them, and as the dance finished, he stepped up and accosted her.

"Your hand, fair maiden," he said, gently taking her hand in his. "But that I think you have fatigued yourself, I would dance with you."

There was so much sweetness in his voice and expression, as he said this, and his action was so gentle, that the maid resigned her hand, and, as she gazed at his handsome face, she unconsciously put her arm in his, and adopted him as her protector. In such cases the parties understood each other in a moment.

If there is one thing more likely than another to excite a desperate quarrel amongst men, it is rivalry in the affairs of love and gallantry. The veriest cur upon four legs can hardly brook being cut out unceremoniously before the eyes of his favourite, and to the tall forester, with the forbidding countenance, the fact of being thus outbraved by a stripling, was matter, at first, of astonishment more than anger. The fellow was a sort of champion too, one hired and kept by the knight of Charlecote as a sort of terror to evil-doers in his parks and preserves; an impudent, reckless, and quarrelsome companion; one whom most of the youths present would fain have avoided fastening a quarrel upon, inasmuch as he had kept the ring on Kenilworth Green for a whole Christmas, against all comers, a few years before.

Slightly bowing her head in courtesy, Anne Hathaway would have tripped off with her new friend and protector, but the keeper was not the man likely to put up with so unceremonious a parting. He stepped on a few paces, and presently overtook them.

"How now, young Master," he said to Shakespeare, "methinks you carry this matter as bravely as rudely? A word with you ere you walk off so quietly with my partner there."

As Anne, in some alarm, had rather urged her protector on, the forester unconsciously laid his hand upon his arm to detain him.

The youth snatched his arm quickly away. "Lay no fist of thine on me, sirrah," said he, "as many words as you like, but touch not my doublet."

The forester looked surprised at the eye of fire with which Shakespeare regarded him.

"And wherefore not?" he said.

"Simply," reiterated Shakespeare, "because your putting affront upon me will oblige me to wipe off such rudeness by a blow of my staff."

"Thou art a bold young springald as ever it was my lot to fall in with," said the forester, stepping a pace back and regarding his rival with a scowling look; "and by my fay, for your inches, as likely a young fellow as ere I looked upon, well limbed and clean made as a good bred colt. But I must take this sauciness out of thee. I cannot sing small before so young a champion; come," he continued, "unhand the lass, lest I pluck her from thee, or rather thee from her."

"The maiden seeks her home for a space," said Shakespeare, "and I attend her; after that I will hold converse with thee. Fear not," he whispered to his fair companion, as she shrank back in alarm at the threatening aspect of the forester, "this is but a drunken dissolute fellow, and I shall be able to protect you from his violence, depend on it. Those who threaten loudly are oftentimes but weak in action."

The pair were again about to move off. But the evident aversion of the maiden to the rude forester was indeed gall and wormwood to him, and roused him to stop her progress homeward.

"Nay, Mistress Anne," he said, "you carry it not thus with your gallant; come, I will bring you to your cot myself," and as he said this, he stretched forth his hand, and would have rudely seized her by the arm, but Shakespeare, who had anticipated something of the sort, dealt him so severe a blow over the knuckles with the staff he carried, that the hand fell powerless, and the forester, with a cry of pain, started back for the moment unable to return the blow.

"Make amongst your companions," said the youth, "I must bide this act now, for good or ill. I have struck the first blow."

The controversy had, indeed, already collected several spectators; "A ring, a ring!" they cried. "Here's Black Dick challenged to a bout at quarter-staff by a boy."

"Ha," said Grasp, who had come up amongst others, and now pushed into the circle, "assault and battery here, eh? Keep back, my masters all; keep out of range, lest we get a flout from their cudgels. There'll be smashing work anon, for look you, yonder's my wild slip of a sometime-clerk, John Shakespeare's unthrift son. He's going to catch it this time, and right glad am I therefore. Stand back, Master Dismal, stand back. Ah, there they go at it right merrily."

"I see evident chance of a broken skull in this business," said Dismal. "That fellow with the green frock seldom amuses himself by a set-to in the ring but he either maims or lames his adversary for life."

The parties indeed had quickly engaged, for as speedily as the forester could shake the numbness from his fingers, he dealt a most uncompromising blow at his adversary, which had it taken effect would certainly have knocked out his brains. But the youth received it on his staff with great coolness, and shifting his right hand, returned it as swiftly. The forester in an instant lost his temper; he rushed upon his opponent with the intention of seizing him in his powerful grip, and throwing him to the earth; but he received so severe a check full in the teeth as he did so, that he stopped short, and shook his head with rage and pain.

"Well struck," cried the villagers, "Black Dick has met his match!"

Coolness and self-possession will always tell in a combat of this sort. The temper once lost, the conflict within tells more against the combatant than the blows of his adversary. Every available function is over-exerted and blind rage baffles the skill.

Thus it was with the bulky forester. Strong drink and violent anger rendered him tremulous as he fought. He dealt his blows thick as hail, most maliciously, and without any regard to the rules of such a combat. He would have killed his opponent if he could, and so young Shakespeare found, and dealt with him accordingly, quite aware that the slightest mistake on his own part would result in his either being killed or lamed for life. The youth, who in reality possessed greater strength than his appearance seemed to warrant, kept well away from the shower of blows, till his antagonist was completely out of breath. He then stood more up to him, returned his blows with interest, and at length dealt him so severe a stroke on the head, that the forester reeled under the shock and almost fell.

Nothing but his own consummate skill could, however, have saved young Shakespeare up to this time from the fury of his antagonist. Nothing now but his own chivalrous feeling could have saved his antagonist from a severer lesson than he actually received at his hands.

The blow he gave the forester, and which struck him on the head, for the moment placed him at his mercy. The strong ruffian reeled and nearly fell, and as he still endeavoured to smite furiously with his weapon, it flew out of his hand, and he was at the mercy of his antagonist, who immediately dropped the end of his staff upon the ground, and waited for him to recover it.

At this moment several of the forester's comrades, who had been shooting at a target at the edge of the Green, attracted by the sound of the fray, came up. They were enraged at beholding the discomfiture of their companion, whose opponent they seemed inclined to handle roughly; and the villagers immediately taking part with Shakespeare, a general fight ensued, and with the true English bull-dog resolution, blows with fist and stick resounded on all sides. Master Grasp was overturned and trod under foot, swearing action and imprisonment against all and sundry the combatants. Master Dismal was fain to betake himself to flight, and Doubletongue said, as he made off also, that such a scene was a scandal to the whole country; whilst the village maidens, in a state of alarm, stood looking on at a distance, and calling to their lovers, cousins, and brothers, to desist for the love of heaven and their own sweet sakes.

In short, such was the rage of the combatants,—the keepers being for the most part Gloucestershire men, and objects of dislike to the Shottery lads,—that it seemed more than probable lives would be lost ere the matter ended.

In the midst of the fray, however, a stately-looking man, mounted upon a large grey horse, accompanied by a couple of cavaliers, and attended by half-a-dozen serving-men, or falconers, rode up to the scene of action. The badge worn upon the arms of the attendants bore the same device as that upon the coats of several of the foresters engaged, being three white lucies, or pike-fish, and the spectators immediately recognised Sir Thomas Lucy, of Charlecote.

No sooner did the knight observe the nature of the business in hand, and his own people engaged, than he clapped spurs to his horse, and dashing into the midst of the fray, called, in a voice of thunder, to the combatants to desist, overturning at the same time, with the shoulder of his horse, the two first persons he came in contact with.

"Give me the names, Huntsman," he said, turning to the man who seemed his own particular attendant, "of all in my service engaged in this disgraceful riot. Now, I will not only discharge, but punish them severely!"

"May so please your honour," said one of the foresters, "we are not altogether so much in fault as you may imagine. One of our comrades hath been assailed and beaten, and we did but take his part here, when all set upon us."

"And what do you here at all, caitiffs?" said Sir Thomas "when ye should be in your walk in Fulbrook Park. Whilst such fellows as you dance and fight at wakes and fairs, my park is broken, and my game killed and carried off."

"We came but in to-day to drink your honour's health, hearing you had given a sheep for the revels," said the chop-fallen keeper.

"You shall drink the health of another employer henceforth," said the knight; "and who is the person you say hath beaten your fellow?"

"A youth, who hath more than once done the like," said the keeper; "one whom I myself have oft-times caught in our woods and warrens, and as continually warned off."

"His name?" said Sir Thomas. "Let me know his name, and I will take sharp measures with him an I catch him."

"Shakespeare," said the keeper; "he hath beaten me myself some time back."

"Shakespeare!" said Sir Thomas, "'tis well. I will remember. Hath the fellow no Christian name?"

"William, your honour," said the forester; "the elder son of John Shakespeare, of Stratford."

"William Shakespeare!" said Sir Thomas, with emphasis. "'Tis well. Now point this William Shakespeare out to me, if he be present on the Green."

"If your honour looks but amongst the knot of men yonder," said the forester, "you cannot fail but see him."

"What, is it that fellow there with the broad shoulders and long back? By my fay, a strong and able caitiff."

"Not so," said the keeper, "'tis the youth standing next him, in the gray doublet."

"Fetch him hither," said Sir Thomas; "I would speak with him."

As young Shakespeare approached Sir Thomas, the knight regarded him with a scrutinizing and searching eye.

"A goodly stripling," he said, turning to Sir Jacob Astley, of Hill Morton, one of the gentlemen with him, "a goodly stripling, and a bold looking withal."

"It hath been notified to me, sirrah," said Sir Thomas, addressing Shakespeare with infinite stateliness and hauteur, "that you are much given to evil ways, inasmuch as you are wont to make frequent trespass upon my parks and woods hereabouts; and that, too, to the detriment of my property and the disturbance of my deer."

"I am sorry such rumours have reached you," said Shakespeare coolly, "since there is, I fear me, some sort of foundation for them. I *have* trespassed in your woods. Albeit, I have never intentionally molested the deer."

"I am glad you have the grace to confess so much," said Sir Thomas; but sith you have not disturbed my deer, you have, at least, beaten my foresters during your trespass, and again to-day have you repeated the offence."

"Your foresters rated me in ungentle terms," said Shakespeare; "railed at, and bestowed vile epithets upon me. Nay, even laid hands on me."

"They are hired by me so to do," said Sir Thomas. "Their roughness is their virtue; and *by* such roughness are they told to deter all trespassers and poachers from my parks and warrens."

"I am no poacher, to be so railed at and roughly treated," said Shakespeare coolly.

"Well, henceforth come no more into my woods," said Sir Thomas, preparing to ride off, "lest I give directions to have thee used in a more rough fashion than heretofore."

"I cannot promise that," said Shakespeare, "since I am much given to wandering; and, truth to say, I know not exactly which are, and which are not, your grounds. I would not willingly anger Sir Thomas Lucy, of Charlecote, *but* an he keeps men for the preservation of the game, and the amusement of himself, methinks such men have small right to domineer and tyrannize over those of poorer sort, who seek but the free air and the wild woodlands."

"Thou art over bold and insolent for thy years," said Sir Thomas; "I will have thee whipped and imprisoned the next time my men take thee. So come not in Charlecote woods an ye be wise." And Sir Thomas, who found his choler getting high, put spurs to his palfrey, and, after ordering his keeper to quit the Green, rode off with his company.

It would be difficult to describe the expression of mingled scorn, contempt, and ridicule which was expressed upon the countenance of Shakespeare, as he regarded the departing figure of the knight of Charlecote.

He stood for some moments leaning upon his staff, looking upon the party as they rode off the Green and disappeared in the woods. He then turned his glance contemptuously upon the keeper, and laughing to himself as he repeated the words, "whipped and imprisoned," turned and was about to leave the spot.

"We shall meet again," said the keeper, in a deriding tone. "I know we shall."

"Not if I can avoid it," said Shakespeare.

"An we do," said the keeper, "you hear what is in store for you."

"He you serve can hardly tell what is in store for himself, much more for another," said Shakespeare, "an he could have done so, he had prophesied thy likely reward both here and elsewhere."

"What would that be?" inquired the keeper, coming close to the youth.

"Present beating, if again insolent," said Shakespeare, "and the gallows in reversion."

The keeper drew back; he remembered his comrade's discomfiture, and the skill the youth had displayed.

"Well, fare thee well," he said, "we shall cry quits anon. An Sir Thomas keep word with thee we shall lay thee by the heels yet."

"And, an he keep word with thee, he will have one knave the less in his service. Adieu, I waste time and speech upon thee." So saying, Shakespeare turned his back upon the forester, who, joining his companions, after exchanging a few angry words with their late opponents, they left the Green, and the sports were resumed.

CHAPTER XXV.

THE TWELFTH-TIDE REVELRY.

The rudeness of the keepers and their overbearing style towards the villagers, was by no means an uncommon occurrence. Backed up by their employers to display as much roughness towards all trespassers as they chose, the foresters were usually a coarse and brutal set. They were mostly chosen too, at this period, for courage, strength, and skill with their weapons; consequently when they came into collision with the peasantry, the latter frequently had the worst of it, and the conflict seldom ended without serious consequences.

On the present occasion, several of the village lads assembled vowed war to the knife against the men they had fought with. They had so often experienced their *outrécuidance* and overbearing rudeness, that they swore to annoy them in every possible way they could.

"Sir Thomas Lucy," said Ralph Coulter, "doth ever take part against us, let his men use us vilely as they may; nay, we shall soon have no leave to step either to the right or to the left from the beaten road. For look ye, an we steal but into the meadows to whisper a word into a fair lass's ear, we are warned off, and ordered to keep the path; an we take a dog to hunt the ducks in the stream, we are threatened with imprisonment for poaching."

"As well do the thing at once as be blamed for it," said another peasant; "who'll go down with me to-night, and shoot a buck in Fulbrook?"

"Have with you for one, say I," said Ralph Coulter, "an we miss the buck and hit the keeper, so much the better shot."

"Nay, this is but folly," said a third, "and may bring all into trouble, so to speak before strangers; you do but jest, I trow! Look ye, we are overheard too."

"An ye mean this lad who hath so well cudgelled Black Dick," said Coulter, "I dare be sworn he is not a sneak to turn informer upon us." "Wilt take a part and bring in a buck some night? Methinks it would be rare sport," he continued, addressing Shakespeare.

"Marry will I," said Shakespeare, whose daring disposition was instantly aroused at the idea of the exploit. "Any night you like I should dearly love to do some despite towards those overweening knaves."

"Well," said Coulter, "we shall talk further of it anon; meantime see the dancing is over, and the indoors diversions are beginning. I am for old Hathaway's orchard and the cider revel."

"And I am for goodman Thorne's," said another; and so the party separated.

The shadows of a January's evening were now beginning to descend over the surrounding scene, and the several parties to retire to their different homesteads, there to continue their twelfth-tide diversions, and to partake of such fare as the good wives had prepared for the swains accompanying their daughters home.

Young Shakespeare, who had made acquaintance with Ralph Coulter, accordingly accompanied him to the cottage of Master Hathaway, where he again met with the handsome Anne, and renewed his acquaintance with her.

The maiden indeed seemed nothing loth to receive his attention, for his handsome figure and gallant conduct had already made some impression upon her.

According to an ancient custom in this and other counties of "Merrie England," Master Hathaway assembled his guests in the principal apartment of his domicile, a good-sized and comfortable-looking room, and which (as was usual in those days) served the jolly yeoman for "parlour, and kitchen, and hall." There was the huge gaping chimney, with its comfortable bench on either hand, together with those stout timbered rafters and oaken beams at the roof, from which hung such store of bacon and other good things appertaining. There was the diamond-paned window and its seat beneath, with the stout timbered doors, the high-backed chairs, and the one massive and cumbrous oaken table, and which seemed from its thick supporters to be fixed into the floor, or growing out of it; and there sat the grandsire in his old accustomed seat under the chimney, "sans eyes, sans taste, sans teeth, sans everything," yet looking with some sort of recognition upon the sports he had witnessed, man and boy, for near a century in that very room. In short, it was a perfect picture of rural comfort and old world contentment that kitchen and its appurtenances, filled as it was with those happy, smiling, and rosy maidens, and their stout-limbed ruddy village swains.

As soon as Master Hathaway had assembled his guests and family, he filled a huge pitcher with cider, and the whole party, young and old, male and female, filed out into the orchard in rear of the cottage. Here they immediately took hands around one of the best apple trees, and dancing round it, the whole company hailed the veteran in the following doggrel, in the gladsome feeling of their light hearts, flinging and capering, shouting and hallooing, like so many bacchanals.

"All hail to thee, thou old apple-tree,
Whence thou may'st bud, and whence thou may'st blow,
And whence thou may'st bear apples enow.
    Bonnets-full! caps-full!
    Bushel-bushel-sacks-full,
    And our pockets-full eke also;
Here's for thee, thou old apple-tree, huzza! huzza!"

Whilst this was being sung, the females of the party, seizing the opportunity of the jug passing round, made their escape within doors; and then the joint intended for supper being clapped upon the spit, the doors were all immediately made fast. Meantime Master Hathaway, having finished his "all hail" to the patriarch of the apple family, bestowed a libation on its mossed stem from the remains of the cider, and then, at the head of his party, made the tour of his orchard, singing the same exquisite piece of doggrel over again.

This done, as the sharp and biting blast of a January night began to be apparent, and the snow to fall, the whole of the men assembled filed off to the house. Here (according to the custom of the time and the sport toward) the doors were found to have been secured by the female portions of the revellers; and they were put through the ceremony of a formal demand for admittance, and as formal a denial.

Exposed to the pitiless pelting of the snow-storm, whilst the damsels jeered them at advantage from the casement, they were told that no lock could be turned, no bolt withdrawn, until one amongst their party (himself a guest and a bachelor) could guess the name of the joint roasting upon the spit.

"And what guerdon," inquired Shakespeare, "to him who guesseth the same?"

"The best portion of the joint," said Dame Hathaway, "the first draught from the cider with the toast and hissing crab in it, and a kiss from the comeliest lass in the company."

"The latter reward, then, at least, I claim," said Shakespeare; "for an you have not spitted the chine to-night, I would I might never see a porker again."

The scream of laughter with which this was received, (the withdrawal of the bolts, and the rush of the lasses to hide themselves from the penalty incurred), proclaimed that the guesser had made a lucky hit; and Shakespeare, in right of his guess, entered first to claim and obtain the reward.

Our readers need scarcely be informed that the handsome daughter of the host was the maiden sought for and selected; and that Anne Hathaway received on this night the first kiss from William Shakespeare.

In the games which were to follow this ceremony, the more mirth displayed was superstitiously imagined to give greater promise of a full apple season that year, and accordingly, fast and furious grew the fun.

If we were to say that young Shakespeare entered into these revels with feelings of unmingled enjoyment, we should indeed belie him.

As he looked upon the joyous faces around him, he felt delighted at the scene; and as his eye occasionally met that of the handsome Anne, he certainly at each glance felt more and more struck with her beauty; yet, still the remembrance of Charlotte Clopton, and the dear friends he had lost, ever and anon "stopped the career of laughter with a sigh," and he, at such moments, felt almost unfitted for the scene.

There was, however, a charm to one of his disposition in these old wild rites and superstitions; and, as after midnight the revellers sat round the hearth, and each one was called upon for the tale of grammarie, the ghost story, or the fairy tale, he at length gave himself up to the enjoyment of the hour and season.

The peasantry of our times have scarce an idea of the enjoyment consequent upon the old creeds and superstitions of their forefathers. Their dispositions are soured, their lives squalid, their style brutal, and in comparison to the good old English peasant, the jovial hearty yeoman of Elizabeth's day, they are a miserable race. The innocence of the old age is fled, and 'tis now all driving harshness, and hard selfish utilitarianism.

Our fairy creed, amongst other things of more moment, and which was wont to be so cherished amongst the superstitions of the peasantry, is gone from their memories.

Not a sprite is left to skim the cream from the bowl,—not a silver piece is now ever lent to the *favoured* maiden, *without the rate of interest*, and found by her at early dawn.

Puck and Robin Goodfellow, and all their elfin throng, *have fled ever* from the scene. At the period of our story, however, these imaginary beings held a prominent place in the minds of our rural populations. Nay, so firmly was the existence of these *elfins of power* believed in, and so much influence were they supposed to have over mortals *for good or ill*, that many an old crone spoke with bated breath when she named the merry or mischievous pranks of Robin Goodfellow. Many a bold youth glanced with eye of fear at the acknowledged haunt of the fay in the forest glade, and many a maiden held the household sprite in religious awe, as she swept her kitchen at early dawn.

That such feelings and superstitions were idle and ridiculous (amongst the bold peasantry of England in a former age) is true. Still, they gave a charm to each shadowy grove and unfrequented wood, and caused an interest in the different wild scenes of beauty where the elfin crew, "those merry wanderers of the night," were wont to hold their moonlight revels, and dance their ringlets to the whistling wind, which to our own times is unknown.

The more noisy sports of the night had finished. The party, nothing loth, for even pleasure is fatiguing, were now seated round the blazing hearth. To noise and loud laughter succeeded the cough of the crone—the saw of the old man's tale—the tale "of woeful ages long ago betide," and the chirp of the cricket; whilst the ruddy glow of the fire was reflected upon the faces and forms of the listeners sitting around. The maidens, too, crept more closely to their admiring swains, as they glanced fearfully behind during the progress of the tale; more than one kiss was taken on the sly, by way of assurance against the spectre. The last pipkin of good liquor simmered upon the hearth, and, in short, it was now the very "sweet o' the night."

To Shakespeare this was a delightful moment. His mind seized upon the secret feelings of the assemblage. He saw them in their ignorance and superstition: and though conscious of his own superiority over the rude throng, "sitting 'mongst men like a descended god,"—nay, in after days, remembering these meetings and the feelings they had engendered, he founded an elfin world of his own on the traditions of the peasantry, and clothed them in the ever-living flowers of his own exuberant fancy. Yes, he who was to astonish the universal world, sat in that cottage like one lost in a dream—a dream which these simple superstitions had conjured up. The snow-storm still rattled on the casement, the fire grew dim on the hearth, the room darkened down, the wind whistled without, and sounded drear amongst the mossed trees in old Hathaway's orchard, as he listened, and, as his arm stole round the waist of the sweet Anne, he forgot his recent troubles, and already felt himself half in love, whilst the tale and the song still went on.

That gentle and unassuming mortal was the last person to presume upon his own feelings and knowledge; he felt pleased and delighted with the company he was thrown amongst, and extracted amusement and instruction from the veriest clod-pate there. Perhaps the enjoyment of the circle was the more perfect, too, from the growing storm, which as it rattled sharply against the casements, added to the comfort within, by the apparent discómfort without.

Remembrance lingers o'er such scenes, and the lapse of time gives them an interest which at the period they scarcely seemed to possess. Yes, time hallows in after days the scene and hour, and softens the remembrance of it even as age softens the touches of a picture.

"Ugh-ugh," coughed the old grandsire, when called upon for his story. "There have been many tales told of Robin Goodfellow in my young days, an I could but remember them. Nay, I can recollect myself sad pranks he used to play. Both him and Hobgoblin, as we used to call t'other sprite. In those days the witches were more plentiful than now, though their evil deeds are rife enow at all times—God 'ild us; but even the witches themselves were no more terrible than was Robin and his rout. Mass, I wish I could remember one half of the merry jests, mad pranks, and mischiefs he used to do."

"Nay, grandsire," said Anne Hathaway, "but this Robin doth no harm now, except it to be to knaves and queans, as he is Oberon's own son, so his royal father hath enjoined him not to harm the good and thrifty."

"Of a verity," said the elder Hathaway, "such is the case in some sort. Nevertheless, Anne, in my time, sad pranks have been played in the night season by Robin."

"Aye, and as many good turns done too by him in mine," said old dame Hathaway. "What, hath not the elf oft-times ground the malt, swept clean the house, and washed all the children's faces in the night?"

"Aye," said the other, "and pinched the maids black and blue for laziness; and even carried them out fast asleep into the green meadows in the night, and led poor wayfarers out of the way to perish in some deep wash." *

"Well, well," said Master Hathaway, "cleanliness and thrift, and a good hunk of bread in one's pouch, will do much; not only to keep off the elf, but to keep one from hungering in the quagmire, for what saith the rhyme." †

"Thy fairy elves who thee mislead with stories
Into the mire, then at thy folly smile,
Yea, clap their hands for joy. Were I used so,
I should shake hands with them, and turn their foe.
Old country folks, who pixie leading fear,
Bear bread about them to prevent that harm!"

"Come, tell us, grandsire," said Anne, "how you met the fairies coming one night from Monkspath."

"Gad-a-mercy, lass, I had almost forgotten all about it," said the old host, who indeed had most likely dreamt the adventure one night in his cups, and then related it till he himself believed it was a fact. "Why, you see, when I was a yonker, there were terrible deeds done in England.

* All these were popular beliefs.

† Clobie's "Divine Glimpses." I adopt these lines because they allude to the curious old opinion, that bread carried about the person was a charm against tricks of Robin Goodfellow, though they bear date 1659.

We didn't live then so peaceable-like, as we do now, under our blessed Queen Elizabeth. A man's life in those days warn't thought o' so much value as in ourn; by the same token, stabbing, smashing, hanging, and heading, and all sorts of wild work, were the order of the day,—more the pity. We hadn't then either such goodly dwellings, at least so many on 'em. Men were men then, and hadn't such luxuries as now. Ugh-ugh, Gad-a-mercy! I have seen the time when we used to sleep o' nights in the open fields as comfortably as under a roof. Nay, we hadn't such beds either then. A shake-down of the fern, or a clean bed of straw, with a log of wood for the head, was enow for most folks. I struck a good strike for Harry at Bosworth Field what time old Shakespeare——"

"Well, well," interrupted John Hathaway, "Bosworth bye and bye. The fairy story now, father."

"Nay, I war only going to say that yonder lad's grandfather (old Shakespeare of Stratford) could have borne me out, had he been alive, since he war at the battle of Bosworth too. Both he and I were together, jammed in amongst the spearmen, when King Richard pressed up on his white horse, and nearly struck young Richmond down. Mass, he were a fierce devil that day, and raged like a fiend. Richmond, I remember, bore back, as well as he might, an Richard had not been beaten off by the good knights around, the hot king had fairly brained him. Two I saw him fell with my own eyes ere he was forced away. Ah, he were a goodly sight to look on that day; and if deeds of daring and good soldiership could ha gotten the day, Richard had had it. He wore his crown upon his helmet, I remember, and (albins men liked him not) by my fay, he looked a king. No man that lived and beheld him but saw that."

"But the fairies, grandsire, the fairies?" said Anne.

"Well, well; bide a bit. Where war I? Ah, I see. I had a mad horse in Shottery—what time I came back from Leicestershire—and I would fain have sold him; so I e'en rode him along with some other youngsters to Kenilworth Green, where there war a wake holden underneath the abbey walls. Folks spoke darkly of old Kenilworth then. Now I'm told there be rare new buildings reared up there."

"There are," said Ralph Coulter. "A fine new castle hath been built by the Earl, glorious to look on, and called Leicester's Buildings, and ornamented, that it would do you good to look on 'em."

"Ah," said the elder Hathaway, "times are changed hugely. At the time I speak of old Clinton's Tower was ornamented and hung with the bodies of caitiffs, traitors, and outlaws; for the whole country round was full of disturbance, famine, and war. Howbeit, as I was saying, I went to Kenilworth to sell my sorrel nag; but I couldn't do so. So after I had taken a draught at the Leicester Arms there, I rode away to a relation I had at Monkspath. Travelling was very unsafe then, as you may believe—worse than now-a-days—and I hastened on to get through the woods before nightfall; and when I had got within about a mile of Monkspath, I saw a man, just as it began to grow twilight, coming towards me. He was dressed in a bright green doublet, and either my eyes deceived me, or the good liquor of the hostel made me see double, but he had a sort of *familiar* flitting at his back. He was very small in make and height, and wore a bright golden bugle at his waist. My horse stopped of himself as the little man came up, and seemed all of a tremble, and wouldn't pass him nohow; so I dismounted, and tried to lead him past. But it wur all one; the horse wur fixed as firm as one of the old oaks beside us. 'Will you sell that brute?' said the little hunter. ''Tis what I wish,' I answered. 'It is very ugly: is it a cow or a horse?' said the little man. 'He was a horse a minute ago,' I answered; 'but now he seems turned to stone: I can't make him go, no wise.' 'My people have got him fast,' said the little man; 'he can't go. What do you ask for him?' inquired the little wretch. 'Fifteen pieces,' I said. 'There's thirty,' said the little man. 'Now stand aside whilst I mount." So saying, the little gentleman gave me the thirty pieces, and got upon the horse. No sooner had he done so than the beast went mad outright, I thought. He flew about, capered, and kicked out his heels, as if a flame of fire had lighted on his crupper. I ran to get out of the way, for fear of being struck, and when I turned, lo, horse and man were clean gone—sunk into the earth as it were, and vanished, leaving me in the greatest of terror and confusion; whilst a wild and beautiful strain—a sort of hollow winding note of a bugle—seemed to pass through the air."

"Strange," said several of the listeners. "Was it not?"

"As soon as I had a little recovered myself," continued the quaint old man, "I hastened on to Monkspath, and sought my relation. He took me to an old monk belonging to the abbey beside the castle, to whom I told the story, and asked his advice about the money, and whether I might use it. The monk gave me leave to use one-half the money, provided I gave him t' other half; 'for,' said he, 'as you in no way circumvented or endeavoured to cheat the buyer, be he witch, devil, or fairy, you are fully entitled to what you asked. The other fifteen pieces,' said he, 'I will lay up in store for the use of our abbey.' On this assurance I was well satisfied, so I hastened to get out the purse the little gentleman had given me; but the worst of it all was that no purse could I find; my pocket was empty, my purse gone, and the monk rated at me for a knave, whilst my relation laughed at me for a fool."

"He, he, he—ugh—O dear—O dear!"

"And the horse," said Anne—"the horse? you forgot the horse, grandfather."

"The horse—oh, ah, true enough—the horse. Why I found him, on my return home here, grazing quietly in the orchard, with his saddle turned under his belly, and covered with mud and mire, as if he had been drawn through all the mosses and sloughs between this and Coventry."

"And you was not at all flustered that night?" said Shakespeare. "Pardon the question, but I thought the little man in green might have treated you to an extra cup."

"Body o' me,—what I drunk! Not a whit. I had had just enough to make me all right. I'd a drunk about as much that night as I have to-night, or perhaps a quart more."

"And who do you then suppose the buyer was?" inquired Shakespeare.

"Who?" said the old host, "why, who but Robin Goodfellow, his own self! Who else should it be?"

"True," said Shakespeare, laughing; "there's no question on't."

"A song, a song," said Dick, the shepherd. "Let fair Mistress Anne sing the song about Robin."

Anne Hathaway accordingly, in a marvellously sweet voice, and to the old tune of Dulcina, sang some verses, which, although not word for word the same, in some sort were like the following stanzas:—

I.

From Oberon, in fairy land,
  The king of ghosts and shadows there,
Mad Robin I, at his command,
  Am sent to view the night sports here.
What revel rout
It kept about
I will o'ersee
And merry be
In every corner where I go,
And make good sport with ho, ho, ho!

II.

When house or hearth doth sluttish lie,
  I pinch the maidens black and blue;
The bed-clothes from the bed pull I,
  And lay them naked all to view.
'Twixt sleep and wake
I do them take,
And on the clay-cold floor them throw;
If out they cry,
Then forth I fly,
And loudly laugh I, ho, ho, ho.

III.

By wells and rills, in meadows green
  We nightly dance out hey-day guise
And to our fairy king and queen
  We dance our moonlight minstrelsies.
When larks 'gin sing
Away we fling,
And babes new-born steal as we go,
An elf instead
We leave in bed,
And wind out-laughing, ho, ho, ho! *

* This song has been attributed to Ben Jonson, and in the old black-letter copies it is directed to be sung to the tune of Dulcina. As it embodies some of the freaks of Robin, I have given it here.

How much longer Mistress Anne Hathaway's song might have continued it is impossible to say, but as she finished the last verse steps were heard without the door, followed by sounds, as if some one in a faint voice demanded admittance, and then a dull heavy blow, like a person falling, and which shook the door violently.

The wind piped loud and drear, whilst all paused and listened, and presently a deep groan, which appeared to come into the very room from beneath the door, still further startled the party.

The village maidens were too much frightened to cry out, but each threw herself into the arms of the swain next her, whilst Master Hathaway rose from his seat, and Shakespeare felt obliged to bestow a kiss upon the ripe lips of Anne, in order to reassure her.

"Gad-a-mercy," said Hathaway, "'tis surely Robin himself come amongst us."

"Ah!" said Dame Hathaway, "this comes of singing ribald songs to offend him. Now the good year; what shall we do to appease the sprite? Ah, mercy on me, there is another groan, as I am a true woman."

"Some one is surely in distress," said Shakespeare, rising, "suffer me to unbar the door."

"Troth, I'd rather not," said Hathaway; since it may be a device of the evil one to come amongst us."

"Nay, but it may be some wayfarer lost or misled on this inclement night," said Shakespeare. "A few minntes' neglect may cause death. I pr'ythee allow me to open and look out. There are enough of us here," he continued, smiling at the horror-stricken peasants, "to cudgel Puck and all his crew."

So saying, Shakespeare stepped across to the door, and, drawing the bolts, quickly opened it, when the body of a man to all appearance dead, rolled into the apartment.

CHAPTER XXVI.

THE MISLED WANDERER.

The visitation we have just described caused a sufficiently startling interruption to the cozy comfort of the entire party. Young Shakespeare started back in some surprise, and the whole circle, springing from their seats, stood gazing upon the object so suddenly introduced amongst them.

The villagers looked upon the visitation as something supernatural, and were afraid to move; but Shakespeare, after closing the door, with main force against the driving wind and snow, stooped down and examined the object at his feet.

"Move the log upon the hearth, Master Hathaway," he said, "and make it send up a flame, so that I may see better. Ah, 'tis as I thought, some poor devil caught in the storm. He seems dead."

"Dead!" cried Dame Hathaway, regaining courage, when she found the visitor was not a fairy, or perhaps Robin Goodfellow in *propriâ personâ*. "Dead! Gad-a-mercy, how dreadful!"

"Best warm his inside," said Master Hathaway, approaching. "Here, let us drag him close to the fire, and give him something to drink."

Suiting the action to the word, Master Hathaway took the inanimate body by the shoulders, and, drawing it before the fire, laid it along upon the hearth,—a ghastly object,—appearing, in the blazing light, the prostrate form of what had once been a tall strong man. The face was now, however, pinched and ghastly, and the limbs already stiffening.

The readiest remedy at hand being a portion of the hot cider, with the hissing crab in it, some was immediately poured down the throat of the prostrate wayfarer, whilst all hands set to work to draw off the heavy boots, and divest him of some of his outer garments, in order to rub and chafe his body. In the progress of this operation it became apparent that the person of the visitor had been exposed to all the vicissitudes of flood and field; since the mud frozen upon his outer garments, and the peat-moss which was incrusted upon his long boots, doublet, and torn belt, shewed that he had wandered through more than one morass in his progress.

He was evidently a person of condition, as was apparent from his dress, which, torn and soiled as it was, proclaimed the rank of the wearer, by its fashion. He was completely armed too, having a long heavy sword in his belt, and poniard in his girdle.

"Ah!" said old Hathaway, as he gazed upon the man's face, after pouring a draught of hot cider down his throat; "I surely know that countenance."

"See, he's coming to," said Dame Hathaway; "he opens his eyes, aye, and his mouth too. Give him more liquor."

"'Tis so," said Hathaway, after regarding the prostrate form; "I thought I knew that face. Dame," said he, calling his wife aside, "this is a somewhat dangerous visitor, inasmuch as he is one whom it is considered treason to shelter."

"And who then is it, husband?" inquired the Dame.

"'Tis Eustace the priest," whispered Hathaway, "who used to lie up at Clopton, and through whom 'tis said the old knight got into so much trouble. His coming bodes no good to us, I fear."

"Gad be here" said Dame Hathaway, "that's ill tidings to give us on a twelfth-night, or rather morn. But be he priest or sinner, traitor or faitour, or whatever else he may turn out, we cannot do otherwise than help him in his present need."

"Right," said Hathaway; "we must shelter the man, that's certain."

In accordance to this humane resolve, and which was indeed at the period sufficiently hazardous, the priest was conveyed up stairs, and laid upon a four-post bed. But although every attention was paid to him, it was soon apparent that his hours were numbered.

Calling Dame Hathaway to his bed side, as he somewhat recovered, the priest desired that Master Hathaway might be summoned.

"I fear me your kindness, good Master Hathaway," he said, "may possibly get you into misfortune; and were I able to rise and leave your cottage, I would rather do so, than lay you under the danger of succouring me."

"Heed it not," said the good farmer, "a belated wayfarer should ever find shelter in an Englishman's cottage."

"But, in me," said the priest, "you behold a man condemned to death, and whom the officers of justice are now in search of."

"I know you only as one in need," returned the farmer. "Those who search know for what they search. You are welcome to my roof whilst needing it. When you no longer need it, go forth."

"I shall never leave it alive," said the priest. "Listen whilst I relate the causes which have driven me to this extremity."

"Go to," said Hathaway, "sleep would do you more good. But an it pleases you to be a talker, I am all attention."

"You doubtless know me," said the priest, "and so much of my history as led me to fly from Clopton what time the good Sir Hugh was arrested and sent to the Tower."

"Hap I do, hap I don't," said the farmer. "Take another sip of the warm sack my dame hands you, and go on from thence. At least I've heard of the events of that night."

"I escaped pursuit on that night," said the priest. "They sought me in the south, but I fled north, across the border, and took refuge in Scotland."

"Ah!" said old Hathaway, "I dare be sworn there you found plenty of your own sort. Scot and plot hath rhymed together pretty often during this reign."

"It hath," said Eustace; "and I speedily entered into a plot there."

"One you found ready-made to your hand," said Hathaway; "Eh?"

"I did," said the priest. "I fell in, whilst in the mountains, with one Morgan, also a fugitive from England: he introduced me to Babington, Savage, and others, who were zealous Catholics, and engaged in a project for dethroning Elizabeth, and restoring by force of arms the exercise of the ancient and true religion. The Pope, the Spaniard, and the Duke of Guise, had all emissaries amongst this company. I, however, persuaded them of the vanity of any attempts upon the kingdom, so long as one so prudent and popular as Elizabeth was suffered to live. An assassination, an insurrection, and an invasion, must at one and the same time be attempted, I told them, that they saw at once the force of my arguments. We met, during this discussion, in an old castle situate in Strathdon, and called Corgarff—a wild and desolate place. To you who dwell in fertile and pleasant England, my good folks," continued the priest, "the aspect of the wild region in which we held our meetings, would have appeared sufficiently terrible. No shrub, no tree, not a blade of grass was to be seen on this drear mountain land. Nothing but blasted heath, rocky glens, and deep morasses. The people wild, desperate and fearful, as the land they inhabit."

"In few," continued the priest, "having assumed the disguise of a soldier, and the name of Geffrey, I left this place for England, with the purpose of obtaining a secret interview with the Queen of Scots, during her imprisonment. This opportunity I found whilst the queen was in custody of Sir Amias Paulet, rigorous as that confinement was. To her I communicated tidings, that on the event of Elizabeth's death, her own deliverance would be attempted; all the zealous Catholics would fly to arms, and that foreign forces taking advantage of the general confusion, would fix her upon the English throne, and re-establish the Catholic religion."

"Alas! alas! what terrible doings you who meddle with religious matters think upon," said Master Hathaway; "better to kneel down under the blue sky, and worship God without form and ceremony, if such is to be upheld by treason and bloodshed, from one end of the kingdom to the other."

"Alas! thou speakest wiser than thou art aware of," said the father, "and after a life of intrigue and dark underhand doings, in death I find that all such measures are but a serving the cause of the devil, in place of doing our duty towards God."

The dying priest now became so faint and exhausted that he could scarcely proceed.

"I feel," he said, "the hand of death rapidly approaching, and bitterly doth it now weigh upon my soul, that I have in some sort aided the enemies of my country in raising that dreadful tempest which sooner or later must now fall upon the land."

"Truly a heavy weight to lay upon the breast of a sick man," said Hathaway, shuddering. "And how then came you thus?"

"Our scheme," said the priest, "was discovered. Nay, it had been all along known. The Queen of Scots approved the project, and even when we were ripe and ready for action, one of our party, named Ballard was seized. This indeed so alarmed us, that finding we were also strictly watched wherever we went, we dispersed in parties, and under cover of night, and in various disguises, we fled from London a week back.

"Of all who were engaged, however, and we numbered fifteen individuals, all, I have since learned in the different towns where I have ventured, have been taken, some in woods, some in barns and outhouses where they sought shelter; nay, I have myself lain in concealment beneath the straw in the barn adjoining your cottage here for the last few days. This morning I stole out, and whilst you were engaged with your village dance, I endeavoured to reach a secret refuge known to me at Clopton, and which place I concluded was uninhabited. Unexpectedly, however, I found as I entered the private part of the mansion, that I was mistaken. I was encountered by one Martin Delville, who it seems hath remained in charge of the hall. He attempted to seize me, and in defending myself, I received a shot in the breast. Still I managed to escape, and wandering through the country, I endeavoured to find some place of refuge, some roof where I might be sheltered. Faint with loss of blood, I still held onwards in the hope of reaching Stratford, but a dancing light, which at one moment seemed to await my coming, and the next went bounding from me, and by following which I have been more than once nearly drowned, at length led me back to the spot from whence I had started. As the light vanished from my eyes, its place was supplied by the distant appearance of your comfortable fire, seen through the casement, and the driving snow. I but managed to reach your door, and that was all—life is fast ebbing away with the blood that flows from my wound."

"Nay, cheer up," said Dame Hathaway, "perhaps it may not be so bad; I have some Friar's balsam here at hand which will do wonderful things."

"It's no use, goodwife," said Hathaway, "I see death in his face. He bleeds inwardly as thou see'st, and is almost choked. Not all the friars that ever lived could save him, and to speak truth he hath had already quite enough to do with such cattle, for see what sloughs and pitfalls they have led him into."

"Nay," said Dame Hathaway, "it was Robin Goodfellow, you see, who led him into all these sloughs and pitfalls he describes, and at length brought him to our door."

"Robin Goodfellow, or Robin Badfellow," * said old Hathaway——

"Hist, hist!" said Dame Hathaway, "never abuse Robin if you wish to thrive."

"Well, go to," said her husband, "the man is sped, and there's an end. Do thou and Anne remain with him whilst I go down to the lads below. 'Tis almost dawn. Alas, alas! this is a sad finish to our twelfth-tide sports; but we must still not suffer our guests to depart without their breakfast."

As Hathaway spoke, he descended to the apartment below, where the guests were still sitting around the fire, and discussing matters appertaining to the appearance of the misled wayfarer, and telling of woeful tales and dire stories, which suited the hour and the circumstance.

At old Hathaway's re-appearance amongst the circle, all were set to work to clear up the apartment, put it to rights, and prepare for the breakfast it was customary to partake of before the company finally broke up. The first faint streaks of dawn were beginning to appear as they departed. The snow-storm had cleared up, the diamond panes of the windows were fretted with frozen crystals, and as old Hathaway threw open the door and looked forth, the trees in the orchard were

* The sprite was sometimes so named at this period.

heaving with congealed snow, the ground was covered with the same white sheet, icicles hung in clusters from the roofs of the outhouses, and all around was softened and rounded by one white feathery crust. In short, it was one of those delicious winter mornings so often seen after a driving dreary and tempestuous night,—a morning in which the old world look of the buildings and barns around, seen in the clear wintry air, and the white flaky look of the country, gives so delightful an aspect to a rural hamlet.

Old Hyems seems then to smile as benignantly as he can,—to have smoothed the icy furrows of his brow, and consented to give to human mortals a slight respite, ere he fetches from the frozen bosom of the north more cutting blasts and angry winds.

"Then icicles hang by the wall,
And Dick, the shepherd, blows his nail,
Then Tom bears logs into the hall,
And milk comes frozen home in pail.
When blood is nipp'd, and ways are foul,
Then nightly sings the staring owl,
Tu-whit, to-who, a merry note,
While greasy Joan doth keel the pot."

CHAPTER XXVII.

THE SUITOR.

The confession of the dying priest will doubtless recall to our readers the state of England at this period. Matters indeed were fast hastening towards that great event of Elizabeth's reign, which, for its mighty import, and the magnificence of its preparation, is, perhaps, without a parallel in the history of the country. The minds of men indeed were at this time fully impressed with the certainty of some great and terrible convulsion being at hand. It seemed that a fearful storm was surely and slowly gathering above their heads, and which, sooner or later, was to burst upon the land like some torrent breaking bounds. There was no occasion for men to ask each other from whence this ruin was to come. The great enemy of the country,—the haughty, vindictive, and cruel foe of England at this period, was the iron-hearted bigot of Spain: and upon Spain were the eyes of all men turned with apprehension. 'Twas the general theme of conversation, the all-absorbing topic of the day; and torture, murder, and every sort of evil that fiends could inflict upon the inhabitants of a conquered country was to be expected, should a successful invasion take place. Yes; Spain was then the bugbear of nearly every Englishman's fireside. One or two startling events, however, which made men "whisper one another in the ear," were to take place, ere this grand convulsion shook the nation; and yet, amidst the anxieties consequent upon such a state of things, it is curious how mankind continue the even tenor of their lives.

The twelfth-tide revel at Shottery had introduced young Shakespeare to some new acquaintance in that place. Amidst the youths he had met there, he found one or two lads of spirit; and, as he bent his steps across the fields towards the village, he would fain have persuaded himself that it was to renew his acquaintance with them that he had set forth. Ere he had reached the village, however, he felt obliged to confess that the real desire of his heart was neither for the companionship of the lads of the village, nor to learn tidings of the wounded priest, but really and truly to see again and hold converse with the handsome Anne.

"Oh heaven, were man but constant
He were perfect. That one error
Fills him with faults."

Mortals indeed are prone to error; and he whom we reverence as the greatest of men, was no more secure from the failings the flesh is heir to than his fellows. In truth, the youthful Shakespeare was again in love.

Those of the most generous sentiments and finest feelings are perhaps more subject to this passion; for,

"Eating love inhabits in the finest wits of all."

It is not to be supposed that the melancholy fate of the beautiful Charlotte was so soon and entirely forgotten; but youth is not the season for ever-during melancholy. Bright thoughts will then spring up amidst the most gloomy recollections; and if one thing more than another can soothe the cares, and help to "pluck from the memory a rooted sorrow," it is the sweet companionship of woman in all the brilliancy of her glowing charms: and so thought Shakespeare as he took his way across those pleasant fields betwixt his own town and Shottery. "Yes," he said, as he came within sight of old Hathaway's cottage,

"To heal all grief, to cure all care,
Turn foulest night to fairest day,
To breathe delight, Anne *Hath a way*."

In youth we are more prone to fancy one elder than ourselves. The modest lad seems to look up to the full-blown woman, and to feel that his attentions, if received, are bestowed upon a worthy object; that he is indebted to her who consents to regard one so inferior (as at that moment he conceives himself) for women profess, in general, whatever they may feel, a contempt for the attentions of a mere boy, as they term the lad of seventeen or eighteen—a foolish lad, whom we laught at for his simple folly and childish admiration. This is dangerous sophistry, however, for a fair maid to indulge in.

In the middle period of life the fancy of the lover strays towards the fresh and budding flower, and the coy maiden is often sought out for a wife. In age, alas, 'tis but second childishness.

When Shakespeare reached the cottage of Master Hathaway, he felt his heart palpitate as he knocked at the door. His was a new acquaintance, and he hardly knew how the good yeoman might receive a visit so soon repeated. The voice of the old dame, however, bidding him come in, reassured him, and he lifted the latch and entered.

"Ah, Master Shakespeare," said the old dame, who was sitting at her spinning-wheel, "troth am I right glad to see thee. My husband and I have been oft-times talking of you since the night you was here."

"And the goodman," said Shakespeare, "is he hearty?"

"Troth is he, and away to Warwick to-day with Goodman Coulter, Hodge the smith, and others."

"And your fair daughter?" said Shakespeare; "I see her not here. How fares she?"

"A little dashed in spirit with this matter you wot of—the wayfarer whom we had to bury yesterday," said the dame.

"He is then dead. I thought his end was near."

"He died soon after you left," said Dame Hathaway. "The crowner sat on's body, and the man Martin from the Hall was examined with Lawyer Grasp and Master Dismal, and the man were known to be an escaped traitor. And so he's buried in a hole like a dog; and there's an end. And a good end too, if men will go about to compass such mischief as he seems to have been hatching all his life."

"And fair Mistress Anne," said Shakespeare, "is she too busied like yourself, 'weaving her thread with bones'?"

"No," said Dame Hathaway, "though she *is occupied*, she is out in the orchard with Mopsy, and Lawyer Grasp, and Master Doubletongue."

"Grasp!" exclaimed Shakespeare, as a sort of strange feeling shot across him; "what doth the scrivener at Shottery?"

The dame smiled, knowingly. "The bright day hath brought him forth mayhap," said she.

"'Tis the bright day that brings forth the adder," said Shakespeare; "and that Doubletongue too. I am sorry they are acquainted with Mistress Anne."

"Why so?" said the dame. "Master Grasp is rich. He hath store of moneys 'tis said. He hath been saying some pretty things to Anne; nay, in good sooth I think he, *in some sort*, affects her."

"May the pestilence strike the crafty knave!" said Shakespeare to himself, as a slight pang of jealousy shot through his breast. "He affect the handsome Anne Hathaway!"

"You know Master Grasp?" said Dame Hathaway, inquiringly.

"I do," said Shakespeare, drily.

"I thought as much," said the good dame, "for I heard his discourse to Anne, and, sooth to say, he did not speak well of you; nay, he speaks vilely of you."

"Thank Heaven, therefore," said Shakespeare, smiling; "the praise of the wicked is less to be coveted than their censure. By your leave I will seek your daughter in the orchard."

"I pray you do," said Dame Hathaway, "and bid them in to dinner."

When Shakespeare entered the orchard he found the two damsels engaged in removing apples from a sort of store-house erected at the further end of it, to another outhouse nearer to the dwelling; and, as the two elderly swains had gallantly volunteered to assist them in their labours, the damsels were amusing themselves by taxing their good-nature and strength to the utmost.

Accordingly as the youth strolled amongst the trees towards them, he beheld the unhappy Grasp bent double under the weight of an enormous basket, so filled with apples that he could scarce stagger beneath it, whilst Anne Hathaway, with both hands, was still piling up more fruit. Master Doubletongue was similarly loaded, and both the maidens were laughing till their sides ached at the rueful figures their patient lovers exhibited.

The situation was indeed felt by the suitors as sufficiently ridiculous, and when they saw some one approaching both would fain have thrown down their burthens if they had been able.

"Nay, I pray thee, Good Mistress Anne," said Grasp, "give me not the entire produce of the orchard at one turn. I am neither Hercules nor Atlas. My back is well nigh broke, as well as my heart, by your cruelty. I would fain stand upright. Heaven relieve me," he muttered to himself, "from this pestilent load."

"My strength sufficeth not to remove so large a load," said Anne, still laughing, "all I can do is to take them out by degrees, as I have placed them *one by one!*"

"I should die ere relieved by so slow a process," said Grasp. "Oh, my back, my weary back is cramped with long suffering and weight of apples."

"Then trudge off, and throw them into yonder wood-house," said Anne. "I'll never entertain your services if you are thus idle."

"I cannot budge a foot," said Grasp, "I am, as it were, rooted in the snow. Heaven help me."

"Stop whilst I give you this small basketfull," said Anne, emptying more apples into the load.

"Nay, then, I can no longer bear it," said Grasp; and he sank upon his knees, whilst both the lasses kept piling more apples upon his head.

"I am utterly foredone, and must fain succumb," said Grasp; "my better parts are vanquished, lo, I fall," and, as he sank under his burthen, the huge load rolled in heaps around him.

"I shall be crushed, altogether crushed and flattened like a shrove-groat shilling," said Master Doubletongue. "I pray you, fair damsel, to help me down with this burthen. I would fain do my best in your service, but I am not able, I find, to do the work of a younger man."

But the saucy maidens, having brought their two admirers to their present doleful state, as soon as they saw young Shakespeare approaching, ran, shrieking with laughter to meet him, leaving their swains to extricate themselves as they best could.

"I do perceive that I am made an exceeding ass of by this lively virgin," said Grasp, gathering himself up from amongst the rolling apples; "nevertheless her comeliness and favour hath quite entamed my spirits to her worship. I would fain contract a marriage, and the good yeoman her father is right willing to receive me for a son-in-law."

"And I," said Doubletongue, "should greatly like to wive also, an I could achieve the maiden Mopsy. Mass, but she is fresh as an April morn, and strong as a porter. Would to Heaven she had relieved me of this burthen ere she fled! Help me down with it, good Grasp, an you love me."

"Who was that I saw approaching when the maidens deserted us?" inquired Grasp. "See, they are now returning with him into the house, without so much as 'I thank ye,' for all we have done for them."

"'Tis surely young Shakespeare," said Doubletongue, "your sometime clerk."

"Oh, the young scapegallows," said Grasp, "by my fay, and so it is. His presence here bodes no good to my suit, and I have already possessed Mistress Anne with my opinion of him. Nay, Sir Thomas Lucy hath spoken with me about him, too. The dare-devil lad hath somehow offended Sir Thomas, and he vows to deal hardly with him an he can catch him trespassing on his domain. I'll stir him further to't."

"He hath trespassed upon our domains here too, I think, and carried off my sweet friend Mopsy," said Doubletongue. "I'll abuse the varlet where'er I come."

"Thou canst not say worse of him than he deserves," said Grasp; "an I can but once catch him tripping, I'll be his ruin yet."

"Methinks we had better wend our steps back to Stratford this morning," said Doubletongue. "I am sore wearied, and sorely nipped with the cold blast. The pestilence seize this Shakespeare, I had rather not encounter him."

"I would we were both rid of him," said Grasp; "albeit I am somewhat sorry to leave him in the company of the fair Anne; such a smooth-tongued varlet is sufficient to corrupt a whole village."

"Let us slink by and get a peep in at the window," said Doubletongue; and the worthy pair of friends left the orchard.

On that evening a youth and a village maiden were seen strolling quietly along the footpath leading from Shottery to Stratford-upon-Avon. The youth, with head inclined, was telling a soft tale in the ear of his companion—a tale such as evidently was pleasing to her, for her handsome face was radiant with smiles. There was something in the step and bearing of both which proclaimed them superior to the common run of mortals: albeit their costume was but a degree removed from, and in somewhat better taste than that of the peasant of the period. Both were extremely handsome, and it was evident they were lovers, inasmuch as (although the occasional passer seldom failed to stop and turn to regard them) they were so entirely wrapped in each other's society that they seemed lost to all external objects.

As they reached a part of the path which is crossed by the high road, they stopped, and a stately knight, accompanied by two ladies, and attended by several mounted serving men, rode by. The ladies seemed struck with the form of the handsome maiden; and the cavalier, after passing, turned and leant upon the cantle of his saddle, and steadily regarded the youth.

"'Tis he," said the Knight of Charlecote, to himself, "and the girl is Hathaway's daughter. 'Tis pity she should mate with so reckless a youth."

"Who, said ye, they are?" inquired the elder daughter of Sir Thomas; "methinks I have seen the youth at Clopton Hall."

"See him when and where thou wilt, Alicia," returned the knight, "I fear me you will have seen but a graceless suitor, from all I have learned through the scrivener Grasp. 'Tis the woolcomber's eldest son, young Shakespeare of Stratford."

After this brief discourse, the party rode on.

CHAPTER XXVIII.

SHOTTERY HALL.

WITH lovers, days, weeks, and months pass swiftly by. The fair and witty Rosalind is made to tell us, however, that time trots hard with a young maid, between the contract of her marriage and the day it is solemnized, for "if the interim be but a se'night, time's pace is so hard, that it seems the length of seven years."

With the swifter foot of time, however, during the even course of love between young Shakespeare and Anne Hathaway, we shall pace over some few months in our history.

Angry winter must be supposed to have departed; the fields and meadows to have thrown off his livery, and the woodland scene around Stratford-upon-Avon, to be dressed in the green investiture of the coming spring.

The hard pace of time therefore must be now imagined to be progressing with the fair Anne, inasmuch as she has been wooed and won by the youthful Shakespeare. She is indeed between the contract of her marriage and its solemnization.

It was one lovely evening, about this period of our story, that an exceedingly handsome female was sitting pensive and melancholy in her own apartment at Shottery Hall, a large mansion situated just without the village.

Our readers have before had a glimpse of this lady, during the eventful night of the party at Clopton, what time she was engaged in the dance with Walter Arderne. Clara de Mowbray had, indeed, been one of the intimate friends of the fair Charlotte, her confidant and associate from childhood. She was herself an orphan, and possessed of great wealth; and although but one-and-twenty years of age, seemed to have already given up the pleasures of the world, and dedicated her days to good and charitable deeds in and around her own neighbourhood. She was, therefore, as a matter of course, the lady patroness of the little village near which she dwelt.

Whether it was that she mourned over the fate of the early friend, whose death had been attended with such awful and melancholy circumstances, or whether the loss of her parents had left a sad impression upon her spirits, we cannot tell; but certain it is, that Clara de Mowbray seemed to labour under some secret and deep-seated grief, which rendered society a burden to her.

As she sat on this evening in her own apartment, her attendant announced a maiden from the village, who was desirous of seeing her.

"'Tis the handsome Anne Hathaway—is it not?" inquired Clara. "Indeed I sent to request she would come hither."

"It is, lady," returned the attendant.

"Set a chair for her here beside the window, and wait on her in."

"They tell me she is soon to be wedded," said the attendant, as she brushed the chair with her apron, "and that she hath refused a good offer for the sake of her present lover."

"I have heard as much," said the lady; "and 'tis of that I would speak with her."

The Lady Clara had known Anne Hathaway from childhood, consequently, there was little of form or ceremony between her and the more humble friend.

"I have sent for you, Anne," said Clara, as soon as the damsel entered, "to talk about your future prospects. I have been so great a recluse, that I have only just heard of your intended marriage. I trust you will be happy, Anne."

"I hope so, lady," said Anne.

"And do you *think so?*" inquired Clara.

"Wherefore should I not, lady?" inquired Anne.

"There are one or two things," continued the lady, "I have heard of your betrothed, which leads me to ask the question, Anne; and also because we are old friends, and I love you. In the first place, I hear your suitor is younger than yourself. Is't not so?"

"It is, lady," said Anne.

"And I hear also that he is of no calling; that he is poor, and his friends needy."

"All that you have said is true," said Anne Hathaway; *but*—" and she paused.

"But you are in love," said Clara. "Well, I suppose there is no advice I can give you which will avail against that argument. I would have you, however, consider well; and (as I know neither of the parties) I cannot judge in how far your own judgment is right in this matter."

"I would you could see the two together," said Anne, smiling, "you would then have little left to urge in favour of my richer suitor."

"Indeed!" said Clara, smiling; "yet one word more, Anne. I hear the youth—let me see, how is he named?"

"Shakespeare," said Anne, "William Shakespeare."

"Well, then, I hear that this lover of yours—this young Shakespeare, is of a daring spirit; that he associates with youths as reckless as himself; and that, in very sooth, he bears altogether a character for idleness even in the town where he dwells."

"What do you charge him with in particular?" said Anne, smiling.

"Nay, nothing more than I have hinted at," said Clara. "He is slightly regarded by the townsfolk of Stratford, from his idle propensities. If there be a bear to be baited at Kenilworth Green, who so sure to be there as this younker. If there is a wrestling-match and a bull-baiting at Coventry, thither is your swain sure to go. If there be, in short, a wake or fair, or revel, in this or the adjoining county, young Shakespeare is as certain to be seen upon the Green as those resident on the spot. Nay, I have been told that he hath himself beaten one of our Warwickshire champions here at Shottery last Christmas, and that he is giving to poaching withal."

"In respect ye have named his delight in all sort of out-door sports, you are right, lady," said Anne; "but that he is given to poaching is a malicious rumour."

"Well," said Clara, "I see your affections are set upon this match, and far be it from me to oppose your will. I too well know the misery of blighted love. Heaven guard you, Anne. Ere you wed, it would please me to see *the youth*."

"You have seen him," said Anne.

"I remember him not," said Clara.

"'Twas at Clopton you met with him," said Anne. "William hath told me he met you on the night of that unhappy ball, and that Master Walter Arderne shewed you to him in the room."

Clara started. She then said, in some surprise, "Did your lover know Walter, then?"

"They were sworn friends, lady," said Anne.

"Shakespeare!" said Clara. "'Tis a name I remember. Was not the youth who saved Charlotte Clopton from death in the park called Shakespeare? If so, him indeed have I met at Clopton, and have heard both Charlotte and Walter Arderne speak of."

"'Tis the same youth, lady," said Anne.

"Indeed," said Clara; "that doth indeed surprise me;" and Clara remained for some time lost in deep thought. "I have a relic," she said, "of Charlotte's given me by Martin, and which was much treasured by poor Charlotte. 'Tis a small piece of verse of exquisite beauty. If I recollect rightly, Martin told me it was written by this lad—this lover of yours. Stay, I will shew it you;" and Clara, after searching in a small casket, brought forth a scrap of paper with some verses written on it, which she read aloud, and then handed to Anne.

"I am not much given to poetry," said Anne, smiling; "but I see by the character they are written by William; but methinks I should have known them for his by other tokens. He often repeats such verse in our walks. He hath written scores of such pieces as the one I now hold in my hand."

"Nay, then, I cannot wonder at what I have heard," said the lady; "neither am I surprised at such a man being the friend of Walter Arderne. There is one thing more I would ask," said Clara, blushing. "You know my secret, Anne, and can perhaps give me some news of him you wot of, through means of your lover. Where now is Walter Arderne?"

"I shall grieve you, lady, if I say that for some time no accounts have been received of him, and it is greatly feared he hath perished amongst the adventurers with whom he left England."

"How is this news derived?" she said.

"William hath learnt so much from Martin, whom he has occasionally seen whilst Martin remained at Clopton; but latterly Martin seemed to grow uneasy, and as reports were circulated relative to the loss of that part of the expedition with which Master Arderne sailed, he at length left Clopton, where he had been residing almost alone, and went to London. Whilst there he met some of the adventurers who had returned with Sir Francis Drake, and of them he heard dire accounts of the dangers and hardships they had encountered. From them too he learned that Walter Arderne had greatly distinguished himself amongst the followers of Christopher Carlisle at the taking of St. Jago, near Cape de Verde; that he had afterwards sailed for Hispaniola, and assaulted and taken St. Domingo. He was also heard of on the coast of Florida; and it was at the burning of one of the towns, either St. Anthony or St. Helens, on that coast, that Master Arderne is supposed to have perished."

"Was he then not seen and identified amongst the slain or wounded?" inquired Clara.

"It appears not," said Anne. "The expedition, with the exception of some smaller ships separated from them in a storm, sailed along the coast of Virginia, where they found the remains of a colony previously planted there by Sir Walter Raleigh, and which had almost gone to decay. The miserable remnant of adventurers," continued Anne, "who were found by Sir Francis Drake at this place, and who are described to have appeared more like living mummies than Christian men, abandoned their settlement, and prevailed on Sir Francis Drake to bring them to England."

"And have no further tidings been since heard?" inquired Clara.

"Nothing certain. A small portion of the fleet which separated from Drake's squadron after this, and sailed along the coast of Florida, inflamed with rage against the Spaniards and the riches they had already gained, after a short cruise, returned with an account of their having observed a wreck near Raleigh's ruined colony;* and that they had even seen some individuals apparently again located there. They had, however, steadily pursued their course without inquiry; albeit they judged this wreck to have been one of the ships Walter Arderne had held command in."

"So then," said Clara, "these unfortunate men may have been left to perish, exposed to all the vicissitudes of war and climate, and half-naked in an enemy's country?"

"'Tis to be feared so," returned Anne, "although the dreadful mortality which the climate produced amongst Drake's followers is but a feeble restraint on the avidity and sanguine expectation of the young adventurers of England; nay, other expeditions are said to be about to set sail; should it be so, that coast may be again visited."

"And this you have learnt from your lover?" said Clara.

"I have, lady; he loves to talk to me in our walks about the wonders seen in these islands of the sea in the far West. I would you could hear him describe what he has learnt from one or two of the youths who have adventured and returned: how they have seen and landed upon islands inhabited by people of wondrous appearance; islands full of strange sounds, and in which the most ravishing melody floated in the air, the musicians being spirits and invisible to sight."

"Methinks," said Clara, "I should much like to hear your lover's account of such wonders."

"Nay, so interested is he in these accounts, and the riches to be found on the Spanish main, that had I not over-ruled his design, he would himself have adventured this year with Martin Frobisher."

"I have heard something of Frobisher's former expedition," said Clara. "What were the particulars?"

"Nay, I can but inform you as I have learned it from the lips of others," said Anne.

"They set out, I have heard," said Clara, "for the purpose of discovering a passage to Cataia, in the Indies, by the north-west seas. I do not myself quite understand such matters, but I believe they sailed beyond Friesland, where they came in sight of land inhabited by strange and savage people. In this land they discovered some black substance like sea-coal, and on their return shewed it to a goldsmith in London, and he found it to be rich in gold ore, was't not so?"

"It was, lady," said Anne; "this encouraged Martin Frobisher to make a second voyage, when he freighted two vessels home with this

* This was the first attempt of the English to form such settlements; and although they have since surpassed all European nations, they had been so unsuccessful, that they abandoned the place.

black stone, and his project is now so risen in credit that he is about to set sail a third time, with fifteen goodly vessels; nay, had I not used my influence, as I before said, William Shakespeare had surely adventured amongst the crew."

"And so would you as surely have lost a lover, as he would have lost his venture," said Clara. "I have no opinion of these wild schemes —and yet I have half a mind to fit out an expedition and venture myself in quest of a treasure."

"You, lady!" said Anne; "but you are not serious?"

"I was never more so," said Clara.

As she said this, Clara rose from her seat—a hint to her visitor that the interview had lasted long enough.

"Yet stay," she said, as Anne was about to depart. "We have been long friends, Anne Hathaway, and if I find the choice you have made a worthy one, I will befriend you both. One thing I have forgotten to mention, and that is the report I have heard of this match between you and young Shakespeare being disapproved of by your father. Is that also true?"

"My lover is at present poor," said Anne.

"Enough," said Clara. "Farewell, Anne, I intend leaving Shottery for some time, but when I return, remember you have a friend in me. Here," she continued, "is a present I had intended to have given you after your marriage. Take it now, as we shall not meet again for many months. I leave Shottery to-morrow."

And so the friends parted.

The fair Clara remained buried in thought for some time after the departure of Anne Hathaway.

At length she arose from her seat, and her eye fell upon the sonnet she had received from Martin. "The verse is indeed beautiful," she said. "Happy, happy Anne, how much is thy lot to be envied! In thy rank in life there is little impediment to the affections. Thou lovest and art beloved again: there is no drawback in regard to inequality, or matching in degree. The village lad loves and chooses his mate as the turtle, unembarrassed by wealth or worldly interest. This youth must, however, be in mind at least far superior. Well, thy prospect is a happy one! Whilst mine, alas! he I love is perhaps lost in the watery wastes of unknown seas—perhaps starving on some desert shore."

As Clara thus indulged her melancholy thoughts, she rang a small silver bell, and desired her attendant to summon to her presence the steward or major-domo of her household.

"Hubert," she said, "I am about to leave Shottery for London. My horses have of late had but idle times, and an excursion will do them good. I ride with twenty followers."

The orders of Clara were law with Hubert. He therefore bowed; and she continued, "I take this strong escort," she said, "because I shall have great charge with me in gold and diamonds. To you I will at once confess the purpose of my journey to London, and my farther intentions when there. I am about myself to fit out an expedition to the coast of Florida, and in person to visit the strange lands said to exist in the New World."

"In choosing amongst my people," she continued, "pick out those youths who you think would be likely to volunteer for such an exploit."

"And when do we depart, lady?" inquired the steward.

"The day after to-morrow," said Clara.

And again the steward bowed, and then withdrew.

CHAPTER XXIX.

THE LOVERS.

THE very name of the New World during the reign of Elizabeth, was suggestive of boundless wealth, and the wildest hopes of gain. The islands already visited by the adventurers of the period, were said to be scenes of enchantment—a sort of demi-paradise, where the most lovely Indian females wandered about in all the innocence of the golden age.

Such was the idea men entertained of the New World, as it was then called, and in consequence, albeit those who had returned from this land of promise, presented in their own worn appearance but small encouragement to others to try fortune in their boasted region; still the voyage, as it was designated *par excellence*, was in great repute amongst the "rash, inconsiderate, and fiery voluntaries" of Elizabeth's reign. And, under these circumstances, sea-faring men of all sorts, and even those who had never beheld the sea, occasionally made up the file as soldiers for the various expeditions in vogue. The hardships and dangers these men encountered beneath the hot sun of the tropics at this time; their endurance under difficulties, whilst exposed to privation in their marches through unknown forests, defiles, and mountains, is wonderful to contemplate. Nay, perhaps, the very difficulties to be encountered, and the watery wastes to be traversed, even enhanced the desire these desperadoes felt in undertaking the venture; added also to this spirit of enterprise, and the prospect men beheld in the sunny distance, of lovely lands, and scenes of enchantment in the bright islands they thought to find, there was in the breast of the Englishman at this period a rankling and deep-seated hatred of the Spaniard—then the stoutest soldier of the civilized world—a foe not only worthy in that day of the Englishman's sword, but who bore away from him the palm of soldiership, and, of whom, he felt in some sort jealous. The Spaniard, at the same time, whilst he had been drilled into wonderful efficiency by long conflict with the Moors, the French, and Italians, surpassed all other men in the qualities which conquer kingdoms, even at fearful odds.

The Spanish hidalgo still possessed all the chivalry of the crusader, with augmented bigotry and superstition. Fighting was his element, and greed of gold and religious fanaticism his stimulants. His pride was beyond description. He was—

"The man of compliment, a most illustrious wight,
A man of fire, new words, fashion's own knight."

'Twas against soldiers of this stamp that such men as Drake were now waging war. The stern hearts and iron fists of his sailors and men-at-arms, were turned against wretches, whose cruel hearts had shewn no mercy to the harmless Indian; and fierce, bloody, remorseless, was the conflict when the Englishmen met the Don.

The great success of the Spaniard in both the Indies, too, was an additional stimulant to the emulation of the English adventurers.

He was indeed considered a hero, who returned safe from the horrors of murderous conflict, and the sack and siege of town and settlement in the tropics. His sun-burnt visage was gazed on with curiosity; and his account also of hardships endured amidst swamp and thicket, together with exaggerated circumstance of horrid animals, fearful reptiles, and wonderous beings in human form, was listened to with awe and wonder.

The morning Clara had fixed on for her departure dawned brightly. Hill and dale, and wood and park, were faintly gilded with the early morning sun; she looked around, and sighed as she reflected, that perhaps for the last time she beheld the domain of her ancestors.

As her party left the grounds of Shottery and took their way through the village, she reined up her palfrey, and, with her female attendant, remained a few minutes behind. She then turned her horse towards Anne Hathaway's cottage, and, as the road ran close beside it, she resolved to pass the dwelling of her rustic friend, and perhaps see her for a moment and bid her again farewell. As she did so, she observed two youths advancing along the road. They carried cross-bows in their hands, and seemed bound for the woodlands.

"Is not the slighter of those youth's Anne's lover?" inquired Clara of an attendant, as the young men entered the garden of old Hathaway's cottage.

"It is, lady," said the attendant. "Yon handsome lad is William Shakespeare."

"Listen!" said Clara; "he is awakening his mistress with a song." And as the lady drew bridle under shelter of the tall trees beside the cottage, they heard a beautiful voice accompanied by a sort of lute, singing these *now* well-known words.

"Hark! hark! the lark at heaven's gate sings,
And Phœbus 'gins arise,
His steeds to water at those springs
On chalic'd flowers that lies;
And winking Mary-buds begin
To ope their golden eyes
With everything that pretty bin,
My lady, sweet, arise.
Arise, arise." *

* "Cymbeline."

The beauty of the verse, and the sweetness of the singer's voice, completely fixed Clara to the spot; and, as she listened anxiously for another verse, she heard the lattice open, and the voice of Anne join in conversation with her lover. Clara felt extremely anxious again to see one who had been the friend of Walter Arderne, and she determined to accost the youth. When she rode round, however, to the front of the cottage, he was gone on his way, and afterwards with his companion might have been observed, concealed in the woods at Fulbrook. Together they lay in the thick covert and watched a sequestered stag, a bolt from Shakespear's cross-bow had wounded, and which he was again endeavouring to gain a shot at. 'Twas his first poaching offence; and whilst he lay thus crouching in the thick brake, and again sought to get near the stag, his comrade, Dick Snare, kept watch somewhat aloof, lest the keepers came upon them unawares.

Meantime slowly and sadly the maiden of high degree turned her horse's head from the scenes of her childhood. She felt desolate amidst her plenteous fields and domains, whilst the humble friend of her childhood, the village companion, the poor cottager, seemed happy in all the world could bestow worth coveting; and as Clara turned from the cottage, the handsome Anne, unconscious of her near proximity, was intently perusing some verses which Shakespeare had thrown in at her window as he departed,—verses addressed to herself.

I.

"Would ye be taught, ye feather'd throng,
With love's sweet notes to grace your song,
To pierce the heart with thrilling lay,
Listen to mine, Anne Hathaway.
She hath a way to sing so clear,
Phœbus might, wondering, stop to hear;
To melt the sad, make blithe the gay,
And nature charm, Anne hath a way.
She hath a way,
Anne Hathaway,
To breathe delight, Anne Hathaway.

II.

"When Envy's breath and ranc'rous tooth
Do soil and bite fair worth and truth,
And merit to distress betray,
To soothe the heart, Anne hath a way;
She hath a way to chase despair,
To heal all grief, to cure all care,
Turn foulest night to fairest day,
Thou know'st, fond heart, Anne hath a way.
She hath a way,
Anne Hathaway,
To make grief bliss, Anne hath a way."

CHAPTER XXX.

THE ADVENTURERS.

About three weeks after the departure of Clara de Mowbray, a stout-timbered vessel, built after the peculiar fashion of the time, and yet in something improved in its construction from the unwieldy craft in general use, might have been observed beating up against wind and tide on the Kentish coast. The weather, for the time of the year, was unusually rough, and to a heavy rolling sea was added a driving rain, and a roaring gale of wind. There is considerable danger, too, as the mariner well knows, around him on this part of the coast. His craft has been driven out of its course, and the fearful Goodwins are close at hand; still labours on, however, that gallant barque, manned by stout English adventurers. She is trying, amidst the driving rain and furious winds, to make out the mouth of the Sandwich haven; and, whilst her timbers creak, and the blast whistles amongst her rigging, a delicious strain of melody seems to float around her. The notes of a lute are heard by the sailors accompanied by a voice of ravishing sweetness; and, as it issues from the cabin of the vessel, it sounds as if some angel is trying to soothe the fury of the winds and waves.

Dangerous as is this part of the coast, even in the present time, when its perils are so well marked out to the navigator, at the period of our story, it was, by comparison, almost an unknown sea. No secure harbour was then constructed close opposite the Goodwins. No buoys and revolving lights pointed out the dangerous proximity of rocks and shoals; those dread quicksands, whose depths retain the wrecked treasures of successive ages; sands which

> "Will not bear our enemy's boats,
> But suck them up to the top-mast."

Bravely, however, keeps on that labouring barque. One moment she seems engulphed in the boiling waters, and the mist rolls over the spot where her hull was last tossing. The next she is trembling upon the crested wave, and again about to be hurled from its summit into the waters beneath.

One eye there is, on board, which seems especially to watch over her,—an eye which calmly scans every part around, watches every cord of her rigging, and rectifies every mishap consequent upon the violence of the gale.

Meanwhile, on the waist, the deck, the poop, are to be seen, besides the sailors who work the vessel, lying, sitting, and holding on by the ropes, the forms of fierce and bearded men, clad in the buff leathern dress which formed the usual costume of warriors of the period, their half-armour being doffed during their voyage along the coast.

Suddenly the eye of the chief, as the driving rain for the moment seems to subside, catches sight of a range of white foam. Another and another follow after, till they seem to overtake each other, and mingle in a perfect cauldron of boiling sea.

Then his voice sounds amidst the roar of winds and waters—the sails flap—the cordage strains—and every eye looks anxious, and every heart beats quicker; for that moment is to decide whether the living, and warlike freightage, are to ride safely past the gulf, or to be sucked down amidst the depths of the awful Goodwins.

As the chief mariner leaps upon the bulwark of the vessel, and, grasping the rigging, looks out upon the boiling sea, a slight and graceful youth has emerged from the cabin, and placed himself beside him.

"We are in peril," said he, in a low voice; "these are the fatal sands you thought you had safely passed an hour ago."

But the mariner for the moment heeds not the question of his superior. His whole attention is given to his craft, and the horrible depths she is every minute apparently about to be engulphed in.

It was an awful moment for one so young and delicate-looking as that boy. Yet his cheek blanches not at the prospect of a death so fearful. He clings to the slippery ropes, and awaits the event with a courage worthy of one of firmer frame and maturer years; whilst the vessel, dashing amidst the waves, still holds stoutly on.

As she did so the mariner leapt down, and, as his feet again touched the deck of his craft, he drew a long breath.

"'Twas a fearful moment," he said, "I ne'er before looked down whilst so close upon the eternal bed of many a tall and stately vessel. 'Twas a moment that told of life or death."

"'Tis passed, then," said the youth; "see, we are driving away from yonder white gallopers, who seem to course each other in an endless chase."

"'Tis passed, *for this time*," said the mariner; "but we are on a fearful coast on such an evening as this. Methought I knew each foot of these waters; but in such a driving gale 'tis scarce possible to know our course."

"And what then will you do?" inquired the youth.

"Still make for the mouth of the haven I told you of," said the captain; "and which leads us to safety, if we can hit it."

"No easy matter, methinks," said the youth, "in such a gale, eh?"

"Nevertheless, I do not despair," returned the mariner. "My youth has been passed upon these very seas. But this is no weather for your Excellency," he continued respectfully, taking the youth's hand, and leading him towards the cabin of the half-decked vessel.

"You forget I am the commander in this expedition," said the youth, smiling.

"Only of the land-forces," said the mariner, returning the smile; "the vessel, by our compact, I am to be captain of."

Half-an-hour after this conversation and the gallant barque was quietly and slowly winding its course along the muddy stream which flows up to the Dutch-built Cinque Port situated at this part of the coast.

The Cinque Ports in Elizabeth's day, albeit their grandeur had in a great measure departed from them, were still of great importance to the nation. There was a pride and pomposity of manner still to be found amonst the barons, and burgesses, and townsfolk, which had descended to them from their warlike ancestry, during the days when kings honoured them with their especial favour, and granted them privileges and immunities unknown to other towns. With all the pride of their mail-clad ancestry, therefore, and whose constant sufferance had been sack and siege, fire and slaughter, the more peaceful Cinque Porter of Elizabeth's day considered himself still a sort of a *magnifico*. 'Tis true that in place of the chain-mail and two-handed weapons of the iron-men of the Norman period, whose only trade was war, the present race were clad in the high-crown hat, the short cloak, and the full trunks of the well-dealing merchant. Yet still, albeit the portly, lank-haired, Flemish-looking burgher stood upon his gentility as he walked the key of this muddy haven,—yet still, we say, steel corslet and military pride was not altogether laid aside, and the *trade of merchandize* had not entirely superseded efficiency in the *tradè of war*.

On the morning following the night on which the strange barque entered the haven of Sandwich, two portly townsmen greeted each other in the Fish Market.

"What vessel was that same which crept up last night and lies moored before the Fisher's Gate?" inquired neighbour De Bock of Master Cramp.

"I ca'nt observe," said Cramp. "She looks queer, methinks. There's an armed sentinel upon her deck, to keep any one from leaving her without license, and another man-at-arms upon the shore with loaded caliver, who walks up and down forsooth, as who should say, keep off Sir Curious, and pry not too closely into our affairs."

"Is she from Holland, think ye?" inquired De Bock.

"I should say nay to that," said Cramp.

"Is she from London, laden with serge, baize, and flannel, think ye?"

"I rather opine not."

"What is her rig, neighbour?"

"Nondescript, I think."

"What is her build?"

"Indescribable, I should say."

"Hath she any freight at all on board?"

"As far as I can judge, she hath a freight."

"And what is it?"

"Principally arms of various sorts—rapier and dagger pike and arqebus."

"Ha, sayst thou? Then must she be seized, and her destination inquired into."

"That might cause some sort of controversy—some arbitration—since each weapon I have named hath a man tacked to it, and a hand to exercise it."

"What, *is* she then filled with armed men, neighbour?"

"She is. So much have I learned by looking down at her just now from the tower of St. Clement's Church."

"'Fore Gad, she may be a Spaniard then."

"I think nay to that, too."

"Or a pirate?"

"*There* thou *hast it;* methinks she *is* a pirate. Nay, certes she is a pirate who has been forced to take shelter in our haven by yesterday's gale."

"My life upon't thou art right, Let's e'en go look upon her, and then to the mayor with our report." And the worthy burgesses immediately threaded the narrow streets, and approached the Fisher's Gate, which looks upon the flats on the Thanet side of the town.

Just within the Fisher's Gate, and in the narrow lane which leads down to it from the town, there is still to be seen an ancient hostel called the Checquers. Its low arched doors, its narrow passages, its comfortable sanded parlour, its ample kitchen, diamond paned windows, and small comfortable rooms, low in roof, and ponderous in beam, bespeak its early date. It had been the hostel of the Fisher's Gate full half a century before the period of our story.

If curiosity was a ruling passion with the two burgesses, love of good liquor was equally strong, and accordingly as they necessarily passed this old hostel, they turned in for their morning's draught.

As they did so, they found it was occupied by two persons belonging to the very vessel which had so much excited their curiosity. One was a slight and effeminate looking youth, of most graceful form, and features of exceeding beauty. His long curled ringlets hung over either shoulder, which, as it was not the fashion of the day, rendered his appearance even more remarkable. His dress, although it bespoke the seafaring man, was evidently fashioned after his own whim. Perhaps it was more in the style of the Venetian sailor than the English seafaring man. Such as it was, however, it added much to the graceful beauty of him who wore it; and as it was accompanied by a certain rakish swagger, an assumed easy manner, the appearance of the juvenile stranger altogether considerably astonished the two grave, staid, and simple-minded Cinque Port functionaries, who entered the hostel.

The companion of the youth was a man in no way remarkable, except for his high forehead, intelligent countenance, and well-knit and somewhat athletic form. His costume was that of a sort of amphibious adventurer of the period, half sailor, half soldier—a man equally serviceable either on the deck of his vessel, or in the tented field, and alike trained to the arts and manœuvres of war on the rampart or in the trench, on horseback or on foot. His twisted-hilted and long rapier was carried in a broad buff belt; his gauntlets reached to his elbow; his thick leathern doublet carried the marks of the breastplate he wore on service, and the wide-topped boots reached his full trunks, like those of a fisherman of the present time.

The youth before-named occupied an arm chair, situated near a table on which the appliances for a substantial breakfast were placed, and which he occupied in a sort of lounging, jaunty style, ever and anon picking a small portion from the plate before him, and conveying it to his lips with the point of his richly-guarded dagger, the whilst his stalwart comrade applied himself to the viands like one who especially relished a good meal.

"Your Excellency," said this latter sailor, without seeming to notice the entrance of the native burghers of the town, "scarce seems to have found the benefit of these Kentish breezes. Your appetite is somewhat dainty this morning, methinks; and yet this bread is white as the snow-flake, and sweet and wholesome withal. Let me give you the veriest taste of this Canary wine, 'twill coax you into trying yonder pastie."

"I thank thee, good Captain Fluellyn," * returned the youth, "I cannot bear Canary so early. Indeed, my breakfast is already made; I eat but slightly in the morning. At dinner I will drink with ye turn and turn about, an you list, till your brain reels like a top."

"Ah, so thou ever sayest," returned the Captain, "but when dinner comes your Excellency still evades the wine-cup."

The title given to the youthful navigator, his distinguished appearance, and the luxuries by which he was surrounded, rather astonished the natives as they observed the pair.

It was plain that the silver goblets from which they drank, and the elaborately ornamented plates and dishes upon which the viands were served, together with the handsome case of liquors, all of which belonged to a sort of canteen which stood open near the table, must have been brought for the use of this noble from the ship then lying but a few yards off.

The curiosity, therefore, of the two townsmen was considerably excited to know who and what he was, and as both himself and the stalwart captain continued their conversation and meal without taking the slightest notice of their presence, their self-importance was a trifle injured, and Master De Bock addressed himself to the handsome sailor.

"If I may crave permission of interrupting your exertions for a moment," he said, stepping up to the table, "I would fain know if our presence here is intrusive, and, if so, I would crave permission to retire with my worthy townsman here."

At this sage address from the lank-haired round-faced burgher, the tall captain laid down the small dagger with which he was helping himself to a portion of the savory pastie before him, and, twisting the end of his moustache, stared at him for a few moments, and then throwing himself back in his chair, looked inquiringly into the face of his companion.

* A name at that time to be found at Stratford.

The youth was evidently inclined to laugh; there was, indeed, a sort of twinkle in his eye as he returned the stare of the sea-captain.

"Is it your Countship's pleasure to be private?" at length, said the latter, as the burgher stood gazing with his fishy eye upon the youth.

"We do in some sort court seclusion," said the Count, "and to that end, have engaged and hired this hostel, for the especial use of ourselves and followers during the stay of our vessel in yonder haven."

"Shall I signify the same unto these worthy traders?" said the Captain.

"His lordship hath himself spoken it," said the burgess, "we take our leave. May we, however, crave to know the honoured title of the distinguished personage visiting our town, and the name of the vessel in which he has arrived? It is necessary we should convey to his honour the mayor intelligence of such visitation, in order that he may wait upon his lordship in proper form."

The youth again smiled. "I am myself called," he said, "'the Count of the Saxon shore.' The vessel in which I am passenger is named the 'Phantom,' commanded by this worthy gentleman, my esteemed friend Captain Fluellyn, a gallant seaman, who hath sailed with Drake, and fought the Spaniard by sea and land."

Upon this introduction, the Captain thought it necessary to rise from his chair, and bow to the two townsmen in due form, which they as formally returned. After which, at a sign from the Count, he offered them a glass of Canary from the high-necked bottle upon the table.

"The Count of the Saxon shore," said De Bock, smacking his lips with ineffable relish as he sat down the glass. "That is, indeed, an ancient title, and one I knew not was still in existence. Doth your lordship claim to be lineally descended from the Roman whose authority extended in former days along this coast, and whose castle walls are still to be seen at hand here, and called Rugulbium or Reculver?"

"By the father's side, most assuredly," said the Count. "Maternally, I am of Kentish extraction, since, on the female side I claim descent from the god Woden, whose effigy was as you know, or ought to know, enthroned upon the hill a mile westward of your town, and called to this day Wodnesborough."

"A most respectable lineage," said the burgess, quite awe-struck at so glorious a descent. "His worship the mayor, attended by the hog-mace, the supervisor of the gutters, the several beadles in commission within our walls, will have the honour of waiting upon your lordship forthwith."

"The honour will be to us," said the Count, rising and bowing as the burgesses were about to leave the apartment. "For the next four hours we shall be engaged here in consulting with our gallant friend, and certain messengers we expect to arrive; after that, if it so please your mayor, we will receive him."

"And now, Captain," said the Count, reseating himself, "since we have got rid of those cane-bearded worthies, and you have finished your meal, we will, if it so please ye, discuss certain matters appertaining to this venture of ours."

"I am all readiness to give attention, Sir Count," said the Captain, also sitting himself comfortably in his chair, and drawing the case of liquors close beside him.

"In the first place, then, I trust you clearly comprehend my intentions in this voyage?"

"I think as much," said the Captain, filling his glass; "nevertheless, perhaps you will oblige me by repeating your wishes?"

"My voyage, then, I would have you to understand, is more a voyage of discovery than of profit. I neither wish to work mines, nor burn and sack towns. I would avoid all chance, if possible, of coming into collision with the Spaniard; and, unless I see occasion for other course, I would rather fly from, than seek an enemy."

"But," said the Captain, "you scarce gave out so much before. This somewhat exceeds what I expected. The Falcon is constructed after some improved notions of my own, and will assuredly outstrip any vessel upon the seas; but I like not to be always upon the wing. You forget I am one of Drake's first comrades, and have learned to love powder as devotedly as I hate the Spaniard. Body o' me, I shall lose what reputation I have gained! We shall be taken for little else besides knaves and cowards."

"You will find me ready enough to fight where fighting is my cue," interrupted the Count; "and if our voyage is successful, I will be myself an East and West Indies to you, inasmuch as you shall never again be obliged to seek fortune in the wide seas. And now we understand one another perfectly?"

"Your last argument is all-powerful," said the Captain. "I admire your love of adventure, coupled as it is with so much humanity, and am yours for the voyage, making peace or war as you affect either the one or the other. Nevertheless, I may as well remind your lordship, ere you embark on the enterprise, that we sailors of Drake and Frobisher, since the time we have interfered with the Spaniard, have a proverb, that there 'is no peace beyond the line.'"

"I have heard so much," said the Count, "and now methinks, whilst we wait here for the person appointed to join us, a short history of your adventures in these seas would serve to while away the hours."

"The history of my life might prove both distasteful and tedious to you," said the Captain; "but a brief account of it is at your service. Where shall I begin?"

Just as the sea captain was about to commence his narrative, and whilst he refilled his pipe with the weed he professed such veneration for, the sharp-ringing sound of horse's hoofs were heard beneath the arch of the gate-house, which indeed was so close to the old hostel that it almost formed a part of the building.

At this period there was no drawbridge across the stream which separated the town from the Island of Thanet, and communication was kept up by a ferry-boat, which plied exactly opposite the Fisher's Gate.

As the horseman was ferried across, he hailed the craft which had caused so much curiosity to the Sandwegians.

"Hillo, ho, ho! Falcon there! Is the Count on board?"

"Gone on shore," was the brief answer returned.

"Captain on board?" inquired the horseman.

"Ashore with the Count."

"Where do they lodge?"

"At the hostel within yonder gateway."

Accordingly, the horseman, after landing, rode straight up to the Checquers, and unceremoniously entered the apartment in which the Count and Captain were seated.

"Welcome, good Martin," said the Count, rising, "you see we keep time and tryst here."

"I am here at my time," said the traveller.

"I am right glad you have so soon joined us," said the Count; "for, sooth to say, both the Captain and myself are most anxious to be on the broad waves of the Atlantic."

"Our necessaries are by this time on board," said the Captain; "and as this honourable person makes up the file of gentlemen engaged for the expedition, what stays us, but we warp out to sea at once? In an hour I will undertake to be under weigh."

"Be it so," said the Count. "In an hour myself and friend will be on board."

And the Captain rose, and, after another cup of Canary, proceeded to his ship.

"Have you succeeded in learning any fresh tidings?" said the Count to our old friend Martin.

"I have journeyed far, and in something profited by my travel," said Martin. "I have visited the Netherlands, and also been in Warwickshire, since I met you in London, and now I keep tryste, and am here as appointed."

"You are ever worthy and zealous in the cause of your friends," returned the Count; "what are your tidings?"

"Briefly, then," said Martin, "I have reason to believe the good Walter lives; but, if such be the case, he is prisoner to the Spaniard—the worst sort of captivity—since he is in the hands of those who know no touch of pity, and are incensed against the English. This letter will better inform you of his situation."

The Count took the letter and perused it. "We will speed to his assistance," he said, as he refolded it. "And, now, how goes all in Warwickshire. Hath Sir Hugh Clopton returned?"

"Of Warwickshire I have not much news to give," said Martin. "Sir Hugh is still in the Low Countries. At Shottery all is as usual. Your steward commends him to you. Yet, stay, there is some further news of your own neighbourhood. Your old playmate, Anne Hathaway, is married to young Shakespeare."

"That I concluded must have taken place," said the Count, "since, when I left Shottery, they were to be united in a few days. I trust she will be happy. The bridegroom is, however, somewhat young to make a steady husband. I think I have heard you say you knew something of the lad: report speaks of him as a wild youth."

"Report is in something correct," I believe," said Martin. "To say I knew him well would be to say more than I should be warranted in affirming. What I did know of that young man served me for matter of reflection. For his wildness I cannot offer excuse, except that he hath a mounting spirit; nay, I will venture to affirm, that had your expedition been delayed a week, he would have joined in it."

"'Tis better as it is," said the Count. "I would not that my good friend Anne should so soon lose her husband."

"There is, however," continued Martin, "startling news from London, and which I rather think I am the first to announce in this town, as I overrode a foundered post between this place and Canterbury. The Queen of Scots, 'tis said, is again involved in a dangerous conspiracy to destroy our brave mistress, Queen Elizabeth."

CHAPTER XXXI.

THE BENEDICT.

THE course of events connected with our story has necessarily obliged us to deviate from the locality in which we have heretofore progressed. We must, however, now again, after such brief excursion, return to the spot from whence we started, and as the sun shines brightly upon park and field, and wooded glade, once more look upon fair and fertile Warwickshire.

Sweet Stratford-upon-Avon! those who know thee, and know thee well—who have lingered in thy old-world streets, and wandered in thy neighbourhood, breathing the scented air which smells so wooingly amongst the shadowy groves and unfrequented glades around, will acknowledge that there is no place in England, for situation and beauty, thy superior.

There is a freshness in thy neighbourhood, a quiet beauty in thy streets, a cozy comfort in many of thy dwellings, and a venerable and impressive grandeur in thy religious edifices, belonging alone to an English town of good and ancient descent. Was a stranger to be dropped suddenly in the centre of this town, whilst he looked around, and noted the sweet aspect of the locality he had so suddenly arrived in, methinks he would say to himself that he had reached a spot noted and celebrated in the world's esteem beyond most others in the kingdom. Yes, in this rural picture we think the stranger might find all these peculiar features characteristic of the old haunts in which Englishmen of a former age dwelt so happily. Those verdant villages, which made the English, however much they loved military adventure the whilst they formed the hosts of kings in the vasty fields of France, look back from the splendour of the tented field upon their own pleasant woodlands and quiet homes with fond yearning.

Tuck of drum might sound, the horn's sweet note be carried by the evening breeze, as it floated over some stricken field during these splendid wars of the Edwards and Henries. The gonfalon might flutter, and the knight, with all his train, ride stately amidst the white range of tents; the archer might lean upon his bow and gaze upon the splendour of the host. But the noble, and the knight, and the peasant-born soldier of England, alike sighed in his heart of hearts for the hour that was to see his foreign marches over, and himself amidst the scenes of his island home.

"That England hedged in with the main,
That precious gem set in the silver sea."

If then our readers love fair Warwickshire, and admire the grandeur and beauty of its scenery as we do, they will scarce be angry with us for again leading them back toward Stratford-upon-Avon.

And Shakespeare is married. One great event of his life is passed. He dwells with his wife in his native town; beyond the precincts of which he is comparatively unknown, or, being known, but little regarded.

He is scarcely more than eighteen years of age, and his wife is four-and-twenty. Their means are small, and their comforts few. The prospect before them is not of the brightest, but they are young, and in youth all seems beautiful because all is new. A female, however, of twenty-four, wedded to a youth of eighteen—*a mere boy*, as she terms him—will be likely to have her own way in everything; at least she will try to have it, and that is almost as bad. We fear, too, the blooming Anne is a "little shrew." She hath a high spirit withal, and we opine that her tastes and dispositions are not in exact accordance with those of her youthful husband. He is all imagination—all fire, energy, and spirit; whilst she is mere matter of fact. The gods have certainly not made her poetical, and she thanks the gods therefore. And then her age. Beautiful as she is in face and form, she is not matched in respect of years, and she knows it.

"Too old, by heaven; let still the woman take
An elder than herself—so wears she to him,
So sways she level in her husband's heart." *

William Shakespeare had married in opposition to the advice of his parents. The handsome Anne had done the same in regard to her's. Such cases are by no means rare in their walk of life. The present is

* "Twelfth Night."

all that is considered, the future unthought of. Old folks do sometimes, however, know more than young ones give them credit for; and in this instance they prognosticated the match would not be a happy one.

That the youthful poet felt some sort of disappointment when he found how widely his disposition and tastes differed from the companion he had chosen, there can be little doubt.

His extraordinary flights of genius, his wondrous conceptions, she had no part in. She, indeed, could scarce understand them; and that which she could not comprehend she looked upon as the rhapsodizing of a boy. Even those beautiful descriptions, and the music of his honeyed vows, for Shakespeare, although married, was still a lover, were now listened to without the smile of appreciation. "Alas!" he said to himself, "maids are May when they are maids, but the sky changes when they are wives." In short, the youthful poet found that he had matched unhappily. There was little sympathy in feeling, although there might have been in choice; and so their loves passed

> "Swift as a shadow, short as any dream,
> Brief as the lightning in the collied night."

They dwelt in Henley Street, in the house next to that in which the youth's parents inhabited; and he occasionally assisted his father in his business as a dealer in wool.

In Stratford, at this time, there was a knot of young fellows celebrated for little else beside their idleness, their wit, and their reckless daring. One or two of these were apprenticed to different trades in the town. One had made the voyage, and returned a reckless desperado, although a jovial and most amusing companion; another had served for a brief space in the Low Countries, "the land of pike and caliver," where finding hard knocks more plentiful than either pay or promotion, and his courage none of the greatest, he had deserted his colours, and returned home with a marvellous capacity for imbibing strong liquors, and relating wondrous stories of his own exploits whilst a soldier:—

> "Of healths *five* fathom deep,
> Of palisadoes, frontiers, parapets,
> And all the current of the heady fight."

With these youths young Shakespeare had before been in the habit of associating. Their eccentricity amused him; there was a kind of character in their lives which he loved to contemplate. Before his marriage he had loved however to indulge his thoughts a good deal alone, to wander and meditate amidst the delicious scenery in the neighbourhood. Now it was somewhat different, he had home and its duties to attend to, besides matters connected with his father's business, to keep him from so continually excursionizing as heretofore.

His meetings with these choice and master spirits, these jolly companions who "daffed the world aside, and bid it pass," were, therefore, for the most part, in after hours, and when the business of the day was over.

Besides these lads of mettle, there was another person whose company young Shakespeare had of late much affected, and in whose society he found a perfect fund of entertainment, a feeling which was quite mutual, as this friend was of a capacity as fully to appreciate the extraordinary talents and delightful society of the juvenile poet, as the latter was to enjoy the wit and humour of his entertainer.

This person, who was a resident at Stratford, although not a native there, was a most singular compound. He was possessed of some property in the town; but his expenditure was generally greater than his means warranted, and he was consequently obliged often to eke out his funds by laying his companions under contribution. He was ever in difficulties, and yet ever jovial, hospitable, and with his friends around him. His eccentricity, his wit, and his follies were a continual feast to young Shakespeare; his absurdities, and the scrapes he got into, a continual tax upon his intimates to get him respectably clear of. By the sober and puritanical of the townsfolks he was detested, for he made them the subject of his biting jests. By the respectable citizen he was feared as an intimate, for his tongue was a continual libel upon all his acquaintance. By the more light-hearted and careless, who laughed *with* him and *at* him, he was tolerated, and even sought after, for his amusing qualities.

In his person, the man was as singular as in his disposition—fat, and unwieldy in figure; he was upwards of six feet in height, with a round ruddy face, in which the laughing features were lost amidst the puffed-out cheeks and double chin—a sort of figure and face, which looked as if the owner had been fat and full of jollity at the time of his birth, and gone on increasing up to his present age.

What was the history of his former life none could tell, for he had come a stranger to the town. Some said, however, that in his youth he had been engaged in the wars of the Netherlands, and cashiered for cowardice; others affirmed that he was the discarded steward of some noble, dismissed for arrant knavery and dishonest practices; whilst by others, again, he was said to have been the host of a low tavern, situated in the purlieus of Whitefriars of London, and, that having amassed a small competency, he had since pretty well dissipated it, and was now living at Stratford to be out of the way.

Be that, however, as it may, at the period of our story he resided at a sort of tavern or hostel, situated in the suburbs of the town, and which hostel himself and yoke fellows principally occupied, leading a roaring, rollicking life, to the great scandal of the more steady portions of the community.

In this society young Shakespeare heard many things which considerably augmented his store of knowledge. The soldier described "the toil o' the war," and the abuses of the service he had been in, where "preferment went by letter and affection." The adventurer told of seas, "whose yeasty waves confound and swallow navigation up;' of islands full of noises, and peopled by strange monsters; and the fat host spoke of the "cities usuries," "the art o' the Court," and the adventures and intrigues himself had been the hero of in various localities from his youth upwards.

In proportion to the pleasure young Shakespeare took in this society, was the dislike entertained for it by his wife; for the character of the presiding genius of the tavern she was well aware of, together with his fondness for, and capacity of, imbibing strong liquors, and carrying them steadily. His professed libertinism, and light opinion of the whole sex, —his impudent boast of favours received from several of the good dames of the town, and the various cudgellings he had received from their husbands—each and all of these matters had been industriously poured into her ear by her female gossipers, with the additional information, that the unwieldy gentleman, notwithstanding his unfitness for such exploits, was much given to walking, or rather riding, by moonlight; and, with his more active friends, making free with a stray haunch occasionally, at the expense of the neighbouring gentry. Nay, it was even affirmed, that some of the midnight excursions of himself and followers had not been entirely for the purpose of coney-catching and deer-stealing, but that more than once they had stopped certain travellers between Coventry and Warwick, and eased them of their cash.

As he was, however, well known to be one of the most arrant cowards that ever buckled on a rapier, this latter story was for the most part disbelieved, as far as he was concerned.

Be that as it may, the companionship of the eccentric John Froth and his yoke-fellows was not likely to lead a youth of the free, unsuspicious, and generous disposition of young Shakespeare into any good employment, and that his wife well knew and as roundly told him of. Had her advice been well-timed, and gently given, perhaps it might have produced its effect; but unhappily, the fair Anne possessed a shrewd temper and little tact.

"In bed he slept not for her urging it,
At board he fed not, for her urging it,
Alone, it was the subject of her theme;
In company she often glanced at it."

And therefore came it that the man was wretched. In short, his sleep was hindered by her railings; his head made light, and his meat sauced with her upbraidings; so that he was driven, for relief, to associate the more with the very companions his wife was so jealous of.

"Sweet recreation barred, what doth ensue,
But moody and dull melancholy—
Kinsman to grim and comfortless despair;
The venom clamours of a jealous woman,
Poison more deadly than a mad dog's tooth."

Perhaps one great charm young Shakespeare felt in the society of his fat friend, was the faculty he seemed to possess of enjoying every moment of his life to the utmost. He turned everything to mirth. Nothing could for a moment damp his spirits, unless his fears for his own personal safety were aroused; and, even then, he was the more amusing, from the very absurdity of his apprehensions, labouring, as he did, to persuade those who so well knew his infirmity, of the heroic nature of his disposition.

It was, indeed, in consequence of the amusement to be derived from this latter failing, that he had been once or twice invited by his companions to join in several of their poaching expeditions. The state of alarm he had been in, and the difficulties his associates had led him into, having furnished, even himself, with an endless theme of amusement after the exploit was over.

CHAPTER XXXII.

THE HOSTEL.

At the present time, when every street and thoroughfare of a country town has its public-house filled with the noisy refuse of an overwhelming population, and absolutely roaring with ribaldry, many of our readers have but a faint idea of the quiet comfort and cozy appearance of a hostel in the olden time. Its ample kitchen hung around with articles and implements of the good wife's occupation, the chance guests, for the most part, assembled in such apartment, and the quiet retirement of its other rooms, engaged, as they not unfrequently were, by some well-to-do retired person, half sportsman, half soldier, who paid his shot weekly, and was dependent upon chance customers, and mine host, for companionship.

Such guest not unfrequently dubbed himself gentleman, upon the strength of possessing a half-starved steed and a couple of greyhounds. Sportsman he was, of course, for every man professed knowledge of, and had a taste for, field sports, when England was less cultivated, and her woods and wastes teemed with game.

The tavern we have named as the residence of Master Froth, was called the Lucy Arms, because upon its sign were displayed the three white pike fish, or lucies, which had been the cognomen of the knights of Charlecote from the time of the Crusades downwards.

Inn signs were, indeed, in former days for the most part of an heraldic character. Many of the town residences of the nobility and the great ecclesiastics were sometimes called inns, and in the front of them the family arms displayed. Such inns afterwards became appropriated to the purpose of the hostel, and the armorial decorations retained, under the denomination of signs, directed the guest to them as places of accommodation and refreshment. This we retain even in the present degenerate age, the signs of the white, red, black, and golden lions of the Crusades; and the blue boars, golden crosses, swans, dragons, and dolphins, which ornamented the knightly helmet or shield, now do duty at the entrance of the beer-shop.

"Thus chances mock and changes fill the cup of alteration."

It was one evening in the merry month of May, about a year after the marriage of young Shakespeare, that Jack Froth, and several of his associates, were assembled at the Lucy Arms.

The apartment in which they were congregated was one which Froth had appropriated to his own especial use,—a good-sized room, whose windows looked into the orchard in rear of the hostel, one of those sweet and verdant orchards peculiar to the time, and which are now, for the most part, destroyed; but which, in Elizabeth's day, were attached to every goodly dwelling, or hostel, in a country town.

A half-open door, on one side of the apartment, gave a peep into a smaller room, in which, as the sun streamed from the lattice-window, its rays fell upon, and lighted up, the deep red curtains and square-topped hangings of an antique bed; and at the same time gilded the high-backed chairs with which the room was furnished.

On the ample hearth of the first-named apartment two enormous deer-hounds were to be seen, sprawling at full length, their occasional disturbed sleep, and short sharp bark, shewing that their dreams were of the woodland and the chase.

The occupants of the room were five in number. They were seated round a massive oaken table, which placed near the window, gave them a delicious view of the green and bowery orchard.

The fat and jovial Froth, "the lord o' the feast," as he leaned back in his strong oaken chair, whilst he occasionally looked out upon the orchard, listened to the recital of some verses his opposite neighbour was reading aloud. Seated directly opposite the window was a tall thin man, of about five-and-twenty years of age, clad in the faded suit of an officer of pikemen, an enormous rapier tacked to his waist, with dagger to match. His chair being drawn so close to the table that he sat bolt-upright, and, as he dallied with the glass he ever and anon carried to his lips, he also listened with attention to the words of the poem.

Opposite to him sat another man, about thirty years of age, clad in a tawdry suit, which in our own days would have been shrewdly suspected of having done duty on the boards of a theatre. Beside him, with apron doffed, and his cap thrown aside, sat mine host of the tavern—a portly and jolly-looking companion.

Such was the party assembled, and, as the reader finished the fragment of verse, his hearers seemed so much interested in its recital that for some moments there was a pause of expectation. It was like the expiring sound of sweet music, which has a soothing effect upon the listener, making him long for a renewal of the melody.

"There is more?" said Froth, inquiringly, as he turned his eye upon the reader.

"No more have I written," said young Shakespeare, who was indeed the reader of the poetry; "nor deemed I this deformed offspring of my brain worthy of notice."

"Then I pr'ythee, good William," said Froth, "repair thy voice by another draught of Canary, and give the two first verses over again."

"Has my verse, then, so much pleased you?" inquired Shakespeare.

"It hath more than pleased, it has delighted me," said Froth; "so to't again, lad."

"Two verses you shall have," said Shakespeare, smiling, "but no more." And he again read from his manuscript the following lines of a poem he had that morning commenced writing,—

"Even as the sun with purple-coloured face—"

"'Fore gad, bully host," interrupted Froth, "but thy countenance at this moment, round, fiery, and covered with huge angry welks and knobs, must have suggested that line. Was't not so, sweet William; didst thou not call the sun's face purple-coloured from the reflection of our host's mulberry visage?"

"Go to, go to," said the host; "'fore gad, if my face took but a tithe of the good vivers to keep it in colour that thine doth, I were altogether a ruined landlord."

"I cry you mercy, good William," said Froth; proceed with thy stanzas. Mine host here is one of those prating knaves who would rather talk than listen, let who will be the orator."

And the poet again read from his manuscript,—

"Even as the sun with purple-coloured face
  Had ta'en his last leave of the weeping morn,
Rose cheeked, Adonis hied him to the chase;
  Hunting he loved, but love he laugh'd to scorn.
Sick-thoughted Venus makes amain unto him,
And, like a bold-faced suitor, 'gins to woo him.
'Thrice fairer than myself'—thus she began:
  'The field's chief flower, sweet above compare,
Stain to all nymphs, more lovely than a man,
  More white and red than doves or roses are.
Nature that made thee with herself at strife,
Saith that the world hath ending with thy life.'"

"And how call ye the poem?" inquired Froth, as young Shakespeare finished the second verse, and then thrust the paper into the breast of his doublet.

"I think of calling it 'Venus and Adonis,'" he said, "for fault of a better name."

"Call it what thou wilt, lad," said Froth, "'tis a glorious commencement. Like everything else thou dost, 'tis excellent."

"Ha, ha," said Pierce Caliver, "thou art full of thy ropery, Froth; thou word'st him, thou word'st him. See, he blusheth at thy praise."

"I word him not, but as I mean," said Froth; "an his cheek blusheth, 'tis more than thine was ever guilty of. I hate flattery as I hate an unfilled flasket in the woodlands at midnight. He hath but one fault, that lad."

"Ah, a fault," said Caliver, "can Will Shakespeare own a fault in thy eyes? I pr'ythee let's hear it."

"Nay, 'tis not a fault, either, 'tis a misfortune," said Froth, "he's married."

"Gad-a-mercy, that is indeed a scrape to get into!" said Ralph Careless. "I have been twice across the Atlantic, escaped shipwreck as often, been left for dead amongst the burning huts of a Spanish settlement; and yet have I never had such an escape as when I offered marriage to the Widow Crooke, and she altered her mind a week before the day fixed."

"That widow must be worthy looking on too," said Froth; "for truly her own escape exceedeth all thine put together."

"How so?" said Careless.

"In escaping from thee," returned Froth.

"Nay, the evil-favoured old hag," said Careless; "but she escaped not altogether scot-free either, since I drew a handsome forfeit ere I consented to let her break off."

"Had she given thee all she possessed," said Froth, "so she kept herself free of thee, she had the luck on't; but, come, the very name of marriage hath made our good William here a melancholy man. Oh! 'tis monstrous that tying together of couples for life, to claw and tear like a brace of tabbies cast over a clothes' line! Said I well, William? Why, fill again, and pass the flasket."

"Nay," said Shakespeare, "wooing, wedding, and repenting is, after all, but a Scotch jig, a measure, and a cinque pace. The first suit is hot and hasty, like a Scotch jig, and full as fantastical; the wedding mannerly and modest;* and then comes repentance, and with his two legs fallen into a cinque pace, faster and faster, till he sink into his grave."

"Methinks, bullies," said the Host, "since we are on the subject of matrimony, that we must quaff a health for the nonce. Heard'st thou not that our good William here is the honoured father of a fair son—a goodly boy?"

"Ah, by St. Jago and charge Spain!" said Caliver, "and is it so? Why, then fill to the brim, my masters all;" and the health of the infant was pledged in flowing bumpers of Canary. After which, the long-necked glasses were flourished to a loud huzza, and being cast overhead, smashed upon the rushes with which the apartment was strewed.

"And now," said Froth, "thou shalt give us a song, William—a song of thine own, for what man amidst us could produce a verse worthy of thee to sing? Come, warble, and let it be to thine own words, Will."

"A song—a song!" said Caliver; "give us one, William, in praise of the wine-cup."

Shakespeare smiled, and then sang:

"Come, thou monarch of the vine,
Plumpy Bacchus, with pink eyne;
In thy vats our cares be drown'd,
With thy grapes our hairs be crown'd:
Cup us, till the world go round,
Cup us, till the world go round."

* "Much ado about Nothing."

Whilst the chorus was ringing out, till every room in the hostel echoed with it, another individual entered the apartment.

The new comer was a tall, good-looking youth, clad in a worn leathern jerkin, which seemed as if it had endured the worst spite of the elements, and done duty in the woods for many years. His russet boots were drawn up to the thigh, and his well-worn wide-brimmed beaver was without feather or ornament, except a large assortment of fish-hooks, with the horse-hair twisted around it. In short, he looked what he really was—a dissolute hanger-on of a country town, and yet a good fellow withal, one given to the sports of the field, without means or license to pursue them—one of Diana's foresters, a poacher, a professed deer-stealer.

"You keep a goodly revel here, my masters," said he, drawing a chair, and seating himself unceremoniously at the table.

"Ha! what, Diccon Snare, is it thou, thou wandering knight of the hollow woods?" said Froth. "By my troth, thou art welcome; fill thyself a chalice for the nonce. How goes all at Warwick?"

"I scarcely know," said Snare, "since I have not been there for some days. If I have news at all, it is of these parts, and farther afield. There is work for you to-night an ye listen. The old Pike of Charlecote hath ridden forth, and taken in his train some thirty followers. The moon is up to be sure, but then the woodlands are but badly watched."

"And how know'st thou this, thou sworn enemy of an outlying stag?" inquired Shakespeare.

"How know I it? Why, from sure intelligence, and careful watching. How else should I know my trade?"

"Nay, thou hast served a pretty apprenticeship to the poaching trade, Diccon, that's certain," said Froth, "as the hangman's brand can testify! And what takes Sir Thomas to town with so strong an escort?"

"It seems there is more trouble at Court about the Queen of Scots," said Snare, "and her name is again mixed up with all sorts of intrigues and plots against our Queen. My Lord of Leicester hath stroked the beard of consideration upon the matter, and set on foot an association for the nonce. They are sworn keepers of the Queen's safety in life, and doubly sworn to revenge her death, should she fall by these malignant conspirators. A great many of the gentry around have gone up to join in this association, whilst the Queen of Scots is again placed in more severe keeping."

"Ha!" said Froth, "I heard somewhat of this before; and so—"

"And so," continued Snare, "Sir Thomas in great state hath set forth towards town, and sleeps to-night at Kenilworth, where the great Bear-ward at present lies."

"So that several of his foresters follow in his train, eh! is't so?"

"They do; he rides in state, for, as thou knowest, 'tis the pride of the old Pike to be followed by a whole troop. I saw him pass along the road as I lay perdue in the covert. Twenty of his fellows in coat and badge, with green and yellow feathers in their hats,* and as many falconers to make up the train."

"And that in truth makes a fair field for us," said Shakespeare. "What say ye, my masters all? Shall we be minions of the moon tonight? Shall we strike a buck at Charlecote?"

To men of the wild and peculiar disposition of the assembled party, nothing could be more pleasant than an excursion of the sort.

A midnight visit to the woodlands was by no means an uncommon circumstance in their lives; but hitherto they had pursued their sport in localities somewhat more removed from the town in which they dwelt. To the bold and imaginative Shakespeare, as his eye glanced into the moonlit orchard, the excursion had charms known only to himself. He had once or twice before watched the deer in the glades of Fulbrook, and he now joined in the expedition heart and hand.

Preparations were accordingly forthwith commenced, and the entire party made themselves ready for an exploit, which in those days, and with such men, was attended with something more of circumstance than in our own.

In the first place, a large closet in the bedchamber of the portly Froth was ransacked for such change of garment as was necessary for pushing through the more thick and tangled cover. Cross-bows and other weapons of the chase were then lugged out, and, amongst other articles, a sort of theatrical dress was produced; and being carefully packed up, was strapped upon the shoulder of Diccon Snare, to be used as occasion might serve.

This latter article of apparel had been purloined from the wardrobe of a company of masquers, who were in the habit of visiting Stratford. It was neither more nor less than the dress of "*Mors, or dreary Death*," a character then enacting in one of the tedious moral plays of the period.

It was fashioned so as to represent a skeleton; and seen in the woodlands in the night, would be likely to scare a forester out of his wits, and consequently, should the party be molested during their exploit, enables them to escape without collision or discovery.

By the time the party had indued their forest gear, the curfew proclaimed that it was time for them to set out; and once more seating themselves round the board, they arranged their plan of proceedings.

"Now, my masters all," said Froth, "a cup to hearten us, and another to the success of our venture, and then to horse."

"Let him whose courage fails remain here," said Caliver; "and let those to horse whose feet cannot prop up their bodies."

"No scoffing, lads," said Froth. "Thou knowest I am not able to travel on foot so far, or so fast as thou art; but in the field, I have twice thy skill at a shot."

* People of condition in the country generally rode with numerous followers at the period.

"I have heard thee say so often," said Caliver. "To-night I hope to see a specimen of thy skill."

"Thus be it, then," said Snare. "You and I, Will Shakespeare, will go straight to Charlecote Park. By 'ur Lady! we'll strike the best buck in the herd. You, Froth, being mounted, will accompany us, and remain without the park in readiness to receive the deer when we have struck it. You, Careless and Caliver, will walk apart lower down, and give us notice in case of approach."

"I like not that lying-out work, and alone too," said Froth. "The last time I played receiver on Wolvey Heath, I was nearly captured. He that dies a martyr, 'tis said, proves that he is not a knave. But, methinks, 'tis not so sure that he proves himself no fool."

"And wherefore art thou and Will Shakespeare to have the best of the sport?" said Careless. "Methinks, since you say the chase is left to take care of itself to-night, we might all four be strikers, and make a good venture on't."

"Nay," said Snare, "be it as you will. Will Shakespeare here is sound in wind and limb. You are both of ye but broken-down hacks at best, and, if you take my advice, will lie perdue without the palings; for, an we be molested, we shall have a smart run for it, I promise ye."

Having made their arrangements and laid the plot of their proceedings, the party soon after divided, and left the hostel by different doors. Shakespeare, Snare, and Froth, the latter mounted on horseback, and disguised in a sort of countryman's frock, took the road; whilst Caliver and Careless, leaving by the back door, crossed the orchard, and making a slight detour to the right, joined them about a mile from the town.

Scarcely had the party left the Lucy Arms a quarter of an hour ere Pouncet Grasp, accompanied by Master Doubletongue and a couple of ill-looking companions, entered it.

"Ah," said Grasp, peering about, and snifting like a terrier dog in search of a rabbit; "ah, Host, is your honoured guest, Master John Froth, within?"

The host of the Lucy Arms had an instinctive dread and a most unalterable dislike to the lawyer. He considered a visit from him little inferior in omen to that of a visit from the plague. He accordingly busied himself about some matter or other, and pretended not to observe Grasp.

"Not within?—eh, Host?" said the latter, making a sign to his two attendants, who immediately planted themselves at the front and back doors of the premises. "I am sorely unlucky in my visits, Host. An it please you, permit me to observe *myself* if Master John Froth hath in reality gone abroad."

"Hast thou business, Master Grasp," inquired the Host, "with mine honoured guest to-night? If so, I take it the best way would be to confide it to me, or call again. I have said it: Master John Froth *hath* gone forth to-night."

"Business," said Grasp; "ah, to be sure; 'business, like time, stays for no man,' as the saying goes. Why, yes, I have a slight trifle of business; albeit I may not confide it to thee. Certes, I *will* call again. Wilt thou meantime draw me a tankard ere I depart?"

Whilst the host busied himself in drawing the liquor called for, and which he immediately set about, in the hope of speedily getting rid of the trio, Grasp sauntered into the passage, and peeped into the private apartment of Froth, in order to be sure he was really out, and then whispered to his two neighbours to make a shew of leaving the house by the back way, and quietly conceal themselves in the orchard.

That done, he returned to the kitchen, drank off his liquor, and bade the host good night.

Scarce had he gone a dozen paces, however, ere he returned stealthily, and watching without the window till the host for some purpose left the kitchen, he very quietly re-entered it, and concealed himself there.

CHAPTER XXXIII.

THE DEER STEALERS.

The Lucy family we have already had occasion to notice as descended from an ancient and honourable house. They might indeed say with Christopher Sly—"We came in with Richard Conqueror," since they have in truth, occupied an important position in England for many centuries.

The mansion of Charlecote, at the period of our story, stood in the midst of a park or chase much greater in extent than at the present time.

The ground plan of the building forms in shape the Roman capital letter E, perhaps in compliment to the virgin Queen, with whose arms it is decorated. The soft and gentle Avon gliding at the base, and the park, which immediately surrounded the building, was shadowed by oaks of great age, which gradually gave place to brake and thicket, almost impenetrable in some parts to aught save the hound or the game he followed. This again was relieved at intervals by open spaces of great beauty, in which the fern grew in wild luxuriance, and hundreds of broad short-stemmed oaks, at distant intervals, threw their huge branches over the green surface, as if rejoicing in their unconfined luxuriance. In such spots, so bright and fresh in the pale light of the moon, the fern decked with liquid dew, and the branches of the trees glittering with bright drops, the fairies might well be imagined to hold their sequestered revels.

Every glade and bosky bourne, every tree and fern-clad undulation, was a scene peculiarly adapted to the elfin and the fay. They seemed to tell, in their sweetness, and their unmolested seclusion, of the innocent ages of an early world, when faun and satyr, and nymph and dryad, revelled in the open glade, or reposed on the mossed bank beneath the sheltering boughs.

Stealthily, and with the utmost caution, not a word even whispered, but communicating to each other by signs as they advanced, young Shakespeare and Diccon Snare slowly emerged from the more thick cover upon one of these picturesque glades, and took their stand behind a huge oak—

> "An oak whose boughs were moss'd with age,
> And big top bald with dry antiquity."

"We near the herd," said Shakespeare, in a gentle whisper to his companion.

"We do so," said Snare, "a few yards more and we shall get within shot, thanks to our care in gaining the wind, and, look ye, there they be! You can just see their antlered heads above the long white grass in yonder open space."

"We must be wary in our approach," said Shakespeare, in a whisper; "tread softly, that the blind mole may not hear a footfall."

"'Twere best to lay along and drag ourselves to yonder blasted oak," said Snare. "Be careful and keep where the fern is less thick. The slightest unnatural movement of the herbage, and they are off."

So saying, Snare lay flat on the ground, and began to worm himself towards the tree he had mentioned, Shakespeare doing the same and following close in his wake; and so quietly and cautiously did they continue their serpent-like course, that a looker-on would hardly have discovered the track they took except by the occasional movements of the long grass and fern.

Every now and then the crafty Snare lay perfectly quiet for a few moments, and then cautiously raising his bare head, looked forth to see if the herd were still unconscious of their approach.

Nothing could be more lovely than the entire scene, as it was looked upon by Shakespeare. Before and around him lay the wild chase, the deer couched "in their own confines," and nearly hidden in the long thick grass of ages—himself in a spot which, except under the peculiar circumstance in which he sought it, he could scarce have beheld the game so near,—those magnificent and antlered monarchs of waste, be it remembered. For in Elizabeth's day, and in the extensive parks of the great, the stag was a wilder and fiercer creature than the same animal domesticated as they are, from the confined space in which they are necessarily kept.

The danger attendant on the situation also lent its charm to one of his bold and ardent spirit. As his eye glanced amidst the magnificent scenery, his imagination was instantly carried back to the days of the early English kings, when Britain was one entire forest, waste or wold; and when, even at an after period, the conquering Norman had lain waste whole districts to give room for the chase. Then again, with the shifting change of thought, his imagination bodied forth the fabled beings of an earlier age. The mossed carpet on which he stood, the venerable trees around, the sweet scent of the fern, and the perfumed air of the fresh forest, as the dews of summer night fell around him, suggested those magnificent thoughts, peculiar to himself, and which in after life produced descriptions unequalled for beauty in any age. He was

"With Hercules and Cadmus,
When in a wood of Crete they bay'd the bear
With hounds of Sparta.
Besides the groves,
The skies, the fountains, every region near
Seemed all one mutual cry."

Meantime whilst the mind of Shakespeare was impressed with the beauty of the situation, as well as interested in the sport, the less imaginative Snare, with his whole soul intent upon slaughter, and with all the cunning of his craft, his body flattened against the huge tree, one hand keeping his companion back, the other grasping his cross-bow, again cautiously peered out into the glade before him.

This was a moment of intense interest to the deer-stealers. They found themselves so close upon the wild and magnificent animals that they could see their slightest movement.

There is, indeed, something inexpressibly exciting to the hunter or the deer stalker in thus finding himself in the midst of the herd, a spy upon them in their security, conscious at the same time that the slightest movement or mistake on his own part will ruin the hours of toil he has previously spent in gaining his position.

A magnificent stag lay a little to the right, and nearest to Shakespeare; he touched his companion lightly on the shoulder, and by a sign signified that he meant to fire at it.

Snare stretched his neck and peeped over his shoulder. As he did so, Shakespeare saw, that with the instinctive knowledge and jealousy of their nature, the herd were becoming aware that danger was in their close vicinity.

In an instant their heads were thrown back, the next moment Snare heard at some distance that short guttural noise, so peculiar to the deer at particular seasons of the year, and as the splendid animal upon which Shakespeare had fixed his eye caught the sound, it leaped to its feet and bounded from the spot, the whole herd in an instant also flying like the wind towards the cover, seemed to vanish into the mists of night; but ere his companion could stay his hand, Shakespeare had raised his bow to his shoulder and fired. The shot struck the deer just behind the shoulder, and the animal bounding into the air, fell struggling amongst the fern.

"Hark!" said Snare, as the same guttural sounds were again heard in the woods. "You should not have fired. 'Tis the signal from our comrades. The keepers are at hand."

"May the fiend take them," said Shakespeare.

"So say I," returned Snare; "but an we take not especial care, they will take us; for look ye, the startled herd will sweep by them yonder, and they will be upon us anon; and see, that huge beast is kicking and struggling like a dying ox,—quick, good William, strike roundly in and cut his throat."

So saying, Snare gave all his attention to the direction in which the sounds came, whilst Shakespeare, dashing upon the stag, seized the animal by the horns. There was then a short and desperate struggle, and with his sharp dagger he cut the creature's throat. He then as swiftly rejoined his companion. Scarcely had he done so ere they were both aware of the approach of the keepers, who having observed the affrighted herd, and at the same time noticed the peculiar sounds given by the watchers, and which were somewhat out of season, came directly upon them.

"We might easily shew them a clean pair of heels, and join the bulky Froth without the palings," whispered Snare; "but we must have yonder beast at all hazards; and we can but make a fight of it if it come to the worst. Down with thee, good Will, flat in the fern. Here they come—I see them plainly in yonder glade." So saying, Snare threw himself on the ground close beside Shakespeare, and immediately divesting himself of his jerkin and hat, rose up again a most grisly object—neither more nor less than Mors, or Dreary Death. Meanwhile the rangers came quickly on, four in number, and each armed with cross-bows and a short barbed spear.

They advanced to within about a bow-shot from the tree behind which Snare and Shakespeare were concealed, when the former, slowly gliding from behind its stem, advanced directly upon them.

The first sight of such an apparition, seen but indistinctly amongst the huge boughs, brought the whole party to a stand, They but half made out its hideous outline, when it emerged into the clear moonlight, and seemed gliding upon them, "a bare-ribbed death, horrible to sight." To say the keepers were frightened would be to say little. They were at first paralysed, and then turning, they fled like the wind; whilst Snare immediately again threw himself flat on his face, and was lost to sight amongst the fern; so that, as the keepers looked back whilst they fled, the apparition had apparently vanished into the earth.

Rejoining Shakespeare, Snare now resumed his outward garment; and taking advantage of the panic, both hastily approached the deer, and securing its legs, fastened them on a quarter-staff which they had supported on their shoulders, they then hastened across the glade.

So soon as they had gained the park palings, and which at this period, and at this part, ran across a deep sandy lane, they threw down their burden; and casting themselves on the ground to regain breath after their rapid flight, listened attentively. In a few moments a huge broad-backed countryman, clad in the loose frock of a miller's man, mounted upon a strong-jointed horse, and carrying an empty sack on the pommel of the saddle, rode past.

"You ride late, Master Miller," said Shakespeare, as he clambered over the palings.

"Nay; rather I ride early, Master Forester," returned the other. "Hast anything for the mill to-night?"

"I have, good Froth," said Shakespeare; "but is there a clear coast?"

"By the mass! I think there be. Be quick, however, for three of Sir Thomas's fellows have passed this spot not a quarter of an hour back."

"Good!" said Shakespeare. "Then hand me thy meal bag." And the horseman threw his sack to Shakespeare, as Snare at the same moment heaved the carcase of the deer over the paling, and then following himself, the sack was quickly drawn over the body of the deer, and it was thrown across the horse, the trio making the best of their way along the deep sandy lane towards Stratford.

As they emerged from the lane upon a rushy mead, and left the boundary of the park, a low whistle was heard, which they answered. Soon afterwards they were joined by their companions, and enveloped in mists of the swampy ground they traversed.

It was about the hour when "night is at odds with morning which is which" that the party we have before seen assembled at the Lucy Arms once more entered its hospitable doors. Quietly, and with considerable caution, however, they stole in, one of them bearing upon his shoulders, nay, round his neck as it were, with the hind and fore legs protruding before him, the carcase of a goodly stag. This latter bent his tall form, as he was ushered into the kitchen of the hostel, and threw his heavy burthen upon the floor, whilst his companions and mine host, by the light of the fire, and in great glee, proceeded to examine it.

"By 'ur Lady, a fine beast," said the host. "Why, Will Shakespeare, this is even a better night's work than when you shot that beast in Fulbrook."

"A stag of ten, my masters all," said Froth. "'Fore gad, I am well nigh exhausted with long fasting and sharp watching. A cup of wine, mine host, a cup of wine to Sir Thomas Lucy's health."

Whilst the host produced his wine, and Froth and Careless seated themselves on the settle beneath the chimney, Snare and Shakespeare were busily engaged in skinning the stag, which having quickly accomplished, they as speedily cut it up, and disposed of the several portions in such places of security and concealment as the host pointed out. After which, the skin and the antlered head were thrust into the meal-bag, and carried into the orchard, where Shakespeare dug a hole and buried it.

That done they returned to the kitchen, and mine host having spread a table and furnished it with liquors, some rashers were cut from the carcase of the deer, and fried, and eaten with a relish only known to men who had spent a night in the forest glades watching and killing the stag from which they were taken.

"By 'ur Lady, my lads," said Froth, as he washed down these delicious morsels, hot from the fire, with large draughts of mine host's best ale, "this is the best part of the night's work. O I like not that lonely watching beneath the moon's rays. Give me the tankard and a savoury collop after the deed is done, and spare me the toil of the action. And yet, lads, an I had met yonder caitiff-keepers, I should have found them in work, I promise ye."

"No doubt," said Caliver; "it would have taken them all four to have carried thy fat paunch to the cage."

"I taken to the cage!" said Froth, "I would have cudgelled them to mummy."

"Ha, Cavaliero," said the host, "thou would'st have smote, thou would'st have foined, thou would'st have traversed, eh, ere limbo should have held thy portly body? And that reminds me, Lawyer Grasp, with two imps of the evil one, was here to-night inquiring for thee."

"Ah!" said Froth, turning rather blank, and setting down the tankard. "The peaking knave, then, hath entered the action against me for Master Doubletongue's debt. Would I had been at home, my lads, we would have tossed the caitiff in a blanket."

"Nay, Host," said Pierce Caliver, "I had rather myself not come in contact with that Grasp; by the same token, I owe moneys too. Therefore keep fast your doors while I am within them."

"My hand upon it," said the host; "I will keep all fast till noon; and none shall have egress or regress. Said I well, lads, eh?"

"You did, Host," said Careless' for I, too, would as lief walk with the receipt of fernseed by daylight."

"And now, my lads all," said Snare, "let us have one song, and then a nap; after that to seek our several destinations. I am for Warwick when day breaks."

"And I for Monkspath," said Careless.

"And I for Stoneleigh," said Caliver.

"And I for home," said Shakespeare, with a look of mock solemnity, where——"

"Where thou wilt be finely clapper-clawed for being out all night," said the host. "Such it is to be a married man—ha! ha! A young man married is a man that's marred. But truly, Will, thou art not yet married; thou canst hit a buck by moonlight with the best of us; so, I pry'thee, give us that song of thine about the horns, and we'll all join in chorus."

Shakespeare accordingly commenced the following glee, Snare and the others taking part, and joining chorus:—

Shak. What shall he have that killed the deer? *
Snare. His leather skin and horns to wear.
Shak. Then sing him home.
Chorus. Take thou no scorn, to wear the horn,
It was a crest ere thou wast born,
Shak. Thy father's father wore it.
Snare. And thy own father bore it.
Chorus. The horn, the horn, the lusty horn,
Is not a thing to laugh to scorn.

* "As you like it."

The first faint light of the breaking dawn, as it gradually appeared through the diamond-paned window, found the entire party wrapped in slumber.

The fat and jovial Froth, with his huge legs stretched out before him, his portly body thrown back, and the tankard fast-clutched in his hand, showed by his apoplectic breathing, the heaviness of his slumbers.

Shakespeare, somewhat fatigued by the night's exertions, sat opposite, with his head on his folded arms.

Snare was down full length before the expired fire upon the hearth; and the others were disposed on either side.

Not a sound was heard, except the prolonged chorus of the sleepers, and the chirping of the cricket; when from beneath a large table at the farther end of the kitchen, and where he had lain concealed, the head of Pouncet Grasp was protruded. Stealthily, and with the greatest caution, he listened to the heavy breathing of the sleepers. He then as carefully emerged from his hiding-place, and stole on tip-toe towards the party, identifying each individual as he did so, and putting down his name in a small tablet he drew from the breast of his doublet.

"Oh, oh," he whispered to himself, as he closed the tablets, after writing down the name of William Shakespeare; "here is a precious nest of ye."

"Ah! ah!" he continued, as he stepped to the door, and carefully opening it, looked back ere he departed. "Here's a delicious job for a man to stumble upon! A good night's work you have made on't, Master William Shakespeare, have ye? Yes, and a precious piece of work have ye all made on't. A Star-Chamber matter will Sir Thomas make of this, as sure as my name is Grasp." So saying, he quietly opened the back door, and stole out to join the followers whom he had left in the orchard.

"Shall I call the other men, and make the capture, Master Grasp?" inquired one of his myrmidons in a whisper. "Not to-night, good Giles," said the lawyer. "By no means to-night. There is a precious fellowship within there; and they may capture us! Besides, I have found out a plot—a monstrous plot—a damnable plot—and yet a lovely plot—a most sweet piece of villany!"

"A monstrous plot!" said the constable; "What is't, another conspiracy to murder the Queen?"

"Worse," said Grasp. "Now, listen and perpend. Thou knowest Sir Thomas Lucy hath of late lost more than one deer?"

"I do," said the constable.

"Well, an he hath lost them, I have found them."

"Where?" eagerly inquired the constable.

"Here, in this veritable inn," said Grasp.

"And when?" inquired the constable.

"Why, now, even now: go to—see what it is to bear a brain."

"Nay, then, Master Grasp," said the constable, "if su the case, I also have a discovery to tell of."

"Ah!" said Grasp, "what is it?"

"Whilst we lay perdue in yonder corner of the orchard. But, stay, dost see that tree there with the spade against it?"

"I do," said Grasp, eagerly.

"With that spade, and under the third tree in line therewith, did Will Shakespeare dig a hole this night, and into that hole did Diccon Snare bury a something concealed in a sack."

"Ha! say'st thou; by my faith the skin of the stolen deer," said Grasp, "as I'm a lawyer. Let us mark the tree; and now, my lads, I have ye emmeshed in a lovely web. No noise, ye knaves," he continued to his men, "but get through the hedge and away."

"Ha! ha! Master William Shakespeare," he said, as he followed his two ill-looking myrmidons. "Now, will I to Sir Thomas Lucy, of Charlecote, knight and magistrate, and then will we let the law loose upon ye."

CHAPTER XXXIV.

THE ADVENTURE.

OUR situation as recorder of events connected with this history, whilst it enables us to look from an elevated position upon those connected with our story, enables us also to transport our readers, with a thought, from pole to pole. Nay, we can even rival the swift flight of Puck, if we so will it, and "put a girdle round about the earth in somewhat less than forty minutes."

In virtue of this power, we therefore take leave to transport our readers upon the "sightless couriers of the air," and bid them look down upon the main of waters several thousand miles from the scene of our last chapter—even to the watery wastes which wash the coast of Florida.

A small speck—an atom—is seen slowly and laboriously making its way over the broad waves of the Atlantic. Steadily and beautifully, as we obtain a nearer view, does she seem to mount upon the rolling surge, and then again sink down into the vale of waters, almost lost to sight between the liquid mountains which follow each other in succession, apparently from end to end of the world.

How awfully grand is the situation! How curious to consider is the intellect, courage, and perseverance of those who guide that barque through such an unknown waste! The dreadful winds roaring above them, and beneath the multitudinous waters descending, "where fathom line would never find the ground," one touch of an unseen rock, one bolt starting in the vessel's hull, one unmarked and uncared-for blast of wind, one spark alighting in a crevice, and that vessel and all that it contains, unknown, unseen, is resolved into the vast tide, and washed amidst the atoms contained in its dark waters. Months have passed since the Falcon left the river which flows up to that old Dutch-built Cinque Port where our readers may remember to have last seen her. Steadily hath the wanderer held on day after day, through fair and foul, into the dark waste, alone, like some atom upon the surface, and still breasting the wave, as if eternity was before her in those rolling seas.

Strange that the spirit of adventure should sustain men in such a hopeless-looking wilderness! That the desire of finding new worlds, or their greed after gold, should take them from all they hold dear in their own land. Such, however, is the motive which actuates the major part of the crew of that labouring barque, whilst to one alone amongst them, and who seems the chief of the party, the secret spring which is indeed the prime mover of the adventure, is love.

The youthful Count, then, whilst he leads on his followers under the idea of new discoveries, great gains, and hatred of the Spaniard, is, in truth, seeking for one who has either perished by wreck or starvation, or is still living in hopeless abandonment or captivity, somewhere amongst these far-away seas.

One only confidant is aware of the secret motive, and that person is our old acquaintance Martin. If then we look within the hull of this small craft, we shall find its interior peopled by some sixty stern-looking and bearded wanderers, high in courage, stern in resolve, the captain and crew who work the vessel, the eccentric and faithful Martin, and one female in disguise, the latter "a count of wealth as well as quality," to all appearance, and who, as proprietor of the vessel and leader of the expedition, seeks ostensibly but to pursue his love of adventure.

In consequence of the inferiority of size, form, and fashion of this vessel, and the unknown ocean they traverse, the Falcon and her war-like fraughtage have been beating about for many a weary week.

It was after being exposed to one of the fearful hurricanes so frequent in these seas, that we now look upon the Falcon and her devoted crew. Tempest-tossed as they had been for some weeks, to their great relief they at length began to find themselves approaching land, and by the delicious fragrance with which the air was loaded—an air which seemed as if it blew from some garden abounding with sweet flowers—they found themselves amongst "the still vext Bermothees," where they resolved to remain for a short time in order to refit.

Strange and unnatural appearances, however, whilst in this, as it first seemed, region of paradise, so astonished the sailors, that after a brief sojourn, the Count was necessitated to hasten his departure—

"The Isle seemed full of noises,
Sounds and sweet airs, that gave delight, and hurt not."

The sailors, too, with characteristic superstition, declared they heard strange voices commanding them to leave the shore,* and, as if to enforce their orders, a dreadful storm of thunder and lightning seemed to

* Such an account was in reality given by the adventurers who sailed with Sir Humphrey Gilbert, the father of our plantations, and the brother of Sir Walter Raleigh, and who was lost in the storm following the portentous sounds we have described. Might not this very incident have suggested to Shakespeare the description of the island in the "Tempest."

rend the very heavens, and darkness settled as a pall around them. Fearful shapes too were said to glare through the murky atmosphere around the ship, and the apparition of the ominous flame, called by seamen "Castor and Pollux," flitted above the mast. These portents were the prelude to a yet more tremendous storm, which threatening to swallow up the little vessel, eventually drove her on an island which runs parallel nearly to the coast of Carolina.

The Count here disembarked, and refreshed his followers, by rest amidst woods and groves of tall cedar trees, around whose trunks wild vines hung in festoons, and the grape seemed so natural to the soil, that the clusters covered the ground and dipt into the ocean.

Again they put to sea, and again they made a strange land filled with new wonders. Here, whilst the adventurers sought the interior of a country they had been led to believe contained cities in which the houses were studded with pearl, the Count and his immediate attendants sought the ruined colony from which Drake had carried off the remnant of followers, previously left by Sir Walter Raleigh. "They after riches hunt; he after love." The dangers and difficulties encountered by both parties it would be difficult to picture; for hunger, heat, wounds, and disease were the portion of the adventurers of Elizabeth's day. Through gloomy swamps they penetrated, and through interminable forests they hewed their way. Many were pierced by the poisoned shaft of the Indian, many died of despair, and many were the victims of serpents, reptiles, and savage beasts; whilst others again died of loathsome diseases unknown in their native land.

Still the Count, the faithful Martin, and their immediate followers held on. They had gained some tidings by which they learnt that a party of wrecked seamen had been carried captive by the natives to a city in the interior of the country; and they resolved to reach them, or perish in the attempt.

'Twas indeed an edifying sight to behold the stripling youth who led that small band. One evidently nurtured in luxury and ease, enduring the extremity of danger, fatigue, hardship, and privation, and lending a fire to his jaded followers by his heroic fortitude and example. What mattered it him, that for days hundreds of half-naked Indians, with their clubs and bows, hovered around his mail-clad band. One moment swarming to the close attack, the next showering flights of arrows from the distance. Still himself and party were resolved to penetrate to the rescue of their countrymen or die; and the little band at length reached the place they sought.

'Twas lucky for the young Count that he had steeled his mind to bear disappointment when he donned the light cuirass which adorned his breast; for himself and followers, on arriving at the capital of the country, found literally nothing to repay their toil. In place of boundless wealth and temples of the sun, the adventurers found a wretched Indian town, which had been sacked and partially burned by a detachment of Spanish soldiers, and who had apparently carried off those they sought as prisoners to their ship.

Here again, therefore, the Christian fortitude of the young Count supported his followers. "Murmur at nothing, comrades," he said. "If our ills are repairable, it is ungrateful; if otherwise, it is vain. There is comfort yet. The Spaniard is assailable, and the Falcon swift of pinion; we will return, embark, and swoop upon the enemy."

Well knowing that the Spaniards always went into the Gulf of Mexico by St. Domingo and Hispaniola, and directed their homeward course by the Gulf of Florida, where they found a continued coast on the west side, trending away north, and then standing to the east to make for Spain, the Captain of the Falcon directed his course accordingly; and guided by report of some barques he fell in with, managed to gain sight of the very vessel they were in search of.

The Spaniard was a huge carrack loaded with treasure; and when the English vessel sighted her, she was labouring heavily in a gale, and which the lighter and better-built Falcon rode with ease. Displaying his flag, the Count instantly gave orders to bear down and near the enemy; and disregarding the increasing winds which now blew almost a hurricane, the two vessels encountered each other.

How strange it seemed that amidst the fury of the elements, and which in a few short hours might overwhelm both vessels in the deep, the natural hatred the crews bore each other should urge on and help the destruction. And still more edifying was the gallantry with which the smaller English vessel bore down upon the huge golden prize, received her heavy fire, and, crashing upon her, whilst they were locked together, attempted to storm her bulwarks, and gain a footing on her deck. Then might have been seen a fearful sight,—amidst the tearing of masts and rigging consequent upon the vessels being locked together for the moment, and whilst they were simultaneously heaved upon each wave, was heard the ringing sound of musketry, the clash of weapons, and the despairing cry of agony, mingled with rattling sails and roaring wind.

Enveloped in smoke, none knew whether they were sinking amidst the dire confusion and horrible sounds around. Navigation was suspended whilst rage lasted, until the vessels separating with the increasing violence of the storm, in a crippled state, and, as if pausing for want of power to renew the fight, they were now gradually driven from each other. Not as they had met, however, did they part. In the confusion of the fight, and owing to their tearing apart ere the English adventurers could master the Spanish craft, and which by their valour and impetuosity they had nearly accomplished, several had fallen into the hands of the Spaniard, whilst a similar capture had also been made by the Falcon.

The young Count and Martin were unluckily amongst those left upon the deck of the Spanish vessel, and one or two of the before wrecked sailors, of whom the Count was in search, together with some Spaniards of condition, were the prize of the English.

This was a dire consummation to the crew of the Falcon after all their toils. The Spaniard was known to be a cruel devil on the high seas. The prisoners would be tortured or made to walk the plank. In addition to this, there was no possibility of rescue or renewal of the fight in such a sea, and in so crippled a state. Both vessels, therefore, lay rolling upon the waters, the crews glaring at each other till night.

Notwithstanding their crippled state, the Captain of the Falcon, with the characteristic industry of the English sailor, set about preparing for a renewal of the engagement, and, after giving a multitude of directions, he found time to address himself to a tall noble-looking cavalier, who seemed the principal of those whom the chance of war had introduced into his vessel.

"This is an unlucky issue to our adventure, Seignor," he said, "unless we can repair the mischief by a second fight."

"A lucky one for me, good Captain," returned the cavalier, "I was forced with other prisoners upon the deck of yonder Spaniard, and ordered to fight against you, my own countrymen. In the *melée* I managed to gain a footing upon your craft. Another day had perhaps seen us all committed to the deep."

"Whilst I," said the Captain, "in gaining that for which I adventured in this voyage, have lost my venture by losing my employer. Is not thy name Arderne,—Walter Arderne?"

"It is," said the cavalier, in some surprise, "How have you discovered so much?"

"There are those in this vessel who know you," said the Captain; "men from your own neighbourhood, and who are the followers of the owner of this craft, a noble gentleman who set sail from England for the very purpose of discovering and rescuing certain of his countrymen said to be cast away on the coast of Florida."

"You still more astonish me," said Arderne. "What was the name of this person?"

"My employer, and who has unluckily become a captive in yonder carrack, is called the Count Falanara, a noble having large estates in Warwickshire."

"We have no such name, or proprietor of land, in that county," said Arderne; "you have been deceived."

"In some sort I think so," said Captain Fluellyn; "will you favour me by stepping into the cabin of this noble, and in which, until his absence gave me opportunity of entering, I have never yet been?"

So saying, the Captain led the way into the small cabin the Count had occupied during the voyage, which had been fitted up under his own directions.

Nothing could be more elegant than the interior of this cabin; the curtains of the small sleeping-berth were of common silk, fringed with gold; the window beneath which the waves rippled was elaborately carved, and also framed and gilt; a splendid mirror of small dimensions, being framed in gold, ornamented the opposite side; the lamp which was suspended from the ceiling was also of pure gold; an elaborately-carved seat, with velvet cushions, was opposite the small round table fastened in the centre of the cabin, and upon it was placed a lute. In short, everything shewed that the recent occupier was a person of somewhat effeminate tastes and habits, and so the Captain seemed to think. "A soft nest," he said, "for one vowed to adventure, and the dangers of the New World. One would think a noble possessing the means for luxuries such as these need scarcely seek for treasure."

"Truly so," said Arderne.

"And yet," said the Captain, "it all depends upon the treasure sought. This Count, as you have said, hath in some sort put a cheat upon me; inasmuch, Master Arderne, as he was not what he seemed."

"True," said Arderne.

"These things are not the usual accompaniments of a sailor, or a rude son of adventure," said the Captain, somewhat contemptuously, touching the lute and the framed mirror with the end of his sheathed rapier. "On my first acquaintance with this youth—this noble—and when I took instructions anent our voyage, I looked upon him as a coward. He was for avoiding all unnecessary danger and collision with an enemy. Subsequent events, however, and his endurance under toil, and his ardour after that he sought, caused me to change that opinion. A week ago, as I listened to the melody of the voice which accompanied yonder lute, it suddenly struck me the Count was a female."

"A female!" said Arderne. "Had she no familiar friend—no confidant with her—who was aware of her real name, think ye?"

"She had," returned the Captain, "a shrewd and faithful friend, who seemed her confidant; albeit I could make him out as little as I could his superior. He also is captured or lost in the confusion."

"We must take that vessel, Captain, or perish!" said Arderne.

"We will at least do our best," said the Captain, preparing to leave the cabin, and look to the exertions of his men. But at that moment a sudden cry arose in the vessel, which made both him and Arderne hasten their steps. The Spaniard was on fire.

This was indeed a terrible consummation. The night was dark—the burning vessel some miles off.

Regardless of the billows rolling mountains high, Arderne and a resolute company got out the boats of the Falcon, and attempted to approach the blazing vessel.

'Twas, however, all in vain. The conflagration rapidly increased; so that ere the boats neared her, she was on fire in many places; her ordnance thundering off as the flames reached them, rendering it impossible to approach near. That several escaped in their boats was likely; but the English sailors, in spite of Arderne's desire to keep near, rowed back to the Falcon, whence they remained gazing upon the flaming craft—a terrific spectacle thus seen by night. The shape, cordage, masts, her high and towering poop, and all her gilded furniture, displayed in the hot flames, as if some painter had drawn out every portion.

All night and part of the next day did the haughty-looking Spaniard burn, till she was consumed to the water's edge, and then, as the Falcon neared her, there arose ever and anon a column of smoke from the rolling sea, consequent upon the close decks, full of spices, exploding under water, and which the fire had not taken hold of.

CHAPTER XXXV.

MORE MATTER FOR A MAY MORNING.

STRATFORD-UPON-AVON, like most country towns, possessed at this period, amongst other and worthier inhabitants, a certain amount of fragments, who were indeed in themselves nothing, but who wished to make themselves, as they fancied themselves, something.

These stuck-up portions of humanity, besides being extremely chaste in their ideas of propriety, were perhaps the most intolerant and unforgiving Christians in the world.

Brotherly love and charity were as often and as forcible in their mouths as real humanity was wanting in their hearts. Did a poor maiden err, and allowed her failing to be discovered, she was to be utterly cast out, abandoned, destroyed—no redemption allowed. Did a youth but shew the germs of a generous spirit, and fling out never so little, he was to be hunted down as one of the wild and wicked, irrecoverably disowned, and driven from society. Such folks are, as we have said, always to be found in a small community of citizens—the unwholesome impurity which circulates in its veins and arteries, and poisons by degrees the stream of its life.

Should any of these envious censors happen to observe one whom they consider of mark and likelihood beyond the common herd, they endeavour to make shipwreck of such superiority, by nipping it in the bud. They feel conscious of their own commonplace inferiority. They know themselves in reality nothing, and they resolve to reduce, if they can, the superiority of others to their own level, or to trample and destroy it utterly, if possible.

" Such a commodity of warm slaves " in Stratford had for some time looked with evil eye upon young Shakespeare. There was a superiority about him which, as it was more observable to their envy, they could by no means behold with quietude. They regarded him with a rankling dislike, and received, invented, or promulgated with avidity any thing they could gather to his disadvantage.

Our readers will perhaps think it odd, that one so young should already have found enemies in his native town. They will, however, remember, that " Envy always dogs merit at the heels," and that Shakespeare, as he was no common person, was at the same time the most open, generous, and unsuspicious of mortals—a man likely to expose himslf to censure, and care little about it either.

Back-wounding calumny, as he well knew, "the whitest virtue strikes." With every aggravation of circumstance, therefore, the somewhat desultory life young Shakespeare led, became canvassed by these good citizens of Stratford.

He was noted as one of irreclaimably wild and dissolute habits—"quoted and signed to do some deed of shame;" and through the industry of Grasp and Doubletongue, the Charlecote exploit got wind all over the neighbourhood.

No sooner did Grasp hear of the return of Sir Thomas Lucy from Kenilworth, and which happened a few days after the adventure, than he hastened over to Charlecote, and demanding audience of the stately knight, laid all he knew before him.

Our readers will readily picture to themselves the ire of Sir Thomas on hearing this piece of intelligence, and which, as Grasp related the conversation he had heard whilst lying in perdue at the hostel, plainly shewed the knight that his park had been broke, and his deer shot under his very nose.

"Ha!" he said, as he rose from his chair, and looked forth into the lovely chase; "and is it so? and are we bearded thus? Now, I will teach these knaves a lesson they shall not easily forget! The *outrécuidance* of that wild young fellow—that young Shakespeare, it shall go hard, but I will punish. A slight touch of the whip would do much towards taming so fiery a spirit. Ah! and what then, nothing but my parks, my woods, and my forest-walks will suffice for the recreation of that young springald.

"Master Grasp, I am much bounden to you for this intelligence. At once we will proceed against the whole gang of desperadoes. Let me see your list again. Ah! I see. And now, with regard to the Lucy Arms, we will begin there first. No more shall that swaggering Host make mine own property the den in which these ruffians congregate, and lay their plots to rob and plunder me."

"Master Fillpot was soliciting a fresh lease of the Lucy Arms, was he not, honoured Sir?" inquired Grasp.

"He was so," said Sir Thomas. "His lease expired last Midsummer, and I was about to renew it. I will renew it with a vengeance, Master Grasp, as you shall see anon."

"Marry and amen," said Grasp. "The Lucy Arms, grieved am I to say it, since they are pertaining to so honourable a house, hath been for some time a sign of disrepute in the town, a rallying point for certain dissolute and shameless characters to assemble at."

"They shall no longer be so," said Sir Thomas, ringing a small bell on his table. "We will incontinently proceed there. Let the head keeper be sought immediately," he said to the domestic, who answered the summons.

"He awaits in the court with the hawks, Sir Thomas," said the domestic.

"Order him hither," said the knight, "and inform the ladies I shall not go to the marshes this morning. I have business at Stratford which will employ me till after noon."

The man bowed and withdrew, and immediately afterwards the head keeper, a tall, athletic-looking man, holding his falcon on his glove, entered the room.

"Your fellows keep good watch, Oswald," said the knight. During my absence at Kenilworth, I have been again robbed; one of the best bucks in the park has been stolen."

"I heard not of it, Sir Thomas," returned the falconer.

"So it appears," returned the knight. "Nevertheless it hath been done; by the same token, this worthy, honest person saw the deer brought to the kitchen of the Lucy Arms at Stratford, where it was skinned, cut up, and actually some part of it eaten by William Shakespeare and his companions."

"You amaze me," said the keeper; on that night some of those I left in charge of the park were scared by a horrible apparition, the same which has been sometimes seen in the chase of Kenilworth, and so alarmed Roger Watchum, the Earl's head keeper, that he took it as a warning of death, and never joyed after. It hath grievously scared our people too, and they are afraid to go out at night, except in couples."

"Let them quit my service in couples then," said Sir Thomas, "since they are such cowardly hounds, and do you put a bullet through that ghost wherever you find it. I am well served by fellows who, scared by a shadow, run scampering about the woods, and leave the deer to the mercy of caitiffs and common robbers the whilst."

The head keeper well knew the stern disposition of his master, he therefore only bowed and waited further orders, whilst Sir Thomas walked up and down the apartment for some minutes without speaking. After a while, however, he again addressed the keeper.

"Go, sirrah," he said, "get together half a score of my out-door serving-men with pick and crow-bar. Send them forward to the Town-end at Stratford; and do thou and half a dozen of thy fellows, prepare to attend *me*."

"And now, Master Grasp," he said, "we will take your's, and the depositions of the men you have brought with you, who saw this Shakespeare in the act of burying the buck's-hide in the orchard of the Lucy Arms."

Meantime whilst these transactions were taking place at Charlecote, the unconscious delinquents were again assembled at the hostel, where we fear, it must be confessed, more mischief was being plotted against the quieter portions of the community.

The spirit of mischief, and the love of sport, was, after all, the chief mover of the whole party. They enjoyed those stolen pleasures, and, indeed, doubly relished the banquets they furnished forth, from the very circumstances of their being so procured.

On the present occasion, the presiding genius of the tavern—the jovial Froth, with Pierce, Caliver, and Careless, were the parties assembled in the parlour of the Lucy Arms.

'Twas the time, according to the magnificent wight Armado, "when beasts most graze, birds best peck, and men sit down to that nourishment which is called supper,"—about the sixth hour.

The meal was accompanied by sauce of the best quality, hunger, and savoured by good humour and hilarity. It consisted of a smoking haunch from the very buck we have already heard so much controversy about, and which was washed down by large draughts of liquor, various in kind, and exquisite in flavour.

It would have done the reader's heart good to have beheld mine host of the tavern, with the sleeves of his doublet tucked up, standing at the table to carve the savoury joint, and whilst he ever and anon partook of a morsel and pledged his guests in a bumper, waiting upon them and uttering his quaint sayings.

William Shakespeare and Diccon Snare had promised to be of the party on this evening, but from some cause or other which was unexplained, neither had kept the appointment.

Meanwhile the supper was finished, the haunch devoured down to the very bone, the napkin was removed, and the sparkling liquors in their quaint-cut bottles and flasks being placed upon the board, the party sat in for a carouse. They had all been over to Warwick on that day, and pleasure and action gave a zest to the evening's entertainment and the enjoyment of the hour; still the absence of Shakespeare and Snare made the evening's enjoyment, after all, seem incomplete. There was a feeling of something wanting to crown the joy of the party; for those who had once been in the society of the delightful Will, would be likely, without knowing the extent of their feelings at the moment, to experience a terrible void if he disappointed them.

The assemblage, however, were not men to allow the hours to hang on hand; and in the hope and expectation that their friends would join them, they carried on the war in jovial style. Their jests principally were levelled against Sir Thomas Lucy, whose rude and overbearing keepers they were the more pleased at gaining a triumph over; inasmuch as one or two of their own party had before been severely punished for offences against the game laws—offences, which men of their sort looked upon in the light of no offence at all, and rather as a sort of feather in their caps, anything but a theft; or, if a theft, a species of stealing which those of spirit, and ranking as gentlemen, had a right to indulge in: for what says the old doggrel?

"Harry and I in youth long since
Did doughty deeds, but some nonsense;
We read our books, we sang our song,
We stole a deer; nor thought it wrong;
To cut a purse deserves but hanging,
To steal a deer gets merely banging."

"Ha, ha!" said the Host. "Art thou there, bullies? Why, then, confusion to these Bohemian tartars! and we lads of mettle will still feast at their expense. What we must hedge, we must lurch. An we are borne down by the vile in spirit, we must resort to cozenage,—we must filch,—we must steal,—we must coney catch,—we must cozen the dappled deer from the fern."

"Truly thou art in the right, Host," said Froth; "but I most especially marvel what keepeth the jovial Will to-night. He struck the buck, and should be at the carving of the haunch. We lack him—we lack him much. By my fay! the cup lacks flavour, whilst expectation is thus defeated. Oh, 'tis a glorious boy! Come, lads, let us in his absence cheer our spirits with a catch. Give us Will's own song of the horns: an we have not himself, we'll have his verse." And the party sang,—

> "1. What shall we have that kill the deer?
> 2. His leathern skin and horns to wear.
> 3. Then sing him home.
> Take thou no scorn to wear the horn,
> It was a crest ere thou wast born."

The chorus was trolled out again and again, the singers applauding their own exertions vigorously, by repeated raps upon the table. Mine Host sat with his hands clasped before him, his head keeping time with drunken precision:

> "The horn, the horn, the lusty horn,
> Is not a thing to laugh to scorn."

When just at this moment the whole company were startled by an apparition nearly as appalling in appearance as the spectre they had themselves scared the keepers of Sir Thomas Lucy with in Charlecote, and which indeed was neither more nor less than Sir Thomas Lucy himself.

The knight advanced a few paces into the room, accompanied by several of his men, and stood to regard the party. Mine host was the first to catch sight of him, and the lusty chorus he was trolling out died away in a faint quaver, and as the rest of the company, following the direction of his staring eyes, turned and beheld the tall knight, conscience made cowards of them all, and, with a desperate rush, they endeavoured to get out of the room. Two dashed into the sleeping-chamber of Froth, whence they escaped into the orchard, whilst mine host, Caliver, and Careless, bolted through the open window.

Following the example of these latter fugitives, Froth made also an attempt to escape by the window, but his huge body became fixed like a wedge, as he endeavoured to throw himself forwards upon the grass without, and his nether man presented so fair a mark that the irate knight pointing him out to his head keeper, the sturdy forester stepped up, and by a most industrious application of his hunting-whip, so stimulated the exertions of Froth, that, bellowing with pain, he at last managed to get through the opening.

If the stately knight had been given to mirth, the sight of this swollen porpoise, during his efforts to escape,—his huge legs kicking at his tormentor,—his great body fast jammed,—would have furnished him with laughter for some minutes.

Sir Thomas, however, was too irate to be so moved; he sought for proof of the guilt of the parties in this their sanctum, and, quickly proceeding to overhaul the lodgement of Froth, he found sufficient evidence of their poaching propensities; crossbows, matchlocks, and snares of various sorts, were rummaged out and brought to light; and even the costume of Dreary Death, and other disguises, were produced. In fact, the query which had been often suggested by some of the more staid neighbours of the vicinity, as to how the swash-bucklers and rollicking blades constituting the society of the Lucy Arms, managed to live, was brought to light. They lived by their exertions on the road and the glade. They were squires of the night's body—Diana's foresters—gentlemen of the shade.

No sooner was Sir Thomas fully satisfied on this point than he retired from the interior, and, mounting his horse, ordered the men awaiting him at the town-end to be summoned.

"Master Grasp," he said, "I have more than once given this caitiff host notice to quit, and he hath still hung on and craved to remain my tenant. You have seen him this day evacuate the premises of his own free will, and I will now give my own people possession."

Thus saying, Sir Thomas ordered his men to enter the hostel, and proceed to unroof it,* after which he desired them with pick and spade to demolish and destroy as much as they could effect that night, and in the morning to return and level the Lucy Arms with the ground. That done, he reiterated his commands to the obsequious Grasp to proceed against the whole party as aiders and abetters in the robbery—William Shakespeare, in particular, as principal. To *prosecute* and *persecute* with the utmost rigour of the law. After which he turned his horse, and, grave and stately, attended by his keepers, rode off to Charlecote.

CHAPTER XXXVI.

THE LAMPOON.

On the morning of the day on which Sir Thomas paid a visit to the Lucy Arms, William Shakespeare, seated in a small parlour at the back of his house, was employed reading from a somewhat bulky volume certain matters which appeared deeply to interest him.

So much so, indeed, that albeit his attention was often called from the subject of his studies by the little crowing baby he held in one arm; still he ever returned with renewed avidity to devour a few more pages, as often as the playful infant gave him an opportunity of doing so.

The volume Shakespeare was reading from was a thick squat folio, then some thirty years printed, and called Hall's Chronicles. Many and various were the histories contained in this thick volume; and the deep interest young Shakespeare felt in their perusal, and the impression they made upon his mind, may be imagined when we enumerate them

* This sort of ejectment was not uncommon in Elizabeth's reign.

as set forth. First, then, there was "the unquiet time of King Henry ye Fourth." That was indeed a stirring page in England's history, "when trenching war channelled her fields," and intestine jars and civil butchery "daubed her lips with her own children's blood."

Then followed the victorious acts of King Henry the Fifth—a glorious epoch—a "record of fair act," and which, as we read of, he already saw before him, "the warlike Hal, in the vasty fields of France,"

"Assuming the port of Mars, and at his heels
Leash'd in, like hounds, famine, fire, and sword,
Crouching for employment."

Then came the troublous season of King Henry the Sixth, when

"Cropp'd were the flower-de-luces in our arms,
And England's coat one-half was cut away."

Then followed the boisterous reign of King Edward the Fourth, the pitiful life of King Edward the Fifth, the tragical doings of King Richard the Third, the "politic governance" of King Henry the Seventh, the triumphant reign of King Henry the Eighth.

How diligently young Shakespeare perused this book; and how carefully he remembered the impression made upon his mind, his after-life has shewn us.

At the present moment, like many a less elevated genius, his studies were disturbed by civil discord, domestic brawls, and the matters of every-day life around him.

Such, however, was the fine disposition of the man, that it took much to disturb the serenity of his temper and the equanimity of his mind.

We have seen that, in the amiability of his disposition, he was snatching an hour's leisure from the business in which he was engaged, and helping to nurse his child whilst pursuing his studies. This employment in itself would but have enhanced the pleasure afforded by such study. But unluckily (albeit he gave as little attention thereto as possible) he was at the same time subjected to the observation and sharp rebuke of his somewhat shrewish better half.

The stolen hours spent with his associates of the Lucy Arms had caused him a series of lectures and upbraidings, which completely shipwrecked his domestic peace.

All this he suffered in silence, for, as he could not compromise his companions by disclosing their confederacy in his deer-stealing exploit, he wisely held his tongue; not that he, however, deemed it right to keep secret counsel from the wife of his bosom; but in this case, where others were concerned, honour bound his tongue. In his own words he could have told her—

"That he knew her wise, but yet no further wise
Than William Shakespeare's wife. Constant she was,
But yet a woman: and for secrecy
No lady closer, for he well believed
She would not utter what she did not know,
And so far would he trust the gentle Anne."

In the present instance the gentle Anne appeared determined to have a serious quarrel with her husband. She flatly told him she would never rest till she had discovered where and with whom he had passed the night; and her upbraidings, as is frequently the case with females in her station of life, were by no means mild.

> "The venom'd clamours of a jealous woman
> Poison more deadly than a mad dog's tooth."

And William Shakespeare found it, and accordingly at length his patience gave way, and he arose, laid aside his book, placed his child in the cradle, and notwithstanding his stomach warned him it was near the dinner hour, he donned his castor, left the small apartment, and was about to leave his house for the Lucy Arms, when, just as he reached the door, he beheld Diccon Snare.

Dismounting from his horse, Snare entered the front-room of Shakespeare's house; and having desired the lad to whom he gave charge of the steed to lead it round to the shed in rear, he closed the door behind him carefully, and then threw himself into a chair, as one who had ridden far and fast since he had taken to the saddle.

"There is ill news abroad, Will," said he; "the Charlecote business is blown—Sir Thomas Lucy knows all. That much concerns you, for you are made the principal in the affair. Other matter hath also come out regarding some transactions in which Caliver and Careless are concerned. Caliver is in custody. Careless hath escaped, and, as I am not altogether exempt, I am for London with all speed."

"For myself I care nothing," said Shakespeare; but for Pierce, Caliver, and Careless, I am grieved. But whence is all this derived?"

"I met one of Grasp's lads at Kenilworth this morning," said Snare, "who with an officer was searching for Caliver; he gave me a hint to convey intelligence to the lads of the Lucy Arms; and I have ridden hard to give you the first notice."

"This doth indeed look ugly," said Shakespeare. "Sir Thomas hath ever held me in his hate, and undeservedly so. Wherefore he hath this dislike, I partly guess; now he has me on the hip, I doubt not he will do his utmost against me. But I pry'thee come in, Snare, you look pale, and lack refreshment. Our meal is about to be served."

"Nay, but," said Snare, "your wife, Will,—she likes me not; nay, she forbade my coming hither last Martinmas."

"Heed it not," said Shakespeare, smiling; "believe me, she meant not what she said. A friend both tired, hungry, and in need of shelter, shall never be turned fasting from my door. Besides, hath not thy love brought thee hither to warn me? Tush, man! Do you tell me of a woman's tongue—

> "That gives not half so great a blow to the ear,
> As doth a chestnut in a farmer's fire."

And Shakespeare threw open the door, and ushered his friend Snare into the inner-room, where they found the dinner spread, and the wife not best pleased at having to tarry.

"Not a word of matters appertaining," he whispered to Snare, as they entered. "Mistress Anne will not endure thee long, Diccon. After the meal is finished, she will take herself off to the upper-room."

Snare therefore followed his friend, and looking somewhat scared, made a leg, and paid his compliments to the hostess as he best could.

'Twas exactly as Shakespeare had surmised. The handsome Anne, whose brow grew somewhat contracted when she saw her husband usher in Snare, left the pair to themselves, as soon as she had finished her meal.

After her departure, Shakespeare placed liquor before his guest; and over a social glass they debated seriously of their affairs.

The high spirit of Shakespeare, however, would not permit of his long remaining under dominion of care or apprehension; and, under influence of a cup or two of Canary, he began to rail upon Sir Thomas, and lash him alternately.

"Out upon the clod-pate," he said; "his brains are as thick as Tewkesbury mustard. He imprison me—he have me whipped! Pshaw! I laugh at the dull ass! I will make him a jest to the whole country!"

"O' my word, Will, he will be more likely to drive thee from it," said Snare; "for Launcelot Quill, Grasp's head clerk, vows he never saw man more angered than the old knight is against thee."

"Tush, man!" said Shakespeare, "never tell me of his anger. Let him do his spite. He hath already done me several ill turns, from the bare suspicion that I have broke his park. Now, I doubt not, he will fine, imprison, and what not, if he can but catch me! Come, another cup, and then to inform our companions of the Lucy Arms of this matter. Best, however, clap-to the outer door, and make all fast," he said, rising and drawing the bolt across the fore-door, "lest this Cavaliero Justice hath already let loose his myrmidons against me. Ha! ha!" he continued, reseating himself, "he a Justice of the Peace! —he a Parliament Member! Why, I will fashion a better justice after supper out of a cheese-paring. I pr'ythee, Snare, reach me that ink-horn. I will write a lampoon upon the peaking Cornuto, and fasten it up against his park-gates—I will, indeed, lad!"

"Nay, but Will," urged Snare, "thou wilt scarce venture, daring dog as thou art, further to irritate the knight? I tell thee, being married and settled here, this business will already go far to ruin thee."

"Ruin me!" said Shakespeare, somewhat bitterly. "Ruin me, saidst thou? Why, man, dost think me in a thriving condition here in Stratford?"

"Not entirely so," said Snare, looking around; "I would I could see thy nest better feathered, Will, and I trust I shall yet do so."

"I think it not," said Shakespeare; "business decreases apace with me. I am called wild, inattentive, dissolute,—nay, I have had one or two slight misunderstandings with my family; and, as thou sayest, this last business and the rancorous hatred of Sir Thomas, will go hard with your poor friend. But, come, here we have a couplet or two in his condign praise: for a taste—

"A parliament member, a justice of peace,
At home a poor scarecrow, at London an asse;
If lowsie is Lucy, as some volke miscalle it,
Then Lucy is lowsie whatever befall it."

"'Fore heaven, Will, stop," said Snare, laughing, "Thou hast indeed touched up the knight; thou hast tied him to a post, and wilt lash him into madness."

"Nay, but stay," said Shakespeare, "I will give him another stanza yet. Hearkee to this:

"He thinks himself great.
Yet an asse in his state,
We allowe by his ears but with asses to mate;
If Lucy is lowsie as some volke miscalle it,
Then sing lowsie Lucy, whatever befall it."

"Nay," said Snare, "an thou stick that up, thou hadst better put the seas between thyself and Britain. The Knight of Charlecote will be driven stark staring mad."

"Well," said Shakspeare, "we shall see how matters progress. If Sir Thomas bears me hard, as true as thy name is Diccon Snare, I will nail this lampoon to his park-gates, and have it sung to filthy tunes through the town."

CHAPTER XXXVII.

THE GARDEN.

It was one bright morning, a few days after the events we have recorded that a gay and gallant-looking party rode into the grounds of Clopton and approached the Hall.

The mansion, which had for some time remained shut up, now appeared to be resuming something of its former state. Its latticed windows were once more open, whilst servants were to be seen moving about the offices and gardens, and even the bark and bay of dogs were heard in the kennel.

The good Sir Hugh had suddenly returned to his home from the Low Countries. Time had gradually ameliorated his deep grief, and restored the equilibrium of his mind. He felt tired of camps and military service, and his thoughts turned to the green woods and sweet scenes of his own home.

A feeling we suspect which almost all soldiers, however much ambition and the love of profession may keep them in harness, more or less experience. There is a period in the lives of all men in which the occupations of a country life form a sort of recreation after the toils and cares of the world. That which we disregard in youth, amidst the gaieties and frivolities and ambitions of life, in age seems to come as a natural repose. A wise provision of nature, and which in earlier times was perhaps better exemplified. To youth, the bright weapon, the helm, the shield, and the defence. To riper age, the plough, the hoe, and the dibble.

Sir Hugh had returned to his sweet home, and, albeit a settled melancholy was on his spirits, he could better enjoy that home now that absence had rendered it less painful to him to look upon, and he returned with renewed zest to his old employments. He was in his garden, giving directions to his gardener about the different plants, and flowers, and shrubs, and turning over in his mind the varieties which in his daughter's time she had loved to cultivate—

> "Daffodils
> That come before the swallow dares, and take
> The winds of March with beauty. Violets dim,
> But sweeter than the lids of Juno's eyes
> Or Cytherea's breath; pale primroses
> That die unmarried, ere they can behold
> Bright Phœbus in his strength."

He was busied amongst his "somewhat o'erweeded garden," when an attendant announced that Sir Thomas and Lady Lucy were advancing towards the house, with the intention, no doubt, of paying him a formal visit on his return. Upon which the good Sir Hugh set his dibble in the earth, smoothed down the cuffs of his doublet, belted on the long rapier, which he had laid aside upon the walk when he commenced work, and, adjusting his short cloak and starched ruff, entered his house to receive these distinguished guests.

Sir Thomas Lucy, in the kindness of his heart, had hastened to pay a visit to his old friend the moment he heard of his arrival, and, well knowing there would be many things to excite the feelings of Sir Hugh on his return, he was resolved to carry him back to Charlecote.

"I will have no denial, Sir Hugh," he said, "I have come hither to bring ye forth to Charlecote. We have wanted you long, and by my fay we cannot away without ye."

"Nay, but," said Sir Hugh, "I am but now returned. Methinks in a few days I should be more prepared to leave home again."

"Prepare me nothing," said Sir Thomas. "What the good-year, dost think we will let thee sit down to a solitary meal here, when we have shot the buck, and dressed the haunch on purpose for thee? Come, man, Lady Lucy takes no denial; and, see, my daughters are here to fetch thee."

There was no resisting this, so Sir Hugh, sighing as he glanced upon the lovely daughters of his neighbour, ordered out his steed at once.

It was a lovely morning, as the party rode through the grounds of Clopton, and emerged upon the road to Stratford. Many matters were discussed by the two friends after their long separation.

Sir Thomas rode, as was customary at the period, with his falcon on his glove, his falconers being in attendance. Nay, even the ladies carried their favourite hawks, which they petted, and even talked to as they rode; a favourable opportunity for giving them wing being not altogether neglected occasionally.

"We must have a day on't in the marshes, Sir Hugh," said the Knight of Charlecote, "and you must away with me next week to the Cotswold Hills, to the coursing, Sir Hugh. By 'ur Lady, I have a pup of old Snowball, which, an I am not mistaken, will win the match. 'Tis a goodly cur, I promise ye."

"I will see him run," said Sir Hugh.

"And that reminds me," said Sir Thomas, to tell thee I have of late been much molested by a knot of young fellows breaking my parks and shooting my deer."

"Ah, the caitiffs," said Sir Hugh, "can'st not take them?"

"In sooth can I, and will trounce them too. One, especially, have I marked for punishment; and my lawyer hath him in hand. A wild lad of the town here, named Shakespeare."

"Shakespeare!" said Sir Hugh; "not young William Shakespeare, the eldest son of the woolcomber?"

"The same," said Thomas. "I shall impound the knave ere many hours more are over his head."

"Nay, I am truly sorry to hear this," said Sir Hugh, "for I have reason to think well of that lad."

"'Tis more than any one else hath, then," said Sir Thomas "He hath been a bitter thorn in my side for some time."

"Truly, you surprise me; hath he then so altered since I left these parts?"

"I know not that," said Sir Thomas; "but I well know he hath the reputation of the wildest young fellow in the neighbourhood."

"Nay, then I am utterly astonished," said Sir Hugh. "We must talk further of this matter; and I must see if I cannot get you to overlook, in some sort, young Shakespeare's offence."

"I would do much to pleasure you," said the Knight of Charlecote; "but my lawyer hath instruction to prosecute him with rigour. I was resolved to make a Star Chamber matter o't. If he be, however, so much favoured by thee, my good friend, we must look to't. But come, here we are at Charlecote. Ha!" he continued, pulling up his steed suddenly; "what have we nailed up against the gate? Dismount, Hubald!" he said to the Falconer, "take it down, man, and read it, and see what 'tis."

The head Falconer dismounted, and approaching the gates, took down a good sized placard written in large characters, a single glance at which seemed to cover him with dismay.

"What is it, in the name of wonder?" said the Knight. "Read, man, read; don't stand glaring like a driveller. Is my place placarded for sale?"

"An it so please ye," said the Falconer, "a gnat hath gotten into my eye, and I cannot well make it out. 'Tis a verse, too, and I cannot read a verse anyhow."

"Thou art a knave," said the Knight. "Read, I tell thee. I am curious to know what such documents can have to do with my gates. Read, I say, without more circumstance." And accordingly the Falconer, like one affrighted at his own voice, and in doleful tones drawled out the following couplet :—

"A parliament member, a justice of peace,
At home a poor scarecrow, in London an ass.
If Lucy is—"

"Ahem! 'If Lucy is—'" And the Falconer stopped.

"Proceed, sirrah," said Sir Thomas, with the calmness of concentrated rage ; "proceed, a God's name!" And again the Falconer read—

"If Lucy is lowsey as some folk miscall it,
Then lowsey is Lucy whatever befall it."

To paint the ire and astonishment of Sir Thomas would be difficult.

"Here's goodly stuff toward," he said, as the Falconer stopped after the four first lines, and stood looking as much scared as if he had himself been guilty of the composition. "This, then, Sir Hugh, is doubtless the production of thy witty friend. A pestilence strike such wit! say I. Here, hand me the paper. Now may the fiend take me, an I do not give him his full deserts for this insult." And cramming the placard into the bosom of his doublet, to be read carefully and at more leisure, Sir Thomas put spurs to his horse and rode into the courtyard of his mansion.

CHAPTER XXXVIII.

THE FLIGHT TO LONDON.

A week has elapsed since Sir Hugh Clopton paid his visit to Charlecote. He has been a few days returned to his own home again, and is filled with pleasurable sensations on account of a letter just received from London, and announcing the arrival there of his nephew, Walter Arderne. The ship in which Walter has received a passage home is called the "Falcon," it is lying at Deptford; and the letter from the nephew to the uncle treats of strange matter; and promises, when they meet, still stranger news, connected with his escape, and safe return to England. A postscript adds, that as Walter has returned naked, as it were, to his native land, and has little to delay him preparatory to his returning to Clopton, his strong love for his uncle, "sharp as his spur," will help him on his road as fast as his horse can bring him. One only drawback is there to the contentment of Sir Hugh, and that is the account his nephew gives of the loss of the faithful Martin.

Still (although Sir Hugh felt more happy at this intelligence than he had been for some time) he did not let his feelings interfere with a project he had conceived after his return home, of going into Stratford in order to pay a visit to John Shakespeare, in Henley Street. The good Sir Hugh felt, that however much the son of the woolcomber might have disgraced himself, at any rate he himself was in duty bound to try and befriend him. "A deer-stealer," he said, as he mounted his horse and rode forth, "and given to all unluckiness in catching hares and rabbits too; and then that biting satire nailed against the park-gates, and stuck up all over the town: nay, 'twas too bad, and that is the truth on't. Here, too," he continued, (fumbling in the pocket of his doublet,) "is a vile ballad I bought of an old hag, who was bawling it through the streets of Stratford but yesterday. Let me see what saith the doggrel:

"Sir Thomas was too covetous
To covet so much deer,
When horns enough upon his head,
Most plainly did appear."

"By 'ur Lady, but 'tis sad stuff; and here be more—

"Had not his worship one deer left?
What then? he had a wife,
Took pains enough to find him horns
Should last him during life."

"Ah, a very simple lad, and a wilful. Had it not been for these things—these scraps of bad verse—I could have made matters up, I dare be sworn." And Sir Hugh (who by this time had reached Henley Street) dismounted, and entered the house of the woolcomber.

How well the Knight of Charlecote had bestirred himself, and how well he had been assisted in his prosecution of the deer-stealers by the wretched Grasp, was evident, since Sir Hugh found that Snare was in jail at Warwick, Caliver in durance at Coventry, and that William Shakespeare had fled.

Yes, Shakespeare had fled from Stratford-upon-Avon. How trivial a circumstance did that seem at the time! Except his own family, none seemed to know or care much about him. A mere youth was driven from his home to avoid punishment for a trifling indiscretion; persecuted by a man of high and chivalrous feeling, and who knew him not, but by the ill report of the vile; a man who, had he but suspected the great worth and brilliant genius of the fugitive, would have been one of the first to befriend, in place of injuring and driving him, alone and friendless, from his home. And that act, whilst it lent an imperishable *eclat* to his own name, was, perhaps, the exciting cause of the greatness of the offender.

It was dark night when Shakespeare left his home. The resolve was suddenly taken: his high spirit could not brook the thought of degredation and punishment at the suit of the Knight of Charlecote. The misrepresentations, the misconceptions, and the absurd reports of the Stratford noodles, had disgusted him; and (even amidst the laughter caused by the lampoon affixed to the gates of Charlecote) he fled from the town.

Added to these feelings, there was the natural ambition which a young man, a husband, and a father, entertained to enter into some wider sphere of action, and where the talents he possessed might be brought into play. Domestic difference, too, and undeserved reproach, —or, if *deserved*, ill-timed, galled his spirit, and his gentle nature rebelled against the treatment he had received. The fire in the flint, 'tis said, "shows not till it be struck."

'Twas night when he left his home. To his mother alone had he confided his intent, and to her he had entrusted the care of both wife and children. 'Twas two hours past midnight when he donned his hat and cloak, took his quater-staff in his hand, and prepared to start.

Gently he ascended the stairs, and entered his sleeping-room. The handsome Ann was buried in a deep sleep; and as one snowy arm encircled her infant, her dark-brown locks lay like a cloud upon the pillow. What a picture of rustic English beauty did she present! One kiss of her parted lips, and he descended the stairs, and let himself out by the back-door.

He was obliged to be cautious as he crossed the orchard, and gained the open fields in rear of his dwelling. It would, however, we opine, have been somewhat dangerous had the emissaries of Grasp molested him on this night, as his spirit, although bruised, was not broken, and he would have been a difficult person to capture. Ere he left the orchard, he turned and looked long and fixedly at his own and his father's dwelling. He felt that, perhaps, he might never again behold the sloping roofs which covered relatives so dear. All, save one (his mother), were buried in deep sleep, and unconscious of his flight. A minute more, and he was gone from his native town. Hurrying onwards over the meadows and woodlands—avoiding the high-road—across the country towards Warwick—"over park, over pale—through brake, through briar." Without any fixed notion as to his route, London was his destination; and with a mind ill at ease, the solitude of the woods was most congenial to his thoughts. Thus he traversed, alone and at night, the first few miles of that delicious and park-like scene between his native town and Warwick; and still, as his steps were destined towards the latter town, old haunts, and points of interest, lured him from the direct line; and the breaking dawn found him standing, leaning upon his staff, on Blacklow Hill,—a spot, we dare say, well known to the majority of our readers. The sweetness of this locality, and the delicious scene around, for the moment took him from his own particular griefs; his mind reverted to the terrible deed of stern and wild justice it had been the scene of.

In the hollow of the rock beneath his feet, Piers Gaveston, the minion of Edward the Second, had met his sudden fate.

Amidst the fern and on the mossed face of the rugged rock were still to be seen the name of the victim, and the date in which the deed had been done, rudely cut at the moment of the execution.

1311.
PIERS GAVESTON,
EARL OF CORNWALL,
BEHEADED.

Around him were the oaks of the Druids; in the distance, embosomed in softest verdure, gray with age, and softened in the mists of early dawn, were the towers of the magnificent Warwick.

On right, on left, were the deep woodlands, at this period covering nearly all Warwickshire like a huge forest. 'Twas a scene peculiarly adapted to call forth all the chivalrous feelings and historical recollection of such a being. The distant rush of the water from the monastic mill at Guy's Cliff, a sound which the monks of the adjoining abbey in bygone times had loved to hear, soothed the melancholy of his soul;—a sort of dreamy and shadowy remembrance of ages "long ago betide;"—a feeling as if the gazer upon such a scene had been familiar with the iron men who lived in feudal pride, and owned those towers in bygone days, stole upon him. He stood upon the domain of that mighty Earl of Warwick, "the putter up and plucker down of kings;" the blast of whose bugle in that county had often assembled thousands, "all furnished, all in arms." In thought he followed the proud baron in all his stirring career. Knight and esquire and vassal, a "jolly troop of English" swept by with tuck of drum and colours spread; and then he saw the mighty earl dying amidst the dust and blood of Barnet:—

"His parks, his walks, his manors, that he had,
Even these forsaking him; and, of all his lands,
Nothing left him but his body's length."

Any one who could have looked upon that youthful poet at the moment, might have surmised the Shakespeare after-times has been wont to picture. There was the divine expression,—the countenance *once seen*, even in a portrait, never to be forgotten; the eye of fire, "glancing from heaven to earth;" the splendid form, with head thrown back and foot advanced. And thus he stood upon Blacklow Hill—

"A combination and a form, indeed,
To give the world assurance of a man."

Not like a fugative flying from the paltry spite of a scrivener set on by a country squire, but like the herald mercury.

"New lighted on a heaven-kissing hill."

Long did the fugitive linger in this spot, till—

"Light thickened, and the crow
Wing'd to the rooky wood."

He then, as hunger forced him from his retreat, crossed the meadows, and entering the town of Warwick, sought an old hostel situate in the suburbs. No sooner did he enter this town, than he began to find himself one remove from the dull seclusion of his native place. The streets seemed all alive; a huge bonfire was a-light in the market-place, and hundreds of the rough sons of toil were assembled around, and in the adjoining thoroughfares.

Another diabolical conspiracy of the Jesuits had been discovered, and their designs frustrated. The news had just travelled to Warwick, and all was exultation, execration, and wild riot; whilst, added to this was a whispered rumour that the Queen of Scots was to be immediately brought to trial for participation in the plot. Sir Walter Mildmay, Sir Amias Paulet, and Edward Barker,—it was said at the Castle, —had waited upon Mary, informing her of the commission to try her, and also that Mary had refused to submit to an examination before subjects. Thus, then, all was excitement, stir, and bustle, as Shakespeare, unmarked by all, passed through the streets of Warwick and entered the market-place,—a scene, perhaps, not quite so rude and riotous as in earlier times in that old town, yet still sufficiently characteristic of the period.

At one side of the market a company of fleshers, butchers, and half-clad hangers-on, reeking with the "uncleanly savours of the slaughter-house," threw up their sweaty night-caps, and urged their savage mastiffs to the charge, whilst an unlucky bear, tied to a strong stake, hugged and bit and bellowed with the agony of the attack. At another part a rout of fellows were to be seen wrestling and playing at quarter-staff; others, as they sprawled before a low hostel, were dicing and drinking, whilst a whole company danced and shouted around a bonfire, in which the effigies of Philip of Spain, tied back to back to a shaven monk, were being burnt. At another part of the market a considerable crowd was gathered around a sort of rhyming pedlar,—a tatterdemalion poet, who said, and shouted, and sang, the latest news, the newest ballad, and the last lampoon made upon Sir Thomas Lucy of Charlecote:—

"A Parliament member, a justice of peace—
At home a poor scare-crow, in London an ass."

Passing through this crowd, and gathering from several knots of the citizens much of the stirring news, Shakespeare entered a small tavern situate in the outskirts of the town, near the Priory walls, where, although he found less bustle, there was yet a decent assemblage of guests. Here again he had opportunity of hearing those events which at the moment interested the kingdom from one end to the other. Violent philippics were levelled against Mary of Scotland, Philip of Spain, the Pope, and all communicating and consorting with them. The Queen of Scots, it was asserted by one of the travellers, had been found guilty of writing a letter to Philip, in which she offered to transfer all England to the Spaniard should her son refuse to embrace the Catholic faith. Another guest affirmed she had entered into a conspiracy against her own son, and instigated agents to seize his person and deliver him into the hands of the Pope, or the King of Spain.

As the fugitive sat beneath the huge chimney, and listened to the noisy debate of these politicians, amidst the hum of voices, and with the names of Walsingham, Babington, Burleigh, Hatton, Leicester, and others, ringing in his ears, he fell asleep, and with his arms folded, his head dropping upon his breast, his feet stretched out upon the hearth, his quarter-staff fast clutched in his arms, in company with others snoring in different parts of the apartment, did he pass the first hours of the night on which he fled from Stratford.

It was by no means an uncommon occurrence in Elizabeth's day for guests and wayfarers at a hostel of this sort *so* to pass the night. Your traveller oft-times took his supper, folded his arms, drew his cloak around him, and slept in his boots and doublet when on a journey. The comfort of a good bed, as in our own day upon the road, was by no means thought so necessary. Nay, during the reign of Henry the Eighth, the peasant slept upon the floor with a log of wood for a pillow; and a comfortable bed to the hardy English peasant or the yeoman was a luxury indeed. The traveller, therefore, who meant to be early on the road, paid his shot over-night, and departed with "the first cock." Accordingly, the morning broke as Shakespeare brushed the dew from the grass some miles from Warwick, and the sun shone out brightly as he neared the towers of Kenilworth, then in all its pride and magnificence. The parks, and woods, and chase of this fortress were well known to the poet; and the beautiful little village, with its priory situated close to the walls, amidst verdant meadows, and surrounded with thick and massive foliage, had been a favourite haunt. Here, when a schoolboy, he had accompanied his father, what time the Earl of Leicester entertained Queen Elizabeth for seventeen days, "with pomp, with triumph, and with revelling." And here he had taken his first impression of regal pride and power. At the same time he also got an inkling of the theatrical diversions then in vogue; for hither came the Coventry men, and acted an ancient play upon the green—a play long used or represented in their antique city, and called "Hock's Tuesday," and in which the Dane, after a formal engagement, was discomfited. Here, too, as he stood upon the margin of the castle-lake, he beheld another pageant, in which

"Arion,* on a dolphin's back,
Uttered such dulcet and harmonious breath,
That the rude lake grew civil at her song."

Many other rough sports, too, had he seen on this occasion and on this spot; the gracious Queen, sitting patiently the whilst, "kindly giving her thanks to the actors for nothing."

"Her sport to take what they mistook,
And what poor duty could not do,
Noble respect took it in might, not merit;
And where she saw them shiver and look pale,
Make periods in the midst of sentences,
Throttle their practis'd accents in their fears,
And in conclusion dumbly breaking off,
Out of their silence did she pick a welcome,
And in the modesty of fearful duty
She read as much, as from the rattling tongue
Of saucy and audacious eloquence."

As Shakespeare turned from the neighbourhood of Kenilworth, the scene was by no means new to him, yet still it made considerable impression upon his mind; the huge castle and its flanking walls and towers, and the buildings which had been added to it during various reigns, altogether made up a pile of feudal grandeur such as was hardly to be equalled in the kingdom. There stood the new and magnificent buildings of the favourite Leicester—the towers of old John of Gaunt,

* The Earl, besides other things, had represented Arion on a dolphin, with rare music, whilst fireworks were seen in the air. Shakespeare, more than once, alludes to Arion on a dolphin's back. Might not these things have made early impression upon his mind?

"time-honoured Lancaster,"—the lodgings of King Henry the Eighth—the old tower of Cæsar, (built by Geoffrey de Clinton,) the tilt-yard, the swan tower, the water tower, Lunn's tower, Fountain tower, Saintlow tower, and Mervyn's bower. There was the plaisance, the orchard, the huge court, the garden, the glassy lake, and the wild and magnificent chase. All these, much as they had been impressed upon the mind of Shakespeare in former rambles, seemed doubly interesting and impressive now that he was leaving the scene, perhaps for ever, without purse, profession, or prospect. Nay, should he meet some outlaw or common robber on the road, he might have said, with his own Valentine—

"A man I am, crossed with adversity,
My riches are these poor habiliments,
Of which, if you should here disfurnish me,
You take the sum and substance that I have."

Those who have left the home and haunts of their childhood, and all there so dearly loved, can best describe the feeling of desolation which the one solitary wanderer for the first time feels, and which each mile seems to add to. He who has first embarked for a distant clime, leaving all worth living for, to "make a hazard of new fortunes in the world," can best remember "how slow his soul sailed on, how swift his ship."

When Shakespeare left the neighbourhood of Kenilworth, all was strange and new to him; and he might then be said to have entered upon "the wide and universal theatre."

All travel at this period was performed on horseback. Roads were foul, ill-made, and difficult; so much so, that in winter a man might have been dead in London three months before his next heir at York heard the news. The towns and villages, too, were then few, small, and far apart; and as Shakespeare inquired his weary way onwards, how sweet in remembrance seemed the bowery beauty of that sequestered spot he had quitted—sweet Stratford! and where he knew every face he met, where he saw and mixed with his own family every day, every hour. Sometimes, as he lay along, and rested beneath the shade of melancholy boughs, he loved to ponder upon those dearly-loved relatives, and imagine what they were doing, what they thought of his absence, and whether they missed him. His mother, too, she who had always so loved her first-born, who could read his high desert, and appreciate his brilliant talents, when all else passed him by, how would she miss him!

'Oh this will make my mother die of grief."

The tears would then course one another down his cheek, and he would start up and hurry onwards again. He had no fixed route, but inquired his way from village to town, and from hamlet to city. His good constitution, and out-door habits, made it no hardship to him to pass the night upon the mossed bank in the open air. The cottage afforded him refreshment, and the thin drink of the shepherd from his bottle was oft-times offered in return for a few minutes' conversation upon the wold; the hawthorn bush the shade in which he rested; and thus he proceeded onwards in his flight, purposely deviating from the direct road, as well from inclination as that he felt it likely some search might be made after him either by friends or enemies.

The few coins he had in his pocket when he started were soon expended, and he experienced at times, during his progress, the pangs of hunger without the means of allaying it, and this perhaps was an ordeal Shakespeare was fated to go through. He was destined to feel the "uses of adversity" ere he rose, by his own mighty efforts, above the world. He was to see human nature in all its varieties. To experience the depressing weight of poverty, ere he surmounted his worldly cares, as the lion shakes the dew-drops from his mane. Adversity was to be the finishing school of his studies—nature the book presented. In this school he took his degree, and which all the learning of the ancients, all the pedants of the antique world would have failed in teaching him. Nor was his attention confined to the actions of men as he mingled amongst them. He was the exact surveyor of the inanimate world as he travelled through it, and his descriptions in after-life were grafted from the contemplation of things as they really existed.

To a solitary traveller on foot at this period there was considerable peril. The resolute ruffian, the "resolved villain," who lived by levying contributions on the road, was often to be met with. Nay, even strong parties of travellers were frequently attacked, and robbed, and murdered, 'twixt town and town. Still all unarmed, except the stout staff he carried in his hand, and the small dagger worn at his girdle, and which served to cut up the food he ate, Shakespeare held on his way. The lowly ruffian as he emerged from the thick cover which overhung the road occasionally scowled upon him as he passed, and then let him proceed unquestioned. There was something in the eye, which met his glance, which told the robber of hard blows and desperate resistance, whilst the unfurnished manner in which he travelled promised little in the shape of booty. Once or twice the wayfarer had joined a party of carriers, who, with other travellers in their company, were going the same route, but, as he frequently diverged from the road, he soon lost such companionship and made his way alone, through by-roads and foul ways, and across the dreary wastes and commons, at that period extending occasionally for many miles. It was on the fourth evening of his journey that, having made a long detour from the main road, he again came into it about five miles from Stoney Stratford. The day had been lovely, he had wandered far, and as he laid himself down beneath some huge trees and watched the bright track of the setting sun, he fell into a sound sleep.

'Twas "the middle summer's spring." The bank upon which he lay looked a perfect haunt of the elfin crew, but whether or not, on *this* night, Shakespeare dreamt a *dream of Midsummer*, or whether he dreamt at all, we are unable to say. Whilst he slept, however, he was suddenly awakened by the sound of voices near.

As he opened his eyes, by the moon's light he observed three persons standing a few yards from him. The spot on which he reclined was so shadowed by the overhanging branches and thick with fern that he had himself been undiscovered, and a few moments' observation convinced him that the men he beheld were "squires of the night's booty." Their heavy boots, their soiled doublets, the rusted breast-plates they wore, their slouched hats, and untrimmed beards, altogether indeed convinced him they were thieves.

Whilst he regarded the ill-favoured trio they descended from the overhanging bank into the road, where they were joined by a fourth person, who stole from the covert on the other side, and for some minutes remained in conversation with them. The situation was not without its interest, albeit it was fraught with danger to Shakespeare. He had, indeed, unconsciously intruded himself into the trysting place of a band of robbers, and, as he rose to his feet and removed somewhat behind the tree, he watched them narrowly.

They were evidently laying in wait for passengers, as he more than once observed one of the party throw himself flat upon the road, with his ear to the ground, in order to listen for the tread of hoofs. To remain behind the oak (whose antique root peeped out upon the overhanging bank) would have been dangerous. Still, as he resolved closely to watch these men, he cautiously withdrew into the deeper cover of the trees. As he did so his head struck against some obstacle pendant from one of the boughs, and, as he raised his eyes, he beheld the dead body of a man suspended, a ghastly object thus seen in the gloom, and which sufficiently shewed the evil nature of the neighbourhood. He had, in fact, reached a spot called the "Crooked Wood," a part of the road at that period famous for robbery and murder, and the bodies of several malefactors were hung *in terrorem*.

Shuddering at the sight, he withdrew from the vicinity of this object, which swinging backwards and forwards looked yet more horrible in the deep gloom. The next moment he heard the distant sound of hoofs upon the road, and at the same time observed the figures beneath drawing cautiously off on either hand, concealing themselves completely in the deep shadows, one only remaining prostrate in the very middle of the highway. Although the horsemen approached rapidly, it was some time ere they neared the spot; now the clatter of hoofs appearing close at hand, and then (as some turn in the road intervened) again for some moments totally lost to the ear.

At length they advanced down the hill which led immediately into this dark defile. Two horsemen he distinguished; the foremost immediately reined up his horse, and signed to his companion to do the same. The heart of Shakespeare beat quickly as he observed one of the travellers dismount and stoop down to render assistance to the prostrate form before him. As he did so the robber suddenly grasped the traveller by the throat and pulled him down, at the same moment his three companions darted like lightning from either side of the road; whilst two assailed the horseman, the third aided their comrade to despatch the traveller who had been entrapped.

The struggle was desperate: the mounted cavalier had in an instant unsheathed his long rapier, and manfully defended himself; and the woods around rang to the blows of the combatants. Meanwhile the prostrate traveller, whose horse had galloped off at the commencement of the fray, was also in an unpleasant plight. This latter, being a powerful man, had more than once heaved himself up by main force, and nearly cleared himself from his adversaries. But, with heavy blows and desperate exertions, they at length succeeded in pinning him down. In an instant, however, the fallen man succeeded in drawing a pistol from his belt, and discharged it into the body of one of his opponents.

All this happened in as short a time as it has taken the reader to peruse it. Life and death, in such deadly conflict, is taken and received by the combatants like the lightning's flash; and, albeit the travellers struggled manfully, yet a very few minutes sufficed to tell against the lesser party. The horseman was on the point of being dragged from his saddle, and his fellow-traveller was growing exhausted with the violence of action. At that moment, however, a heavy blow fractured the skull of the ruffian who held the bridle-rein of the rearing steed, and as the new combatant afterwards opposed himself to the robber, who had by this time succeeded in bringing the rider to the ground, after a short and rapid combat, the latter turned and fled.

This turned the tide of battle instantaneously in favour of the travellers, and as is oft-times the case in such conflicts, it ended in the same rapid manner in which it had commenced. The travellers stood panting with their recent exertions, and whilst three bodies lay before them in the road, their deliverer, leaning upon his heavy quarter-staff, stood regarding one of them with curious eye.

Meantime, after the person, who seemed by his appearance the principal of the travellers, had somewhat recovered himself, he stepped up to the hero of the quarter-staff, aud poured forth his thanks for the service rendered.

"We are indebted to you for no less than our lives," he said, "and would fain repay the obligation by something more acceptable than thanks."

The moon was at the moment hidden, but as Shakespeare caught a nearer view of the features of the speaker, he plucked his own hat over his brow, and withdrew still further into the shadow of the trees. At the same time he courteously refused all requital for the aid he had rendered.

"Can we do nothing to requite this favour?" said the taller Cavalier.

"You can," said Shakespeare, "since, if I guess aright, your name is Arderne, and you go towards Stratford-upon-Avon."

"Such is my name," said the traveller. "How can I serve you?"

"By giving this token," said Shakespeare, tearing a leaf from a small tablet he carried in his breast, and writing a few words on it.

"No more?" inquired the traveller, endeavouring to get a better view of the speaker.

"Tell those to whom you give the token," said Shakespeare, "that he who sends it is in life and health—no more."

"But will you not bear us company?" said Arderne. "This place seems dangerous, and alone you may be met by others of the gang."

"'Tis no matter," said Shakespeare; "I cannot consort with thee. Our paths to-night, as through life, lie in different directions. Farewell!" and hastily darting off, he was quickly lost in the gloom.

"Strange," said Walter Arderne, as he glanced closely at the small slip of paper in his hand, and which the moon's light now gave him an opportunity of reading. "Ah! this paper is directed to the woolcomber in Henley Street. Methought I knew the voice. 'Twas then William Shakespeare who so opportunely befriended us."

So much was Arderne surprised at this meeting, that he would fain have followed Shakespeare, but his companion dissuaded him.

"The man is gone suddenly as he came," said he, "and we are not wise to remain longer in this place. Come," he continued, as Walter remained looking in the direction his sometime friend had taken, "let us on, and endeavour to catch our horses. We may be met again in this dark pass, and, by my fay, it is not every night in the week a man meets with a—let me see—How called ye this friend in need?"

"Shakespeare," said Arderne, whilst he still lingered in the hope of catching another glimpse of his deliverer—"William Shakespeare."

"Ah, Shakespeare!" said the blunt Fluellyn, sheathing his rapier. "Truly so; but come on, a' God's name, I say; for 'tis not every wood at midnight that can produce a Shakespeare."

CHAPTER XXXIX.

OLD LONDON.

Our scene shifts now from the pleasant fields and sylvan retreats in which we have so long lingered, and changes to the great metropolis of England—London, in the olden time—a vastly different place, as our readers are doubtless well aware, both in size and aspect, from the same metropolis of the present day; since three parts of that which is now crowded with houses, intersected with streets and squares, and crammed with an overwhelming population, was then the haunt of the deer, the form of the hare, the park, the thicket, and the chace.

It is curious to imagine the appearance of this metropolis in Elizabeth's day. Its peculiar houses, with their sloping roofs and beetling stories, its narrow thoroughfares, and the variety of antique buildings, which still remained to tell the tale of former reigns, altogether producing a picturesque and beautiful effect, such as our readers have doubtless often dwelt on with pleasure in the old paintings of the time. Added also to the peculiar architectural beauty of that day, many of the better sort of edifices being detached, surrounded with tall trees, and standing within the rounding of their own gardens, presented a delicious and bowery appearance ere the very interior of the city was reached. The silver Thames, too, at this period, still flowed for the most part through green banks, until its tide passed the dark gates of the Tower, when for a small space the buildings were reared one upon another, as if they had apparently been thrust forward from the more crowded parts, and only hindered from toppling into the stream by the piles and heavy timbers of the crushed-up cabins underneath.

Thus the whole together, seen from the water, with their diamond-paned bay-windows encroaching over the stream, looked like the bulkheads of innumerable vessels crammed and cast in confusion along the margin of the river.

After passing this crowded mass, however, and which, in Elizabeth's reign, stretched out for a short distance, the eye of the passenger was again relieved by edifices both of a noble appearance, and by no means stinted to space, the banks even at this part of the river occasionally displaying a verdant appearance, and such buildings standing in their own proper grounds. For instance, the very important hostel of the Three Cranes, with its porch, its huge chimneys, and its ample rooms, was reared upon the grassy bank, its deep bay-windows looking out upon the stream. The frowning towers and dark water-gate of Barnard's Castle next appeared. Then came the ominous-looking tower of Bridewell. A few strokes of the oar, and the pleasant gardens of the White Friars met the eye. Then came the Temple Gardens, and after them the pile of buildings, with battlement and strong tower, called the Sauoye; after that, amongst many other important edifices, were to be seen the castellated towers of Duresme Place, York Place, the Courts, the Starre Chamber, Westminster Hall, with a sort of pier running out from the open court in front, and the Parliament House; then came the huge Abbey of Westminster, not as now, choked up by encroaching squalor, but standing in its magnificence in the midst of verdant meadows; and lastly came the Queen's Bridge.

On the Surrey side, the aspect of the Thames and its banks would have yet more surprised a modern eye, since there the wind still sighed amongst the reeds and long grass of centuries. On Lambeth Marsh stood the palace and church, together with some two dozen straggling edifices. But the Oxen's low was heard along the whole of that over-crowded part, so well known to the Londoner of the present day, and now so teeming with a squalid and overwhelming population. All along the banks on this side, trees and gardens, with an occasional row of houses, a goodly edifice, or a countryfied hostel were to be seen until the passenger came to Winchester Place, St. Mary Over, and London Bridge, with the gate-houses, towers, and multitudinous buildings, built all along it. Nay, the spectator, standing upon the top of one of the towers of the bridge and looking beyond the great blackened wall of Old London, beheld a large tract called the Spital Fyelds, in which the sheep fed beneath the shade of tall trees. Bishopgate Street, too, with its one long straggling thoroughfare, seemed a trifling village. In Finsburie Fyeld stood the windmill, and the kennel for hounds. Clerkenwell seemed but a single church with its surrounding wall. Gray's Inn Lane appeared a remote thoroughfare, leading to the open country, and Broad St. Jiles was a trifling village; whilst in Convent Garden, then comcompletely surrounded by a high and massive wall, stood a single edifice —the Convent, from which it took its name, and beyond it green meadows studded with trees.

Such, then, were the environs of London, at the period of which we write. Its interior we shall perhaps again have occasion to speak of during the progress of our story.

It was on the afternoon of the fifth day from his leaving Stratford-upon-Avon, that William Shakespeare, standing upon Hampstead Hill, looked upon London for the first time. The spot on which he stood (albeit it has now, like others we have mentioned, become one vast region of brick and mortar) was then studded with oaks, which had perhaps witnessed the gathering of the kightly and the noble for the Crusades. Immediately on his right, was the massive buttressed wall, inclosing the grounds of a half castellated and moated residence, a country seat of the Earl of Southampton.

As Shakespeare stood thus and gazed down upon the metropolis, he beheld many of those time-honoured edifices, yet remaining, which he had read of whilst studying the history of his native land.

Long did the future poet gaze upon the scene before him, and the setting sun was pouring down his softened glories, and bathing tower, and steeple, and wall, in a flood of molton gold, as he entered the suburbs. Suburbs which the traveller of the present day would have likened more to a row of hucksters' shops, or temporary buildings run up for a fair, than the outskirts of a great city.

Far as the eye could reach were to be seen those pent-house stalls, which, projecting into the highways, displayed the different articles of the different trades and occupations of the indwellers, and which being relieved by innumerable signs, tubs, long benches, stalls, smiths' forges, and quaint-looking inns or hostels, gave a most picturesque and diversified appearance to the whole.

It must have been a singular sight to behold that friendless young man, wending his way along the suburban streets of Old London. The dust of many miles upon his worn shoes, his spirits weary, and, like his own Touchstone, his legs weary too, and not a cross in his pocket. He was in London now, and the hard selfishness of the citizen he found somewhat different from the good-natured hospitality of the cottager. His last coin had been spent that morning, and he was weary and hungry withal. Yet still the first sight of the streets of London, as he gradually got into the interior, so much interested him, that he forgot both hunger and weariness and kept wandering on.

To the right he turned, now stopping to admire some relics of the days of the Plantagenets; and then to the left, now looking up at some edifice whose beetling stories, projecting over the street above, so nearly met a corresponding edifice on the opposite side, that the inhabitants might almost have shaken hands out of the upper floor windows. The increasing bustle of the great town he was every step becoming more involved in, he at first disregarded, being wholly taken up with the buildings he passed, and the curiosities every moment presented to his view. Occasionally, too, his attention was arrested by a group of cavaliers, dressed in all the magnificence of the period, as they rode gallantly through the streets. Then again, the furtive glance of the merry-eyed citizen's daughter, and which she threw at the exceeding handsome, though somewhat country-clad young man, as she tripped down some narrow passage, arrested him.

These matters caused Shakespeare ever and anon to stop and consider curiously, and, as he gazed around, the continual passers as constantly interrupted the current of his meditations.

Then he was rudely thrust from the causeway, as a swaggering party, ruffling and rustling in "unpaid-for-silks," and attended by a whole retinue of followers, passed on towards the court-end of the town, talking loud, swearing gallantly, and even singing snatches of songs as they progressed; elbowing the men from, and thrusting the females as unceremoniously to, the wall. Their huge trunks and short cloaks fluttering in the wind, their chains and various ornaments glittering in the sun, and the feathers in their high-crowned hats brushing the overhanging stories of the houses as they walked.

All these varieties, so new to the pedestrian, continually excited his curiosity, more especially as, from the conversation of several citizens, he found that rumours of events of importance were filling men's minds with the anticipation of events to come.

"Heard ye the news, neighbour," said one staid-looking burgher, "just brought in from Milford Haven? A Spanish fleet hath been sighted off those parts."

"Nay, neighbour," said another, "I heard not of the Spaniard. They do say, however, that the Duke of Guise hath landed in Sussex with a strong army."

"And I heard," continued a third, "that the Scot hath made an irruption into England. Nay, 'tis even whispered that Queen Mary hath escaped, and that the northern countries, have, in sooth, commenced an insurrection."

"Aye, and harkee, neighbours all," said a fourth, "only let it go no further, I heard tell in Paul's to-day of a new conspiracy to assassinate our good Queen Elizabeth, and set on foot, 'tis said, by L'Aubespine, the French Ambassador. Nay, I can tell thee that a mob hath beset the Frenchman's house, and he hath been ordered to quit the kingdom without delay. Aye, and 'tis said the Queen is much troubled with these things; that she keeps close, and much alone; that she muttereth much to herself, and seems in great tribulation."

"Not much wonder, either," said another. "'Tis certain she is in great terror and perplexity; and if she hesitate much longer to order the execution of the Queen of Scots, the kingdom will be burnt up in an *auto-da-fé*."

As Shakespeare listened to these rumours he still continued to wander on amidst the labyrinth of lanes, alleys, and buildings in which he found himself. Now he progressed through a dense mass of wooden tenements called Shoe Lane, the streets crooked and narrow, and overshadowed by a perpetual twilight, from the abutments overhead, rising, as we before said, story above story, until they almost closed upon each other. Then, again, he turned down another street, retraced his steps, wandered back through Crow Lane into Gifford Street, and was brought up by the huge black-looking mass constituting Old London Wall. Gazing up at the ramparts of this dark boundary, he made his way along the Old Bailey, passed through Lud's Gate, and found himself in the large open space in which stood the then gothic-looking structure of St. Paul's. Here he found a large concourse of people, men, women, and children, leaping, shouting, and holding a sort of revel around a huge bonfire kindled just at the part called Ave Maria, whilst a second rout were collecting in the vicinity of a sort of stage erected opposite the houses named Paternoster Row.

Leaning upon his staff, in the shade of the old gothic building, he gazed upon the scene before him as the chimes rung out from the tower. He stood apart from that crowd alone, unknowing any, unknown to all, on a spot now covered by the vast building since reared upon those ancient foundations: and, as he stood, he looked upon a scene which called up associations no longer likely to be engendered in such locality; for all is gone which could impress the mind with the times in which he himself lived, or with the deeds of a former age.

The edifice itself, at that period, told of monkish intolerance and monastic grandeur; when the knightly and the noble bowed their necks, and walked bareheaded on the flags beneath, and even kings did penance amongst the mean and miserable at its shrine.

He was amidst the mighty dead—the men of whom he had read in his home at Stratford! The Norman kings, in all the pomp and circumstance of their feudal pride, had walked upon that spot. Then, again, as he seated himself upon an ancient tomb, his thoughts turned upon his own welfare and prospects, and he began to ask himself, for the first time since his arrival in London, what course he was to pursue? Now that he had reached this aim and end of his journey, what was he in reality the better for it? He knew no one: he had neglected to make inquiries of his own friends as to persons to whom he might have got a recommendation; and money—the best friend of the traveller—he had none. But then, he was in London. "Truly so," he thought to himself. "The more fool for being there, when in the country he was in a better place." And then he thought of home, of wife, children, and other relations, and then his heart softened, and he wept. Yes! there, amidst the bustle of Old Paul's, whilst the Londoners recreated themselves before a sort of moveable stage, on which certain dramatic representations were exhibited to the gaping crowd on one side, and the bonfire raged on the other, and all was uproar and hilarity,—there did Shakespeare sit and weep, "in pure melancholy and troubled brain." At length, overcome with weariness, he leant back against an old tomb, and fell asleep amidst the hubbub.

And, as he slept, came swaggering by, the gay fop—the gallant of the city—the tavern-haunter—the ruffler—and the bully. Then paced by the more staid and sober citizens, "merchants our well-dealing countrymen;" but they stopped not to glance upon the tired stranger. Then came flaunting along, tempted out by the beauty of the evening, the city madam with her gossip, the merry wives of Chepe; and, as they passed, they stopped for a moment to glance upon the well-knit limbs and handsome face of the homeless Shakespeare. They marked his travelled look, his dusty shoes, and his worn doublet, and they felt inclined to arouse him, and ask the cause of that pallid cheek, and his sleeping in the open air at such an hour. But then, a titter from the rude gallant as he passed, sent them forward amidst the throng. Then came the cut-purse, as the shadows deepened, and he stole a furtive glance around the dark old building. But the night was not far enough advanced for him safely to rifle the pockets of the sleeper, or slit his windpipe unobserved; and so Shakespeare slept on amidst the throng. Quietly, sweetly did he slumber, until, as night approached, the crowd gradually dispersed, the stage disappeared, and all deepened down. Soundly, heavily, slept that wonderful man amidst scenes which he was ere long to render famous in all time. One touch of his pen was to picture Old Paul's and Lud's Town, as no other could picture them. He was to revel in these scenes amidst which he now unconsciously slumbered, so as no mortal ever revelled before. He was to call up those bright kings, and all the glittering host, and shew them in harness, as they had lived, and to render all that would else have been unknown in Old London—a dream of delight. Nay, those even who dwelt hard by in East Cheap, knew not East Cheap; and London itself was to have an interest lent to it, such as the dwellers in it at that moment little thought of. And so Shakespeare slept the sleep of weariness—of "weariness which snores upon the flint."

By-and-by, an old poor man, clad in scraps and tatters, "his whole apparel built upon pins," his ragged beard descending to his waist, and carrying a filthy wallet on his back, as he poked about, and picked up bones in the churchyard, came and looked upon him, and after a few moments' contemplation, stirred him with the end of his staff and awoke him. "Best not sleep here so late, young master," he said; "'tis unsafe."

Shakespeare rubbed his eyes, stared at the crooked object before him, and thanked him for the caution. "I have," he said, "no cause for fear, since I have nothing to lose. Nevertheless, I thank thee."

"Nothing to fear!" said the tatterdemalion, "nothing to lose! What call ye nothing? Have ye not life to lose? Have ye not clothes? By my troth! there be those haunting Paul's at night, young man, that will take the one for the sake of the other, and so rob ye of both."

"Both are valueless, or at least worth little," said Shakespeare, smiling. "Hark, the chimes! how sweetly they sound."

"Sweeter to those who hear them in a good bed," said the man. "They are the midnight chimes! wherefore dost thou not seek thy home, young master?"

"I should seek that which I should hardly find," said Shakespeare. "I have no home, good friend, at least, not in London."

"Neither home nor coin?" said the aged man.

"Neither one nor the other," returned Shakespeare; "and but a few hours old in London."

"But you've friends here?" inquired the old man.

"Poor in that as in all else," returned Shakespeare.

"Wilt come with me?" said the old man; "I can find thee a roof for one night, perhaps food too."

"I almost die for food," said Shakespeare; "and thankfully follow thee." And so the tatterdemalion led the way from St. Paul's, and Shakespeare followed him.

Through dark alleys and curious thoroughfares did that lean old man thread his way, ever and anon, as he trampled along and turned the corner of some fresh street, stopping for a moment to observe if his follower took the right turn, where so many closes, alleys, and courts existed; for as they made their way to the water-side, he occasionally came amongst houses so thickly and irregularly placed, that, by night, he himself could scarcely thread the labyrinth. Passing through Dowegate, Bush-lane, and Pudynge-lane, he at last stopped before a house in Bylyngsgate. The tenement before which the old man stopped would have been termed in our own days but a shed, since, seen from the street, it apparently consisted but of one large bay window, thrust out from a square wooden building, a large brick chimney sprouting out in rear.

On opening the door, which was situated within a sort of blind alley on one side, the proprietor of the domicile signed to his guest to follow, and entered the one apartment, which indeed constituted the entire dwelling.

Not only was it the parlour, kitchen, and sleeping-apartment of the occupants, but, as the guest glanced around it, he observed, by the light of a lamp placed on a table near the window, that it was fitted up as a sort of laboratory; and its walls being accommodated with shelves, were crowded wlth vials, gallipots, and vessels of antique formation, containing precious unguents, filters, and compounds, perhaps in the present day no longer to be found in the Pharmacopœia. In addition to this, there was also means for experimentalising in the deep science of alchemy,—all which was apparent from the crucibles, retorts, and other vessels scattered around the hearth. Such as the apartment was, the needy-looking hollow-eyed proprietor, and who, Shakespeare surmised was a medical practitioner of that squalid neighbourhood, welcomed his guest to his poor dwelling; and with an alacrity which was hardly to be expected from his appearance, placed wine and refreshment before him; and then opening an ample closet at the further end of the apartment, shewed him a mattrass on which he could repose for the night.

"I have little to offer, young master," he said; "and seldom offer that little. But I saw that in your face which interested me as you slept. You reminded me of a bright youth, my hope in better days, my only son, long since dead; and as I watched thy countenance, I read a bright fortune in store for thee."

And Shakespeare wrung the hand of that old man, so needy-looking and pinched, and slept without fear under his roof, in the then dangerous locality of Bylyngsgate, and where perhaps he might never again awake alive.

CHAPTER XL.

THE POOR PLAYER.

On the morning which followed the events narrated in the foregoing chapter, the traveller took leave of the exceedingly poor but kind old man who had so hospitably sheltered him. He thanked him for his goodness, and bestowed upon him a small ring, which he took from his finger, the only trifle of value in his possession. And that old host attended his guest to the door, and bestowed his blessing upon him, and followed him with his eyes as he wended his way along the narrow thoroughfare, and then still stood and looked in the direction he had gone long after he was out of sight. And then he turned with a sigh and re-entered his dwelling. "Ah, well-a-day," he said, "we may grub on in misery for years and years, and forget the goodly beings we have known in youth and happiness, outliving all that we loved and honoured in the world, and still amidst the contaminating filth of poverty and woe pass our weary lives, and then some superior specimen of goodness and grace as suddenly revives in our recollection of the beings we have seen in bygone times. What would I give, an I were amongst the crowned monarchs of the world, to have yonder youth to companion me? To hear his words, as I have this morning heard them? to see him as I have seen him but now, within this lowly hovel?" And then the old man took the platter from which his guest had eaten, and washed it and put it aside, and set back the three-legged stool on which Shakespeare had sat, and then he wept as he said to himself, "An if I look not upon him again, I will keep these as relics, never to be used by others, for, God forgive me, but I think, as I recollect his words, that yonder man was something more than mortal." And then the old man examined the gold ring his guest presented him with, and as he did so, he gradually approached the crucible upon the fire, and again he looked upon the gift, and, hesitating for a moment as his eye fell upon the crucible, he sighed and dropped the ring into it.

It is evening, and the sun shines upon the banks of the Thames on the Surrey side.

The scenic hour oft-times presents to our readers such a picture as we now invite them to look upon. The houses on this side the river are both irregularly placed and situated, as we have before described, namely, standing here and there apart, amidst trees and gardens, and occasionally neighboured by some edifice of a bygone time, and whose build speaks of monastic grandeur and castellated defence.

Looking from the grassy bank upon the Thames at this part, we behold the stream rushing impetuously through innumerable arches of a dark heavy-built bridge—a bridge which frowns with towers and turrets of curious form and ancient architecture, and which turrets and towers are graced and garnished with the ghastly heads of criminals and traitors lately executed.

As the red glare of the evening sun falls upon these buildings, it is reflected in the innumerable windows with which they are accommodated, at the same time it displays each "coign of vantage," each grated embrasure, each coping-stone, buttress, and battlement of the complicated structure in colours of gold.

The arch and flanking tower, and the iron portcullis and cresset, are all there as if in a heated furnace.

Turning again towards the shore as we stand upon the bank, after passing the ancient edifices called Winchester Place, we behold a long row of buildings near the water's edge, and somewhat removed in the open space behind them, a curiously constructed and somewhat ugly building of a round form. On its top is a small and quaint-looking structure—a sort of "*watch-case to a common 'larum bell*,"—and the whole surmounted by a flag, on which is written "*The Globe.*" A few shrubs and stunted trees are immediately around this building: and the space beyond that, for about half a bow-shot, is gravelled, and even, in some parts, strewed with fresh rushes recently cut from the river's bank.

Some fifty yards to the left of this is a rival structure, composed of stakes and high palings—a sort of stockade, round which flutter half-a-dozen little markers or flags; and over the gateway which admits into the arena, is written in large characters the words "*The Bull Bayting.*"

A little removed from the former of these buildings, stands a hostel of the commoner sort, with its garden in rear, several goodly trees before its porch, and a bowling-green pleasantly shadowed. Benches are before this inn, and also under the trees, and the actors upon the scene are both many and rather uncommon in appearance.

The inn is indeed the haunt of those persons who find employment in the two houses of entertainment we have described. The hangers-on of the Globe Theatre, and the employés of the Bull and Bear-bayting, men of a character and disposition somewhat peculiar. They are indeed, many of them, *sui generis*, something in style and demeanour between the magnifico and the mountebank, and yet amongst them are men of appearance and talent worthy of a better station.

As they congregate about this rallying-point, they seem the very genii of idleness; and, in their listless indifference, above the doings and events of this work-a-day world.

Here a fellow, with his beaver cocked, and swaggering gait, throws out his arm, in order to display a cloak of three-piled velvet, whilst his toes are seen peeping from the foot of an ample russet boot. There a comrade, evidently "a horse of the same colour," an "affected fantastico," points a toe in attitude, twists a moustache with a grace, plays off a gauntlet with a flourish, and struts "like chanticleer i' the sun." These are the magnificoes of the walk. Then come a crowd of under-strappers, whose vocation is in their very look, who even play their parts hourly, and *live* in character—either aping the grandee, the gallant, the swaggerer, or the lisping idiotic driveller; the clowns and jesters making up the file.

Each speaks with an accompanying gesture, and walks with a circumstance. Some have a sort of sad hilarity, and utter dull jokes with a grave brow, or laugh *in a sort*. They even wear a ceremonious observance towards each other, and look upon the world in general in an inferior light. The free-masonry of bombast is rife amongst the fellowship. If one hands the tankard to his fellow, standing with mine host beneath the porch, he does so with a flourish, and receives it again cross-handed. In short, as they are seen congregated about their haunt, or place of call, they seem uninterested in the common-place events of the world as other men. Their ideas are inflated and dreamy; their world, their kingdom, is their theatre, and their lives felt to be but passed whilst they strut their hour before the admiring throng. "The best actors in the world, either for scene individable, or poem unlimited." "Seneca could not be too heavy, nor Plautus too light for them." Whilst these characters walk and talk, flourish and attitudinize, a trumpet sounds from the roof of the round building first described, at which some amongst them seem to start like the war-horse aroused; others pay their shot to mine host; others again wave a hand gracefully to the buxom landlady at the latticed window; and all take their way to the theatre. They are indeed summoned to prepare for the scenic hour, to rehearse their parts—such as those parts are.

Amongst these men there were, as we have hinted, some individuals of a superior stamp, men of high attainments, considering the period in which they lived, and who, finding no vent for the talents they were in possession of, passed their hours amongst the choice spirits of the Globe.

There was a romance in the lives of some of these latter, in keeping with their appearance; and one or two had attempted a higher flight, and endeavoured to improve the style of dramatic composition. Nor had they altogether failed, for many dramas had been written by them possessing real and absolute excellence.

Scarce half-an-hour had elapsed after the trumpet sounded from the Globe, when a man passed through the various portals upon London Bridge; and, as chance directed, turning to the left upon the Surrey side of the river, quickly took his way amongst the ancient buildings then lining the bank.

Wearied and faint from lack of food—for he had been all day wandering through the streets of London,—he stopped beside the Norman structure, built during the crusades by William Pont de l'Arche, and called St. Mary Ouer.

The curious in antiquities will, we fear, look in vain for any vestige of this remnant of the early English, which nevertheless, in Elizabeth's day, with its church and monastery, extended down to the very edge of the Thames.

Leaning upon his staff, undecided in which direction to turn his steps, Shakespeare stopped beside the dark walls of this ancient edifice; and, after gazing upon the building with interest for some moments, entered the porch of the old monastery.

Whilst he remained there, several cavaliers on horseback rode past —gay youths, tricked out in all the extravagance of that age of extravagant costume; their loud laughter, and joyous converse, as they careered along, shewing that their spirits were gay as their habits. They came from the bridge over which he himself had just crossed, and took their way along the massive wall then skirting the antique buildings of Winchester Place.

Whilst Shakespeare continued to remark the several parties occasionally passing, he also observed that boats, containing companies of ladies, also put into a small landing-place near at hand; and these latter parties took the same direction the horsemen had gone.

The beauty of the evening, the fresh air from the river, the monastic grandeur of the old buildings, and the cheerful appearance of the various companies he at the moment beheld, somewhat revived his drooping spirits. He felt it impossible to be quite unhappy, whilst all around was gay, and the scene so lovely.

Listlessly he continued to watch the various boats; and as the parties disembarked and passed on, in their thoughtless hilarity, he arose, and bent his steps in the same direction.

He passed through the open field along that strong buttressed wall, then inclosing Winchester Place; and a few paces brought him to the close vicinity of a building, around which several persons at that moment were congregated—the Globe Theatre. The place and scene altogether interested him, and again he stopped to observe the throng, and which, as it altogether presented a somewhat singular appearance, we shall ourselves stop with him to observe.

The entrance of the building was accommodated with benches on either side, on which were seated various of the hangers-on of the establishment, and one or two of the actors, waiting for their call. Amongst these, a couple of clowns or fools were conspicuous; and as they uttered their witticisms, and performed divers tricks, for the amusement of themselves and their companions, they collected an audience without, which frequently recruited those within—cracking their jokes, and familiarizing themselves with the various companies as they came up. These were, indeed, the all-licensed fools of the time, and without whose presence and aid no performance was considered perfect; they bore off, in some sort, the tedium of the long dialogue then in vogue.

Whilst Shakespeare stood to regard the scene before him, the flourish of drum and trumpet within the building recalled these motley-minded gentry and their companions to their various duties; and at the same moment a gay party of mounted cavaliers approached, dismounted, and entered.

Still that tired stranger, as he stood beside the portals of the theatre, continued to feel an interest in all that was going on there. The merry glance of the citizen's wife, as she passed in,—the answering look of the gallant as he followed,—the gay and flaunting party from the Court-end of the town,—the loud laugh, the sharp rebuke, the coarse jest, the retort courteous, and the counter-check quarrelsome,—all were there.

By-and-by a couple of cavaliers, splendidly mounted and magnificently apparelled, came galloping up. They dismounted at the door, and the one nearest Shakespeare threw the rein of his steed to him, and desired him to hold the horse, at the same moment thrusting a silver coin into the youth's hand. His companion meanwhile had confided his charger to the care of one of the employés of the theatre, and the next moment both these gallants were within the Globe. They had passed so quickly, that Shakespeare found himself in possession of the coin and the steed, ere he had time fully to observe the person of the cavalier who had favoured him with his custody.

As he looked at the money, a slight blush tinged his cheek, but he repressed the feeling of shame which at first intruded itself, as he reflected the money was honestly come by. He then looked more curiously upon the noble animal intrusted to his charge.

Passionately fond of a horse, like most men bred and born in the country, he examined its points with interest. It was in truth a noble animal, answering in every point the description he has himself given of a perfect courser:

> "Round hoofed, short-pointed, fetlocks shag and long,
> Broad breast, full eye, small head, and nostril wide,
> High chest, short ears, straight legs, and passing strong,
> Thin mane, thick tail, broad buttock, tender hide.
> Look, what a horse should have, he did not lack."

Pulling the arched neck of the noble steed, he then led him towards the man holding its fellow.

"Know you the owner of this goodly horse?" he inquired.

The man was evidently a sort of character, a swaggerer who wished to pass for a gentleman and a soldier, albeit his elbows were ragged, and his whole dress patched and furbished up.

"Know I Master Edmund Spencer?" he said, looking contemptuously upon Shakespeare. "Where canst thou have lived, boy, to ask the question. Best inquire me next for the rider of *this* nag, Sir Walter Raleigh. Thou knowest not the choice spirits of the Court. Ergo, thou art strange to the town."

"I am, in sooth, a stranger to the town," said Shakespeare; "but a few hours old in it."

"And from whence?" inquired the other.

"From Warwickshire," returned Shakespeare.

"The county I know," returned the other; "my grandsire was of Warwick, eke also. Hast coin in pouch, camarado mine?"

"I have," said Shakespeare, producing the silver piece given him by Spenser the moment before.

"Ha!" said the other, "then will we adventure to yonder hostel in search of liquor and food wherewith to repair ourselves, for sooth to say thou lookest both pale and hungry. Come ye of the Ardens of Warwickshire?"

"One way I do," said Shakespeare. "But Arden is not my name. Call me William."

"'Tis no matter," said the other; "thou art a proper fellow of thy hands, and I have taken a fancy for thy companionship. Lead on thy steed good William; a cup of Canary and a toast will cheer thee."

And thus did Shakespeare make a friend and procure the refreshments he so much required, and with the poor player sitting beside him on the bench, whilst they held the horses beneath the tree, under the influence of "the good familiar creature, wine," he unbosomed himself to this new comrade.

"I will befriend thee in all I can," said the player, and who in truth, being but a sorry stick, was himself rarely employed, "I will myself advocate thy fortunes, good rustic," he continued. "I do spy in thy face and figure marvellous proper attributes for certain parts, for the which we are in want of actors. Ah, by Apollo! thou hast the limbs, and thews, and form, to captivate the fancy of ladies fair."

CHAPTER XLI.

THE TAVERN REVEL.

The general aspect of London in the reign of Elizabeth is so singular, when contrasted with the same great metropolis of our own day, that we must again refer to it.

The houses in the heart of the city, like those in the suburbs, were still chiefly built of wood, or of wood and brick; the poverty of their appearance being the more apparent from their being, ever and anon, relieved by the stately and massive building of former days. The dark monastery, the massive wall, or the castellated edifice, were constantly to be seen amidst streets so crooked and narrow, and so dismal from the abutments overhead, that foreigners, as they threaded their way, and amidst damp and wind, are said to have likened London to the vale of death. In wet weather the streets were especially dismal, and so prevalent were consumption and pestilence that bonfires were ofttimes kindled in order to purify the air and avert the plague. Nay, even kites and ravens were to be seen hopping about the various thoroughfares, being kept by many inhabitants for the purpose of devouring the filth.

Nothing, indeed, could well exceed the contrast during Elizabeth's reign between the splendid, though somewhat barbaresque, magnificence of the mansions of the nobles and gentry, and the houses of the commoner sort of people. Yet still, although the houses of the citizens were for the most part poor and ill-contrived, yet every now and then would be found amongst them, the dwelling of some richer trader which broke the uniformity of the general mass; such edifice having a quantity of gable ends at all heights and in all directions, with chimneys of fantastic shape and profuse ornament, and covered with decorations; the multitudinous frames in its windows completed the picture.

These were the dwellings of some of the merchant-princes of the town, whose strongly-barred and iron-studded doors shewed that where wealth was to be found defence was necessary against the lawless spirits roaming through the dark thoroughfares at hand.

Another contrast to the filthy, unpaved, and uncared-for state of the streets and thoroughfares at this period, was the costly style in which many of the houses were ornamented on any occasion of rejoicing or pageantry. At such times every window and pent-house was garnished with banners and strips of tapestry, or hung with rich fragments of velvet, damask, or silk, whilst the city functionaries and the various companies "in robe and furred gown," and attended by a host of proper fellows, apparelled in silk and chain of gold, contributed to make up the show.

On the morning which followed the night Shakespeare made acquaintance with the poor player he awoke in a small, low roofed apartment in the upper floor of the hostel of the Globe. He felt himself considerably refreshed, and rising from his truckle bed he threw open the window and looked forth upon the well wooded hills of Surrey. It was a pleasant picture at that time, and the inn itself, being of considerable size, presented a stirring and bustling scene. Immediately beneath him was the ample stable-yard, with long rows of out-buildings and sheds appropriated to the varieties of cattle usually driven from the country on certain days of the week, the horses of the carriers being on one side, and the stabling for those of travellers of a better sort on the other. Then there were other buildings appropriate to the large quantities of poultry which it was customary at this period to rear, besides the ample dove-cot, which stood beyond the bowery garden, and which harboured such flights of pigeons that their rush through the air was heard at considerable distance as they wheeled and circled about.

"Tired nature's great restorer, balmy sleep," had laid so heavily upon the wanderer that it was somewhat late when he awoke, and the bustle in the inn-yard below proclaimed that the business of the day had commenced.

Returning from the window he sat himself down on the bed to consider his prospects. After awhile he took from an inside pocket of his doublet a small roll of paper. It was an unfinished poem, "the first heir of his invention," and which he had carefully preserved and brought with him, intending to finish and, if possible, get it into print at some futnre opportunity.

The composition seemed to please him, for his countenance brightened as he read it, and he quickly lost all thought of self in the thoughts conjured up. Taking out his tablets, for pen and ink were articles not so readily found at hand as in our own times, as he gazed upon the well-wooded hills in the distance "burnished with the morning sun," he added the following stanza to his poem—

"Lo, here the gentle lark, weary of rest,
From his moist cabinet mounts up on high,
And wakes the morning, from whose silver breast
The sun arises in his majesty;
Who doth the world so gloriously behold,
That cedar tops and hills seem burnished gold."

Scarcely had he thus commenced when a slight tap at his door disturbed him, and his new friend the player entered.

"Ah! by St. Paul," said the player, "have we writers here? How, Sir traveller, inditest thou thus early? I aroused thee not—I called thee not—I disturbed thee not; for much toil maketh the limbs weary, and I would have thee, good rustic, freshened and refreshened. But lad, I find thee up and working with brain and pencil. Come—I have brought thee a chalice for thy morning draught. Indue thy habiliments—descend to the lower world—and I will take thee before Master Marlow, who will, peradventure, find thee apt, and capable of preferment."

Shakespeare thanked the player, whose bombast considerably amused him; and putting up his poem, accompanied him to the common apartment of the tavern, then filled with a motley assemblage. After procuring something by way of a breakfast, which the remaining portion of the money given him the night before enabled him to do, he accompanied his new acquaintance over to the Globe.

Early as was the hour, the business of the morning had commenced, and many of the actors engaged in rehearsing a new play.

The scene altogether was a new and striking one, and instantly engaged his attention.

As his eye took the whole interior in its glance, a forcible impression was made upon his mind. The stage—the rude half-circle of seats and benches, seen thus in the shadowy light admitted from several small openings—the various picturesque figures sitting and lounging about, some of them being on the centre of the stage, and rehearsing their parts—the melody of the tragic rhythm—all impressed him. He even, at the moment, conceived a visionary project of one day making the means and appliances he beheld around subservient to his own mighty conceptions. In an instant, the want of something long sought seemed found; and then again, as he looked round, and his mind grasped the possibility of his project he said to himself—

"But, can this cock-pit hold
The vasty fields of France? or may we cram
Within this wooden O, the very casques
That did affright the air at Agincourt?"

Whether it could or not, he was not then permitted further to consider. The possibility of such an event, time was to shew; and in the meanwhile the player disturbing the current of his thoughts, tapped him on the shoulder, and invited him to follow to a small apartment, situated on one side of the building, and which constituted a sort of manager's room.

The proprietor of this apartment was at the moment engaged in the composition of a new piece; and as he wrote, he ever and anon rose from his seat, and with voice and gesture, recited a portion of his composition, though, perhaps, had he better known the man introduced into his presence, he would have been less verbose before him.

As it was, he continued to rehearse in a ranting tone, sawing the air with his hand, and strutting up and down to give effect to the lines.

During a pause of consideration, he observed the player and his companion, "Ah!" he said, "what wants that youth?"

"Pay and employment, good master mine," said the player.

"Hath he wit?—can he speak?—are his legs strong?—arms pliant?"

"He is young, strong, and of good parts," said the player—"I can avouch it."

"Then will we find him in employment," said the manager; "he shall have charge of the footlights, and snuff the lamps." And so Shakespeare became attached to the theatre.

CHAPTER XLII.

MORE STRANGE THAN TRUE.

In a former chapter we have seen Walter Arderne, after many and various adventures by flood and field, returning to the home and haunts of his childhood. The good and gallant youth (although from station and prospects he might reasonably have hoped for ease and happiness in life) had hitherto seemed but a step-son of fortune after all. And now, "like a younker and a prodigal," lean, rent, and tattered, having endured shipwreck and been sold to slavery by the insolent foe, by a sudden freak of fortune was once more safe in Warwickshire and with his beloved uncle at Clopton. The meeting between Sir Hugh and his nephew was extremely affecting. They were now all in all to each other, for both had experienced losses which to both were irreparable. The grief, however, they experienced for past sorrows had now considerably abated, so that they could hold converse upon bygone events and even find benefit from such communion.

Still, when Walter looked around him in his old neighbourhood, like Sir Hugh when he had first returned, he felt at times a sense of desolation which was almost insupportable. The loss of his old and tried friend, the eccentric Martin, was also a heavy blow to him; and in addition to this the absence and delinquency of the singular friend, whose conversation had made so great an impression upon them all, during their short acquaintance, especially grieved him. The breath of slander, when he came to inquire into the facts leading to young Shakespeare's departure, had rendered that youth's conduct so reckless and even criminal that Walter was as much surprised as grieved at all he heard.

"It was a good thing," Mr. Doubletongue said, "that the *Ne'er-do-well* had made off with himself, or the Lord knew what he would be after next. Stealing of deer by night, and catching rabbits by day, would perhaps have been the least part of the story. Nay," he continued, "the lad (albeit he had a most comely female to wife) had as sharp an eye and as devilish a tongue for the lasses in Stratford as—"

"Thou thyself hast, neighbour," said Dismal. "Howbeit he hath departed this town, and peradventure this life too, for since he shook the dust from his shoes and fled hence, I believe no word hath been received of him. Let us hope he *is* dead and buried."

"Nay," said Doubletongue, "such ill-weeds die not so easily. I rather think he hath quitted the kingdom—peradventure joined the Spaniard." And so the ill-tongued gossips of Stratford shook their heads in answer to Arderne's inquiries, and he forebore all further questions from that time. Nevertheless, a few days after his arrival at Clopton, Walter repaired to Stratford in order to inform the young man's friends that he had met with and received an essential service from the wanderer whilst upon the road; and at the same time he delivered the small autograph which announced the welfare of the writer. In doing this he found how greatly the flight and its cause had grieved the father and the mother of Shakespeare, and all his family, whilst the wife of the errant youth had been taken home by her parents to Shottery.

The stately woolcomber, who had all the pride of a good old English yeoman of his day, deeply felt the disgrace of having a son thus "given to courses wild," and although he would by no means allow that his dearly loved William had done aught to be ashamed of, yet still as he had always said such courses would lead to ruin, he now bitterly felt the truth of his own words. And so, as Walter observed all this, he forbore to make further inquiry. The captain of the Falcon had accompanied Walter Arderne to Clopton on his return, and as the company of the adventurer was agreeable, and he was, on the whole, a good-natured, open-hearted seaman, he remained there for some time.

It was about a year after the return of Arderne to Clopton, that one morning, whilst seated with Sir Hugh and Captain Fluellyn in the oak-pannelled room, Pouncet Grasp was announced. This announcement caused some little surprise, as neither Sir Hugh nor Walter knew of any business likely to bring the shrewd lawyer to Clopton.

"I like not the fellow's name, even," said Sir Hugh, "since that pestilent matter which sent me to the Tower. What doth he here?"

"'Tis ever a bird of ill-omen," said Walter; "a wretch who lives by trickery and deceit. Was it not this Grasp whom Sir Thomas Lucy employed to prosecute young Master Shakespeare, and whose activity drove the lad from the town?"

"Ah!" said the Captain, "what then? 'Tis a sort of stormy-petrel, whose presence is always the forerunner of storm and tempest. Eh? is't not so?"

"Even so," said Sir Hugh, "'tis a dangerous caitiff."

"I would have such rascals hanged in clusters!" said the captain. "As they *live* by the law, they should *die* by the law! Let's out and see him tossed in a blanket!"

"That would be but an inhospitable reception," said the old knight, after stroking his beard, and considering. "By 'ur Lady but we will see the knave, and hear what he really wants at Clopton. Hubald," he continued to the serving-man, "shew him in."

When the lawyer accordingly entered, he made so many contortions of body, and bent and bowed so often and so humbly to the three gentlemen, never even venturing to lift his eyes from the floor, that the Knight of Clopton desired him to desist from his prostrations, and deliver himself.

"Come forward, man," he said, "and cease these ceremonious observances. We are neither pagan deities nor eastern despots, but good and true-born Englishmen. Hold up your head, speak plain, sooth, and fear nothing!"

Upon this Master Grasp muttered some words about his sorrow for past passages, and his desire to oblige the good Sir Hugh, and ended by depositing on the table the eternal blue bag he always carried; saying, as he did so, that he had no particular business at that moment with Sir Hugh Clopton at all.

"Then, if such is the case," said Sir Hugh, "as I especially hate law and all appertaining, Master Grasp, as speedily as convenient, remove yourself from our premises."

"Nay," said Grasp, "good Sir Hugh, I pray you bear with me, since I come to bring joyful tidings to one *near* and *dear* to you—even your worshipful nephew there, Master Walter Arderne. And in order to convince you thereof, with permission, I will enter upon the matter at once." As he said this, Grasp emptied the contents of his bag upon the table, and forthwith began to fumble amongst a whole heap of parchments, strewing them about in most admired disorder.

"Gad-be-here!" exclaimed the old knight, as he looked with astonishment upon the vast quantity of documents and deeds. "Here be matter enough to undo half the families in Warwickshire. 'Fore Heaven, I ne'er looked upon such a mass of parchments before. Lord help thee, Walter, and keep pen and ink out of thy hands, for an thou settest thy name to these deeds, thou'lt never be thine own man again. I pr'ythee," he continued to the lawyer, "leave sorting that mass, and explain thy business."

"Grasp, however, had now made good his footing, and produced his impression. And, as he pointed with fore-finger from paper to paper, he began to recapitulate the various tracts of land, domains, and estates and all and sundry thereunto belonging, with messuages, tenements, and matters appertaining, so rapidly that Sir Hugh stood aghast, with eyes starting and face of wonder, as he listened.

At length, the knight put a stop to it all with a voice of thunder, and insisted upon a more clear demonstration of the matter in hand. "What, in the fiend's name," he said, "hath my nephew to do with your heirs male, your tenures, domains, your castles, windmills, your fee-simples, your tails and entails, your arable lands, wastes, commons, fishponds, and woodlands, and all the litany of impertinence you have been uttering for the last half hour?"

"In fact and in right," said Grasp, *de facto* and *de jure*, all and every thing hath your nephew to do herewith."

"How so?" said Arderne. "I know nought about the lands you have named, unless it be that here, in Warwickshire, I have heard such places exist."

"Nevertheless, as sure as they exist, they to all appearance are at this moment your own, good Master Arderne," said Grasp.

"Mine?" said Arderne. "The man is mad. I pray you explain."

"I will so," said the lawyer. "May I be permitted to sit in this presence."

"Take a chair," said Sir Hugh. And the lawyer accordingly seated himself, wiped his glasses, and commenced again.

"You doubtless are aware that, by the father's side, you can claim kindred with the noble house of Plantagenet," he said.

"It's a far-away relationship then," said Arderne. "Nevertheless I believe such is the case; but what of that?"

"You know it well enough, good Master Arderne," said Grasp; "for it is a thing to thank God and to be proud of; and you also know that the Lady Clara de Mowbray was also akin to you. As thus:—Geoffrey Plantagenet wedded with ——."

"Well, a truce with all matter of that sort," interrupted Arderne. "I know my lineage well as thou canst tell it me, Master Grasp. But what of Clara de Mowbray?" Granting I am her distant kinsman, and distant indeed must the relationship be ——."

"Nevertheless it is true, as I am in a condition to prove," said Grasp. "Nay, not only are you her kinsman, but you are her sole remaining kinsman, and to obviate all controversy about succession, she hath constituted and appointed you her sole heir."

"You do, indeed, astonish me," said Arderne; "is then the beautiful Clara de Mowbray dead?"

"'Tis so rumoured, set down, and given out," said Grasp.

"She is said to have gone to foreign parts," said Sir Hugh; "died she there!"

"She did," said Grasp.

Alas! my poor daughter's dear and only friend!" exclaimed Sir Hugh. And then there was a pause of some moments amongst the party, whilst Grasp, whose heart was as hard and dry as the parchment he idolized, became again so deeply involved amongst his papers, that he seemed to lose sight of everything else around him; nay, even Sir Hugh and Arderne seemed totally to have forgotten his presence. Arderne, indeed, was lost in the thoughts this intelligence had conjured up. He called to mind the exceeding beauty of the high-born lady who thus had made him the heir to all her vast possessions; and as he did so, many little passages between them, during his intimacy with his cousin Charlotte, flashed across his brain. At length, as his eye fell upon Grasp, he again questioned him.

"You were apparently employed," he said, "by the Lady Clara de Mowbray as her lawyer, Master Grasp?"

"I had that honour," said Grasp. "I was the instrument by which, under direction of her major-domo, or house steward, she gathered in her various rents. May I hope for a continuance of favour for the like, from your honour?"

"Know you the circumstances of the lady's decease, and where she died?" inquired Arderne.

"I do," said Grasp, "inasmuch as having been bound for the term of one year to keep the circumstances pertaining to the event secret; that time having now expired, I am at liberty to divulge to this honoured company all I know thereof."

"I pray you to proceed," said Arderne.

"It seemeth, then, said Grasp, "as I am given to understand by the steward or major-domo before-named, that since the melancholy fate of the daughter of the honoured master of this house, and who was (under favour for mentioning it) buried alive ———"

"How! buried alive?" said the captain, laying down his pipe, whilst Sir Hugh groaned aloud, rose from his seat, and walked to the window, and Walter Arderne started as if he had received a bullet through his brain.

"Buried alive!" iterated Grasp, as he watched his auditors with the utmost satisfaction and curiosity. "I conceive it is no libel to say so much, *inasmuch* as it is well known, and has indeed made some talk at the time."

"I pray you," said Arderne sternly, "to continue your relation, without further circumstance. You pain us all by such unnecessary particulars."

"Nay," said Grasp, "I crave pardon; but as the particularly horrible nature of that young lady's end was in some sort necessary to what follows, I felt obliged, in some sort, to refer to it. Howbeit, I will now expedite my narrative, taking it from the events I have thus brought back to your remembrance. It seems, I say, that the particularly awful nature of the said Miss Charlotte Clopton's death made a great impression upon the mind of the before-named Lady Clara de Mowbray, and whose intimate friend the before-mentioned Charlotte was; and that moreover the said Clara de Mowbray mourned over her said friend's sad fate with strict observance of privacy for many months. Nay, that on the news first being told her of Mistress Charlotte's having been buried, she, in fact, shut herself up from all communion with the world."

"We heard as much," said Arderne; "I pray you to proceed. She resided at Shottery Hall at that time I think?"

"She did so," continued Grasp, "and where, somewhat on the sudden (as I learn from her confidential servant,—also my client,) she conceived the idea of changing the current of her thoughts and ameliorating her grief by seeing foreign lands. In pursuance of which design she fitted out a vessel, hired a crew, engaged a gentleman of approved valour as captain, and sailed for the New World."

"How! said ye," exclaimed Captain Fluellyn, "fitted out a ship, engaged a crew and captain, and adventured to the New World?"

"What ship did she sail in, Master Lawyer Rasp?"

"Grasp, good sir, and it so please ye," said the lawyer.

"What ship, quotha—let me see. I have a document here, signed by one of her followers, and which states the name of the ship, the number of her crew, the title of the said captain, and all thereunto appertaining and belonging. Ah! let me see," he continued, (fumbling about amongst his papers.) the 'Eagle'—the 'Estridge'—the 'Heron' —the Hawk'—no, it was none of those. The—ah! here it is—the 'Falcon,' that was the vessel; Fluellyn, captain commanding; owner, Count Falconara."

The Captain looked at Walter Arderne, in whose face was reflected the astonishment depicted in his own; and both, as if by common impulse, rose from their seats, and walked forth into the open air.

Arderne took a turn along the dark walk which led to the rivulet at the bottom of the garden, ere he spoke. At length he approached the Captain (who, out of respect, had remained near the house).

"This is a strange matter!" said Fluellyn.

"It is indeed!" said Arderne. "It seems to me like something unreal. I can scarce believe that Clara de Mowbray hath perished in such a venture."

"You knew the lady, then?" said the Captain.

"I did," said Arderne. "She was the friend and intimate of Charlotte Clopton, she of whom ye have heard me speak, and consequently in former days much here; nay, she rented a mansion at Shottery for the purpose of being near her friend."

"Perhaps said the Captain, "for the purpose of being near her *friend's* friend. 'Tis evident she loved you, and you saw it not."

"Nay!" said Arderne, "she knew I was betrothed to my cousin."

"Tush, man!" that mattered not amaravedi," said the Captain; "she loved you, spite of fate, and against hope. 'Tis not uncommon with women. She heard of your desolate condition through the worthy Martin; and (urged by her strong love) she persuaded him to adventure with her, in the hope of discovering and rescuing you from your desolate situation: so much I can myself answer for. How she bore herself in that adventure, I have also reason to know. All we required to know further was the name of this Count of quality, and, behold! we have it. Come—thou art at least a richer man by the knowledge."

"Would to Heaven," said Arderne mournfully, "she were in the enjoyment of her own wealth. I seem to make shipwreck of all that interest themselves in my welfare."

"Ah!" said the blunt Captain, "I doubt thee not, good Master Arderne. Such a woman were worthy of an emperor's love; one to worship in life, and evermore sigh for when dead. But come—no more sad brow and sighing breath. Thou art the likeliest man in all the country,—hast fair domains, castles, parks, and warrens, according to yonder scrivener. Such an one need not sigh for a wife methinks. Let us in, lest the old knight and the lawman fall to buffets, spite of the news brought."

"Sir Hugh must indeed not know of this," said Arderne, "at least, not at present; 'twould but revive his grief for Martin's loss. Over a cup of Canary after dinner we will relate the story."

And thus did Walter Arderne become the possessor of many fair domains in Warwickshire and other countries; for as there was none at that time to dispute possession, and as their former possessor was fairly identified, and her death deposed to by more than one of her own followers, so there was nothing to hinder him in the succession.

There was, however, a certain degree of melancholy attached to the whole affair, which seemed to throw a gloom over the estates, as he in turn visited them,—a something wanting—a deserted look—an inexpressible feeling of dislike to assume the mastery and ownership of these fair and fertile lands. "I can even yet hardly reconcile to myself the right of proprietorship here," he said to Sir Hugh, as they looked forth one day from the towers at Hill Morton upon a vast chase below. "It seems to me that I am an interloper—an usurper here."

"Tush—man!" said Sir Hugh; "this is to be overscrupulous. Take the good the gods send, and make no words on't."

And thus matters rested quietly for days, weeks, and months, and then there arose matter which took the thoughts of men, throughout the land, from their own particular concerns, and (whilst the whole nation rang with the news) called up the energies of all.

Sir Hugh was with his nephew and friend when the first intimation of the certainty of this event reached Clopton. The day was hot, for it was just at the end of April, and the knight had ordered the dinner to be served in the hall, where they were enjoying the half hour after their meal "with pippins and cheese" and a whiff or two of the pleasant weed.

The soothing influence of his pipe was just composing the old knight to sleep when the sharp sound of hoofs were heard in the court without, and a messenger, "bloody with spurring, fiery red with haste," came clanking into the presence.

The sealed brief he handed to Sir Hugh—with the words, ride, ride, ride, upon the cover, in a few minutes after its perusal effectually dispelled the influence of the weed Sir Walter loved, inasmuch as it was from Sir Walter himself, and dated from Deptford.

"Come forth, my old friend," said the letter, "the time hath arrived for all to be stirring. 'Tis now certain the Armada is about to sail. Let your nephew look to his command and bring up his companions. Our ships are ready for sea and men are wanted. 'Fore Heaven, *we will singe the Dons whiskers for him*,* or smoke for it ourselves."

CHAPTER XLIII.

ENGLAND ON THE DEFENSIVE.

Our story having now (with swift passage) glided o'er some two years, we arrive at a period in which all England was aroused by the alarm of a dreadful invasion.

All corners that the eye of Heaven visited throughout the island were were indeed frightened from their proprietory by the mighty preparation of the Spaniard,—a preparation of such vast magnitude that it shewed the determination of the foe to subdue, and put to indiscriminate slaughter, the whole population of the country, if possible exterminate heresy at one blow, and acquire eternal renown by re-uniting the whole Christian world in the Catholic Communion. England at this period, it must be owned, was in a critical situation. A long peace had deprived it of all military discipline and experience. It was exposed to invasions from all quarters, as it was in reality neither fortified by art or nature; whilst the numerous Catholics, with which it still abounded, it was feared would be ready to join the invader the moment he succeeded in landing.

In addition to this, men began to consider the difference between the English and Spanish forces. To remember the overwhelming power of the naval force of the Spaniard, and the vast numbers, reputation, and veteran bravery of his armies, and then—as they sat and brooded over these matters— they reflected that the fate of England must be decided in two battles, one at sea and one on land. Deep and portentous were the thoughts and fears these things conjured up when the certainty of the visitation became apparent. Whole families, high and low, rich and poor, looked each other in the face with vacant horror and dire apprehension. From the hut to the castle, from the cottage to the baronial hall, spread the whispered fear. Not altogether the fear of being beaten in fair and open fight, but of being overwhelmed by the mighty power of a tremendous foe without chance of a successful defence. Nor is it to be wondered at, if the hearts of the islanders did quail at this juncture, when we remember the three years' preparation which (*now completed*) was about to be precipitated like a mighty torrent upon the shores of England.

* A saying of Sir Francis Drake's at this time.

According to a letter of Sir John Hawkins, written at the time to Sir Francis Walsingham, the main strength of the Armada consisted in a squadron of fifty-four magnificent and invincible ships, embracing nine galleons of Portugal, twenty great argosies of Venice, twenty huge Biscayns, four large Galleasses, and a ship of the Duke of Florence of 800 tons. Besides these were thirty smaller ships and thirty hulks, which, together with others, amounted to 132 ships and 20 caravals.

On board this huge fleet were 8,766 mariners, and 21,855 soldiers, besides 2,088 galley-slaves; and in addition, the Armada contained stores for the army, cannon, double cannon, culverin, and field-pieces, 7,000 muskets, 10,000 halberts, 56,000 quintals of gunpowder, and 12,000 quintals of match. Nay, so confident were these overweening Spaniards of success, that their huge ships even contained horses, mules, carts, waggons, spades, mattocks, baskets, and everything necessary for settling upon the land they meant, at one blow, to conquer and enslave.

Both fleet and army were also provided on a scale of unexampled profusion, and the officers who were to lead, and who were of the noblest families of Spain, even embarked their suites of attendants and their physicians. But, perhaps, the most galling accompaniment to the Englishman, and which this dread Armada had provided itself with, was one hundred and eighty monks and jesuits, carrying with them chains, wheels, racks, and whips to be employed in the conversion of those heretics they might choose to spare from the infliction of a cruel death. In fact, every part of the vast empire of the malignant Spaniard had resounded with "dreadful note of preparation and the noise of armaments," whilst all his ministers, generals, and admirals were sweating in aid of the design.

But this was not all that England had to fear, for the Duke of Parma and Asmodeus of Savoy had also prepared in the Netherlands an army of 30,000 men; whilst the Duke of Guise was conducting to the coast of Normandy 12,000 troops, in order to embark and land on the west of England. So that in the Netherlands also the air resounded with the busy hammer of smiths and carpenters, collected in Flanders, Lower Germany, and the coasts of the Baltic, and who "making the night joint-labourer with the day," were engaged in the construction of vessels and flat-bottomed boats, for the transport of their infantry and cavalry.

The hearts and minds of many for the moment quailed under the thought of this tremendous armament; whilst all Europe apprehended that England was doomed, and must be overwhelmed and enslaved.

A deep gloom and a secret horror was indeed upon the hearts of all. They stooped, however, but for a moment beneath the tide, and then the whole nation seemed to start up at the imperious challenge of Spain, sword in hand, sheathed in complete steel.

Not a county in England, not a town or village even, but seemed to rise simultaneously in arms—not a corner of the land but rang with preparation and muster, and awoke endeavour for defence! Nay, such was the incredible alacrity with which from shire to shire the soldiers were raised, and mustered and marched, that from Cornwall all along southward towards Kent, and thence eastward to Lincolnshire, (as the account of the period is worded) "was there a place to be doubted for the landing of these foreigners; but that within forty-eight hours, on horseback or on foot, 20,000 men, completely armed, with ammunition, provision, and carriages, commanded by the principal nobles of their counties, and captains of knowledge, would be ready to oppose them."

In the interior, also, every man capable of bearing a weapon, rushed to arms.

The green fields, near Tilbury in Essex, gleamed with the white tents of 22,000 foot, and 2,000 horse, whilst another army, close at hand, counted 28,000 men.

The narrow streets of London, too, resounded night and day with roll of drum and blast of trumpet; every church and tower and hall was rummaged for arms and armour. Each citizen stood in harness of proof. The armour, which had "hung unscoured by the walls" even from the Crusades, was taken down and put in requisition; and in addition to this, 10,000 additional troops were raised within the walls, together with 5,000 more as a reserve.

All this, however, against the overwhelming moral force of Philip, in the minds of many experienced men, was thought insufficient; and whilst the bold spirits of the leaders of the host led them to affirm that they were strong enough to cut to pieces the whole Spanish force the moment they land, there were others quite aware that the ocean was the element on which to meet the foe.

"A mighty power," said the great Raleigh at the juncture, "in a goodly fleet of ships, and which neither foot nor horse can follow, cannot be desirable to land where it list in England; unless it be hindered and unconnected by a fleet of answerable strength." It was accordingly under advice of men of approved valour and conduct, that Elizabeth set about to equip a fleet suitable, as far as possible, to the occasion.

Notwithstanding, however, the almost incredible exertions made to meet the foe on the seas, the naval power of England seemed quite inadequate to resist so terrible an enemy upon the waters. All the sailors in England amounted to but 14,000 men, and the size of the shipping was so small that, with the exception of a few of the Queen's ships of war, there were not four vessels belonging to the merchants which exceeded 400 tons. The royal navy consisted but of twenty-eight sail, many of them of small size, and indeed for the most part deserving the name of pinnaces rather than ships.

To counterbalance this disproportion, however, the English felt consolation in the known dexterity and valour of her seamen, their constant custom of sailing in tempestuous seas, and being undeterred by the dangers of the element on which they had now to fight; a virtue which will ever render our glorious sailors more than a match for any foe.

In addition to this small navy, all the commercial towns in England furnished forth ships. The citizens of London fitted out and equipped thirty vessels, and the gentry and nobility hired, armed, and manned forty-three ships.

Such then was the mighty preparation of the Spaniard, and such was the "awakened endeavour of England for defence,"—an endeavour perhaps without parallel in the history of our country, and which we have thus minutely brought to the recollection of our readers, because it was witnessed and keenly observed by one whose mighty mind seized upon whatever came within his piercing ken, and who, whilst he was the most careful of observers, was, at the same time, possessed of judgment as remarkable as his imagination and genius were wonderful; one who treasured up what he then beheld, although he stood, apparently, but as "a cypher to that great accompt;" and whilst he thus in reality, beheld "a kingdom for a stage, princes to act, and monarchs to behold the swelling scene," himself possessed—

"A muse of fire; that would ascend
The brightest heaven of invention;

afterwards giving his observations to the world in descriptions of chivalrous grandeur, such as none other in any age has equalled. One who himself saw that brave fleet so hastily collected and prepared for the occasion.

"With silken streamers the young Phebus fanning,
And in them beheld,
Upon the hempen tackle, ship-boys climbing;
Heard the shrill whistle, which did order give,
To sounds confus'd. Beheld the threaden sails,
Borne with the invisible and creeping wind,
Draw the huge bottoms through the furrowed sea,
Breasting the lofty surge.
Who stood upon the rivage and beheld
A city as the inconstant billows dancing,
For so appeared the fleet majestical."

Yes, whilst the choice-drawn cavaliers of Elizabeth's age stood in arms, and whilst, upon the waves rode those adventurous seamen, Shakespeare stood amongst the file, and as his capable eye marked the big muster, his heart beat with each roll of the drum, as it resounded amidst the narrow streets of old London.

And what, indeed, must have appeared to such a man "this post haste and homage through the land," this "threatening of the threatener," this "pomp and circumstance of glorious war?" What must have been the feelings of that one man as he stood amidst the throng—

"For who was he, whose chin was but enriched
With one appearing hair, that would not follow
Those culled and choice-drawn cavaliers?"

He saw the daily and hourly preparation; he beheld the knightly and the noble "all plumed like ostriches;" he saw the closes, the streets and alleys of Lud's old town swarming with men-at-arms.

"He beheld the strict and most observant watch,
Which nightly toiled the subject of the land:
The impress of shipwrights, whose sore task
Did not divide the Sunday from the week:
And then he put himself in arms."

CHAPTER XLIV.

THE BOAR'S HEAD IN EAST CHEAP.

Whilst London, and indeed all England, was thus aroused by this sound of deadly preparation, a gay and jovial party sat carousing in one of the apartments of an antique tavern in East Cheap.

They sat around a huge table situated in the centre of the apartment, and which was indifferently well furnished with savoury viands and generous wines; and a single glance sufficed to proclaim them the choice spirits of the tavern. Daring, reckless blades, companions who daffed the world aside, men heeding nothing, caring for nothing, dreading nothing, and to whom the spirit of the times was peculiarly delightful. They loved action, those revellers. Their lives were made up of the false fleeting excitement of some four hours' exhibition before the flickey foot-lights of a theatre. They were indeed actors all, but their vocation was over for the time amidst the excitement of the coming war.

And as they sat at supper at one of their old haunts, the Boar's Head in East Cheap, they aroused the neighbourhood with their revelry. Amongst them, however, was one whose voice in an instant caused attention. When he spoke their clamour ceased, and whilst some envied, others wondered at, and one or two even disliked (for amongst men of this sort there is ever a something of jealousy) all listened to and sought to catch his slightest remark. Nor was it at all surprising that such should be the case, for this man, who had joined their company, and become an actor about a couple of years before, had made an extraordinary impression upon them all. He had come amongst them a stranger, a fugitive, and in distress. He had taken the meanest, the most subordinate parts in the dramatic representations then performing; but his words, appearance, and manners had been instantly recognized as something uncommon.

Amongst those men, and whom he had accidentally, and as if by a sort of fate, at once fallen in with, were some who read character deeply and instantly, who caught peculiarities and appreciated talent at a glance.

Such then is the association in which we again, after a brief interval look upon Shakespeare. The actor's of Elizabeth's day—a jovial racy set—men who could play the parts assigned them in the inn yard, or with the hawthorn-bush for a scene, and trust to their own good acting and energy to keep their audience amused.

And these men had Shakespeare astonished by the genius and talents he possessed, whilst his conversation displayed the wildest sallies of fancy, the most brilliant wit, and the utmost depth of observation. In fact, he had become their oracle, their adviser, their leader. He had already altered and improved some of the rude scenes of their dramas, shewn them how to put them effectively upon the stage, taught them to suit the action to the word, and in short shewn a taste and genius for the profession that at once astonished and delighted all.

To many it will doubtless appear strange and startling thus to mark Shakespeare down to a period of our island history, which for stirring import had never been exceeded, to find him thus, with his companions of the theatre, on the eve of so terrific an encounter as was then about to take place "between two mighty monarchies," to behold him a living, breathing man, at a moment when all England was aroused to beat off the invader from her shores, or fall and perish miserably beneath the yoke.

The feeling of the thousands then in arms was as of one man; not an islander stood enranked with iron upon his breast, but owned a heart as brave and true as the weapon by his side; nay, every right arm felt a limb of steel, and each fist, as it grasped the rapier's hilt, was ready to rain its storm of blows upon the crests of the overweening Spaniard, and smite him dead upon the earth he came to invade. And such will it always be in "this sceptered isle."

'Twas a picturesque-looking party that assemblage in the old room of the tavern in East Cheap. The chimes, sounding from the tower of St. Paul's, proclaimed the hour of midnight through an open casement which admitted the fresh and balmy breeze of May. In different parts of the room were to be seen portions of the arms and armour the wearers had cast aside when they sat down to their carouse,—the heavy rapier, the cuirass, the helmet, and the plumed hat are thrown carelessly into corners, whilst the story, the biting jest, and the song is heard:—

"And let me the canakin, clink, clink, clink,
And let me the canakin clink,
A soldier's a man, and life's but a span,
Why then let a soldier drink."

We have said that Shakespeare had obtained an influence amongst the men with whom he had become associated, and the present circumstance of this tavern meeting shews it,—"that tiger's heart wrapped in a player's hide, had stirred them up to join him in the present enterprise." The players have turned soldiers, and are about to seek service amongst the troops embarking with Drake, Hawkins, and Frobisher. With the dawn they are to take boat, and drop down towards Tilbury Fort, where the Queen in person is to inspect her troops; and this night they hold perhaps their last revel in one of their old haunts, this night perhaps they drain their last cup in old London.

Fast and furious grows the revel. The spirit of the time lends its charm to men so easily excited, so "of imagination all compact." They drink deep to the healths of the bold spirits of the day. To Lord Howard of Effingham, who commands upon the seas; to the Earl Leicester, who defends the capital at Tilbury; to Lord Seymour; to Lord Hunsdon; to the Queen,—

"Cup her till the world go round."

And then that *one man's* voice is heard, as he rises and drains his glass, and his tongue gives utterance to words which still more fire the hearts of his hearers. For he speaks of his native land:

"That England hedged in with the main,
That water-walled bulwark, still secure
And confident from foreign purposes.
England, that never did, nor ever shall
Lie at the proud foot of a conqueror,
Unless she first doth help to wound herself."

And now, as the breaking dawn sheds a faint and pale light upon tower, and church, and lofty roof, gradually redeeming the narrow and overshadowed streets from the gloom of night, the sounds of bustle are heard around. Then comes the rattle and roll of drum, the blast of horn, and the quick tramp of armed men. Up Fish-street Hill, down St. Magnus Corner, rattles and reverberates the rolling sheepskin; now it sounds dead and dull beneath the eaves and penthouses of St. Margarit's and Pudding Lane; and now it beats loud and shrill as it emerges into Chepe, whilst Aldgate, and Houndsditch, and Hog Lane, and Tower Street, and Cornhill, and Budge Row, also are filled with replications of the clamour.

As the tongue of war thus suddenly startles the ears of the revellers, they start from their seats, and hastily resume the defensive armour. A few minutes more and East Cheap seems filled with men, and all the crafts of London to have turned out and put themselves in arms. Then comes the short quick word of command, the halt and front," the trail of the puissant pike, and the ringing noise of caliver upon the hard ground.

Then, as the Golden Cheap, as it was called, displays its rich treasures from each window, its cloth of gold and silver, and velvets of various hue, its arras and rich carpetings and silk, and, more than all, its comely wives and the handsome daughters of the wealthy burghers standing at the casements they have thus adorned,—then on come the levies destined for the defence of the coast, or about to embark in various ships, lying in the Thames, and which, passing through the double rank of the civic battalions, with quick pace and heavy tramp, turn towards London Bridge.

As these sounds, we say, salute the ears of the revellers, they leave their flagons, and, hastily selecting their various arms and defensive armour, call lustily for something substantial ere they join the newly-raised levies. They go forth to the war as to another revel,—those players. They vow to singe the whiskers of the overweening Don. And Shakespeare halloos them on,

> "Hostess, my breakfast, come,
> O, I could wish this tavern were my drum."

CHAPTER XLV.

THE CAMP AT TILBURY.

To describe minutely the magnificent force assembled at Tilbury, and the camp there, would be both a tedious and a twice-told tale. My Lord of Leicester (who had the ordering of all matters thereunto appertaining) had arranged things not altogether so unskilfully. It was at his instigation, and invitation too, that the Queen herself paid a visit to her troops there; for, says his letter to her on this occasion, "If it may please your Majesty, your army being about London, as at Stratford, East Ham, Hackney, and the villages thereabout, shall be not only a defence, but a ready supply to Essex and Kent, if need be. In the meantime your Majesty, to comfort this army, and the people of both these counties, may (if it so please you) spend some days to see both camps and forts." And so the bold Tudor, in martial array, visited the camp; and never, perhaps, did the world witness a more heroic sight. The glorious sun of a summer's day poured its rays upon a glittering host. Line beyond line they stood enranked on either side, and beyond the blockhouse, as the Queen landed; and as the drums rattled, and the cannon roared, when she stepped from her barge, down went ensign, and pike, and caliver.

The Earl of Leicester and his officers received her on landing; and two thousand horse, dividing into two brigades, together with two thousand infantry, formed her immediate guard.

The next day she reviewed her troops on the hill near Tilbury church, attended by the Earls of Leicester and Ormond. She wore a corslet of polished steel upon her breast, (a page bearing her plumed helm,) and thus, bareheaded, and carrying a marshal's truncheon in her hand, she rode through the ranks amidst the most deafening cheers; after which she harangued the host in a speech of considerable length.

The scene was one likely to make a deep and lasting impression upon the minds of all who witnessed it. The assembled troops were, in themselves, worthy of note; for, besides the regular and trained infantry and cavalry of the period, there stood enranked, and *doing the duty of private volunteers*, some of the noblest in England. The gentry of the various counties had donned their harness, and come forth to do the duty of common soldiers; scarfed, and plumed, and belted, they stood there, resolved to lay down their life, ere they yielded one foot of their native land to the invader. As the Queen passed on amidst this steel-clad host, there was one who stood somewhat apart, and in an interval of the lines of infantry; he raised his voice amidst the general enthusiasm, as the royal Tudor rode along the rank near which he was posted; and then he lowered his weapon, and as he leaned upon it, keenly observed the whole scene.

He saw that lion-hearted woman, and who had then borne the sceptre for thirty years; her body cleped in steel; her high pale forehead furrowed with care; her bright and piercing eye, and her majestic form unbent by the pressure of years. He saw her thus, mounted upon her magnificent steed, like a true daughter of the Plantagenet, vindicating the honour of her kingdom. He saw her thus, undismayed by the tremendous armament threatening her coast, pass on from rank to rank, "with cheerful semblance, and sweet majesty;" and as she rode—

"A largess universal, like the sun,
Her liberal eye did give to every one."

Those who have stood in the ranks of an English battalion can perhaps best imagine the proud feeling which must have animated the breast of Shakespeare at this moment. His eye passed rapidly over the glittering files, and then it dwelt with curiosity upon the stern features of the troops, as each glance was bent upon that one form, "so regal, so majestical;" and, as he looked upon the expression of those bearded men, he felt that no power which the invader could bring would be likely to subdue such a host. The English might be struck dead—blasted—annihilated by some wrathful bolt from the skies, but, unless the power of Heaven fought against them, no foreign force could subdue that *island-host* upon their own ground. And then, whilst he gazed upon this inspiriting sight, as the Queen passed off the ground, and took her way "so strongly guarded" amongst the innumerable white tents, a wild flourish of martial music floated through the air, the firm unbent forms of the soldiery relaxed, the sword point was lowered, the pike trailed, drum and fife sounded, and the various companies wheeled off their several positions and followed through the camp. As column after column moved past, still that observant eye was rivetted upon them. The musqueteers in the front rank; the pikemen in a dense column behind; then came the cavalry, slow and stately, with a rushing ringing sound, the horses reined back to keep time to the trumpets' clang. Squadron after squadron, they moved past with stately pace and slow; the several leaders armed in steel, galloping up and down the ranks, and giving the word as they wheeled round and moved off the field. They were led by one scarce two-and-twenty years of age, who seemed, on his magnificent charger, with his beaver raised, "the prince of chivalry, the "arm and burgonet of men." The young Earl of Essex, just then in the zenith of his fame, and to whom the Queen had given command of the cavalry.

And so the eye of the "poor player" pierced through the camp and witnessed all the "pride, pomp, and circumstance of glorious war;" himself, in his humble suit of buff, with back and breast and helm of a common soldier, the greatest man there. He saw the tented field, so as only a nation's "endeavour for defence" could have shewn it him. He mingled amongst the white tents of the soldiery, and he visited the huts made of boughs of trees and poles, beneath which many of the gentry from the various counties and their followers were sheltered.

At this period of his life his profession had made him known to many of the nobles and leaders present, and those who fell in with him were pleased to have a word with "the pleasant Willie" amidst the excitement and bustle of the hour. As he turned from the scene, and, with his companions threaded his way amidst the crowd of soldiers, suttlers, and the other accompaniments of a huge army, he was met and accosted by one high in authority amongst the host.

"Ah! Will Shakespeare," said the noble, "hast thou too put thyself in arms? 'Fore Heaven, man, thou shalt come with me to my tent. See, here is my Lord of Southampton, and other gallants, 'the very elements of the camp,' would fain have a rouse ere they wait upon the Queen. Come, man, a word from thee will spice the cup. No denial," continued the noble, as Shakespeare endeavoured to excuse himself on the plea of wishing to make on toward Dover that night. "No denial. Come, thou shalt cup us this day in the field. I could better lack the best of my followers on the day of battle than lose thee now we have once met here. What says't thou, my Lord of Southampton, thou canst not excuse the gentle William, eh?" And so it was late in the day ere Shakespeare left the tented field of Tilbury.

When he did so he crossed over a bridge of boats and barges which had been drawn across the Thames at Gravesend. This bridge had been constructed for the purpose of opposing the passage of the invading fleet, should any portion of the expedition succeed in crossing the Nore, and to afford a means of communication for supplies of men and munition from Kent and Sussex.

With two or three companions (and who, like himself, were resolved to hasten to the coast and, if possible, get on board some vessel at Dover,) Shakespeare hastened, after leaving Gravesend, along the Old Kent Road, then the most beaten track in England.

Thus then, under circumstances so peculiar, the players found themselves in the county of Kent, that interesting county, which has been the battle-ground of the English for so many centuries, and which yet retains the ancient name Cæsar,* conferred upon it upwards of eighteen hundred years before.

* Cæsar denominated this county, Cantium; time, therefore, has made no further alteration than in giving it an English sound.

Much as was the traffic on this thoroughfare at the period of our story, the road was still in a very primitive state, thickly shadowed by trees on either side, ill kept and full of deep ruts and quagmires, whilst the country on either hand seemed one entire forest, and thus, amidst the bustle of the time, troops marching and counter-marching, "posts tiring on," pack-horses, and wains, and carriers occasionally overtaking them, Shakespeare took his way.

We leave our readers to imagine the feelings of the poet as he passed along this, the old Roman road.

As his eye pierced through the gloom, he beheld the road ascending through a leafy tunnel, and as he mounted a steep hill, he looked into the thick shadow on either hand, and then stopped and contemplated the place with a curious eye. It is more than probable, whilst he looked upon this locality, covered as it was with enormous trees, the road darkened by their shadow, the overhanging bank covered with fern, the crow winging to his nest, the moon just beginning to appear, that some passages he had perused in one of the old chronicles of England flashed across his brain, for in the scene thus beheld at so sweet an hour Shakespeare looked upon Gad's Hill.

And now, as the players left the woodlands, and descended the hill on the other side, a magnificent sight was presented to their view,—looking in the pale moonlight like some romantic view exhibited during the scenic hour, the Keep of Rochester, white and spectral, towered above the flanking walls that surrounded it; the rushing waters of the river flowing just beneath; the old picturesque town (then in comparison but a hamlet) lying dark and sombre on the left. 'Twas a scene that spake of former passages in Britain's history; and as Shakespeare looked upon it he felt the impression. There beneath him flowed the broad Medway, where the Britons had made their stand against the legions of Rome. On the bank, surrounded with battled towers, frowned the tower of the Norman Gundulph, now, as of yore, filled with glittering troops; the flaming cresset glaring from its walls, and reflected in the stream. The "panoply of war, grim-visaged, but glorious war," once again had revived its thick-ribbed towers. And in the old hostel of the Crown, Shakespeare and his troop slept that night,—a locality since immortalised, for 'tis *the inn-yard at Rochester*, of the scenic hour.

CHAPTER XLVI.

THE INVINCIBLE ARMADA.

At a time when every rank of men in England buried all party distinctions, and prepared with order as well as vigour, to resist the violence of the invaders, the Catholics throughout the land were not found wanting. Many gentlemen of that sect, conscious that they could not justly expect either trust or authority, entered themselves as volunteers in the fleet or army, whilst many equipped ships at their own charge, and gave the command of them to Protestants; others again bestirred themselves, and animated their tenantry, servants, and neighbours to join in the defence.

Amongst these, Sir Hugh Clopton and Walter Arderne had manfully bestirred themselves. Sir Hugh had mustered his servants and followers, and putting them under conduct of his good friend, Sir Thomas Lucy, marched off as a simple volunteer to Tilbury Camp, whilst Walter Arderne, with no less zeal, and tenfold means, (for be it remembered he was now the possessor of an enormous fortune,) had equipped several ships at his own charge, intending to join Sir Francis Drake.

And thus having brought our readers to this period of general enthusiasm, we now almost lose sight of the individuals more immediately connected with our story in the universal excitement. The huge Armada, after having by a variety of reports seemed to threaten every foot of the coast in turn, was at length first discerned making its approach. A Dutch pirate brought intelligence to Plymouth that the Duke of Medina Sidonia was in reality in the English Channel. The captains and commanders of the English vessels were at the moment of this intelligence being brought playing at bowls at Plymouth; and Sir Francis Drake, with the true spirit of an English seaman, insisted upon playing out the game. "Play it out," my masters all, he said, "play it out. We have plenty of time to win the game first and beat the Spaniards afterwards."

A south-west wind, however, blew so strongly at the moment that the vessels had considerable difficulty in warping out. At length, however, by the tremendous efforts of all hands, (for the anxiety of the troops and sailors to get at the enemy is hardly to be described,) the English ships were fairly at sea, and, with every sail set, bearing up for the enemy.

"And now sits expectant in the air,"

for whilst the sea bears upon its bosom the opposing fleets, the shores of England are bristling with the armed legions watching the event. The islanders standing "like greyhounds in the slips straining upon the start," and thus, whilst "borne by the invisible and creeping wind," the ships neared each other, was to be seen those characteristics of the islanders which furnished forth descriptions like the blast of trumpet to a Briton's ear.

"On! on! you noblest English,
Whose blood is set from fathers of war proof!
Fathers, that, like so many Alexanders,
Have, in these parts, from morn till even fought,
And sheathed their swords for lack of argument.
Dishonour not your mothers. Now attest,
That those that you call'd fathers, did beget you;
Be copy now to men of grosser blood,
And teach them how to war."*

* "Henry the Fifth."

It is not our purpose fully to describe the action with, and the discomfiture of, the Huge Don, only such portions of the engagement as embraces the fate of those connected with our story being necessary.

Suffice it then that the fleet of the mighty Spaniard came on slowly, awfully, and, according to the description given by Camden, so tremendous in appearance that the very winds seemed tired of propelling and the ocean groaned with its weight. That the English ships, dwarfs as they appeared by comparison, and few as they were in number, resolutely encountered, and, like bulldogs, which never leave the animal they are pitted against whilst life lasts, stuck to and worried the bloated Don till they completely pulled down his pride.

The proximity of Plymouth to the Spanish coast had rendered it probable that that part of England would be selected by the enemy for his first attempt, and there accordingly the Queen had appointed as Guardian one of the noblest and most approved soldiers of her realm. That aspiring hero, the gallant Sir Walter Raleigh, in himself a host at such a moment, was appointed Lord-Warden of Plymouth, with office of Lieutenant-General of the county of Cornwall, and 5,000 men under him.

No post or appointment on land, however, could satisfy such a man, when he himself knew the element on which the English ought to meet their foes was the sea. Accordingly, the blast of war and the thunder of the cannon found Sir Walter amidst the foremost, fighting hand to hand like some avenger, and covered with the smoke and blood of the hot encounter. Sir Walter, indeed, with a brilliant company of nobles and gentlemen, had left Plymouth in a small squadron, and quickly came up with the Spanish fleet. As they sighted the enemy, it was joined by a small force fitted out by Walter Arderne, and the two made into the midst of the fight.

Notwithstanding, however, the desperate valour of Sir Walter Raleigh, and which at times amounted to rashness, in the present instance he displayed his superior seamanship, and used discretion. He was aware that the lighter and less numerous vessels of the English had an advantage over the unwieldy Spanish galleons, provided the former avoided close quarters.

He therefore ran near the floating castles of the enemy, and poured in his broadsides, whilst they found it almost impossible to bring their great ordnance to bear, ere he was off again. This plan of operation was adopted by the whole English fleet. Ever asunder, but always in motion, they took advantage of the wind to tack whenever they could most annoy the foe; pouring in broadside after broadside, and sheering off out of range of the Spanish guns, and then again boldly returning ere the latter could well reload; performing, as Sir Henry Wooton described it, a perfect morris-dance upon the water.*

It was in vain that the Spanish fleet bore down upon their antagonists, anxious, by bringing them to a closer action, at once to destroy

* Oldy's "Life of Raleigh."

them. The skilful English sailors avoided the contact by continually separating into small divisions. Six of the English ships, however, led by Sir Martin Frobisher and Lord Thomas Howard, were so disjoined from the rest, that the galleasses of the Armada came close upon them, and continued a desperate engagement for many hours. At the same time, another squadron of the English fiercely assailed the division of the Armada stationed to the westward; nay, such was the desperation of the English, that they in a short time disabled every ship in the line there.

Amidst the storm of hurling iron, hid from one another by volumes of white smoke which hung upon the waters and enveloped everything around, two individuals sprang from their vessels, and, followed by their crews, sword in hand, clambered with desperate energy up the hull of one of the Spanish ships. The dense smoke on all sides is only relieved by the rapid volume of fire which seemed to pour out of every part of the Spaniard. The tearing of timbers, the shriek of agony, the cry of despair, and the deep curse, is answered by the wild joyous cheer of the jolly Briton. Amidst a storm of blows, the two leaders, the forlorn-hope of the boarders, gaining the high deck of the Spanish craft, sprung upon the enemy's deck, where they were instantly followed by their strong-armed countrymen. What can resist, what can front them and live! Their blows are like the lightning's flash! Their force, strength, and ire, is terrible to look upon! They carve a passage; they bear down all before them! The deck of the Spaniard is slippery with blood; the thunder of the cannon is even hushed for the instant; and then is heard the ringing noise of hundreds hand-to-hand,—the cold dull smite of steel upon the body, the deadly curse, the cry of horror, and the shriek of death.

During this terrible encounter, even whilst mounting the side of the Spanish vessel, the two men we have first described caught sight of, and recognised each other. In the face of him who sprang from a small craft called the Falcon, one of the sometime players of the Globe recognized Walter Arderne; and in that countenance beside him, although now with smoke and powder disguised "as if besmeared in hell," Arderne has for an instant recognised the features of one known in fair Warwickshire in happier days. They see, they recognized each other, but their thoughts are as the red flash of the artillery around them, and the next moment they are in the midst of blows and death. A contest of this sort, so fought and followed, is seldom of long duration. One side or other must generally be overborne; and, accordingly, the entire crew of the Spanish galleon were either driven to the poop of their vessel, or dead upon her decks. So numerous, however, were the Spaniards, that even in this desperate extremity they were formidable; and still the contest raged.

In the midst of the *melée*, the player who we have before seen amongst the first to board the Spaniard, is now fighting hand-to-hand with the Spanish captain.

Hard pressed, (for the rapier of the Englishman bears the *invincible* Don almost to the planks of his vessel,) the latter turns and flies below. Entering his cabin, he snatches up a pistol, and attempts to fire it into a huge barrel of gunpowder, and so blow up his vessel. Like lightning the Englishman strikes the pistol from his grasp, and calls upon him to yield.

The Spaniard, however, renews the contest like a tiger at bay. Rushing upon his foe, for the moment he bears him backward ; he then as suddenly turns towards a youth who, crouched in one corner of the cabin, seemed terrified, and unable to protect himself. Him the Spaniard now rushes upon, and attempts to pierce with his rapier ; but the Englishman again anticipates him, strikes the weapon aside, and pierces the *invincible* Don to the heart at the very moment the vessel is captured; and one loud English cheer fills the air. Curiosity and humanity leads the victor to approach the boy whom he had so opportunely saved. He drags from before him the body of the Spanish captain, bids the lad look up and fear nothing; but, overcome with the terrors of the situation, the lad had fainted. At this moment the cabin is filled with the excited captors—they are maddened with rage and blood, and ready to strike down all before them. Anxious for the poor boy, the gallant player lifts him up, throws him across his shoulder, and carries him upon deck, never leaving him till he has placed him in safety in his own vessel.

Amidst the turmoil, confusion, and horror of such a scene, (for, of all battles, perhaps a sea-fight presents the most savage and desperate picture of warfare,) the "poor player," who had thus rescued the youth from death, and borne him to a place of comparative safety, had but small leisure to pay attention to him.

Nevertheless, as he placed him in the cabin of the English vessel, he could scarcely fail to observe his extreme beauty; and as the lad came to himself, and thanked his preserver, the player found, by his accent, that the lad was English born.

Commending him, therefore, hastily to the care of some of the sailors at hand, (as his ear again caught the wild huzza of the victors,) the player again sprang upon the deck of his own ship, and the next moment was once more amidst the scene of death and slaughter—enveloped in smoke and fire—deafened with the roar of guns, and in the midst of crashing timber and falling spars.

The Spanish galleon had been captured ere he again reached her decks; but still on went those English red-handed from slaughter to slaughter, "with ladies' faces, and fierce dragon's spleens," they assailed ship after ship of the squadron they had become entangled with, and night only arrested the terrible encounter.

Awful indeed is the destructive power of man, when once his rage is let loose upon his fellow. Those stately Spanish vessels, covered with gilding and ornament, and which had come heaving upon the wave, stately in movement, and beautiful in appearance as a bevy of swans, were now dismantled wrecks, blackened, half burnt, and, as if tortured into madness by their swift enemies, they vomited forth their fire at random, their shot flying over the heads of their adversaries, and hurting each other in the confusion of the scene.

In other parts of the engagement the English had been equally industrious; and had it not been for the gross mismanagement of those in authority, and through whose parsimony the ships ran short of ammunition, the success would have been instantly followed up; as it was, the parsimony of the Queen might have cost her her crown, for thrice were the English baulked in the midst of success for want of ammunition, and obliged to take advantage of wind to get out of fire, and as often did they return, like avengers, to smite and destroy.

The sequel of this glorious contest is too well known for us to dwell upon; only so far as it bears upon our story have we followed it. To that poor player, the intrepidity of demeanour, the confidence in the love of her subjects, and the activity and foresight of the royal Tudor, was not lost. He saw of what his own countrymen were capable; and when he dipped his pen in his own heart, and described deeds of knightly fame, he wrote as he felt.

The noble Howard of Effingham, profiting by the faults of the Duke of Medina, and the difficulties experienced by the Spanish seamen in manœuvring their floating castles, made a terrible example of the enemy, and all around is crashing ruin, flight, and pursuit. Those ships which were scattered he followed, and the whole fleet of Medina was already vanquished and flying, when the elements effected the rest.

> "So, by a roaring tempest as the flood,
> A whole Armada of collected sail
> Is scatter'd and disjoined from fellowship."

It was during the continuance of the storm which followed, and whilst the few Spaniards who returned to their own shores were filling the ears of their countrymen with reports of the desperate valour of the English, and the tempestuous violence of the ocean which surrounded them, that two solitary travellers took their way along the old Kent road leading from Sandwich to Canterbury. Having quitted the ships in which they had arrived at the old Cinque Porte town, the two wayfarers were now making their way towards the metropolis.

In our own times they would have come under the denomination of strollers, since one of them was in reality an actor, and, in the form of the other who walks by his side, our readers must recognise the youth rescued during the preceding action with the Armada.

Light is the step and joyous the voice of that player. It almost cheers the heavy heart of the melancholy lad, his companion. "Nay, it does, in some sort, apparently chase from his memory some rooted sorrow; for the large glowing orbs of the boy are oft-times turned towards the player as he speaks, and his step becomes more firm as they proceed.

Scarce a mile has been traversed from the town, ere the eye of the player catches sight of a gray and massive ruin on his right, and the steps of both are turned towards it.

Long lingered their footsteps beside that magnificent relic, and deeply ponders the player upon the surrounding scene.

His companion listened to his words with breathless interest. The glittering helmets of the cohorts of Rome seem to pass within the arena.

Nay, the spirit of the Roman, who reared the fortress, like a rock, upon that elevation, eighteen hundred years before, seems still to pervade the spot. There—where the thistle rears its lonely head, and the long grass of centuries waves in the wind—the shadowy forms of the imperial soldiery seem to glide by.

"And such," said the youth, as he listened to the words of his companion, "is in truth the impression felt in each locality where the pick and spade of the Roman has left trace of his conquering arm. The feelings you have just described, the shadowy remembrance such locality seems to conjure up, I have oft-times felt whilst at Clopton."

The player started. "At Clopton?" he said, as he looked curiously at the expressive countenance of his companion. In both there was a sort of dreamy recollection of having met before. "At Clopton, boy? True, there is a Roman trench in the park there. And so, then, thou knowest fair Warwickshire?"

The youth sighed,—his usual answer when his companion, during their short acquaintance, had inquired his history. "I do," he said.

"And know you Stratford-upon-Avon?" inquired the player.

"But too well," answered the youth, again sighing.

"Ah," said the player thoughtfully, "then well may I."

"And wherefore?" said the lad, looking archly in his face.

"I was born there," returned the player. "Have friends, wife, children at Stratford."

"And your name?" inquired the youth.

"Shakespeare, for fault of a better," said the player. And the pair soon afterwards left the Roman ruin and wended on towards London.

CHAPTER XLVII.

THE PLAYER AT COURT.

AND now a new epoch seems to have arrived, and England (for the time being) may indeed be called "*merrie England.*" The good old days of good Queen Bess are now in full force. The nation seems like a burly giant, who, lately weighed down by some heavy disease, and which it required all the strength of his constitution to surmount, suddenly finds himself again in health and strength.

"Now he breathes again, and can give audience to any tongue,
Speak it of what it may."

The enjoyment of the sometime invalid is tenfold from the sudden rebound. Earth and sea, air and sky, look doubly beautiful, and each hour is one of enjoyment. The whole nation revels in the excitement and the joyous feelings consequent upon its deliverance from a fearful yoke. The anticipation of dishonour, torture, and slavery, are no more. The overweening Spaniard, "that Armado hight," has been smitten with deadly vengeance, and all care is thrown to the winds. The Queen, the courtiers, the soldiers, sailors, citizens, nay, all the realm are dancing a galliard through the country. And of all those dancers none danced more vigorously, or cut higher capers, than the royal Tudor herself and her dancing chancellor, Sir Christopher Hatton.

"Full oft within the spacious walls,
When he had fifty winters o'er him,
My grave lord-keeper led the brawls,
And seals and maces danced before him.
His bushy beard, and shoe-strings green,
His high-crowned hat and satin doublet,
Moved the stout heart of England's Queen,
Though Pope and Spaniard could not trouble it."

Leicester, Essex, Raleigh, and Hatton, the especial gallants of the Court, "glittering in golden coats like images," are amongst those revellers.

In London and its environs, bear-baitings, bull-baitings, masques, morris dancers, theatrical exhibitions, and all sorts of diversions filled up the hours.

Great crowds of noblemen and gentlemen (who had met the Queen on her landing at Westminster after the dispersion of the Armada) attended her to St. James's Palace, and, day after day, entertained her, "all furnished, all in arms," with tilts and tourneys.

Fully did the English at this moment appreciate the merits of their Queen. She was extolled, glorified, and almost deified in the exuberance of their joy and loyalty.*

* Stow mentions a little jobbing tailor who absolutely went mad for love of, and died glorifying the perfections of the Queen.

Oh that it came within the compass of our pen to describe the appearance of the Court. To introduce our reader, but for one short hour, within the walls of the palace; amidst that throng of princely gentlemen and stately dames clustered around one of the most gifted and extraordinary women that ever wielded a sceptre. Alas! the times are so changed, that the might, the magnificence of royalty, the grandeur of the scene within, and the halo shed around even the precincts of the palace, can scarcely be understood. The stately forms of the bearded yeomen; the glitter of the halbert, and the flash of weapons amidst tower and turret; the emblazoned doublet; the measured tread of men-at-arms on every post, and port, and passage; the lounging pages and servants, who throng the courts and offices; the hundreds of hangers-on upon royalty at this joyous period. The very sacred character of much that pertained to a palace seems to have vanished. The bold grandeur of the times seem to have departed with those cloistered and embattled buildings, and the stately beings who inhabited them.

The very precincts of the Court,—the "whereabout of royalty," seemed invested with a sacred character during the reign of Elizabeth. The stern grandeur which pervaded the habitations of the terrible Harry, her father, still surrounded the various dwellings of the no less majestic daughter.

Our readers must now imagine the Court in all its splendour at that old palace whose gateway and flanking towers still bear the cognizance and initials of the burly Harry; not as now, however, where the echoes of the drum and trumpet which rings and rattles out upon occasion of pomp and parade, reverberated from the goodly dwellings and ample streets by which it is neighboured.

St. James's palace, in Elizabeth's day, stood in the open country. It had been built upon the site of the dissolved hospital of St. James, by the bluff King, and its buttressed walls were surrounded by a sort of chase or park, the grounds of which to the north were, for the most part, wet and marshy. The heron flapped his wing in the pool where now the Green Park is situated, and amidst the tall trees upon the hill, at present called Bond Street, the deer couched in the fern. It was indeed a picturesque and noble building, exceeding handsome, as a writer of the sixteenth century describes it, built of brick, embattled for defence, and surrounded at the top with crenelles, the chase always green, and in which the Court can walk in summer. Indeed, every part around St. James's, built upon and populated as it now is, at the period of our story was the occasional haunt of Queen Elizabeth, where she rode, walked, and meditated, considered her household affairs, or disported with her ladies, her courtiers, and her lovers.

And what a picture did the scene without the palace exhibit a few weeks after the dispersion of the Armada, and whilst many of those noblemen and gentry, who, at the moment remained in London, were in constant attendance upon the Queen, and endeavouring to outshine each other in their devices and designs.

It is near the hour of noon; the sun shines upon tower and turret, and glances bright upon the arms of the various sentinels upon rampart and gateway. Within, the courtyard is crowded with men-at-arms and persons of all ranks passing in and out. And amongst these are the stately forms of many whom the page of history has had occasion to tell of. In the park without, numerous youthful cavaliers are careering about, mounted upon steeds splendidly caparisoned, whilst a mounted guard of honour stands enranked about a bow-shot in front of the principal entrance. Huntsmen and falconers too, bedight with the royal arms, their greyhounds in couples, and other dogs of the chase, are seen amidst the clank of arms, as the sentinels are relieved. Nay, the perfume of the scented courtiers pervade the air as they dismount and enter the palace. The steaming smell of hot dishes and savoury viands also salute the nostril, as cooks, scullions, servitors, and pages, are seen in the inner court leading from the kitchen, as the hour approaches for the royal banquet.

Shift the scene to the interior, and a magnificent sight strikes the eye, "the presence strew'd." The walls are hung with rich tapestry, and on either hand are the nobles of the Conrt, "a glittering throng." The Queen is about to pass through, and all are bare-headed. What a picture do those men present! Cloaked, ruffed, and rapiered, their very apparel and arms studded with jewels, their bearded faces, so celebrated for manly beauty,—for the Queen loves to look upon the handsomest men the age can produce,—and limbs, and thews, and features, are sure to find favour in her sight. Whilst the nobility stand thus enranked, (many of lesser note at the bottom of the chamber,) a gentleman usher, dressed in velvet, with a golden chain, suddenly appears, the doors are thrown open, and the majestic Tudor is announced as at hand.

First come forth, with proud step and reared heads, some of those lately so celebrated in the "world's debate." Bare-headed, they have had especial and private audience in the presence. Raleigh, with hawk's eye and aquiline features, his very spirit glancing as he looks good-naturedly, but haughtily around. Then Essex, majestic in mien and regal-looking in demeanour, and seeming to carry on his dress the cost of whole manors. Then Leicester, splendid in person and dress, but with somewhat of a restless, uneasy, and sinister expression; dark as a gipsy, and so haughty and unbending in demeanour, that his countenance freezes the blood in the gazer's veins, and yet withal wearing a sort of smile, ever and anon, to shew his pearly teeth; his hand plays nervously with the hilt of his jewelled poniard, as he bows to the several nobles he recognises. And so they file in, and fall into line on either hand.

And now, whatever of conversation, amidst the assemblage, has been going on, suddenly ceases; and each man standing erect, and with his embroidered cloak advanced somewhat over the left arm, the one hand upon the rapier's heavy hilt, the plumed hat in the other—with eyes of expectation, await the moment of the Queen's appearance. A flourish of twelve trumpets and two kettle-drums immediately ring and rattle out; the battle-axes of the gentlemen-at-arms are lowered; and, lo, the Majesty of England has passed the door.

Elizabeth at this period of her reign was fifty-six years of age. Her face, although exceedingly majestic, shewed the deep furrows of care—the care which is the heir-loom of the diadem; her nose was somewhat hooked; her lips, narrow; her teeth, discoloured. In her ears she wore two enormous pearls with rich drops; and her small crown rested upon a mass of false red hair. Her bosom it was her pleasure to display uncovered (the custom of all English ladies before marriage); on her neck was a necklace of costly jewels. The dress she wore was of white silk, embroidered with enormous pearls, larger than beans. Over this dress she wore a costly mantle of coloured silk, shot with silver threads; and her long train was borne by a marchioness. In addition to all this, she wore, in place of a chain, a magnificent collar of gold and jewels. Her aspect upon the whole was at first sight pleasing; but on a steady view of her countenance, there was to be found the unendurable look of a line of kings. The eye that could gaze down a lion; the fierce glance of the royal Harry, was there; a glance which proclaimed the excitable nature of the Tudor blood.

She remained stationary for a few brief moments as soon as she entered the room, and seemed to comprehend the whole assemblage in one rapid glance. She then advanced, with her bevy of attendant ladies, and, at her pleasure, spoke first to one and then another of the nobles present. To one or two giving her hand to kiss, as a mark of special favour, her favourites (albeit they had already been favoured with a private audience) being every now and then appealed to; whilst the moment her eye detected any person of peculiar note, or nôt immediately belonging to her circle, she fixed him like a basilisk.

"Ah! Master Spenser," she said, as she stopped near the author of the "Faery Queen," "hast thou received the guerdon I promised thee for thy song yet? We rated Burleigh soundly for disobeying our orders, and bringing forth that jangling rhyme of thine, which touched our honour. Let me see how went it;" and the Queen repeated, with good emphasis and discretion, the words of the poet:

"I was promised on a time.
To have reason for my rhyme:
Since that time until this season,
I have had nor rhyme nor reason."

"The radiant Gloriana," said Spenser, "doth overmuch honour my poor couplet by repeating it; nevertheless the rhyme still hath reason. Of that, our shepherd of the ocean* can testify."

"How! Raleigh," said the Queen, "hath not thy friend received the hundred pounds I promised him? This is overbold of Burleigh!" And the eye of the Queen shewed the lioness' glance as she looked

* Raleigh.

around for the offender. Burleigh, however, had anticipated a storm, and sought the lower end of the room; meanwhile Raleigh, who seldom let an opportunity pass for pressing any suit he had to carry, replied that Spenser had as yet received nothing of the promised coin.

"My friend is as unlucky as myself," he said; "for neither hath he received his guerdon, any more than I myself have obtained the grant of lands your gracious bounty half promised."

"Ah!" said the Queen, (who spite of her partiality for the wit, genius, and valour of the adventurous and daring knight, little relished his rapacity). "Ah!" she said, "what, that suit of the fields at Mitcham again? And when will you cease to be a beggar, Raleigh?"

Raleigh saw he had half offended, but his impudence and readiness brought him through. "When your Majesty ceases to be a benefactress," he said, gracefully bowing.

The angry spot left the Queen's brow. She smiled and shook her head. "Thou art an accomplished courtier," she said, as she passed on, "but thou gettest not the Mitcham meadows of us yet notwithstanding."

"What mutterest thou, Tarleton?" she continued sharply, to one of the attendant clowns or comedians, whom she frequently admitted to her presence.

I mutter nothing that I will not stand to, Madona," said Tarleton; "and that which your Majesty calls muttering, was but an assurance to my gossip, Raleigh, of all he requires. Raleigh hath but to open his mouth, and the tid bits from your royal table are sure to be cast into it."

"So!" said the Queen, rather angrily.

"Yes," returned the bold jester, "Look but on my lord there—he of the dark eye and olive complexion. By my fay, he hath swollen to such a huge bulk in the sunshine of your royal eye, that anon we shall all be overwhelmed!"

This sally of Tarleton's against the Earl of Leicester was received with a titter of applause, and Burleigh, who had indeed tutored the poor jester, greatly enjoyed it.

Elizabeth saw the feeling, and affecting to hear it with unconcern, turned to another of the court fools. "Well, Pace," she said, "and now I suppose we shall hear from you also of our faults."

"What is the use of speaking of that which all the town is talking of?" growled Pace.

Although the Queen permitted considerable license to men of this class, she was more deeply offended than she chose to shew, and passed on without another word. A few moments afterwards, however, both Pace and Tarleton were observed, at a hint from one of the gentlemen-at-arms, to quit the presence.

"Ah, Bacon," said the Queen to her ample-browed Lord Keeper, "we are sorry to see thee still suffering from the old enemy, the gout. Remain not standing here, my lord; go sit thee down. We make use of your good head, not your bad legs!"

Lord Bacon, nothing loth, bowed and hobbled off.

"My Lord Bacon's soul lodgeth well," she observed to one of her ladies, and truly do we honour him therefore. We are the enemy of all dwarfs and monsters in shape, and would have all appointments, either civil or military, bestowed on men of good appearance. What sayest thou?"

"Certies, I am woman enough to be of your Majesty's opinion," answered the lady; "and yet your Majesty cannot always suit wit and judgment with a splendid dwelling: witness your royal choice of Sir Robert Cecil."

"True," said the Queen, "Cecil hath both a mean look and an ugly expression; but we cannot want the crook-back."

The Queen now turned, and taking Leicester aside, held him for some time in conversation, during which all kept aloof. She then, as it was near the hour of dining, again passed down the line, still speaking to and noticing all she felt any inclination to propitiate, Leicester, Raleigh, and one or two of the more privileged courtiers following. As she passed into the second chamber, she observed amongst the *élite* several whose rank had not entitled them to be in the presence-chamber; and wherever her eye fell on a handsome face and form, she stopped and made inquiry concerning such persons.

"I pray you, Mignonne," she said, turning to one of her ladies, "who is yonder handsome youth—he who stands there near the door?"

"I know not his name, Madam," said the lady.

"Pshaw." said the Queen, "I have ever those about me who are ignorant. Leicester," she continued, "what is the name of yonder youth?"

"He whom your Majesty's eye hath fascinated, even to the crimsoning of his cheeks," said Leicester, "is Charles Blount."

"Nay," said the Queen, "I could have sworn there was good blood in his veins. He is brother of Lord William Mountjoye, is he not so?"

"He is, Madam," said Leicester, "his younger brother, and now studying at the inns of court. He was in Drake's ship, and did good service against the Spaniard."

"Nay," said Elizabeth, "by my fay, an he was with Drake, he was like to be where blows were rife. Bid him approach."

The youth accordingly came forward and knelt to the Queen, who, still more struck by his handsome form and features, gave him her hand to kiss.

"Come again to Court, good Master Blount," she said, "and I will bethink me of your future fortunes."

The young man again blushed, and being extremely bashful, stammered some incoherent reply of thanks which still more interested the Queen, and again she added words of encouragement.

The Earls of Essex and Leicester smiled contemptuously, and Essex, who stood near the Queen, made some sneering remark, which was partially overheard. Not even, however, could the favourite Essex escape censure at such a moment.

',Ha!" she said (turning sharply upon him), "say'st thou, my Lord? Stand back, lest we teach you manners here."

Essex bit his lip, but he was fain to obey, observing to my Lord Southampton "that every fool he thought was coming into favour."

"Then," said Southampton, who stood near, "'tis fit we introduce something not altogether so silly, and there is one here to-day I much wish her Majesty to notice. Ha! and look ye, she hath already found him."

"Of whom speak ye?" inquired Essex.

"Of one well beloved by thee," said Southampton. "See thou not the man there standing amidst the throng, somewhat behind the beef-eaters?"

"I do," said Essex. "'Tis Will Shakespeare."

Meanwhile, whilst Essex, whose proud spirit being somewhat chafed, had thus remained behind the royal party, the Queen passed on talking right and left as was her wont, and discussing matters of political interest with those near her. "We will think of this matter, my Lord of Effingham," she said, in answer to something that noble had said. "I am ready, as thou hast seen, to arm for defence, but I make no wars."

"Nevertheless, your majesty should strike a blow at Spain ere he recover the effects of his discomfiture. I hear again of formidable preparations being in contemplation to avenge the destruction of his ships. Nay, Philip hath affirmed, and that on oath, that he will be revenged even if he is reduced to pawn the last candlestick on his altar."

"Nay, my Lord," said the Queen, "if the dollars of silver and ingots of gold, and which the wretched Indians work for in their native mines, could effect the conquest of this realm, he would assuredly succeed, but I fear him not. We have stout hearts and heavy blades here in England to oppose to his glittering coin. Whilst you yourself, Raleigh, Frobisher, Drake, and other daring spirits are ready for the sea, we shall hold our own, my Lord."

"Nevertheless, your Majesty will, I trust, hear at a future opportunity what myself and my Lord of Essex have to urge in favour of an expedition against Spain."

"It may be we will hear both," said the Queen, "but in truth Essex is hardly to be entrusted with command. His impetuosity requireth a bridle, my Lord, rather than a spur. He is the soul of chivalry, but rash as he is brave; and see you there now," she said, turning and looking after Essex, "I reproved him but with one word, and his choler is aroused even towards us, his benefactress."

The Queen turned now to a tall, gaunt, but exceedingly noble looking old man, his costume partaking both of the soldier and the courtier. "Sir Thomas Lucy," she said, "we have heard of your gallantry during the action with the Armada. We thank, in your presence, all those gentlemen of fair Warwickshire for their alacrity in fitting out ships, and their bravery in fighing them. We heard of you Sir Thomas, in the hottest part of the battle."

"And where your Highness shall ever find me when the foes of England are to be met," said the old knight, proudly, and at the same time rearing his head as he watched the progress of the royal Tudor. Presently, however, the countenance of Sir Thomas underwent a slight change, he seemed to start at some name her Majesty pronounced. His pale iron-grey visage became flushed; nay, had Sir Thomas received an insult in the presence, the expression of his countenance could not have more instantly changed. Slowly and with contracted brows, his eyes rested upon the person Her Majesty was speaking to, and that, indeed, not five paces from where he himself stood. He was fixed—astonished. He could scarcely believe his eyes.

"What! Master Shakespeare," said the Queen, as her eagle-eye caught sight of the poet standing amongst a crowd of officials, "and so thou too hast come to Court? We have not ourself yet seen thy last poem—thy Tarquin and Lucrece, but Raleigh and Essex have repeated some passages to us."

Shakespeare bent his knee and presented a small roll of paper to the Queen, which she received graciously, and after glancing at it, "'tis well," she said, "we will, good William, be present." She then gave the poet her hand to kiss and passed through the door.

As Shakespeare rose from his knee he was immediately accosted and congratulated by the Earls of Essex and Southampton, whilst many others of the Court came about him.

Sir Thomas Lucy, meanwhile, continued to exhibit the utmost astonishment. The countenance of the poet he could hardly mistake. The name, too, he had caught the sound of, and in the person of one apparently on the most familiar terms with the grandees of Elizabeth's court, nay, one who was received with favour by the haughty Tudor herself, he saw the individual who had broke his park, stolen his deer, and decamped to avoid punishment for his offence.

Whilst, therefore, Shakespeare stood amidst the glittering throng, Sir Thomas still continued rapt in astonishment. Proud as he himself was, he felt (in common with all country squires), that removed from his own little domain, and transplanted into the wondrous world of fashion of London, he was but a "cypher in the great accompt." But a small mite indeed, helping to swell the grandeur of the court.

> "A substitute shines brightly as a king
> Until a king be by, and then his state
> Empties itself (as doth an inland brook,)
> Into the main of waters."

"A parliament member," he muttered to himself, as the lampoon kept recurring to his mind, and as he watched the courtiers, so interested and so joyous, whilst in the influence of Shakespeare's wit. "It must be him—I am sure it's him—I know it's him—A justice of peace," he muttered: "at home a poor scarecrow. And on such terms here at court too! In London an ass," he continued, as he approached somewhat nearer, and took a more keen survey of the unconscious poet. "Yes, it is him sure enough; and yet—I'll make bold to make sure," and Sir Thomas accosted Sir Christopher Hatton, and inquired somewhat tartly, the name of the gentleman who seemed to keep the Lords Essex, Bacon, Leicester, and Sir Walter Raleigh, in such exceeding mirth.

"His name?" said Hatton, who was himself hastening to the feast of wit, "Why, it's our Shakespeare, man—The gentle Will—Knowest thou not Will Shakespeare, the very element of wit and pleasantry?"

"Shakespeare!" said Sir Thomas. "Shakespeare! Thank you, Sir Christopher. Shakespeare! the element of wit and pleasantry! And what may be the present calling of this element of whit?" he inquired.

"His calling; why, he's an actor, Sir Thomas—a poet, and a right good one. A player, sir, and a writer of plays; one, too, who keeps us amused.

"Oh!" said Sir Thomas, "'Tis so, is it? Good!—an actor—a mummer—a morisco."

"Come, Sir Thomas," said Sir Christopher, "I'll make him known to thee; I'll assure you he's a rare fellow, this Will Shakespeare."

"I thank you, la," said the knight truly. "I hold not acquaintance with mummers and wild moriscos. Farewell, Sir Christopher, I am away to Warwickshire. An ass, quotha. Well, this 'tis to have deer, and parks, and warrens—this 'tis to be a player. The world's turned athwart. Farewell, Sir Christopher, (he continued hurriedly to the dancing favorite,) fail not to come to Charlecote, we'll kill the buck there—eh?" And so Sir Thomas left the palace.

CHAPTER XLVIII.

SIR THOMAS LUCY IN LONDON.

The more Sir Thomas Lucy heard, during his sojourn in London on the subject that had so startled him at Court, the more he wondered.

It was but a few days after he had caught a glimpse of the Warwickshire lad, whom he had hunted from his native town, that he found the name of William Shakespeare in the mouths of almost all he met. That his name should be at all subject of conversation at this precise moment, was indeed astonishing, considering the habits and pursuits of the generality of the Londoners. The warm citizens of London were for the most part a staid and grave set. The more juvenile were rude and rough; fond of athletic sports and out-door pastimes. They loved to see the bear tug and hug the hound; to witness the cruel conflict 'twixt mastiff and monkey; to see the bull driven to madness; or to shout over the bout at quarter-staff. Added to these pastimes it must be owned, however, that the patience with which they could sit at a (so-called) theatrical exhibition, and listen to the long-winded orations, speeches, and mysteries then in fashion, and which had been handed from their more ignorant ancestors, was a perfect marvel; for except that the fool or clown uttered here and there a conceit, a theatrical exhibition was a weary business. Shakespeare, who had now spent some time, in a sort of apprenticeship, amongst the players, had already altered this style; and just before the invasion of the Spaniards, he had perfectly astonished the town by producing a piece of his own writing—a play, which, albeit in our own time it is in comparison but slightly regarded, possessed in Elizabeth's day peculiar attractions. This play, which was called Pericles, had greatly delighted the Court and the city. It in some sort partook of the style of production most suited to the taste of the time, and prepared the way for more perfect productions.

It is not therefore matter of so much surprise, that just at this precise moment, when the fierce revelry consequent upon the dispersion of the Armada was beginning to pall upon the "monster with uncounted heads," the circumstance of William Shakespeare being about to produce another play, should make some stir.

As Sir Thomas passed through the Golden Chepe, he found, by the conversation of many whom he met, that the Queen intended to be at the Blackfriars Theatre that afternoon.

Now Sir Thomas had never in his life been inside a theatre in London. He had seen mysteries, mummeries, morris-dances, and Christmas revels in his own hall at Charlecote. But other sort of dramatic representation, in common with others of his class, he had no conception of or care for.

"Diccon," he said to one of the attendants who walked behind him (for Sir Thomas always promenaded the town with half-a-dozen serving-men at his back,) "What is this play we heard my Lord Keeper speaking of?"

"Marry, Sir Thomas, it is a play written, I be informed, by one Sampson Beakspere of this town."

"Ah," said Sir Thomas, "Beakspere, said ye? Art sure that is the name?"

"One cannot be sure of anything, an it so please ye, in this sink of iniquity,," said Diccon, "where lying, thieving, and every sort of villany existeth in open daylight. Nay, one cannot be sure of finding one's throat hale and sound in the morning when one lays down at night. By the same token, at the hostel where I lay, they cut off the badge containing the three silver pike-fish from all our sleeves."

"*Beak*speare," said Sir Thomas, merely glancing at the denuded coat sleeve of his head serving-man. "Art sure it is not *Shake*speare, Diccon?"

"I cannot tell your honour. Beakspere was the name I understood, but it may probably be Shakespeare. Nay, I should not be surprised even if it was the very fellow who stole your honour's deer, and stuck up bills against our park-gates. Nothing is too bad for this town and the people in it. I would we were fairly back in Warwickshire.

Sir Thomas looked hard at his serving-man, so unusually talkative in his presence. "Amongst other things they do in this town, Diccon," he said sharply, "it seems they have taught you to drink more strong beer before breakfast than your brains can bear. Go to, sirrah; less circumstance when you answer." And the stately knight held his way along Chepe.

On this morning he was intending to pay a visit to an old friend residing at Dowe-gate, and afterwards to take boat, at Styll-yard, and cross over to Bank-side, there to see the bear-bayting," and accordingly his serving-men turned down Bucklersbury, traversed Canwick Street, and completely bewildered themselves in East Chepe.

These thoroughfares were somewhat strait and exceedingly intricate in Elizabeth's day, whilst the encroaching stories of the houses grazed the plumes on the tall knight's castor, as he walked, so much so that he was fain to hold down his head. By which proceeding he, ever and anon, run full butt against some tall fellow or other, receiving such abuse as rather kept his philosophy from rusting.

"How now, thou mandrake, thou thin-faced gull!" said a tall man, dressed with great bravery, and who, accompanied by several others, was advancing from the water side; "how mean ye by that? Thou hast run thy hatchet visage full in my breast, and murdered my ruff, thou ass!"

"I cry ye mercy, fair sir," said Sir Thomas, who was always the gentleman. "I am as ready to make amends, as I have unconsciously offended."

"Offended, quotha," said the gallant, as he stood pluming himself, like a bird, and pinching out his crushed ruff, which starched with yellow starch stood out a foot at least from his neck. "Thou hast murdered my ruff, I tell thee, and shalt duly answer it."

"Of a verity," said Sir Thomas, "an I have endamaged thy ruff I will pay thy laundress coin wherewith to re-stiffen it. An I have ruffled thine honour I will give the reparation with my rapier, always presuming thou art a gentleman of coat armour, and fit opponent for my poor person, for thy language, to say sooth, is foul, and thy manner coarse even for this foul town."

"How speakest thou,—a gentleman and fit opponent for thee? Betake thee straight to thy weapon. Know I am a gentleman to the Earl of Leicester."

"Diccon," said Sir Thomas, sheathing his half-drawn rapier and stepping aside, "this is thy business. Tell this caitiff, that the language and behaviour of a menial should be at least civilized when he encounters a gentleman."

"Wilt not fight with me?" said the bully, who, together with his fellow, now rudely pressed upon the knight's party.

"Not willingly will I fight with a scavenger," said Sir Thomas, "the quarrel shall be a good quarrel, for I will fasten it upon the Earl thy master. I stand aside here—smite him, Diccon—well, Diccon—lay on my men all, and clear a passage. I would pass on."

Upon this the followers of Sir Thomas threw the round targets they carried on their left arms, before their breasts, and, spreading out over the whole width of the thoroughfare, drew their blades, and advancing upon the rude followers of the Earl of Leycester bore them back, so that Sir Thomas passed on his way to the bear-bayting.

CHAPTER XLIX.

THE THEATRE OF THE BLACKFRIARS.

In our times the profession of an actor presents a picture of uninterrupted drudgery and discomfort. In Elizabeth's day such was not the case. There was not then that continual craving after novelty, that constant production of pieces, written for the hour and the topic of the day, which gives an actor no rest. In comparison to our own race of actors (excellent as many of them are for the sort of work they have to do,) the actors of Elizabeth's day were a company of magnificoes, "proper fellows of their hands," and "tall gentlemen in their own esteem."

The thing they took easily, and with a certain dignity of deportment. It was indeed edifying to see one of these goodly fellows with part in his hand, his plumed hat, "short cloak and slops," and eke his rapier, taking his early walk, either in the fields or on Bank Side, or peradventure hiring a boat at the Blackfriars, and thus gesticulating, with a short and diminutive bowled pipe in his mouth, studying the author's meaning to the letter, and *getting up his lengths.*

Sometimes they went forth in companies, these men, to some favourite rural haunt, some delightfully situated hostel or tavern by the river's bank, or to the bowery woods near Richmond or Greenwich. On such occasions they would take boat, and make the river echo with their jokes, and puns, and witticisms, as they were wafted along on its glassy surface. At other times a select few would hire horses and beat up the towns of Windsor, Mortlake,* and other places which the occasional residence of the Court made more gay and populous ; for those actors loved to haunt the whereabout of royalty. Their professional knowledge made them exceeding good companions too. Glorious fellows. And then how dearly too did "mine host of the tavern," enter into their joviality, and aid them in those little waggeries they were so prone to engage in.

None but those who have mixed amongst actors of talent, and know them intimately, can have an idea of the charm of their society. The very characters they have to personate, good or ill, and the moralities taught in the pieces they are obliged to study, ought to, and does, render them better men. Their study also is to give peculiar effect to all they say and do. And oft-times with them the most common place sentence is pointed into something witty. They understand the "jest's prosperity," and in an instant they penetrated through the follies, the ignorance and the cunning of the common-place. Their ideas being for the most part free, unfettered, and unshackled by mercantile matters, their sentiments are ennobled by the study of those parts they have to perform.

And oh, what fascination, what delight, what a world of itself, is the scenic hour! The romance of feeling, the inexpressible charm belonging to that brilliant little period, none know but the actors themselves. It is oft-times their all of life ; the rest is flat and stale? they live but for those few brief moments in which they glitter the observed of all observers, the admiration, the delight, nay, almost the envy of the audience. Like the lunatic, the lover, and the poet, they are "of imagination all compact." The actor has thrown himself into the author's conception. The poet's world is also the world of him who enacts the part the poet has written. He lives in his author's period, not only whilst acting, but whilst studying the part. The loves, the hates, the fears, the joys, the doing of all around are pertaining to himself—as if "'twas reality he felt."

* Elizabeth, with her court, frequently moved to these places.

Some of these men were very noble fellows, (if we may so term it), noble at least in sentiment, if not in blood, and who would have scorned to perform the mean acts perpetrated by men in a class far above them. They knew, too, in what the point of honour consisted, and were "sudden and quick in quarrel" where they conceived themselves insulted; and it was this virtue in the better sort of the actors of Elizabeth's day which made them sought for, and associated with, by many of the best of the nobility. Nay, it must be remembered that at a somewhat later period of England's history, and when civil war "channelled her fields," the actors were, to a man, found enranked amongst the cavaliers, and fighting "on the party of the King." Their professional education taught them to "hold in hate the canting round-heads," and they fought and bled for the better cause.

How dearly Shakespeare loved the scenic hour his own doings have, we think, proclaimed. The world around him, too, at the period in which he lived and wrote presented much that was grand and exciting. He had but to note what he observed in the vicinity of Elizabeth's Court, in order to pourtray some of his scenes.

From the first moment of his introduction within the walls of the theatre, he had felt the fascination of the "scenic hour," and become captivated with the society of the actors, even rude as the pieces were which he found them performing. To one of his own natural parts and brilliant wit, there was to be found an endless fund of amusement amongst such men. Their way of life also had its charm. How he loved those summer excursions amidst the sweet scenery of Old Windsor—those country revels in which he mingled amongst the rural throng, in all the sports and pastimes "of the old age." He had now been resident in London some time, and besides being noticed by many of the "choice and master spirits of the age," had become acquainted with some of the native burghers of the city, and their connexions in the country around.

The amusements of the early portion of Elizabeth's reign for the most part consisted in her dearly-loved bull and bear-baiting, with occasionally the more refined masques and pageants. These latter, however, were of rare occurence, and usually called forth by some exciting occasion, such for instance as the visit of a foreign ambassador, the celebration of a victory, or the return of some joyous festival. The votaries of the "deformed thief, Fashion," did not then herd together as now. Factions, jealousies, and fears together with the dangerous intrigues which the great carried on against each other, and which oft-times brought the heads of such contrivers to the block, kept the grandees apart. Added to which, those mediums of varied amusement which assemble the *élite* with one another in our own day, were not in existence.

At the period in which our story had now arrived, however, an event was about to take place which made some little stir, and drew a large concourse from both Court and city into one focus.

This was neither more nor less than a new play, written as was then said, by "a right pleasant and merry conceited companion," named William Shakespeare. It was to be enacted within the walls of an old monastery called the Blackfriars. The performance was entitled "The Lamentable Tragedy of Romeo and Juliet;" and so great was the interest created, that the Queen, with such of her Court as she chose should attend her on the occasion, had signified an intention of being present.

It will doubtless appear somewhat extraordinary to many of our readers to find such a performance taking place within the walls of a religious edifice. But the civic authorities had so often opposed the representation of regular performance in the city that the actors at last sought a place without their jurisdiction, and finally obtained the deserted building within the precincts of the dissolved monastery of the Blackfriars, and fitted some parts up for a theatre.

In the preceding reigns there had been no public buildings exclusively appropriated to dramatic entertainment. The most common places of performance were the yards of the Chaucer-like hostels, in the various towns through which the actors wandered.

Some of these inns are even yet remaining, although altered and modernized, in the city of London, and also along the Old Kent Road. The gateways of such houses formed one side of the quadrangle, whilst the balconies, being accessible from the various chambers, obviated all necessity of descending amongst the vulgar in the yard.

In such galleries kings and nobles, the fierce Norman of the Crusades, the knight, the esquire, and the damsel of high degree, had leant over the rails in the olden time, and witnessed the miracle-plays and mysteries then exhibiting. Such for instance as the miracle-play of the Creation, wherein Adam and Eve appeared "in puris naturalibus," and were, as the play quaintly says, "NOT ASHAMED." The earliest of theatres were churches; the earliest performers, monks and friars; and for the most part their exhibitions being on religious subjects, such as the descent of our Saviour to liberate our first parents, John the Baptist and the prophets from the lower regions. On the accession of Henry the Eighth, acting had become an ordinary profession, and companies of players were attached to each town; but previous to the reign of the bluff monarch, plays on general subjects were unknown, yet long before that period it had been customary for great noblemen to have companies of players attached to their household.

Such, then, is a short summary of theatrical affairs previous to the period in which Shakespeare startled the town by his productions,—making a single vault from the lowest depth of misrule and barbarity to the highest pinnacle of excellence in dramatic art and composition; and, apparently without any ostensible guide whereby to steer his course, at once striking out a path, so exquisitely conceived, so laden with perfumed flowers, so filled with romance and beauty, that all the world of after-times has bowed down in worshipful adoration. Of after-times, however, it is not our hint to speak. The sight and impression of Shakespeare's own play, in the infancy of his career, himself enacting a part, and speaking his own words, is what we have to look upon. To bring before the reader's eye that "poor player, who strutted his hour upon the stage, and then was heard no more." "*Heard no more!*"—his own words! How "rounded in the ear," and yet how strange to reflect upon.

We have already said that the expected performance had on this occasion drawn together a considerable audience both from Court and city.

Such was indeed the case, and taking into consideration in what consisted a considerable audience at that period, and when accommodation was at best but scant, the concourse of persons hieing to witness Master Shakespeare's new play was very great.

The *élite* of the Court, for the most part, took boat from their own residences, or from Westminster, where they waited within the Abbey walls for the arrival of the Queen. The citizens, on the contrary, came thronging through Paul's and Ludgate, and over Flete Bridge, and along Knight Ryder's Street, filling the open space before the Abbey, citywards, and cracking their jokes with each other on that side, whilst other nobles and their attendants being congregated about the water-gate or sauntering within the wall, (at that period extending along the Thames from Baynard Castle to Bridewell), presented a gay and brilliant appearance.

All along this part and up to the point of entrance, through the various gateways and passages, until the theatre itself was reached, the actors had strewn fresh rushes, and to and fro upon these flags walked several whose names were famous in the world; and as they walked they debated of matters appertaining.

And now, as the chimes sounded from Old Paul's proclaiming the hour of 4 p.m., soft music was heard upon the water at some little distance, with the sullen boom of the kettle drum. Soon after which, boats containing the yeomen of the guard touched the Abbey stairs, the men as they landed falling in file by file in extended order beneath the various arches and along the passages; and shortly afterwards, as boat after boat discharged its brilliant freightage and shot off again, the Queen, with several of her ladies attendant, and the *élite* of the Court, stepped on shore. As they took their way amidst the cloisters and gothic arches of that old building so darkly venerable, and besides whose walls flowed the broad Thames, it seemed singular to hear the echo of the gay courtier, to listen to the clash of weapon, and the measured tread of the guard, as they followed the royal Tudor, together with the mincing step and affected voice of the Court fop. On the other side, and in the same precincts was also to be heard the ribald jest of the 'prentice of Chepe, and the ringing laugh of the city madam, as they entered the theatre.

Within, too, what was the sight there? Methinks our readers will be anxious to look within those walls, where their own Shakespeare was living, breathing, nay, at that moment, perhaps, dressing for his part, and about to fret his hour.

The aspect of the interior, as it bursts upon the gazer's eye, is indeed curious.

Here was no vast triumphal specimen of architecture; the whole seemed got up for the nonce. But oh! how exquisite—how characteristic of him who was then striving against so many difficulties.

The partition-wall between two large apartments of the monastery had been cut through, so as to form the stage, the proscenium, and the circle. Nay, so rude was the whole construction, that, to a modern eye, it would have seemed only suited to some "play of ten words long," wherein there was not "one word apt, one player fitted." And yet doth a single glance within this rude theatre present all we can expect to find. The boxes were a sort of gallery, along which stood and leant the gallants and ladies of the Court. The Queen and her own especial party being enthroned in a sort of canopy in the centre—looking indeed very like the lady in the lobster.

The rude throne on which she sat was merely railed off from the other seats, and standing behind her chair, on either hand, were several of her favourites. On her right stood Leicester, on her left Essex—both magnificent in look and apparel. Immediately behind her also, on the right of her chair, (stepping down whenever she addressed him), was Sir Philip Sidney. Beside him stood Sir Christopher Hatton, and Bacon was seated near, not being able to remain long on his gouty foot. The rich costume of these magnificent looking men, and their splendid jewels, and weapons, glittered in the reflection of the many torches held by some of the Queen's servants, and even several of the guard held flaming torches in their hands.

In what would now be called the pit, were congregated the citizens. The members of the inns of court, &c., they stood (for there were no seats in that part of the theatre), leaned upon their rapiers, and intently *watched*, as it was then termed, the play.

The stage, which was somewhat elevated above the pit, was on each side furnished with three-legged stools, and strewed with rushes and seated thereon, and even, (one or two of them throwing their careless lengths along), nay even smoking their diminutive pipes, were also several of the privileged of the Court. Raleigh was upon one side, Spenser on the other; my Lord Southampton was also half reclined upon the rushes, whilst others of the privileged sprawled about.

Such was, indeed, a custom of the time (albeit it was exceedingly distasteful to the audience), as these gallants, whilst they swaggered with their rapiers, or combed their long curls, interfered frequently with the business of the hour, mewing like cats, hissing like serpents, tickling each other's ears with the rushes, and, if they had any pique against actor or author, "damning him utterlie." Nay, it was extremely fashionable at this period for a gallant to salute his friend in the boxes, in the midst of the performance, or carry on a loud conversation so as utterly to discontinue and distract the business of the hour, and being thus in the very midst of the actors, perhaps, himself and company would then get up and withdraw, making as much noise as possible. In addition to this was the rudeness of the "all licensed clowns," who laughed in order to set on the barren spectators to *laugh* too, though, in the mean time, "some necessary question of the play had to be considered."

On the present occasion, however, albeit the conversation was somewhat of the loudest, the company were necessitated to be somewhat restrained within the bounds of propriety out of respect to the Queen.

The orchestra, we fear, must have *rather* "split the ears of the groundlings." The performers were, for the most part, situated behind the scenes. It consisted principally of wind instruments and two kettle-drums, which, ever and anon, sounded out a wild flourish of martial music, whilst a viol-de-gamba and several fiddles occasionally created a sort of relief to the troubled ear.

In our own times, indeed, magnificent as the whole scene must have appeared, it would have been criticised severely. The loud talking of those on the stage, the impertinence of the clowns, the rudeness and small dimensions of the stage, and whole theatre, and which latter indeed was calculated to give the actors a gigantic appearance, bringing them too close to the audience, would have been cavilled at. In addition to all this, was the lack of scenery and decorations; nay, so great was the dearth of painted scenery at this interesting period, that the spot on which the scene was supposed to occur, was indicated by a board or placard, upon which was written the particular locality.

Still, with all these deficiencies, the whole aspect of the interior would have presented an extraordinary effect to a modern spectator.

The Queen, beneath her canopy of state, for so was it be-fashioned; her splendid guard standing immediately beneath, and bearing "staff torches," which threw their glare upon the spectators, and lit up the Gothic architecture of that abbey playhouse. The stage itself being also, on this occasion, lighted by torches held by servitors having the royal arms emblazoned on their doublets. Then those choice spirits of the Court too, sitting or lying on either hand, and several of the gentlemen-pensioners on guard at each wing. Altogether, rude as was the theatre, the entire scene was, as we have already said, one of peculiar splendour. Meanwhile, during the few brief minutes before the curtain rises, a lively conversation was going on amongst the audience.

"Ah, what, Sir Thomas Lucy, art thou, too, come to see the play to-night?" said Lord Burleigh to our old Warwickshire acquaintance, who was elbowing his way into the gallery amongst the *élite*. "By cock and pie, but 'tis long since thou and I have met at masque or revel."

"Fie! my lord. 'Tis so indeed," returned the knight, "some twenty winters is it since we foregathered at Arundel Castle."

"Go to, Sir Thomas," said Lord Burleigh, "By 'ur Lady, 'tis thirty years come Martinmas. Rememberest thou the revels there, what time we saw enacted in the great hall the Castle of Perseverance?"

"Truly, I had forgotten that," said Sir Thomas Lucy. "Yet now I do remember me thereof."

"Go to," said Lord Burleigh, "those were princely revels. Dost remember in the performance how rare it was to see the seven deadly sins do their parts?"

"Ah, and how featly the dancers tripped it?" struck in Sir Christopher Hatton.

"I do now remember me," said Sir Thomas, "of those deadly sins. Let me see, there was Pride, Wrath, Envy, Luxury, Sloth, and Gluttony. By the same token they came mounted on their hobbys, and assailed the castle."

"Aye," said Hatton, "and then Humanum Genus (who defended it) was sore bested; truly it was excellent, and then came Mors, or Dreary Death, and took Humanum Genus and carried him off."

"Aye, but then the fool, Sir Thomas!" said Burleigh, "rememberest thou the scurvy knave of a fool? By my fay, he was the life o' the night. Truly, Sir Thomas, the fool was a most worthy fool; not altogether an ass,—eh?"

"Ahem!" said Sir Thomas, who liked not the word ass, "methinks Her Majesty doth glance towards this part, nay, now she peradventure wisheth a word with you."

"Go to," said Burleigh, "I will attend. Oh, that fool! methinks I had as lief go hang as go see a play without a fool in't. Oh! that ass, Sir Thomas; and Sir Thomas, and Lord Burleigh, and Hatton sidled up towards the Queen, and joined in the conversation carried on there upon theatrical subjects.

"Your Majesty will understand," said Lord Revel (who was something of a fop), "that this Shakespeare hath a new style, which is very commendably excellent. A most perfect style, altogether his own. Hast seen anything yet of his producing, my Lord Burleigh?"

My Lord Burleigh shook his head, an old custom with him. "I have not," he replied, "but I hear great things of his poetry."

"Go to," said the Queen, in answer to some remark of Sir Philip Sydney's. "Those matters, Sir Philip, were good, but here be better. Didst thou witness the former play of this man's writing, Sir Thomas Lucy?" she enquired of the Knight of Charlecote.

"If it is so, please your Majesty, I did not," he returned.

"'Fore Heaven, then, thou hadst a great loss. You heard of it? peradventure."

"Truly, your Majesty, we hear not of such matters in Warwickshire as these your London plays," said Sir Thomas drily.

"But you have heard of Master Shakespeare, and seen his verse? Nay, methinks you must have seen his verse."

Sir Thomas coughed (he glanced at her Majesty in order to see if she was bantering him), "His verse, your Majesty," he said.

"Truly so," said the Queen. "How like you Master Shakespeare's verse, Sir Thomas."

"Very scurvily, in verity, what I have seen of it, that is to say. Ahem!"

"That is singular," said the Queen. "Methinks there could hardly be a double opinion upon Master Shakespeare's verse. It is most exquisite and unmatchable."

"I cannot say I have seen anything I particularly admire in it nevertheless," said Sir Thomas, drily.

"What verse have you seen?" inquired the Queen. "Can you repeat a stanza?"

"Ahem! Your Majesty," said Sir Thomas, "I am not altogether good at repeating poetry. I like it not. Sir Philip Sydney was about to observe something,—he understands these matters."

"I am but saying to my Lord of Leicester," said Sir Philip, "that according to the present system, these stage matters are managed in a somewhat more rapid style than was wont to be the custom. Now, for instance, we must tax our imagination. For look ye, if in the play the ladies walk forth before one's eyes and gather flowers, what skills it but your Majesty is forthwith to imagine the stage a garden. By-and-by two wet mariners speak of shipwreck in the same place. Then indeed, are we to blame an we accept it not for a barren sand or rock. Upon the back of that cometh out a hideous monster with fire and smoke issuing from his nostrils; and then the miserable beholders are bound to take it for a cave, whilst in the meantime two armies flying in are represented by some half-a-dozen swords and bucklers, and then what hard heart will not receive it for a pitched field?"

"By my fay, Sir Philip," said the Queen, "we must then have imaginations as fertile as him who writeth these changeful varieties."

"Truly so, your Majesty," said Sir Philip, who was rather affected in his ordinary style. "Doubtless such sights are edifying, but then of time, madam,—of time,—we must be even more liberal, for look ye, if (as is not uncommon) two royal persons fall in love, we may see these lovers become parents of a chubby boy. Then, your Majesty, such boy becomes stolen and lost, and after many traverses he groweth to man's estate, falleth in love in time, and *in time* is ready to marry and all this (an it so please ye) in some two hours' space."

"Nay, Sir Philip," saith the Queen, "methinks you are now taking some pains to appeal to our imagination yourself, lest we should weary ere the performance commences. But, look ye, in good time the drums have ceased and the curtain rises."

CHAPTER L.

THE SCENIC HOUR.

When the curtain rose, it discovered the representation of a private street, very rudely painted upon a sort of hanging screen at the back of the stage, with a couple of wings to match, and upon a board or placard was also written in good-sized characters an intimation for the benefit of the spectators, worded thus:—"Scene during the greater part of the play in Verona; once in ye fifthe act, at Mantua," a flourish of trumpets meantime rung out as the stage was displayed, and one dressed in character as "Prologue," entered, and bowing low towards the royal box, delivered the well-known but now omitted argument of the piece:—

"Two households, both alike in dignity,
In fair Verona, where we lay our scene,
From ancient grudge break to new mutiny,
Where civil blood makes civil hands unclean.
From forth the fatal loins of these two foes,
A pair of star-crossed lovers take their life;
Whose misadventur'd piteous overthrows
Do, with their death, bury their parents' strife.
The fearful passage of their death mark'd love,
And the continuance of their parents's rage—
Which, but their children's end, nought could remove,
Is now the two hours' traffic of our stage:
The which if you with patient ears attend,
What here shall miss, our toil shall strive to mend."

"Methinks, my Lord of Essex," said the Queen, who had listened with great interest to the words, "Master Prologue promiseth well. Marked you how much was contained in those few lines? And lo, here begins the piece."

As the Queen spoke, Sampson and Gregory, with their swords and bucklers, and clad pretty much after the fashion of serving men of their own day, entered, and instantly commenced their animated dialogue.

Not, however, be it understood "slubbered over" by inferior actors, as in our times, but with exceeding humour, and with force and emphasis in every word; for even these minor characters were performed by actors of great talent.

Nothing could exceed the curiosity and interest in the audience even at this, the very commencement. The lively and sharp dialogue, the action so suited to the times in which the spectators lived; the animosity of the Capulet underlings towards the servitors of the Montagu family—and which bore so hardly upon several nobles present, whose followers frequently brawled and fought in the streets—produced a great effect; till, at length, as the lie was given, and Gregory, being prompted to remember his swashing *blow*, drew out his weapon, and the whole four engaged, the excitement, especially in the pit, was extraordinary. A murmur of delight was heard, and whilst some clapped their hands upon their rapiers, others shouted and seemed half inclined to jump upon the stage, and "fight on part and part." The entrance of Benvolio and Tybalt, however, produced a deep and silent attention.

"What, art thou drawn amongst these heartless hinds?
Turn thee, Benvolio, look upon thy death."

There was, indeed, now amongst the audience no inclination to pursue their accustomed practical jokes—no mewling of cats, squeaking of pigs, and tickling each other's ears with the rushes. The wondrous words of the poet held them in a state of enchantment. The nobles of the Court for the moment forgot the accustomed homage of eye and ear. Their bearded faces betrayed their interest, and the templars and students, as they stood leaning upon their heavy-hilted rapiers, sent their eyes upon the stage as if they could have devoured each line.

Indeed, to have any ideas of the interest created, we must again call to the reader's remembrance how great was the contrast between that which *had been* and that which *was*; and if the melody of the verse of Shakespeare can, in the present day, make such an impression whilst we have so many and such varied productions suited to the hour and the time, in how much more was it likely to strike the senses of all present, when it seemed to have descended at once, in all its glorious beauty, like the music of the spheres!

There is that in theatrical representation, it has been observed by one of the greatest writers of our day, which perpetually awakens whatever of romance belongs to our characters. The comic wit, the strange art that gives such meaning to the poet's lightest word, the fair exciting life that is detailed before us, crowded into some little three hours—all that our most busy ambition could desire, love, enterprize, war, glory, the exaggeration of the sentiments which belong to the stage—like our own boldest movements.

Meanwhile the interest increased momentarily. The audience, from the Queen down to the meanest person there, seemed held in a state of enchantment as the piece proceeded. How different was it already from anything they had ever conceived of theatrical representation! It was a picture of life, such as is in the order of nature; there was the buoyant spirit of youth in every line! The Knight of Charlecote even became young again; he cast his eyes for a moment around, and was edified at beholding the deep, the breathless attention of the audience. The royal Tudor, "with eye and ear attentive bent," the lovely faces of her attendant ladies, each thrust forward and eager to catch the words of the poet, and the fine features of the attendant cavaliers, lighted up and animated with an expression of deep interest; the whole assemblage seeming, he thought, to hang upon each word.

As the eye of Sir Thomas again turned from the audience and rested upon the stage, he observed that the scene had been fresh placarded, and was now "a street in fair Verona." Indeed the serving-man who had announced to Lady Capulet, in the preceding scene, that "supper was served, Juliet asked for, the nurse cursed in the pantry, and everything in extremity," had before his own exit changed the placard, and the next moment, as a gay party of revellers filled up the back of the stage, Romeo, Mercutio, and Benvolio, clad in masking costume, vizors in their hands, entered.

The masquing robes of Mercutio were partially dashed aside as he spoke the few words which constitute his opening speech.

"Nay, gentle Romeo, we must have you dance."

At the same moment, too, the vizor which had been held before his face was lowered, and as the glance of the torch-light fell upon his rich Italian dress and elegant figure, Sir Thomas started, whilst a murmur of applause ran through the theatre, gradually breaking into loud plaudits, for in Mercutio they beheld the author of the piece—Shakespeare was on the stage.

The applause, however, was hushed almost at its commencement in the interest of the scene, and then came those startling lines which have since become as household words:—

"O, then, I see Queen Mab has been with you."

They came from the tongue of him who composed them, now uttered to an audience for the first time. Who shall attempt to describe their impression upon the hearers? Who shall describe the manner—the look—the utterance of him who then gave them? Shall we go too far if we say the world had since nothing to compare with that representation? The life, the brilliancy, the style of the character was suited to the actor. He was all fire, energy and spirit,—Mercutio was Shakespeare's self,—the most mercurial and spirited of the production of his comic muse; and the impressive manner in which he gave the words of the character, and their fire and brilliancy, his exquisite intonation, nay, the very dash of his look was irresistible.

The Queen, as he finished his speech, glanced around her. "'Fore Heaven, my Lord of Essex," she said, "but is not this exquisite?

The answer of Essex was drowned in the applause which at the moment burst from all around as the graceful actor continued his part.

To ourselves, perhaps, at this moment, it would appear extraordinary that even greater approbation and louder plaudits had not followed. Shakespeare upon the stage, and speaking his own words, would seem to call forth acclaiming shouts within the walls of that old monastic playhouse which should almost have rent its roof in twain. To ourselves it would seem that the spectators should have almost expired with their enthusiasm; that "throats of brass, inspired with iron lungs," should have greeted him. But, be it remembered, that, exquisite as the whole performance was, as yet the audience knew little of the man, that the consideration of years had to mature the judgment of the world. He was actually giving them that which was too exquisite for the rudeness of the age in which they lived.

And so the play went on, new beauties every moment coming over the ears of that courtly audience, and at the same moment filling with delight those of inferior degree.

Amongst the audience constituting the Court circle were two spectators who stood somewhat apart, and beneath the arched entrance which admitted to the rude gallery constituting the dress-circle. With folded arms they watched the performance with, if possible, greater interest than any there.

They were an old and a young man, who had been drawn to see this performance from having heard the name of the author on their arrival in London. Both were from the neighbourhood of Stratford-upon-Avon, and (albeit they could scarce believe this play was the production of one whom they had long lost sight of), still they came.

As the play proceeded they became convinced from the language that it was indeed the production of the youth they had formerly known.

"By 'ur Lady," said Walter Arderne, "this must be our sometime friend!"

"No man else could have written even what we have already heard," said Sir Hugh Clopton.

"I am amazed," said Walter; "and yet I ought not, for well do I remember what the lad was."

"Hist," said Sir Hugh, "the scene is changed. Ah! and see, too, yonder masquer just now speaking those lines of fire. Is it not he?

"It is himself!" said Walter. "O glorious fellow!"

"Soft, good Walter," said Sir Hugh. In God's name let us hear."

As Mercutio finished his speech, the uncle and nephew looked at each other. The tears were in the eyes of Sir Hugh. "My poor Charlotte prophesied this," he said. "Rememberest thou her words about this Shakespeare when we first became acquainted with him?"

"I do," said Walter; "and she was indeed the only one amongst us who fully appreciated his merits. Nay, from the very first, an you remember, she said he would one day surprise us."

All further attempt to describe the progress of this play, and its effect upon the minds of the spectators, we feel to be a mere impertinence. It seems indeed to ourselves, as in imagination we after eye it, a play within a play—where all is like romance. The audience, that theatre, the players, that "foremost man of all the world" speaking his own words; all is like the fabric of some vision seen before,—a shadowy recollection of some brilliant hour set apart from the dull stream of life, and that too, during a glorious epoch.

As the play proceeded, and the progress of Romeo's sudden passion developed itself, the thoughts of that stately Queen returned to her early youth, ere the sterner feeling of pride and power had obliterated all gentler sensations. She thought upon the days when she loved the handsome Sudley, with all the violence of a first passion.

And if the royal Tudor and all around her were delighted with the delicious picture presented before them in the halls of old Capulet, and the masque held there, they were still more charmed with the garden scene. They felt enchanted whilst they listened to the images of beauty which appear to have floated in such profusion before the poet's mind.

The richness of that glorious Italian picture held them in a state of enchantment. It had the sweetness of the rose, and all its freshness in every line. All was bright as the moonlight which tipped with silver the fruit-tree tops of the orchard, and yet all was soft as a southern spring. The very air of that garden seemed to breath a transport of delight; one almost expected to hear the language of the nightingale's song. And then the refinement and delicacy of the author's conception of the female character delighted the hearers as they listened to the words of Juliet.

"Thou know'st the mask of night is on my face,
Else would a maiden blush bepaint my cheek
For that which thou hast heard me speak to-night.
Fain would I dwell on form, fain deny
What I have spoke—but farewell compliment;
Dost thou love me? I know thou wilt say, ay,
And I will take thee at thy word. Yet, if thou swear'st,
Thou may'st prove false; at lovers' perjuries,
They say Jove laughs. Oh, gentle Romeo,
If thou dost love, pronounce it faithfully;
Or, if thou think I am too quickly won,

I'll frown and be perverse, and say thee nay
So thou wilt woo: but else not for the world.
In truth, fair Montague, I am too fond;
And therefore thou may'st think my 'haviour light;
But trust me gentleman, I'll prove more true
Than those who have more cunning to be strange."

"The world hath nothing like this," said Raleigh to Southampton.

"'Tis heaven on this base earth," returned Southampton. "Said I not the master-mind of this man would produce wondrous matter?"

"Nay," said Sir Courtley Flutter, who was an ancient fop of the first water, "Fore Gad, my lords, 'tis indeed perfect paradise sent down upon us poor worldlings here. I feel inspired altogether—repaired as it were; my heart palpitates—my blood circulates! Ha! I am young again, positively in love myself. Look, how these exquisite ladies, with the Queen there, are overcome. Nay, my Lord Burleigh seems to have forgotten the cares o' the state, and Bacon his gout. An we have another such masque as that just now represented, Sir Christopher Hatton will assuredly fling out amongst the dancers, and give us a coranto."

"By 'ur Lady!" said Sir Christopher, "I would ask no more beatitude in life, during the mighty changes of the world, than what appears in this changing drama, and the stuff of which it is composed. This lower world hath no such bliss. Let me see how went it:—"A hall, a hall,—give way, and foot it, girls!' Oh, 'twas exquisite stuff!"

The limits of the chapter we have dedicated to a description of "the play" permits not of a full dilation upon all therein enacted, neither can we describe the particular excellence of each actor; for each and all performed their parts with a richness and appreciation of the author's meaning the very tradition of which seems to have worn out from the stage.

To the want of scenery during this period we are perhaps indebted for many of those glorious descriptions with which the author has favoured the world in his works.

One thing, and which with a more modern audience would have gone far to take from the delight experienced, was the circumstance of Juliet's being personated by a youth of some sixteen years of age. This, together with the shambling clowns, who, with loose gait and slippery tongue strolled about and vented their scurril jests amongst the audience,—one moment tagging idle rhymes together, and the next venting truths deep as the centre, shewing a most pitiful ambition to make themselves prominent. These circumstances, in some sort, took from the effect.

As for Mercutio, the fire and dash of his character so excited the spectators that they could hardly contain themselves within bounds. He was like some bright exhalation, lending fire to the sphere in which he moved. And when, with the foot and hand, he gave the speech ending "Ah, the immortal passado! the punto reverso! the hay!" the Court gallants, the benchers of the temple, and the citizens, shouted with delight. His death took all by surprise, and his absence from the scene was felt as a shock of reality. It was an age of bright deeds and fierce doers, and accordingly there was a murmur of disapprobation and disappointment when "Tybalt, alive, in triumph," made his exit,—till, as Romeo breaks through his apathy, and, assuming some of the fire of his kinsman's spirit, fiercely encounters and kills "the envious Capulet," a shout of gratified vengeance filled the house. Queen Elizabeth had herself been delighted with Mercutio. "That was a character, my Lord of Essex," she said, "after my own heart. But he was too brilliant to last. His were the faults that travellers give the moon,—

"He shone too bright. But died, alas! too soon."

"'Fore heaven, Sir Christopher Hatton," she continued, "we will not let Mercutio altogether die. An he was so brilliant that the author was enforced to kill him thus early, we will ourself raise him up. Go round, Sir Christopher, and summon that Shakespeare to our presence, in order that we may express to him our approbation of his efforts. What think ye, ladies," she continued, turning to her female attendants, "we will have both the character and the creator of the character beside us."

Shakespeare accordingly, by royal command, entered the royal stand or box, where he knelt and kissed the Queen's hand. After which he remained beside her.

And thus he stood on the right hand of the Queen with his face turned towards the royal countenance, his side towards the stage, and as the play proceeded, he received the compliments of Elizabeth, and answered the various questions she put to him. Nay, she ordered back whoever came so close as to inconvenience the poet, and seemed altogether delighted at having him so near her.

"We will keep you beside us, Master Shakespeare," said she, "and whilst your play proceeds, you shall act as chorus, explaining what may seem wanting to our duller senses."

"Shakespeare bowed his thanks. "I attend your Highness," he said, "with all true duty,"—and thus he remained immovable as a statue during the remainder of the play, the mark of more than one bright glance from the fair bevy in attendance. This was the poet's triumphant hour, and yet the mind of the man was too great to be elevated beyond bounds.

He knew "the art o' the Court," and the uncertain favour of the great; and that there was—

"Between that smile, he would aspire to,
That sweet aspect of princes, and their ruin,
More pangs and fears, than wars or women have."

Amongst the audience, there was a female bright and exquisite as one of the creations of that author's after years. She stood with an attendant, and almost concealed beneath one of the gothic arches of the building, and wore (as was indeed not uncommon at that period) a sort of masking costume. Her features, indeed, were so completely concealed by her mask that only her brilliant eyes were visible.

It was one who, even at this early period of the poet's career, fully appreciated his genius and talents, and (like Charlotte Clopton) at once saw what the world would take years to discover. And what a sight was it for that private friend to behold! She saw him, to whom she owed so much, in his hour of triumph, and marked his expressive countenance as he stood beside the Queen. She marked, too, the surprise and delight pourtrayed upon the countenance of Walter Arderne and Sir Hugh Clopton, as they looked upon the poor player thus honoured in the presence of the mighty Tudor; and then she beheld with a smile, for she knew his story, the astonishment of Sir Thomas Lucy, as the knight's eyes wandered to the stage, and again returned to the figure of the sometime deer-stealer; and whilst his ears drank in the honeyed words of that poet, Sir Thomas felt he could forgive all his juvenile delinquencies, and longed to grasp him by the hand.

Pshaw," he said, "I have been an ass. I am an ass—*ergo*, we are all asses in comparison to this *one* man, this Shakespeare."

CHAPTER LI.

THE TAVERN.

It was about an hour after the performance we have attempted to describe, that a solitary individual stood near the water-gate of the monastery of the Blackfriars. He stood, apparently lost in thought, and listening to the distant sound of music on the waters—the roll of the kettle-drum and the flourish of trumpet, as the Queen and her party returned towards St. James's.

As Shakespeare stood thus alone (after having attended the Queen to the Abbey stairs, and seen her embark), all around seemed dark and sombre. The cloisters of that abbey no longer flashed in the torch-light; the theatre was empty and deserted; all that was brilliant had departed—vanished like the pleasures of the world, and left a dreary contrast behind him.

"Oh, time," he thought to himself, "thou art the most indefatigable of things! The past is gone, the future to come, and the present becomes the past even while we attempt to define it,—like the flash of lightning, it exists and expires."

His companions of the theatre had sought the genial license of the tavern, there to revel over the success of the night, and canvass the merits and demerits of what they had enacted; and whilst he, the poet himself, the idol of the hour, and whom all wished to have with them, felt at that moment unfitted for society.

As he cast his eyes up at the "brave o'erhanging firmament, fretted with golden fire," he felt that "the wide, the universal theatre," was at that moment most congenial to his soul.

Whilst numerous boats continued to pass and repass, many of them filled with companies who had witnessed the performance, he hailed one he observed disengaged; and after rowing to his own lodging, and changing his dress, he re-embarked.

We have already stated that the mind of the man had not been elevated beyond bounds at the success he had achieved. To such a mind as Shakespeare's the prosperity of the hour was more likely to produce a degree of melancholy than any undue elevation. An incomprehensible feeling of contempt and distrust of all worldly success. Perhaps of all mortals this great man was the least given to vanity. The present hour would indeed seem to proclaim as much. He was on that night wished for, sought for, not only by many of the nobles who had witnessed his play, but his companions of the stage too sought for him to join their tavern revel after the performance, and several of the audience had even lingered about the doors, to gain a look at him as he came forth, whilst the unconscious poet, wrapped in his own thoughts, slowly floated down the river. Nay, so utterly careless was he of all he had effected, that the very play which had made so great a sensation scarcely existed but in the memories of the performers who had recited it.

It had, previous to performance, been copied into lengths, as the several parts are technically denominated, and given to the actors to study, whilst the manuscript itself was left casting about amidst the properties of the theatre, to be searched for, if required, at the next performance.

As the gentle Shakespeare, during the silent hour of night, passed slowly along the stream, his thoughts indeed were of other matters rather than his own particular affairs. The ripple of the water, the plash of the oars, the faint sound of music from afar, soothed his thoughts after the false exciting hour.

"Soft stillness and the night,
Became the touches of sweet harmony."

Meantime, whilst the poet floats onwards, we must return to the city, and observe the events taking place immediately after the representation of his play.

In a goodly room of a good-sized tavern, situated in the purlieus of Old St. Paul's, were congregated, on this night, many who had been spectators of the recent performance at the Blackfriars, and several other chance customers.

Besides the more respectable merchants, who had put into the tavern after the play, there were several ruffling blades of the inns of Court, one or two bullying fellows whose means and professions were extremely doubtful—a sort of Alsatian companions, " as ready to strike as to speak," who drank deep wherever they could obtain liquor, and diced whenever they could pick up a cully ; and also several guests from the country.

The Londoners, who constituted a party by themselves, sat at a table extending about half-way along the ample room ; whilst two or three smaller tables were occupied by those parties who had sought the hostel on matters of business, and who transacted their affairs or enjoyed themselves apart from the rest.

The aspect of the room shewed that it had been reduced to its present state from a more respectable occupation. The ample window which ran along one entire side, looked into a good-sized court : and on the capacious stone chimney was carved various coats-of-arms, and all sorts of herald devices and designs.

Those guests who were apart from the sort of ordinary, or common table, were at the upper end of the room, and on either side the chimney. They carried on their conversation amongst each other, and were, for the most part, strangers to the town.

At one of the smaller tables, placed quite up in the corner of the room, were seated a party of four individuals, and two of them being natives of the town of Stratford-upon-Avon, our readers are already acquainted with.

This company consisted of Lawyer Grasp ; a rich client, for whom he was professionally employed ; a member of the Temple, with whom he was in consultation ; and Master Doubletongue.

Besides these, there were also four or five other persons seated upon the long bench beneath the window, and they also carried on their occupation apart from either the guests at the supper table, or the other parties in the room. Some two or three were deeply engaged in play, rattling the dice and staking their coin with an eagerness equal to the absorption of their comrades who watched the game.

Such being the mixed nature of the assemblage, as two fresh guests entered the room and made their way to the upper end of it, the conversation of the various parties formed a sort of confused jargon, very like the cross-reading of a modern newspaper.

Such as it was, it seemed greatly to interest the late arrivals, and, as they stood with their backs towards the fire-place, they lent an attentive ear, more especially to the conversation of Grasp and his small party, and a look of intelligence ever and anon passed between them.

The table at which Grasp sat was covered with the produce of his eternal blue bag, and, as his quick moving fingers pointed to the various documents and deeds, he held forth with his accustomed volubility whilst every now and then a roar from the table, or a dispute amongst the dicers, interrupted his dissertations.

"Here," he said to the Temple lawyer, "here we have the matter duly executed. And here," he continued, "I will prove our right."

"Stay," said the Temple lawyer, "if I remember rightly, there is no mention of this place in the Conqueror's survey."

"A fico for the Conqueror and his survey," cried Grasp; "trouble not yourself upon that subject; mark and perpend—from Geoffrey Clinton it descended to the Verduns in marriage with Leosceline, daughter of that same Geoffrey, as did also the manors of Brandon, and I take it—"

"On my word," roared a tall Alsatian-looking fellow at the long table, "I take it that this Romeus and Julietta, or whatever else 'tis called, is the most exquisite piece ever submitted to a crowned head."

"A pestilence seize Romulus and Julia," said Grasp; "how that fellow bawls. And now, sirs, that same Anselm de Clinton, of whom I was before speaking, was first enfeoffed thereof."

"Up with his heels then," cried one of the dicers, as he threw. "Play. Ha! seven by Old Paul's. More sack, drawer!"

"The fiend sack those dicers," said Grasp, "marry and amen; as I was saying, good sir, by a multitude of testimonies I can prove—"

"A lie, knave, throw again." Ha! ha!" roared another of the gamblers.

"They are certified to hold it," continued Grasp, "of that family by the service of half a knight's fee, and they of the Earls of Warwick. Now my client here—"

"A cheater, I'll be sworn. A murrain take thee!" cried another of the gamblers.

"But how said ye," inquired the Temple lawyer, "that you became opposed to this Arderne? Methinks, when I last consulted you, you were employed and trusted by him."

"At first, *only* at first," said Grasp. "In virtue of my having informed him of his good fortune he did employ me,—entrusted me with management of his estates, and I did but eject—"

"Cheatery, villany!" cried the dicer. "I'll not restore a dernier."

"Pshaw," said Grasp, "I did but eject one or two of the poorer tenants, and put relatives of mine own into their holdings, when he ejected both them and myself. This, my good sir, I liked not, and, as upon careful examination I found one I thought more nearly related to the deceased, and the will distinctly says next of kin, I forthwith sought out my client; there now is our case."

"The case is a good case, an exceeding good case, and so I said from the first," said the Templar. "You have this Arderne fairly upon the hip, an he pay not he must to jail, unless you give him time."

"Not a day, not an hour," said Grasp; "we got a verdict in a former suit, and he shall incontinent to prison."

"Such is the law of a verity," said the Templar, emptying his glass, filling his pipe, and turning now to regard the guests at the ordinary, as they seemed getting up a dispute upon the subject of the play they had witnessed.

"I perfectly agree with you," said a person who sat opposite to the tall Alsatian, "in so far as regards the excellence of the play we have this night seen. But in respect of its newness to the world there I disagree."

"How?" cried the other fiercely, "dost mean to affirm that such exquisite portraits as that lady who loved the youth Romeo, that brilliant Mercutio, and that hot-brained Tybalt were ever drawn by mortal man before? Didst ever behold any thing so like reality as that loquacious, secret, obsequious nurse, or the little Peter who carried her fan? Didst ever—"

"Pshaw," said the other, "I quarrel not with your nurse, neither do I take exception at Peter,—what I say I will maintain with my rapier here or elsewhere. And thus it is: the subject-matter of that play is not new to the world. 'Tis manifestly constructed upon the novel of Italy, written by Luigi da Porto, a Venetian gentleman now deceased—gainsay that who will." And the student rose, drew up his tall form, twisted his mustachio, and looked fiercely around.

"We shall assuredly have a riot here," said Grasp, looking up from the copy of a will he was perusing. "I like it not."

"Nay," said Doubletongue, "'tis but a controversy upon a play. I saw the greater portion of it myself, and came away to my appointment here. 'Twas but a paltry performance methought, full of bombast and fustian."

"Was it not then liked?" inquired the Temple lawyer.

"'Fore Heaven, I cannot answer for that," said Doubletongue. "I only know it liked me not."

"Methinks," said the Templar, "you are hard to please, good Master Doubletongue. Master Shakespeare is somewhat of a favourite here."

"Who, said ye?" exclaimed Grasp, looking over his glasses, and speaking with great rapidity. "Master Shakespeare—methinks I ought to know that name. Comes he from Warwickshire? Is he to be met withal? Canst tell me aught of Master Shakespeare? 'Fore Heaven, I have matter on hand with Master Shakespeare, an' his name be William, and he cometh from Stratford-upon-Avon."

"I pr'ythee settle one thing at a time, my good Grasp," said the London lawyer. "Permit me to glance at that testament you was perusing once more."

"Here 'tis," said Grasp. Nay, you shall find that I do bear a brain; whoso trusts to Lawyer Grasp shall be—."

"Ruined, hip and thigh," cried one of the dicers, hurling the dice-box at the head of his opponent, whilst, at the same time the disputants at the ordinary being also pretty well flushed, a general riot immediately ensued, and swords being drawn the whole room became a scene of confusion.

The two guests who had last entered took advantage of this scene to press close upon the table at which Grasp and his party had been seated. They were both clad in the costume of seafaring men of the period, their sea-caps so completely drawn over their heads that their features were not discernible, though one appeared a slight youth, and the other a middle aged and powerful man.

As Grasp, in some alarm, seized upon his blue bag and withdrew more into the corner, the elder of the strangers, as if to keep from the fray, seated himself in the chair the lawyer had left, and whilst he puffed out huge volumes of smoke from his pipe, abstracted from amongst the papers the will the Templar had been perusing. Handing it then to his youthful companion, the latter seized a pen, and, unobserved, wrote a codicil to it. He then restored it to its place, and as the riot increased and Grasp seized upon his papers and thrust them into his bag, the pair took an opportunity of withdrawing as quietly as they had entered.

CHAPTER LII.

THE PLAYER IN HIS LODGING.

All that Shakespeare had lately seen and gone through made considerable impression upon his mind. In the short period during which the national convulsion we have described was taking place, it seemed to him that he had lived whole years.

Those events, and the great men which the stirring times had produced, seemed indeed to have passed before the poet, for the very purpose of finishing and perfecting the great mind of the man.

He sat himself down on his return to London, and, as he thought over the past experience of his life, such a chaos of bright thoughts and wondrous images presented themselves before and seemed to overflow his brain, that, at first, it seemed utterly impossible to turn them to shape.

Already had his "muse of fire" given him employment at various times, and even taken a dramatic shape; nay, the room he inhabited was filled with fragments—unfinished beginnings; and one or two of the novels of the period had been partially dramatized and then cast aside, after the inspiration which called them forth had, in other pursuits, been forgotten.

His avocations as a player had too frequently led him into scenes of revelry. His way of life was still desultory. He knew not his own value. And whilst his brilliant wit and companionable qualities had kept him too much among the society of men in his own class, he had failed to carry out any of his bright conceptions. His companions hunted him, haunted him, took him from his own thoughts, and dragged him, even when satiated with revelry, into more company; for what party was complete amongst them that had not in it *that one*—that "foremost man of all the world."

His poetry was beginning to be appreciated ere the national danger had fully occupied men's minds, and so fully employed them that all else for the time being was necessarily forgotten. He had written a poem peculiarly suited to the taste of the age, and which was greatly the fashion amongst the gay cavaliers of Elizabeth's Court. This he had dedicated to Lord Southampton, a nobleman, whose acquaintance he had made on the boards of the theatre. Added to this, some sonnets, which had almost by accident found their way into circulation (for no man was more careless or thoughtless of his own works than William Shakespeare) were greatly admired. Nay, the Queen had been so much struck with one or two of them, that she had shewn favour to the poet; and spoken words of encouragement in his ear.

The starched and stately Tudor was indeed becoming extremely fond of dramatic representations, tedious and ill-contrived as they, for the most part, were; and now often frequented the theatre, in place of the bear and bull-baiting arenas. Besides his stage companions, also Shakespeare had, amongst his acquaintance, at this period of his life, some of the most brilliant of the courtiers—Sydney and Raleigh, Essex and Spenser, all were personally known to the gentle Willie. They sought his society for his wit; and they respected him for his fine feelings, his noble sentiments, and his universal knowledge. Nay, these great men felt an internal conviction, whilst in the society of Shakespeare, that great as they themselves were, this man, of almost unknown origin, was immeasurably their superior; that, had his station in life been more elevated and his opportunities greater, he might have risen to the highest eminence in the State. They saw in him—

"The courtier's, soldier's, scholar's eye, tongue, sword."

The war was now for the present over, and amidst the general excitement around him, Shakespeare sat himself down to think upon all he had beheld. The quick result of such consideration our readers will as quickly imagine. The poet seized his pen,—

"Imagination bodied forth the form of things unknown."

His pen "turned them to shape, and gave to airy nothing a local habitation and a name."

Scarce had the joyous shouts for the glorious victory over the invincible Don subsided, ere the poet had completed one of those finished productions which left all competition behind. Yet stop we here for a space in our narrative, even whilst the reader looks upon Shakespeare thus engaged.

This is indeed a period in the man's life which most of us have sought for with the mind's eye.

The living Shakespeare, still comparatively unknown, still disregarded—for, however he might have been appreciated by the very few who were acquainted with him at this time, the wide and universal theatre had yet to discover the greatness of the man. The living Shakespeare, employed in writing that language never equalled, never to be equalled, deserves somewhat of a pause to look upon. The room, the house, the chairs, the tables, each and all, require an especial description. Like his own Iachimo, we must "note the chamber. Such and such pictures. There the windows. Such the adornment of the bed. The arras and figures. Why such and such."

Stay, then, gentle reader, if only for a brief space, and look upon the man—the gentle Shakespeare, as he was denominated amongst his familiars. He sits in a room, which to all appearance has belonged to a building of some pretensions in the palmy days of such edifices. The chamber is large, low in roof, and somewhat gloomy withal. A good-sized bay window, heavy in mullion, and which looks out upon the silver Thames beneath, affording a delicious view of the Surrey hills on the opposite side, gives light to (at least) one-half of the apartment. The morning sun streams through small diamond panes of many colours, which ornament the upper part of the casement, and is reflected in fainter hues, like a fading rainbow upon the oaken floor. The ceiling is richly carved. It displays the cunning skill of the architects of old. And on the heavy oaken beam, which traverses it, is cut from end to end the coats of arms of some city functionary of Old London, for the house (albeit it is now but partially inhabited by one or two of the actors of the Blackfriars theatre, and some portion of it even suffered to run to decay) has, in the preceding reign, belonged to one of the citizen princes—the merchants of Blackfriars. "The chimney-piece, south of the chamber," is elaborately carved, with gigantic figures, "exceedingly ugly;" and tapestry, (albeit it is somewhat faded), displaying pictorial scenes from scriptural and mythological history, hangs to the wall. One side has King David dancing before the ark; the other, "Cytherea hid in sedges."

A massive oaken table stands near the fire-place; a high-backed chair on either hand, and two more in the embayment of the window; and an antique cabinet occupies a place directly opposite the chimney.

The house, we have said, is situated on the river bank, and has once been occupied by a rich merchant, but is now let out in compartments. You ascend to the chamber which Shakespeare occupies, by a broad carved, oaken staircase, and advance along a vast passage which has rooms on either side.

The autumn wind sighs, and soughs, in this old dwelling, as it rushes through the long passages from the water side. In such room our Shakespeare sits and writes. Sometime he stops and considers for a space—thinks, and thinks deeply. Then again his pen glides swiftly over the paper before him, and he writes like the wind. The table at which he is seated is but little removed from the embayment of the window, and his eye, ever and anon, glances out upon the rushing tide, and wanders over the opposite landscape, then consisting of green meadows and stunted trees.

As he thus looks out upon the river, he sees boats filled with gay parties, cloaked and ruffed, and rapiered, attended by other boats, carrying musicians, who make the air resound with their melody—a gay and gallant sight, for these are courtiers going to Greenwich, or Mortlake, or Chelsea, such excursions being common in Elizabeth's day.

As the poet writes, there seems no effort in the composition. His thoughts flow, for the most part, so easily, that it seems but the careless noting down of whatever comes uppermost. He writes as his own Falstaff speaks—as if almost without the trouble of thought. Anon, he smiles and pauses; then he rises from his high-backed chair, takes a turn through the room, and gives utterance to the conceit which has suddenly struck him. The actor predominates over the author at such a moment, and he recites aloud the recent thought, and which his "often rumination" upon the extravagance of action, amongst his associates, has conjured up.

CHAPTER LIII.

THE POET AND HIS PATRON.

Whilst he gives his thoughts tongue, the door opens, and a bulky form seems to fill up the entrance—no other, indeed, than our old Stratford acquaintance John Froth.

"Ah! thou mad compound," said Froth, "and is such thy advice to the fraternity of the Blackfriars?"

"It is," returned Shakespeare.

"Then would we might see it approved in the acting," said Froth; "but 'tis thrown away upon me, as thou know'st. I am not for the personation of aught requiring such rules. If I am to turn mummer, I must enact something fit for a man of my parts to appear in."

"And therefore," said Shakespeare, "will I write a character fit only for thy huge bulk and greater follies."

"Nay, by my fay," said Froth, "I thought thou hadst already put me into shape, for so hast thou promised any time these two months past."

"'Tis better as it is," said Shakespeare, "for till I saw thy vagaries during this last affair with the Spaniard, thy arrant cowardice, thy shifts, for preferment, and then thy desire to keep out of action, I hardly could have displayed such a marvellous compound of frailty and flesh."

"Trouble me not with the remembrance thereof," said Froth; "I received my guerdon, my remuneration, and that was the aim in end."

"And which remuneration thou hast already dissipated in dice and liquor,—is't not so?" inquired Shakespeare.

"Thou hast spoken it, and not I," said Froth, "and so spoken it that I may hardly venture to gainsay it. Wilt furnish me forthwith a few crowns for present need, good William?"

"The more readily," returned Shakespeare, as he handed him the coin, "as I would fain be rid o' thee. See'st thou not, thou idle reveller, that I am busy here with deep premeditated lines—with written matters studiously devised?"

"Well, Will, I will hinder thee not. I will mar not thy labours. I will but fill me a chalice, and drink success to thy muse, and then to the tavern."

So saying, Froth helped himself from the flask upon the table, and pledged the health of his friend, smacking his lips after the draught with a sense of ineffable relish.

"Thou art a wondrous fellow, Will," he said, as he looked upon his friend; "thou wilt thrive. But, in sooth, envy already begins to dog thy heels. Green and Marlow like thee not, William; Green calls thee an upstart crow dressed with his feathers."

"Ah!" said Shakespeare, smiling, "methinks Green hath little reason to speak thus, seeing I have imp'd his wing with some of my own feathers. He will scarce say that to my face."

"Nay," said Froth, "I dare be sworn he will not, for many of them know thee too well to offer insult to thy face. Marlow too speaks of thee as that 'tiger's heart wrapped in a player's hide.'"

"Well," said Shakespeare, "their sayings pass by me like the wind. I pr'ythee be nought awhile, if thou art to remain here, or else betake thyself to other haunts."

"Farewell," said Froth; "you shall find me at the old haunt in Paul's whilst this coin holds out."

Scarcely had Froth departed, ere the sound of horses was heard without, and a man of noble presence, dressed in the extreme of fashion of that age of brave attire, entered the room. Shakespeare instantly rose, and advanced to meet him.

"I am proud to welcome my Lord of Southampton to my poor lodging," said the poet.

"Nay, by my fay, not altogether so poor either," said the noble, looking around him. "I am glad to find thee removed from thy old haunt to so goodly a lodgment, good William."

"And am I not indebted to your lordship's kind favour and friendship for being thus well lodged?" said Shakespeare. "When we first met, my lord, I was somewhat lower in estate than at the present time. A poor unfriended outcast; I do, indeed, owe thee much."

"Not a whit," said the Earl; "you owe all to your own surpassing excellence. I am greatly charmed with thy Tarquin and Lucrece. Nay, Raleigh, Essex, and others do swear by it as the most exquisite thing extant. I, who know thee better, think even better of thee than shall here say."

"You do me too much honour, my Lord," said Shakespeare; "like Venus and Adonis, (and which I had the honour of dedicating to you), Tarquin and Lucrece was but a first effort, when I was green in judgment. I shall hope better to deserve with more experience."

"I pray you to inform me," said Lord Southampton, after a pause, "who and what is yonder companion of thine, and whom I met as I entered the house,—a gross, fat man?"

Shakespeare smiled at the question. "A strange fellow, my Lord," he replied, "and who was known to me in my native town, and whom I have lately fallen in with here. Like myself, he was obliged to fly from Stratford, and being in some difficulties, I procured him employment in the theatres."

"A somewhat bulky actor," said Lord Southampton, "is he not."

"Nevertheless one whom I think even of giving a part to. The man is himself a character worth the studying, and if he exhibits himself before the curtain as he does in his true character, cannot fail to keep the audience in continual laughter. His peculiar humour, tone of voice, look, and jesture, coupled to such a person, are almost indiscribable. Added to this, he is so extraordinary a mimic that no one of us can move or speak before him, but he carries their voice, look, mien, and motion into another company.

"And yet upon the stage he may not be able to execute the same degree of perfection," said Southampton. "Some of your companions of the theatre, I have found prime fellows and witty knaves over their cups, and yet but heavy upon the boards."

"Truly so, my lord," said Shakespeare; "this is one of Nature's secrets, and which I have observed. Necessary qualifications which cannot be well spared in an actor, oftimes exist in men of the profession; and yet, with the assistance of all these united, we see such persons come forth upon the boards but poor and barren. In writing a character for my friend, I shall avoid making him play off his ordinary parts, except to produce himself when I think he will tell forcibly."

"I feel some curiosity to know this witty knave," said the noble "pr'ythee bring him with thee to Southampton House when next you come."

"Providing your lordship can away with his grossness, and resist the attacks he is sure to make upon your purse," said Shakespeare, "you will be amused with him. But, unluckily, 'tis a familiar creature who makes himself enemies as easily as his humour delights."

"And this new play of thine," said Southampton, "holds it still for next week?"

"It does, my lord," said Shakespeare.

"Then have I news for thee of price, good William," said Southampton. "The Queen intends to be present. She takes wondrous interest in all that thou dost, and has of late spoken most approvingly of thy efforts."

"I am much bounden to her Majesty," returned the poet; "and there again must feel grateful to your lordship for having turned her eye of favour towards my unworthy efforts."

"Thou hast sufficiently delighted us all, good William," said Lord Southampton; "and, if I am to judge by the mass of papers I behold here, you intend still further to delight us. Are these portions of manuscript pertaining to another production of the same sort?

"In truth, my lord," said Shakespeare, "they do in some sort tend that way. But at present I am somewhat desultory in my doings. I have so many plans, on so many subjects, that what you behold are but the rough notes of such ideas as pass current. The scraps are of all sorts; perhaps fit for little else but to be cast to the waves without."

"Thou art, at least industrious," said Southampton, "and permit me to say, I believe not in the valueless quality of what I behold here. May I look upon one of these same unworthy scraps?" And Lord Southampton took up a fragment of paper containing some few lines of blank verse.

At first he seemed disposed to read it cursorily, as one slightly curious to know what had employed the pen of his friend. The very first line, however, seemed to strike him, and he read the verse attentively from beginning to end. He then recommenced it, and read it more slowly, observing the wondrous force of the lines more and more as he did so. He then stopped and looked at the pleasant smiling countenance of the writer, so unassuming, so devoid of all self-conceit, and then he read aloud—

"Time hath, my lord, a wallet at his back,
Wherein he puts alms for oblivion,
A great-siz'd monster of ingratitudes:
Those scraps are good deeds past: which are devour'd
As fast as they are made, forgot as soon
As done: Perseverance, dear my lord,
Keeps honour bright; To have done is to hang
Quite out of fashion, like a rusty mail,
In monumental mockery. Take the instant way;
For honour travels in a strait so narrow,
Where one but goes abreast: keep then the path;
For emulation hath a thousand sons,
That one by one pursue. If you give way,
Or hedge aside from the direct forth right,
Like to an enter'd tide, they all rush by,
And leave you hindmost;—
Or, like a gallant horse fallen in first rank,
Lie there for pavement to the abject rear,
O'errun and trampled on. Then what do they in present,
Though less than yours in past, most o'ertop yours:
For time is like a fashionable host
That slighly shakes his parting guest by the hand;
And with his arms out-stretch'd as he would fly,
Grasps-in the comer: Welcome ever smiles,
And farewell goes that sighing."

"Why," he said, "thou hast written here a whole volume in a few brief lines. Not all the learning of the ancients ever produced so much in such compass. I will learn these lines, and have them ever before me. To what pertain they, good William?"

Shakespeare smiled. "Nay, 'tis but a fragment," he said. "My often rumination supplies many such. I shall perhaps adopt them in a play I have been thinking of writing."

"Thou wilt completely alter the old style of representation," said Southampton.

"'Tis my purpose so to do," returned Shakespeare.

"From what thou hast before shewn me," said Lord Southampton, "I think thou wilt do much. But bethink ye, William Shakespeare, albeit thou hast a quick wit and rapid pen, thou must not let things come hastily from thy hands. Good works, I take it, are plants of slow produce. The city lads and the inns of court have, I find, began to regard thee since thou hast remodelled the company of the Blackfriars. And hast thou," continued the earl after a pause, "still the same purpose of becoming a part proprietor in the theatre here?"

"Such is my ambition," said Shakespeare; "but that must be at a future period, when further success shall give warranty to my hopes."

"Nay, want of means shall not baulk thee, good William," said Lord Southampton, "since I see plainly that more power will greatly facilitate the bringing forth thy inimitable works. Look," he continued, taking the pen Shakespeare had been writing with, and scrawling a few lines, "there is an order for a thousand pounds; present it to my steward when thou wilt, and 'tis thine. Nay, double the sum, if required."

Shakespeare thanked his generous patron in terms of manly gratitude; and soon afterwards the noble, after appointing his poetic friend to visit him, took his leave.

After the departure of Lord Southampton, the poet sat for some time, with his forehead leaning upon his hand, gazing upon the order his friend had given him.

Between my Lord Southampton and Shakespeare there was the most sincere friendship. The young noble appreciated the genius of the man, and felt quite a veneration for him; whilst the poet honoured one possessed of the fine feelings and generous and heroic spirit belonging to a more early and chivalrous age.

Since Shakespeare's flight from Stratford some time had now elapsed, during which he had not returned there. He had made a vow not to do so until he could re-appear under circumstances that would disarm the malevolence of his enemies; not until he had achieved a name. Oft-times had he written, and as often heard from his friends, sending them the greater portion of his earnings his efforts continually brought in. This was not the first gift of Lord Southampton; and a considerable sum he had before received had enabled him to settle his wife and children in comfortable circumstances in his native town. The money his noble friend had just now conferred upon him gave him a nearer prospect of revisiting Stratford he thought. And so the poet, with renewed energy, seized his pen, and again gave vent to his wondrous conceptions. As he writes, he remembers former days, and his thoughts revert again to his own sweet home and its neighbourhood, and again he dips his pen in his own heart. Then he revels in the recollection of those orgies amidst the choice spirits of Old London. Those tavern suppers in the quaint dark courts where the hostels of the crowded city are situated. Those secluded taverns of Old London town now, indeed ,no longer to be found. The player's loved haunt, and where the rollicking 'prentice and even occasionally, the nobles of the Court congregated. Where he himself had fallen in with the Alsatian bully, the humourist, and all the varieties of the tavern haunter of the age; and from such he now draws his character, life-like and real, as if they walked and breathed and spoke before him.

And so the first part of the day passes, and still Shakespeare writes, for the fit is upon him, and like many of his class, albeit he spends in whole weeks, at times in joviality, excursionising with his comrades to Windsor and Greenwich, and "dafling the world aside" with the idlest; still there comes upon the man fits of deep thought, which are only to be relieved by the pen.

Whilst he writes, as the clanking tones of the clock of Barnard's Castle strike the sixth hour, the sound of a lute is heard in an adjoining apartment, accompanied by a voice of ravishing sweetness.

CHAPTER LIV.

A CONSULTATION.

As those dulcet sounds reached the ears of the poet, he laid down his pen and listened attentively. That voice, so rich in tone, so sweetly modulated, seemed deeply to affect him; and, as the song ceased, he rose and paced the apartment.

Again, he hears a short prelude upon the instrument, and pushing aside the arras from the wall, he opened a sliding panel, leading into a narrow passage; one of those passages so peculiar to old buildings, and which communicate from chamber to chamber, oft-times along one entire wing of such edifice.

As he did so, the voice of the singer is again and again more plainly heard. How sweetly it sounds in that house, and at that hour, for the shadows are beginning to descend upon Old London.

The poet stands transfixed. His glorious countenance so softened by the sorrowful notes of the musician, proclaim how powerfully the strains affect him—" He is never merry when he hears sweet music."

Again the strains cease and all is silent, save the moaning of the wind without, and which hums through the casement like an Æolian harp. After a pause, the poet again withdrew the tapestry which hung before the doorway, and, traversing the passage, knocks gently against a small door which stood partially open at its extremity.

A sweet voice bids him enter, and the next moment he is in the presence of a young and beautiful female. Traces of recent illness are to be observed upon her cheek, as she sits, half inclined, upon a sort of couch placed near the window of the apartment;—a small lamp, placed upon a table near, giving better light for an attendant female, who is occupied in knitting.

The lady half rises, as the poet enters and as she does so, he sinks upon one knee, and respectfully kisses the hand she extends to him.

Nothing, indeed, can exceed the respectful attention with which the poet stands in the presence of that female. He does not even take the chair, placed near the couch on which she is seated, till she requires him to do so. And well indeed might Shakespeare gaze with interest, and no less admiration, upon that lady, as she again reclined upon the couch from which she had half risen at his entrance.

The perfect proportions of her form and features, softened as they both were in the subdued light of that antique apartment, rendered her in the eyes of the poet even more beautiful. Her dark hair fell in wavy ringlets upon her shoulders, and her large eyes beamed with an expression of sweetness and regard upon him, which made them full of peril to one so impassioned.

Frankly and gracefully she again stretched forth her hand. " My kind preserver," she said, " my generous and noble friend; but that weakness keeps me a prisoner to my couch, 'tis I who ought to kneel to thee."

" I heard the sweet tones, lady," said the poet, " which gave notice that I might approach."

" Alas!" she replied, " how can I ever requite thy generosity? Had it been my fortune to fall into other hands, I might, indeed, have been unhappy; but thou, oh! thou art different from other mortals."

"Beauty, lady," said Shakespeare, " provoketh thieves even sooner than gold. Nay, it is that beauty which has made fearful of trusting you in this evil town, save whilst I can myself guard over you. The wild and reckless spirits who dwell around us here, the desperate characters of many who, in their outward seeming, are of the virtuous, render a sojourn in this city unsafe, and therefore have I brought thee hither; and therefore have I constituted myself thy sole guardian till recovered strength shall enable you to take the journey you contemplate."

"You will forgive me, then," said the lady, "that although I have related to you some portion of my story, I yet conceal my own, and the name of those connected with the tale."

"I am in all thy friend and servant," said Shakespeare.

"And now that I have somewhat recovered," she continued, "recall to me in how much I am indebted to you during my illness. The attendant you have furnished me with hath partially informed me of your goodness, but I would fain hear the recital from your own lips."

"Your disguise," said Shakespeare, "whilst we journeyed hitherward, beguiled me, or I had never so far taxed your strength."

"Ah! but that journey," said the lady, "so travelled, can one mile of it, think you, be forgotten?"

"Nay," said the poet, smiling, "still can I not forgive myself. Those moonlight walks during our route have, I fear, wearied you."

"Could it be possible," said the lady, "for mortal to feel fatigue amidst those scenes, I might have wearied."

Shakespeare again smiled. He felt gratified at the compliment paid him. He was no perfect mortal, and to say that he could look coldly upon the glorious creature before him, would be to belie his nature. He could no more do so than he could have "held a fire in his hand by thinking of the frosty Caucasus." His finer feelings, however, rendered that unprotected female as safe whilst beneath his roof, as if she had been guarded by a host. He seated himself again beside her, and as he calmly and kindly regarded her exquisite form, whilst he again spoke, a bright and pure beam of divine expression was on his bearded face, an expression, which diffused a calm feeling of happiness and contentment over the soul of her who beheld it.

The long crushed spirit of the lady felt the influence of his presence.

"That I had in my ignorance of your sex somewhat overtaxed your strength during our journey," he said, "the result has shewn, since on our reaching London, you was seized with an illness which nearly cost your life."

"I remember nothing," said the lady, "after our arrival at the hotel of the Globe."

"Unluckily," said the poet, "it happened that some seamen who disembarked but a few days before had brought the plague into that neighbourhood. That disease in London is usually so dire in its effect, that, for mere suspicion, the inhabitants act as if for surety. Your ship-boy's semblance, and your illness, gave the host of the tavern a suspicion that you was infected, and he expelled us from his door. Nay, such was the rapidity with which the alarm travelled, that I found it impossible to procure a shelter for you in that neighbourhood; and it was whilst conveying you, still insensible, to the water-side, that I became suspicious of your sex. This discovery increased the difficulty of our situation, till I recollected an asylum in which I could safely carry you, and e'en procure the assistance of medicine. I remembered an old poor man, one so needy, starved, and miserable, that I had oft-times sought, and alleviated his condition. Nay, gratitude had prompted me so to do, since, in my own need, and when, alone and friendless, I first sought this town, he himself befriended me. To the habitation of this man, who indeed, possesses considerable skill in leechcraft, I conveyed you, and to his care, attention, and skill, for night and day did he watch over you, are you indebted for your life."

"And whilst yourself also cared for me," said the lady, "still fearless of the tyrant fever with which I was burnt up; nay, you have since removed me hither, and so continued to guard over me. And all this in favour of one alike hopeless and friendless."

"Such circumstances, lady," said the poet, "should in themselves alone suffice to enlist me in your service. But come," he continued, "we will no more of this. A letter I have just received from my sometime home, in Warwickshire, gives much of news. I have unfolded to you so much of my history, that I may now further inform you there is hope of once more revisiting the friends I left whilst in trouble and disgrace."

"This is, indeed, pleasing intelligence," said his companion. "My own destination is in that neighbourhood."

"To guard over you till I can safely convey you amongst those friends you have hinted at," said Shakespeare, "is my wish; nay, our exertions, and the generosity of a nobleman, my friend, has enabled me to complete a purchase I had in contemplation—a share in the neighbouring theatre here. I have also another play toward, and should it succeed in the represental, I will then attend on you with all true duty."

"But your letter?" said the lady; "pardon my seeming curiosity. In happier days I have owned friends in the neighbourhood of your home. Speaks it of any resident around Stratford-upon-Avon?"

"It does," said Shakespeare. "It is from my father, and gives much gossip of the locality. Amongst other matter it informs me of some difficulties a gentleman, my friend, has fallen into."

"And his name," said the lady, "is Walter Arderne?"

"The same," returned Shakespeare.

The lady's face immediatetely became crimson, and then deadly pale. "And how then hath Walter Arderne fallen into difficulties?" she inquired. "Methought I heard from you, during our journey, that he had succeeded to great wealth."

"It was even so," said Shakespeare, "but I fear I am again taxing your strength. You look somewhat pale."

"'Tis nothing," said his fair companion. "Proceed, I beseech you, I am most anxious to know of the welfare of this Arderne."

"The young man, then," continued Shakespeare, "it appears by the story, after coming into possession of this fortune, and many parks, and walks, and manors, in England, hath busied himself in various acts of goodness. Amongst other things he hath built alms-houses, hospitals, for the use of the afflicted."

"To such a one," said the lady, "fortune should ever belong; but to your story. What more of this Arderne? Methinks I am overfond to hear of so much generosity."

"There is little more to tell," said Shakespeare. "The sums he hath bestowed and the various charities he hath endowed, have involved him in difficulties. His virtues have served him but as enemies. Nay, he seems, I am grieved to say, on the brink of ruin; for, in addition to all I have enumerated, it appears he hath expended large sums during the invasion of the Spaniard, both in fitting out numerous ships, and enrolling and embodying men, all which vessels, through his desperate valour in leading them into the hot encounter, have been either destroyed or returned to port rent and beggared."

"Nay, but," said the lady, "I am still in ignorance how this could possibly involve Walter Arderne in ruin. The fortune he inherited would have borne all this, methinks, and much more, without endamagement."

"Truly so, lady," said Shakespeare; "but it hath suddenly transpired that Walter Arderne is not the lawful heir. A caitiff wretch, named Grasp, and whose ferrit eyes and evil spirit are always seeking mischief, hath, by dint of searching over worm-eaten deeds and musty parchments, hunting out tombstones, and manufacturing pedigrees, somehow found a nearer relation; and all the sums Master Arderne hath expended since the hour he came into possession, the law will enforce him to refund. This, together with the suits he is involved in, will go nigh to ruin both himself and his good uncle, Sir Hugh Clopton."

"And this nearer kinsman!" said the lady. "Does your information extend so far as to name the person of such claimant?"

"'Tis one who is the friend of a powerful noble," said Shakespeare, "of one whom it is dangerous to speak of in other terms but those of respect."

"Methinks I can name him," said the lady. "It is one whose unbounded stomach and high ambition long soared towards a crown by marriage; one whose evil disposition would halt not to obtain power or riches, magnificent as his fortune already is. The Earl with the dark countenance and gloomy soul—he whom Sussex calls the Gipsey; the dangerous Leicester."

"The same," said Shakespeare.

"Nay, then, an Walter Arderne hath that noble for an enemy, let him beware the cup, as well as the law, for Leicester is sure to succeed by fair means or foul. He is the most successful dealer in poison in the kingdom."

"Would to Heaven," said Shakespeare, "some help might be found; for the strait this generous man is like to be driven to sorely oppresses him!"

"Let it no longer do so," said the lady. "Continue to inform me of the progress of events; I will be warranty for his safe extrication from all his difficulties."

Shakespeare looked surprised; but he forbode remark; and soon after this conversation retired to his own lodging.

After the interview, the poet reflected deeply upon the conversation which had taken place, and as he did so, many things which had not previously struck him forced themselves upon his mind regarding his mysterious friend, and which now enabled him in some sort to pluck out the heart of her mystery.

During the time he had watched over her during her illness, and the delirium consequent upon it, she had uttered names which recalled former passages of his life. She had called upon Charlotte Clopton, and bade her leave the horrid charnel-house in which she had been entombed alive, and even named localities familiar to him in his native county.

These things, whilst they contributed to elucidate her story, more deeply interested him. He saw she could appreciate a true heart and bold spirit in man, and could love with all the truth and innocence of a Juliet. There was in her no false pride or prudery, but unconscious of her own excellence, she was indeed one of those bright creatures so often bestowed where they are unvalued. Had such a one fallen to his own share, he thought, how would he have worshipped! But such was not to be. He who was the gentlest, the noblest of mankind, was not to be so companioned. His course was steered, at this period, alone. For him, high birth and bright excellence should have been reserved, because he so well could have appreciated them.

There was, however, to be observed in this singular female a sort of character which even more interested him than her radiant beauty. With all her amiability, she possessed a determination of purpose, which made it impossible to control her designs. From what he could fathom of her intentions and her story, she seemed only anxious to confer or secure some important benefit to the individual she loved, and then to retire from the world, to enter some convent abroad, "and be for aye in shady cloister mew'd." And so, as the poet sat and thought over these matters, he again seized his pen, and wrote.

CHAPTER LV.

ILL WEAVED AMBITION.

The machinations of Pouncet Grasp had not been without their due effect. His evil disposition was as great as his industry, and his very face and form, twisted and contorted as both were, proclaimed the mind of the man as plainly as if he had carried a window in his breast.

Few specimens of the human countenance presented indeed less of the divine about it than did that of the Stratford lawyer. The term *ugly as sin* might, in verity, have been applied to him, for, when he was hatching any particular piece of rascality, the working of his features gave him a diabolical look.

Not only had he succeeded in his design of weaving a web about Walter Arderne, and getting incarcerated within the walls of a prison for debt, but he even managed, by some strange underhand practice, to bring him under the suspicion of the Queen's council for treasonable matter. And yet, with all this malignancy of disposition, Grasp carried about him such an air of *bonhommie* that, until he was found out, he was seldom distrusted. After he had, by the most careful approaches, (like a spider securing a victim in his web, who is too powerful to be openly attacked), fairly enmeshed Walter Arderne, he turned his thoughts upon his old Stratford enemy, William Shakespeare, and whose whereabout he now had little difficulty in discovering, since after the successful performance of Romeo and Juliet, the author's name was in the mouths of many.

Sir Thomas Lucy had departed only a few days before for Stratford, or Grasp would immediately have sought him out, and, as he himself was also on the eve of returning to Warwickshire, together with his new client, in order to take immediate possession of the inheritance succeeded to, he resolved to delay till his arrival the discovery he had made.

Meanwhile, the situation of Arderne was sufficiently disagreeable. He was arrested for an enormous sum, and when Sir Hugh Clopton sought to clear him of the difficulty, by making some great sacrifices, that good old man found, to his further dismay, that some secret foe had denounced his nephew as a conspirator against the life of the Queen.

In Elizabeth's reign, those persons of condition who came under suspicion and were confined within the walls of a prison found it no easy matter to clear themselves, and some, even in the higher ranks of the nobility, without any sustained charge but "for mere suspicion, were treated as if for surety," finding their graves in the dismal chambers of the Tower.

The news of the imprisonment of his early friend greatly troubled Shakespeare. He was just at this time contemplating a return to his native town, for now that he had so far achieved success, and felt within himself the power of future fame, the longing for home, added to the desire of once more embracing all he had dear there, he felt to be irresistible.

To leave London, however, without an effort to serve his early friend was impossible. He visited Arderne in his prison, and afterwards sought Lord Leicester in order to interest that noble in his favour.

The time was, however, somewhat out of joint for making a successful suit to Leicester at this moment. He was in one of those periodical fits of ill-temper which usually attacked him when his "high-reaching" schemes failed. He was out of favour with the Queen too, somewhat on the sudden, and so wide was the breach that, albeit he was seeking by some underhand contrivances to regain a place in her good graces, all his attempts were futile.

To explain this to our readers, we must remind them that after the services of Leicester at Tilbury, Elizabeth had created for the favourite the office of Lord Lieutenant of England and Ireland; an office which would have invested him with greater power than any sovereign of this country had ever ventured to bestow on a subject. The patent for this unprecedented dignity was actually made out, and only awaited the royal signature, when Burleigh and Hatton, by their earnest remonstrances, deterred Her Majesty from investing him with such power.

It was during the fit of rage consequent upon disappointment, that Leicester had behaved with a degree of intemperance so distasteful to Her Majesty, that she dismissed him in anger, and refused to be reconciled.

The despondence which followed the violence of his rage on this occasion brought on an illness, from which he, in truth, never recovered.

At the moment Shakespeare obtained an interview, he accordingly found the earl in so ill a frame of mind, that he refused to interest himself in favour of Walter Arderne.

He was about, he said to quit London for his castle of Kenilworth, and was so utterly disgusted with Courts and all pertaining, that he vowed to Heaven he would no more return.

As the poet looked in the face of this ambitious and still powerful noble, he thought it not unlikely his words would prove true; for the inroads of his peculiar disease were so apparent in his countenance, that the grisly tyrant seemed to have put his mark upon him.

Leicester, at this period of his life, had grown bulky, and lost much of that striking beauty of face and form for which he had been so celebrated. His countenance shewed traces of his ungovernable temper and evil disposition; his hair, lately coal-black, had become a "sable silvered;" his frown had contracted into an habitual scowl; his dark complexion, and from which he had obtained the *sobriquet* of "The Gipsey," had changed to a sickly yellow; his fine features had become bloated; and every part about him seemed blasted with premature age.

As he rose from his seat during the interview, the poet observed that he looked the personification of an evil-disposed but powerful man. One who was torn by the fiend of avarice, the lust of power, and the chagrin of blasted ambition. The Court smile was gone for ever from that once pliant brow, and the scowl of hate seated in its stead.

To the surprise of the poet, whilst he flatly refused interference on the subject of Arderne's imprisonment, he even seemed to experience satisfaction at that youth's danger. The poisonous mind of the most successful poisoner of the age was now recklessly displayed. He seemed to rejoice in the misfortunes of his fellow-men, whilst he felt that his own further success in life was ended. He was indeed at that moment sinking into the grave a hopeless unbeliever, "a bold bad man."

"Sir Thomas Lucy," he said, rudely and abruptly, "hath sought me on the subject of this Arderne, praying of me to intercede with the Queen. But I meddle not again with matters of state or the business of others, my health requires change from the pestilential vapour of this city. I have done with Courts and seek my castle at Kenilworth."

Shakespeare bowed, and was about to withdraw, when Leicester turned and again spoke.

"I advise you yourself, Master Shakespeare," he said, "to keep free of such matters. Peril not your present favour by mixing in treasonable affairs, and so farewell."

"Nay, my Lord," said Shakespeare, "this gentleman, my friend, hath been most unjustly accused. He is one to whom I owe much love. I may not cease from making what interest I can in his favour."

"And I tell thee then," said Leicester, imperiously, "that in me you will find an opponent in his cause; my interest lieth in the very opposite direction, since I am informed by a law-man of your native town that, in right of my wife, I can claim some of those estates in Warwickshire so lately in possession of this Arderne."

Shakespeare felt surprised at this intimation, and immediately the interview terminated.

There was evidently a secret enemy at work, he thought, as he left the house; and, as he passed through the gateway, he ran against a man who was entering.

The poet was so wrapped in his own thoughts that he observed not the features of this person; but Grasp (for it was no less a person who was entering the court-yard) started at the well-known form of his sometime clerk, and, hesitating for the moment, seemed divided as to whether he should not defer his present business and follow the poet.

Whilst he stood undecided, Shakespeare took boat, and so Grasp turned towards the building.

"I shall find the pestilent fellow," he said, "and I shall also penetrate into the mystery of that fair Lindabrides who dwells beneath his roof, and masquerades about the city o' nights. My certie, but I'll spoil his actings, his writings, his inditings, his poetizing, and rhapsodizing. I can myself indite, aye, and play a part, too, as well as he; and so, Master William Shakespeare, look to thyself, for thou art in jeopardy;" and so Grasp turned and proceeded across the court of Leicester House rejoicing.

CHAPTER LVI.

THE ASSOCIATES.

So great were the talents possessed by Grasp for smelling out a plot, whether it existed or not, that he seemed peculiarly fitted for the period in which he lived, and in which conspiracies, either real or pretended, were so frequently agitating the kingdom.

Plot and pestilence, indeed, during Elizabeth's reign seemed the bug-bears of the time. At one moment the Court was driven from its locality, by some of the attendants being seized at the very palace-gates with some infectious disorder, and the next, some dark, evil-minded fanatic was apprehended, dagger in hand, almost in the very presence-chamber.

Since the execution of the Queen of Scots these conspirators had been more hopeless of success; yet still, ever and anon, a new and dangerous attempt against the life of the Queen was brought to light.

Just at the present period of our story, such a design was pounced on by Grasp; but, like all over-zealous persons, he was liable, in his eagerness, to run upon a wrong scent, and lose sight of the game he had started.

It happened, during his visit to London at this time, and in an interval spared from his unmerous avocations, (for Grasp was now a man in full business), that he, one night, amused himself by witnessing an execution in company with his friend Doubletongue.

This execution was one possessing considerable interest, inasmuch as several criminals were to suffer for conscience-sake, and that was always a popular exhibition during Elizabeth's reign. Six were Catholic priests, who were hung, drawn, and quartered, for conspiring against the Queen's life. Two more were laymen, who, having embraced protestantism and returned to the old belief, were to be burned alive in company with a wretched atheist named Francis Wright, alias Kit Wyndham. Besides these there was one other named Word, who was to be executed for concealment of Catholics under suspicion of treason.

The execution took place in Smithfield, and, like those of more modern times, when the cut-purse is seen to exercise his vocation beneath the gallows on which a fellow thief was struggling, so was treason watching within the scorching influence of the fire which burned these traitors.

One Reginald Deville, an usurer and an informer, who also bore the appropriate cognomen of Reynard Devil, had tracked a suspicious character into Smithfield on this very night; a fanatic being, whose husband had been in the service of the Queen of Scots, and who, in the disguise of a man, was known to be in concealment in London for the purpose of assassinating Elizabeth.

In the crowd, and during the excitement of the execution, Deville had lost sight of this person, almost at the moment he was about to gain assistance and pounce upon her; and, as he was prying about, he stumbled upon Grasp, whom he had formerly known.

Now Grasp himself, besides his other business, occasionally did a little in the informing way. Such pursuit formed a sort of afterhour recreation with him. He and Doubletongue, at such times, hunted in couples, and as evil speaking, lying, and slander, were the peculiar talents of his friend, so the more covert villany was his own peculiar forte.

The moment Reginald Deville stumbled upon Grasp and his friend, in his eagerness he half divulged the secret intelligence with which he was furnished.

"Ah," he said, "my good friend Grasp, I am glad to meet. Hast seen a slight rakish figure pass this minute, wearing a cloak of scarlet serge, a red feather in his hat, a brace of petronels in his girdle, and drab trunks with hose to match?"

Grasp was never at fault. "I have," he said hastily.

"Which way went he, in God's name," said Deville. "Quick, or I lose a chance—he's worth the having, I can assure you."

"I will put you upon his trail," said Grasp, "perhaps inform you where he haunts, an you promise half profits and tell me what's his crime."

"Treason is his crime," said Deville, "'Tis a female in man's apparel, one Margaret Lambrun. Her husband died of grief after Queen Mary was executed. The woman was in the service of Mary, and hath resolved on the death of the Queen. I had secret intelligence from a cousin of my own in Scotland, and have been in pursuit for some days."

"Well, then," said Grasp, "I can only tell you in return for your secret that your man, or woman rather, was here beside me in company with four others. Catholics, I dare be sworn, for they looked upon the burning of yonder priests with a devilish expression of horror, in place of viewing it as you and I. They marked me as I watched them, and they are off; but I heard one of them name some place in Blackfriars as where he resided."

"How said ye," exclaimed Doubletongue, "in Blackfriars? then, by my fay, I think I can give ye a clue to this same female."

"As how?" inquired Grasp, eagerly.

"As thus," said Doubletongue. "Dost remember the night on which we consulted with Lawyer Quillet at the Blue Boar Inn?"

"Truly so," said Grasp, "and what o' that?"

"On that night I marked, although you did not, a couple of persons who kept themselves altogether apart from the other guests—a young and a middle-aged person. Nay, I especially marked the younger of the twain, and as I looked upon the tiny foot, the sparkling eyes, and the slender form, methinks I penetrated through the disguise worn, and beheld a female."

"Ah! caitiff," said Grasp, "thou were't ever a devil to spy out a farthingale. And so—"

"And so, I said to myself, where disguise is there mischief is meant, and I resolved to know more. Acting upon this resolve, albeit I lost sight of them during the riot which ensued in the tavern, I followed them out into the street, dodged them to their lair—"

"And that is—?" inquired Deville impatiently.

"In the Blackfriars, at a house down by the waterside, and which I can point out."

"But thou may'st have been mistaken," said Grasp, "appearances may have deceived thee."

"Not a whit," said Doubletongue. "I took some pains to make assurance; for, sooth to say, I was taken with this mysterious female. I watched about the house till I again saw her. I even ventured within, concealed myself during the absence of herself and him who seemed her protector, and I found in the room which she inhabited—"

"What?" said Grasp, who expected a written list of the conspirators. "In God's name what did you find?"

"Her doublet and hose," said Doubletongue. "The very pair of nether garments in which I had seen her masquerading at the Blue Boar the first night I beheld her."

"Oh, monstrous!" said Grasp. "'Tis, undoubtedly the person of whom you are in quest. See, the execution is over and the criminals burnt. Wherefore not at once, proceed to Blackfriars and identify the house? To-morrow we will procure assistance and pounce upon her;" and the two immediately pushed their way through the crowd and left Smithfield."

CHAPTER LVII.

THE POET AND HIS FRIENDS.

THE success of Shakespeare's play of Romeo and Juliet had placed him in a somewhat different situation amongst his companions of the theatre. By the majority he was immediately looked up to as a rising star, and whilst others again viewed him with increasing envy, there were one or two who were so much struck with the extraordinary merit of the composition that they already pronounced him the wonder of the age.

Such, however, was the agitated state of the kingdom at the moment, and fears, factions, and jealousies, so absorded the minds of men of all ranks, that except beyond the circle of his own professional brethren, and amongst his own immediate friends of the Court, my Lord of Esesx, Sir Walter Raleigh, Lord Southampton, &c., the effect produced was, after all, but evanescent.

The English nation at this time was yet struggling to emerge from barbarity. The philology of Italy had been transplanted hither in the reign of Henry the Eighth, and the learned languages cultivated by Lilly, Linacre, More, and others. Greek was now taught in some of the principal schools, and many of the learned read the Italian and Spanish poets. But still literature was even yet confined in a great measure to professed scholars, or persons of high rank. The body public was but gross and dark; and to read and write, an accomplishment valued according to its rarity.

Thus, then, the people who witnessed the great curiosity of Shakespeare's new play hardly knew how to judge. It was welcome even to the most rude and vulgar; they looked at it with a sort of childish wonder. It was a delicious and startling change from the giants, dragons, and enchantments they had been used to. Nay, it even bid fair to supersede the interesting exhibition of the bear hugging the dog to death, or the bull driven into madness by agony. The show and bustle of the new play even charmed the rudesby's, who could scarce even comprehend the beauty and elegance of the poetry.

It was on the morning of the same day on which Grasp had witnessed the execution in Smithfield, that Shakespeare made his unsuccessful application to the Earl of Leicester in behalf of his friend Arderne. After his interview with the fallen favourite, the poet returned, sad and somewhat out of sorts, to his new lodgings in Blackfriars. As was his wont on all occasions wherein his capacious mind had received an impression, he contemplated the object that had furnished it. Indeed, his interview with that ambitious courtier, whose whole life had been a mistake, had been to him a whole volume. "How wretched," he thought, "is that poor man that 'hangs on prince's favours!" and then he seized his pen and wrote,—

"Fling away ambition,
By that sin fell the angels, how can man, then,
The image of his Maker, hope to rise by it."

Whilst the poet wrote, as was not uncommonly the case, a whole levée of visitors continually interrupted his labours. This, however, was a circumstance that seemed rather to aid than disturb the current of his thoughts. He laid down his pen to laugh with the light-hearted, and he thrust aside his manuscript to listen to the more serious. He was all things with all men. The courtier, the soldier, the scholar, all and each found in him something to wonder at and admire. On this day, which was the sixth for the representation of his play, his visitors were numerous. In addition to many of his brother authors, several of the actors and other persons connected with the theatre, the Earl of Essex, Sir Walter Raleigh, Lord Southampton, and the poet Spenser, sought him in his lodging. Master Doubletongue too, who on this day had been seeking an opportunity of introducing himself into the house, as he met with some actor or other visitor coming out, hesitated as to the safety of such espial. Nay, he felt considerably astonished at the number and quality of the persons who seemed, as the day advanced, to come thronging about the locality.

Whilst he continued watching for some person he appeared to expect, he beheld the open space in front of the house filled with the attendants of several nobles of the Court; their magnificent steeds, gaily caparisoned, being led up and down, or held by servitors with the emblazoned badges of the favourites of the Queen.

It is indeed curious to consider the poet himself during the visit of these magnificoes, and who, in the enjoyment of his society, sought a new pleasure; visitors who, like himself, were elevated above "the common cry of curs," and, leaving their high rank out of the question, worthy of the friendship of Shakespeare. The poet himself, too, was perfectly at his ease in the company of these haughty nobles. He sat and conversed with them in all the freedom of unchecked enjoyment.

To attempt any description of the conversation carried on amongst these choice and master spirits of the age would be vain and ridiculous, since it exceeds the power of our pen to describe it. Nay, were it possible so to do, we must of necessity furnish forth to the world a dialogue such as is only to be found in the page of him who acted as the host to the assemblage.

Let us look at the picture, for it is one worthy of regard. Shakespeare sits beneath the ample chimney, his table is before him, strewed with papers. He leans back in his chair; a divine expression, a sweet smile is on his bearded face. Opposite to him is his patron, Lord Southampton, his chin resting upon the hilt of his sheathed rapier, his eyes and ears intent upon the subject Shakespeare is speaking of. Beside Shakespeare, leaning his cheek upon his hand, his elbow upon the table, sits the magnificent Essex; he also is intently regarding the poet, admiration in his gaze. Standing somewhat behind Lord Southampton, his back against the carved chimney, is the poet Spenser. Raleigh sits within the embayment of the window; his plumed hat is carelessly thrown down beside him, and his quick, restless glance is ever and anon turned from the poet towards the different craft which pass and repass upon the Thames below. Beside these, the *élite* of the company, there is Tarleton, the comedian and Court fool, who, under cover of his folly, shoots his bolts upon all the party. One more addition, and the party is completed; and it is made up by the dissolute friend of the poet, the fat and jovial Froth.

Whilst they are engaged in conversation, the drawer from an adjoining tavern enters with wine and other refreshments. From long-necked and quaint-looking bottles is poured the wines of Gascony and Spain. The means, too, and appliances for indulgence in Sir Walter's favourite weed is then handed round, and (as was the custom of the period) each guest takes a whiff; the thin blue smoke mounts into the air, and eddies about the carved ceiling; and, as the mirth and joviality of the party grows faster, time flies unheeded by, the shadows descend upon the Thames, again and again the bottles are renewed, and another day dawns upon the party, ere they recollect how the hours have fled.

Can our readers wonder at this, when they remember of what that party consisted, and their entertainer? Those magnificoes had come to pay the poet a morning visit, and they had stayed half a day and one entire night. Shakespeare was their entertainer!

As the first faint streaks of dawn began to "lace the severing clouds," the poet stood alone in his apartment. His guests had left him, and his room shewed tokens of the revel they had been engaged in.

The revellers had drank deep, for they were such as would be most likely to give themselves up to the peculiar enjoyment of the hour. Shakespeare had cheered the cup for them.

As the glorious poet glanced upon the heap of empty flaskets, broken bottles, remnants of long-necked glasses, and capacious bowled pipes, together with all the *débris* of a long-continued orgie, he smiled, and stepping to the lattice-window, threw it open, and stood to enjoy the refreshing breeze from the river.

Whilst he stood and gazed upon the Thames, the boats containing his recent guests glided past, on their way to Greenwich; for Essex and Southampton, when they found themselves regularly set in for an orgie, had some time before sent away their steeds.

They waved their hands as they passed, on observing the poet, and he remained listening to the music from the boat which followed the barge of Essex, as it grew fainter and fainter in the distance.

As Shakespeare turned from the window, the arras near the fire-place was lifted, and two persons noiselessly entered. He started as he beheld them, for by the faint morning light he distinguished in one of them the beautiful female we have before remarked, dwelling beneath his roof; the other was our old friend Martin. Something more than ordinary he well knew must have caused her to enter the wing of the building he inhabited; in addition to which, he saw she was equipped in her masculine costume, and, together with her companion, prepared for a journey.

"We have come to bid you farewell," she said, as the poet stepped up to her, and took her hand.

"This is somewhat sudden," he returned. "I hoped to have been of your party into Warwickshire."

"Certain spies, good Master Shakespeare," said Martin, "have it seems noted this lady's residence beneath your roof, and she has fallen under suspicion of treasonable matter."

"Yes," said the lady, "my faithful friend and adviser here has discovered so much. My presence here might even compromise you, my kind friend and preserver. We have therefore resolved, at once, to set off on our journey."

"And how then have you learnt this?" inquired Shakespeare.

"Nay, heed not my means of intelligence," said Martin. "Thou know'st I possess the secret of divination, or I could never have at last escaped the Spanish Inquisition, and discovered the residence of this lady in London. Suffice it we know our danger, and must fly."

"And do you then still purpose seeking Kenilworth?" inquired Shakespeare of his beautiful friend.

"I do," she replied. "Lady Leicester is my friend. She will, I trust, be able to do service to him we wish well to. My best hope is from that quarter."

"I have already seen the Earl," said Shakespeare, "and my own expectations, in that quarter, touch ground."

"From the Earl himself I never entertained a particle of hope," said the lady, "his Countess may, however, serve us, for she is my friend."

"All good angels, then, speed you on your journey!" said Shakespeare. "I have myself other chances here. The Earl of Essex hath promised to speak with the Queen, ere another day passes, added to which, Lord Southampton and Sir Walter Raleigh have sworn to back his suit."

"Have you, then, seen the Earl of Essex on this matter?" inquired Martin, in some surprise.

"He and Lord Southampton were here but now," said Shakespeare, smiling, and pointing to the confused state of the apartment. "Behold the witness of their revel. Some ten minutes back they left me to take boat for Greenwich, where the Queen at present stays."

"Farewell, then," said the lady sorrowing, "we dare no longer stay, may we soon meet again!"

"Heaven grant it, fair excellence," said Shakespeare, "until I again revisit my home in Warwickshire, I shall have but small contentment. But until I see my friend out of jeopardy, and clear of imprisonment, I have neither home nor friends there."

"'Tis like yourself," said the lady. "Farewell! We shall soon then meet, I trust. Walter Arderne once relieved from durance, and my task is effected."

CHAPTER LVIII.

STRATFORD AND ITS NEIGHBOURHOOD.

After absence from a well-known locality how fresh and verdant seems every spot there. The mind which has dwelt, again and again, upon every nook and corner, unmarked perhaps and unappreciated whilst in the neighbourhood, becomes enamoured absolutely of trivialities and trifles. How well doth the exile, eating the bitter bread of banishment, perhaps breathing the hot air of the tropics, many, many thousand leagues from the quiet village in which he first drew breath—how well doth he recollect, and dwell with fondness upon each street or lane of the village suburb, the school-boy spot, the home the wanderer longs for with an undying desire!

And if such be the case, how anxiously, and even sadly, do we think upon those relatives and friends domesticated in the far-away home, and see them in their old-accustomed places. Relations so dear and friends so esteemed, yet, perhaps, never again to be met with in life, and therefore more cherished in our thoughts.

And Shakespeare had oft-times felt this anxiety during the time his self-exile lasted. In his own mind he had resolved that, until he had "name and fame," he had "nothing at Stratford." Those dearly loved friends should not again look upon the unthrift younker; and unless the man redeemed the courses wild of the youth, he would no more return.

How far he had already succeeded our readers have seen; and even the little world of Stratford began to feel pride in him they had before so lightly regarded.

Master William Shakespeare, it was affirmed amongst the wiseacres of the Falcon Inn, had indited two several poems, some said three, of such exceeding merit, that they had afforded exceeding delight to the grandees and gallants of Elizabeth's court. Sonnets, too, innumerable, had fallen amongst the fair dames of the palace, like the perfumed flowers blown by the sweet south.

Nay, William Shakespeare was said to be a favourite with the Queen herself. Two plays he had also produced—plays of most exquisite fancy. The Adonis of the Court,—the "wealthy-curled darling of the land," the favourite Essex, was his personal friend. My Lord Southampton his patron. And more than this, than these, than all, William Shakespeare had made money, thriven, purchased property, become a proprietor of one of the theatres in London.

"'Fore Heaven, I wonder what made him ever go away from us?" said Master Mumble, the head-bailiff.

"I always said there was something in him," said Master Lamb.

"He was ever a clever dog though a mischievous one," said Cramboy.

"Dost think he will come back amongst us?" inquired Teazle. "Methinks I long to look upon one who hath written three poems, a whole litany of sonnets, and two masques or mysteries."

"An he do come amongst us again," said the head-bailiff, "I, for one, vote we make him master of the free school."

"Nay," said Cramboy, "I know not how far to agree with you there, before we go to such lengths, let us peruse his works; there is some difference, my masters all, between teaching one's boys their *quis*, their *quæs*, and their *quods*, and writing jingling rhymes for the amusement of the Londoners and the Court."

"Well," said the mayor, "we might make him parish-clerk. Something we ought to offer him, methinks, an he comes back amongst us. Body o' me, hath he not written two poems and a play? There be those amongst us who cannot even write their own names, much more a poem such as 'tis said this William Shakespeare hath produced."

"Hath any one seen these poems you speak of?" inquired Master Scourge.

"Truly, I believe mine host hath a copy of one brought from London by a gentleman of the Court, and left behind him. I saw it myself not a week ago and looked at the title-page, 'tis called Tarquin and Lucrece, a very clever book, if I may judge from the look of the binding."

"We will see that poem," said the bailiff; and the host, being accordingly summoned, produced a small volume, which the head-bailiff with infinite gravity, after laying aside his pipe and adjusting his spectacles, proceeded to read. Scarcely, however, had he got through one verse ere he paused and looked over his glasses at the grave auditors who sat in judgment upon the production, whilst they themselves puffed out such clouds of smoke, that it appeared they were resolved the bailiff should scarce observe the impression produced.

"You do not speak, my masters," said the head-bailiff, "have you heard?"

"Perfectly," returned Master Cramboy.

"And do you approve?" inquired the head-bailiff.

"Ahem," said the mercer, "'Speak that I may know thee,' saith the proverb; proceed;" and the bailiff read another verse.

"F e! fie!" said Master Teazle, "what stuff is here? My service to you, my masters all, and a merry Christmas. How say you now to making Master William Shakespeare master of the free school,—eh?"

"Shall I proceed any further?" inquired the head-bailiff.

"Not a line," said Cramboy. "I feel quite scandalized. What a depraved taste the Court must have! Allow me, however to look at the binding of this volume," and Cramboy quietly noted down where the book was to be bought in order that he might procure and read it as soon as he could, the rest of the company quietly following his example.

"Well," said John Peto, the tanner, "after all what is fame? Here hath our fellow-townsman gained much celebrity by such matter as we have heard. Trash, my masters; lies, conjured up by the fumes of sack and Canary. Marry, the lad hath a quick wit, I dare be sworn, but how he hath gotten himself into the good graces of the powerful by such matter I marvel."

"I remember me," said Master Richard Coomb, (who was known amongst his co-mates by the sobriquet of Thin Beard, from the circumstance of his wearing a starved cane-coloured beard), "I remember me that our townsman, John Shakespeare, father of this William, had from his youth upwards, a quick and shrewd wit. Nay, by 'ur Lady, he must be about my own age; by the same token I played oft-times with him when he was a boy and living with his father at Snitterfield."

"Aye," said Mumble, "he came to Stratford from Snitterfield. He held lands there when he was better off. Did'st know Richard Shakespeare, grandfather to this William? He was well to do, and had lands and beeves at Snitterfield."

"I did know him," returned Coomb; "that is, I do remember me of him. By 'ur Lady, a proper man of his hands as ever you would wish to look on,—aye, and a pleasant man to speak with too."

"Did not your brother, John Coomb, accommodate Master John Shakespeare, at his need, with moneys, not long back?" inquired Cramboy.

"In sooth did he," returned Thin Beard, "more than once, I can tell thee."

"And did I not hear that John Coomb pressed him hard for repayment, and would have clapped him up in jail but for the debt being defrayed by this poet of our's,—this William his son,—so soon as he became aware of it?"

"Nay, 'tis true enough," said Thin Beard; "I may not deny that my brother doth press hard for moneys due."

"Go to," said Mumble; "we all know John Coomb and his usances well enough without your confession. 'Tis creditable to Master William Shakespeare, and he hath shewn himself a good son, albeit he hath been given to courses wild. I like him better for his befriending his father than for his poetry."

"Come," said the head bailiff, laying down his pipe, and rising from his chair, "Let us drink the health of our good townsman, since he hath so far done honour to the place of his birth. Who knows, he may do even better yet! We have not altogether approved of the production here before us, peradventure his songs and sonnets are in better taste than his lampoons. Fill, my masters, to the brim. Since the Queen delights to honour Master Shakespeare, here's his health, and may he soon return amongst us!"

And if such was the feeling entertained towards the poet by the more mechanical portion of the community of Stratford, those of higher degree felt a proportionable share of respect, since they could better appreciate his merits.

And now, having once more returned to the spot from whence we started, we must again re-visit some of the localities in and around that sweet neighbourhood. Sir Hugh Clopton having also returned from London on business of import, is once more to be seen in his old dwelling.

Since we last beheld him located there, many stirring events have transpired. His life, on the whole, has passed, since the action with the Armada, in ease and quietude. At the present moment, however, he is in some trouble, consequent upon the untoward events connected with his nephew. Nay, he has returned to London for the purpose of parting with all he possesses, so that he may but pay off the huge debts Walter Arderne has become liable for, and save him from the other difficulties he is surrounded by.

It is now far advanced in the month of September. The season is wet and dreary,—one of those unhealthy seasons which produce much sickness throughout the land. The continued rain had flooded the country around. The roads, never at this period good, are now almost impassable. The woods are wrapped in mist, and the marsh lands a perfect sea.

"The fold stands empty in the drowned field,
And crows are fatted with the murrain flocks,
The nine men's morris is filled up with mud,
And the quaint mazes in the wanton green,
For lack of tread, are undistinguishable;
Whilst on old Hyem's chin and icy crown,
An odorous chaplet of sweet summer buds,
Is, as in mockery, set."

Sir Hugh, after conferance with his man of business, is preparing in a few days again to set off for London. A journey of such extent is, however, matter of some consideration and considerable danger at such a season, with weather so unpropitious.

As the old knight looks out upon the chase, the gloom of the aspect adds to the gloom of his spirits.

Such a prospect is always calculated to beget a certain share of despondency, even in the most cheerful temper, and Sir Hugh has had enough of sorrow in his time to make him rather a grave than a merry companion.

The old knight, however, is not the man to give way to despair under circumstances like the present.

"Goods news, an Heaven will," he said, as he suddenly descried a horseman, with head bent to the saddle-bow, come spurring against the driving wind, his cloak blown into a balloon, the mire and water flying into the air as he dashed across the chase towards the mansion.

During the prevalence of heavy and continued rain, any object which enlivens the wet landscape, even in our own dull times, becomes of interest. In Elizabeth's day, when so many events of import were transpiring, and when news came but rarely to a country place, the arrival of a post (as the armed and heavily-accoutred horseman was called) was of peculiar interest. He brought, perhaps, intelligence of the danger or death of those nearest and dearest, and now heard for the first time. He bore, perchance, some secret intelligence of warning, some caution against an imminent, deadly foe, some hint to put the seas between the receiver and his native land.

To Sir Hugh the sight of the coming horseman, as he emerged from the belt of plantation, and dashed into the open chase, was fraught almost with alarm.

"God grant," he said, as he strained his eyes to observe if he could recognize the features of the rider, "that this new comer may bring me good tidings of our Walter."

The increasing gloom, however, for it was now evening, hindered the knight from recognizing the person of the horseman. He heard the clatter of the hoofs of the steed along the approach, and, as he threw open the door, the rider having dismounted, unceremoniously entered the room. The next moment his hand was caught in the iron gripe of Captain Fluellyn.

"Thou hast news, Captain," said Sir Hugh, "news of import, or thou would'st scarce have left my nephew in his captivity?"

"I *have* news, good Sir Hugh," said the Captain; "and when I have in something recovered wind enough, I will unfold it to you!"

"Good! an Heaven will," said Sir Hugh; my nephew, good Captain—?"

"Is well," returned the Captain, "and commends him to you. Nay, he is, in some sort, out of his difficulties—that is to say, in as far as the charge of treason goeth."

"Nay, then, Heaven be praised for that!" said Sir Hugh, "for the other matter, the worst is but worldly loss."

"We are not so sure of that, either," returned the Captain, "affairs have altogether taken a new turn. Your nephew hath desired my return at once to inform you thereof, so as to stop your making any sacrifice of property."

"'Fore Heaven, this doth surprise me!" said the Knight, "but come, we will hear such matter at more leisure, and after you have refreshed yourself, for you seem to have ridden far and fast since morning."

"I have," said the Captain. "I am stained with variation of each soil, 'twixt this seat of yours and the town of Oxford, and the ways are wondrous foul and hard to travel over, too. A cup of wine and a rasher will be welcome."

"You shall have the best that Clopton can afford," said the Knight, hurrying out, and calling lustily to his servants to prepare the evening meal without delay.

Accordingly, the Captain, having divested himself of his heavy riding-cloak, and removed the long petronels, rapier, and dagger from his side, was in a few minutes more seated cozily in a high-backed chair beneath the chimney, and opposite his host.

Between the pair stood a small table, plentifully furnished with several sorts of wine. A glorious log of wood blazed upon the hearth, and whilst the servants brought in the refreshments which furnished forth the evening meal, the new comer between each mouthful delivered his news to the greedy ears of his host.

"Many events of import have transpired," said he, as he at length pushed his plate from him, in token that the inner man was satisfied; "aye, and that too in the short period since you left London to arrange matters here. In the first place, I need not inform you that both yourself and Walter Arderne had a secret foe at Court."

"Of that I have long been aware," said Sir Hugh.

"Most probably," said the Captain. "A foe is generally found sooner or later, like the blind mole, by the effects of his progress; but I have unearthed this mole."

"Good," said Sir Hugh, "that's a point gained any how."

"Nay, more, I have discovered you have also a secret and powerful friend at Court, and the friend is more powerful than the foe. Witness the effects. Your nephew is released from all responsibility on the subject of the treasonable charge trumped up against him, and, as he himself bade me deliver to you, is in a fair way of getting rid also of other matters appertaining."

"And how is this derived?" said Sir Hugh. "You amaze me with so much good news. I pray you expound unto me the names of these persons who have interested themselves for and against me and mine. Set this foe before me, that I may know him, good Captain. 'Fore Heaven, I am old, but I have still some skill in fence. Thou shalt bear a cartel to the caitiff."

"It could be easily done," returned the Captain, filling his pipe and puffing out a volume of smoke.

"'Fore gad, then," said Sir Hugh, lighting a fellow pipe, and performing upon it with equal gusto, "you shall find it shall be as promptly done."

"Have you ever had personal quarrel with the Earl of Leicester?" inquired the Captain.

"None, as I am a gentleman," said Sir Hugh.

"And yet," said the Captain, "hath it been through his means that your nephew's late troubles have been brought to a serious issue, so indeed as to threaten his life as well as deprive him of his liberty."

"Were he twenty times an earl," said Sir Hugh, "he shall answer it. Thou shalt seek him, Captain, in my name, and demand the why and wherefore."

"I had much rather be excused," said the Captain, eyeing the gyrations of the smoke, and then peeping at Sir Hugh.

"How?" said Sir Hugh. "Wilt not be then my friend, good Captain? Well, be it so, I will to my good neighbour, Sir Thomas Lucy. He is a man to beard fifty earls, be they ever so powerful."

"Sir Thomas Lucy could hardly do your message either," said the Captain.

"Ha, say'st thou! Truly, then, thou knowest not the goodness and hot-valour of the knight of Charlecote; he is a true friend, and right honest. But wherefore should Sir Thomas refuse to carry a cartel to the Earl?"

"Because Sir Thomas would scarce carry a cartel to one unable to reply to it," said the Captain. "The Earl of Leicester is dead. He died two nights back at Cornbury, on his way to Kenilworth. So much I learnt as I tarried at Oxford, where, moreover, I further heard strange rumours of the manner of his death."

"Gad-a-mercy!" said Sir Hugh, "this doth indeed surprise me. What a world is this we live in. Dead, quotha! and mine enemy too! Well this is news, indeed. But then this friend at Court, good Captain? methinks I should not forget to ask for him."

"Ahem!" said the Captain. "Of that, anon. Bless me! how heavily the rain beats against the casement. Foul weather this, good Sir Hugh, for travellers. Truly the night hath come down dark, as a wolf's mouth, and ways be both foul and dangerous."

"Hast any friend on the road to-night, good Captain?" inquired Sir Hugh.

"I was consorted," said the Captain, "as far as Oxford by one who over-rode me on the way soon after leaving London, and whom I left at Oxford with a purpose of following hitherward. He is a native of Stratford, and one of pleasanter mood I never travelled withal. The man, I think, you know."

"And his name?" inquired Sir Hugh. "Come, fill your glass."

"William Shakespeare," said the Captain. "He who wrote the play we saw in London."

Sir Hugh laid down his pipe, and rose to his feet. "Is Shakespeare coming back?" he said. "'Fore Heaven, thou canst not think, my good friend the pleasure such information gives me. Thou canst not tell what I feel towards that young man—so little known, yet so well appreciated."

"Ha," said the Captain, "so have I heard you say."

"I have before named to thee," said Sir Hugh, "former passages in which my family became acquainted with this Shakespeare, and how we received an inestimable service from him in his early youth. And I tell thee now my very soul yearned to go to that man when in London and clasp him to my heart, but I was ashamed. I gave ear to the tales of his enemies; I believed him to have become worthless and an outcast in the world. And, as I shamed to take part with him in adversity, so I shame to see his face in his hour of triumph. But I love that man. Nay, I am old, Captain, but the words of his poetry, as we listened to it that night, yet ring in mine ears."

"Truly then," said the Captain, whose rough nature was in something moved, "your friendship is not ill bestowed. This Shakespeare hath bestirred himself in your nephew's favour, and procured his release from the graver charge of treason. He hath interested the Queen, through my Lords of Essex and Southampton, and hath given me a clue by which I have discovered the villany of our Stratford lawyer here, Pouncet Grasp, the secret foe through whose influence the Earl of Leicester was made instrumental. Nay, Shakespeare hath been your good friend, Sir Hugh."

"And is he in sooth coming back to Stratford?" said Sir Hugh, rubbing his hands. "In prosperity or adversity, he shall be welcome as if he were mine own son."

"Truly," said the Captain, "I can in some sort almost feel the same towards this friend of thine, for never travelled I with one who so cheered the long miles 'twixt post and post. He was right pleasant and facetious all the miry way 'twixt Acton and Oxbridge. I wished the miles twice as long whilst we pricked across the waste land towards Beaconsfield. Neither wind nor rain, or mud or mire, could alter his merry mood, as, by night, we made our way towards Walting Town; and when we lost our route, and were nearly drowned in the marshes of Abingdon, he turned our danger into a jest. Nothing came amiss to this Shakespeare; he had a saying for every mistake, and a good word for every misfortune."

"Such a comrade," said Sir Hugh, "were worth something on a journey."

"Nay, Sir Hugh," returned the Captain, "I have travelled far and near, yet never met I with such another. By 'ur Lady, I have consorted with your Dane, drank with your Hollander, revelled with your Frenchman, and fought with your Spaniard, yet none did I ever find who could hold comparison with this man."

"I marvel you came not on further together," said Sir Hugh, "since you so well relished his companionship."

"He tarried, as I told you, at Oxford," returned the Captain, "where it seems he had appointed to meet other company. Nay, I myself also tarried one night at Oxford, to rest my horse. We put up at the hostel of the Crown, and, in sooth, a merrier night I never spent withal. This Shakespeare hath a peculiar art. He made himself familiar amidst the various guests, and drew them out to exhibit themselves after the most exquisite fashion. Nay, the hostess of the Crown was herself a woman of exceeding wit and beauty, and seemed to relish the society of the player."

"I know that hostel," said Sir Hugh. "'Tis kept by one Davenant; and the hostess is indeed, as you say, 'a most sweet wench.'"*

CHAPTER LIX.

KENILWORTH.

Our readers, we doubt not, have for some time entertained a shrewd suspicion regarding the somewhat indistinct character latterly flitting about amongst the *dramatis personæ* of our story. The Lady Clara de Mowbray, in her own proper person, has of late been but little seen in the twisted and ravelled skein of this history.

* There is an anecdote extant in Oxfordshire, of the intimacy subsisting between this hostess and Shakespeare Shakespeare is said to have always rested at the Crown, at Oxford, whilst *en route* from London to Stratford.

The fortunes of him who is enshrined in all hearts, has of necessity thrown all minor characters into the shade.

Nevertheless, the doings of so exquisite a creature as Clara de Mowbray, are worthy of the contemplation of our readers, for both in station and disposition she was considerably elevated above the ordinary fragments of the world.

She was a being in whom the best elements were mingled that she might well have been the worshipped idol of the noblest of the other sex. And yet have we seen this female, by one of those curious chances so common in real life, left alone almost in the world, steering her course across the ocean of adventurous deeds, unknown, and, apparently, unappreciated. And is not this oft-times the case? Do we not oft-times see in the world the most paltry portions of humanity, the most impudent and assuming? The most common-place, the most vain, and the most unworthy, exacting the most homage? Nay, succeeding in life better than the good and virtuous?

Clara de Mowbray was one worthy of an emperor's love; a creature we do occasionally, but rarely, meet with in the world; a sort of descended angel amongst mortals, sent apparently as the pattern, the model, for the baser worldlings to "dress themselves by." The world, however, would perhaps be likely to censure Clara, and her virtues to stand her but as enemies—her innocence and her regardlessness of form and ceremony, her recklessness of paltry opinion, be considered unmaidenly and bold! and so might the world think and say, for Clara possessed a spirit as undaunted in the resolve to carry out her projects as she was pure in heart and beautiful in person. If she had a fault it was her unbended determination to go through with any thing she once undertook. She was the creature of romance too, and altogether would have been better suited for a more romantic age than that in which she lived. Albeit her own times gave some scope for the exercise of her peculiarities.

We have seen that from childhood she had loved Arderne; she had had so many opportunities of observing his excellence and worth, that spite of her better reason, and against hope, she had loved. It was one of those unselfish passions which hopes all for the being beloved, and nothing for self. She knew that the object of her thoughts had been engaged elsewhere, that his affections were buried in the tomb of Charlotte Clopton, but that altered not her feelings towards him a jot. Whilst he lived, it was something to breathe in the same hemisphere; and to add to his happiness and prosperity, even by stealth, was her study.

Hence have we seen her in disguise seeking to deliver him from the horrors of captivity or starvation on a desolate shore. Herself enduring the extremity of mishap, and then rescued from captivity of the Spaniard. Hence have we seen her bequeathing, in the event of her own death, all she possessed upon the one so beloved, and hence have we seen her, and her extraordinary disposition revelled in such a situation, the disguised comrade, and then the guest of the wonderful man whose course of life it has been our task to follow. And hence we find her, up to the present period of our story, still bending all her energies to restore the fortunes and happiness of Walter Arderne.

In all things, however, Clara de Mowbray, as we have before hinted, chose to follow her own notions comparatively unknown, certainly she thought unloved by the object of her affections. She shrank from all idea of being recognised as the benefactor of Arderne, lest he should consider himself bound to tender her the devotion of the life she had sought to save. She pursued, therefore, an extremely cautious and erratic mode in all her proceeding. Even Shakespeare, the friend, the wonderful man who had saved her from the Spaniard, she feared entirely to place confidence in. The poet, however, had carefully studied the character of this beautiful female, resolved to thwart her ultimate intentions regarding herself, and if possible, to make her happy.

How strangely then flows the tide of human events. Clara de Mowbray alive, in health, and the real possessor of enormous wealth, was apparently dead to the world as to herself, her affections she thought unrequited. On the object of those affections she had conferred all her worldly goods, and herself she had intended to dedicate to Heaven.

She was a Catholic, and she meant, as soon as she saw all her schemes in a fair way of completion, to seclude herself from the world. She had arranged matters so as to retire to a convent in Navarre. With Arderne the case was as singular. This youth, so much thought of for his excellent disposition, albeit he mourned the beautiful Clara as one dead, adored her memory as a reality, and, had he suspected her of being in life, would have put a girdle round the earth to find her out.

> "Love like a shadow flies, when substance love pursues,
> Pursuing that that flies, and flying what pursues.,'

And that such should be the case,—that the melancholy Walter should become enamoured of what seemed but a shadow, is not surprising in a man of his disposition. The splendid domains he had succeeded to, the romance of the situation altogether, his remembrance of the sometime heiress of these broad lands, at last caused him to be so enamoured of her bare memory that the subject of her beauty formed the entire subject of his thoughts. It seemed to him that she haunted each dell and glided about the stately halls of her fore-fathers, sighed in the winds which swept around the battlements of her ancestry; and, indeed, pervaded every spot around the woods and groves she had conferred upon him. The remembrance of his former love was by a newer object quite obliterated. The good Walter, in short, became a sort of dreamy person. For hours together would he stand in the long gallery at Shottery, and contemplate the picture of Clara de Mowbray; and had not Grasp's machinations, by driving him from these thoughts and from possession of the domains, driven him from the haunts that engendered them, he would most probably have become a melancholy maniac or a misanthrope.

Clara de Mowbray had in her early youth, beside the unfortunate Charlotte Clopton, one other dear and valued friend, the unhappy Countess of Leicester. This beautiful woman, whom the dark Earl had become enamoured of whilst her first husband was alive, he was reported to have "played most foully for." He was said, indeed to have poisoned Walter, Earl of Essex, in order to gain her hand.

The sorrowful Countess, who had ample leisure to repent of her second marriage, had been greatly attached to Clara, and frequently when she could escape from the splendid cares, "the glistering grief," of her own home, had been wont to pour her sorrows into the ear of the heiress. She had consequently been the only person, except the eccentric Martin, who was the entire confident of Clara. She had known of her attachment, and also had been privy to her adventure in search of her lover; she also knew of her determination to retire from the world if she succeeded, and in common with the world, she imagined Clara had perished in the attempt; but as she had been sworn to secresy by her young friend, ere she departed, so she had faithfully kept counsel.

Now, however, but a few days before the Earl of Leicester's death, to her astonishment, in the disguised individual who sought her at Kenilworth, the Countess beheld her dearly-loved friend, accompanied by the long lost Martin. How they had escaped from shipwreck and all the "portance of their travelled history," the Countess had small time to learn, for soon after their arrival she herself was summoned to the sick Earl at Cornbury Park.

The Countess, however, had granted Clara the boon she asked,—a letter to the Queen in favour of Arderne; and this letter, together with the applications of Essex and Southampton, had procured Walter's release; after which, together with the faithful Martin, Clara again sought retirement at Kenilworth.

And, oh! if that splendid record of pride and power could have spoken, what tales of sorrow and suffering, as well as of grandeur, what proofs of unbridled power could it have told. Those magnificent buildings of Leicester, where such princely revels had been held—how could they have uttered forth a wailing lament over the wickedness of unchecked and headstrong will! Those gaudy and tapestried chambers, the last built, the first to go to decay—how well could they have divulged the whispered deceit of human nature, the cunning and the baseness of the *parvenu* Earl who reared them!

For one hour those rooms had "blazed with light, and bray'd with minstrelsy," how many dark and melancholy weeks had they to tell of, whilst sorrow and whispered horror, and surmise that "dared not speak its fear," had reigned there! How had the very domestics feared the descending shadows in those vast rooms, and where the night-shriek "disturbed the curtain sleep!" Deeds of evil note had had their reign in those chambers. The wail of sorrow had been heard oft-times in the long winter's nights, in the dungeons of that castle; and, even to her who was the mistress there, that bright castle-lake, the fair scene without, all had been looked upon from those arched windows with eyes that marked not their beauty,—she, who was the wife of their possessor, slept there in fear.

Through the instrumentality of Essex and Southampton, on becoming better known to those chivalrous men, Arderne had been so much liked, that they had introduced him to the Queen; and Elizabeth was so struck with his handsome form and gallant bearing, that she had taken him into favour, and employed him in her service.

The national spirit of England had been so much aroused by the Spanish invasion, that nothing less than some attempt at retaliation would satisfy the people. Don Anthonia, titular King of Portugal, was a suppliant at the English Court for assistance to establish him on the throne of his ancestors; and as Elizabeth rather relished the policy, albeit she liked not the cost of such a measure, she gave leave to her subjects to fit out an expedition for the liberation of Portugal from the Spanish yoke, always providing they did it at their own proper charge, she lending them ships of war.

This expedition the valiant Arderne resolved, at a hint from the Queen, to join; and, Albeit he was forbidden to have anything to do with it by the doating Queen, the rash and headstrong Essex also resolved to play the knight-errant, and, escaping from the silken fetters of his courtly mistress, as a simple volunteer accompany the expedition.

Clara de Mowbray, meantime, was the guest of her early friend, Lettice, Countess of Leicester, at Kenilworth; the Countess, during the period of her mourning, being resident at the castle. Some three weeks had passed away since the Earl's death, and even in that short space, many events had transpired. Arderne was released from all graver charges; Grasp, although discomfited, terrified and conscience-stricken, was still endeavouring to make a good fight for his client; and Shakespeare was returning to his wife and family. True to his resolve, after his own return to Stratford-upon-Avon, Grasp as soon as he recovered himself, had hastened to Charlecote with intelligence that the "sometime deer-stealer" was at length forthcoming, and would but Sir Thomas give fresh instructions, he, Grasp, would still pursue the delinquent, and bring him to condign punishment.

Sir Thomas had, however, entirely changed his opinion upon the subject of the offence, it appeared. He had also changed his opinion of Grasp, and summoning his head-falconer, old Hubert, he desired him to call together several of his followers, and toss Grasp in a blanket in the park—the knight watching the operations with infinite gusto from his window.

Such happiness, therefore, as usually falls to the share of mortals in this work-a-day world, may be supposed to have fallen to the share of many of the individuals connected with our story.

In outward seeming, such was, indeed the case.

But perfect happiness is, in reality, beyond the reach of mortals. It is the green spot in the distance, and that on which we stand is ever but a sterile promontory.

" What we have not, still we strive to get,
And what we have, *forget.*"

It was one evening, about three weeks after Leicester's death, that the Countess and her interesting friend were seated in one of those magnificent apartments in the buildings to which the Earl had given his name.

Few, as we have before said, as they gaze upon this now ruined shell, can have an adequate notion of its former state and grandeur. The buildings reared by that proud Earl, almost for the sole purpose of offering to the Queen the most sumptuous entertainment ever given by subject to sovereign, seemed, indeed, reared but for that one scene of pomp and grandeur, and afterwards to have remained a sad memento of the mutability of human greatness, and then sank unnoted to decay. As they had added their sum of more to that before enormous pile, so had they, in their vastness, remained almost too spacious for a subject's means. For the castle altogether, with its numerous flanking towers, and the additions which had been made to it from time to time, seemed capable of containing an army within the roundure of its walls.

As the Countess sat with her friend in one of the magnificent apartments of Leicester's Building, she listened to the recital Clara had to give of her own escape from death, when taken prisoner by the Spaniard.

'Twas a delicious evening. The October winds sighed upon the lake without, and scattered the dried leaves from the woodland on the opposite shore. The setting sun shone like gold upon the turrets of the castle, and tinged the massive forest, as the Lady Clara glanced occasionally in the direction where lay Stratford-upon-Avon. The Countess marked that glance as she sat opposite to her friend and beneath the huge chimney, for the coldness of the season, and the size of the room, made the blazing fire upon the hearth anything but disagreeable.

"And after enduring so much," said the Countess, "you mean then, to retire for ever from the world—you will forsake him for whom you have adventured life, fortune, reputation."

"I forsake none," said Clara. "Who knows or cares for one so solitary in the world! I bequeath to him I most love, all my worldly goods—myself I dedicate to heaven."

"There is one other," said the Countess, "and whom I have heard you mention in terms of admiration and respect—will not his persuasion avail."

"He is indeeda man," said Clara, with enthusiasm, "one whose words might do much. But are you quite sure he would not rather approve than censure my resolve? He knows something of my story, but like yourself, he is bound by me to secresy whilst I remain in England."

"Listen," said the Countess, "to what this friend has to urge;" and taking from a sort of cabinet a small packet, she read the following:—

I.

"From fairest creatures we desire increase,
    That thereby beauty's rose might never die.
But as the riper should by time decease,
    His tender heir might bear his memory:
But thou, contracted to thine own bright eyes,
    Feed'st thy light's frame with self-substantial fuel,
Making a famine where abundance lies,
    Thyself thy foe, to thy sweet self too cruel,
Thou that art now the world's fresh ornament,
    And only herald to the gaudy spring,
Within thine own bud buriest thy content,
    And, tender churl, mak'st waste in niggarding,
Pity the world, or else this glutton be,
To eat the world's due, by the grave and thee.

II.

When forty winters shall besiege thy brow,
    And dig deep trenches in thy beauty's field,
Thy youth's proud livery, so gazed on now,
    Will be a tatter'd weed, of small worth held:
Then, being ask'd where all thy beauty lies,
    Where all the treasure of thy lusty days;
To say, within thine own deep sunken eyes,
    Were an all-eating shame, and thriftless praise.
How much more praise deserved thy beauty's use,
    If thou could'st answer—'This fair child of mine
Shall sum my count, and make my old excuse,'—
    Proving his beauty by succession thine.
This were to be new made, when thou art old,
And see thy blood warm, when thou feel'st it cold."

There was a pause after the Countess had read these sonnets, and which she, in common with the entire Court circle, had been delighted with when they first appeared. The beauty of the poetry, like sweet music, placed a spell upon the pair; such verse in those lordly apartments had a double influence.

As Clara gazed around upon the arrassed walls, and then glanced from the window upon the sweet scene without,—when she looked towards the home of the poet, the spirit of that man seemed to breath around. In some sort the Countess of Leicester felt this, for both these high-born ladies knew Shakespeare; his exquisite poetry had stolen over their hearts. They were of the few of their day who already appreciated him.

"Your story, Clara," said Lady Leicester, at length breaking silence, "convinces me this generous man carries with him the remembrance of some early grief—some secret sorrow never to be expressed. I feel as firmly convinced of it, as that you yourself are the excited cause of those sonnets I have just perused. The time of their production and circulation amongst us by Essex and Southampton—the circumstances under which you was rescued by this Shakespeare from the Spaniard—his discovery of your true sex, and subsequent contemplation of your exquisite disposition, Clara, all confirm it. Heaven grant thou sweetest and best of women, that this poetic friend does not himself love, and whilst he has pleaded for license to inform his friend Arderne of your secret, has not indeed felt a pang sharp as the stilleto of the Italian."

Clara started at the words of the Countess, and a slight flush suffused her cheek. The thought was, for the moment, fraught with pleasant reminiscences, but then feelings of alarm pervaded her, lest there should be in reality some truth in the suspicion of her friend. That man, so immeasurably above all other mortals, to love her—that man, whose influence seemed always to pervade every spot around her, where aught noble, refined, or chivalrous breathed—that man, without whose society, even granting she were wedded to him she loved, she must now experience a void, a blank. For be it remembered that Clara de Mowbray had, from circumstances, been the intimate, the companion of Shakespeare, knew his sentiments, been with him in the hour when poetry flowed from lip as well as pen; and that whilst she had listened, his words had produced thoughts and imaginings belonging to the fabled ages of the early world, in Crete, in Sparta, and in Thessaly.

As the Countess remarked the effect her words had produced, she arose and walked to the window. How sad, she thought to herself, that the life of one so amiable should be an aimless one! How sad, that sorrow should inhabit that form where so much grace and beauty dwelt!

Her thoughts, however, were speedily withdrawn from her friend, for at that moment the Major Domo, or steward of the Castle, his white wand in his hand, announced the arrival of a messenger from London bearing dispatches.

"News," she said, as she took the several sealed packets and examined them. "News, Clara, and from my truant son."

"The messenger, an it so please ye," said the steward, "announces the Earl is on his road hitherward, and with a goodly company."

"'Tis even so," said Lady Leicester; "he writes me word he hath returned from Lisbon, where nothing but discomfort, sickness, and mortality attended the English army. Six out of eighteen thousand having already fallen victims to the climate."

"And have you news of others present in that ill-omened expedition?" inquired Clara.

"Nothing save that some of his companions of the expedition are with him. The Queen, I find, by another packet," said Lady Leicester, "is much blamed for permitting this expedition to be undertaken at all since it has thus failed. Nay, she hath been rated by Burleigh. The royal lioness is, therefore, chafed in spirit."

"Ah! and here is another letter," continued the Countess, as she perused a somewhat curious document, as curiously worded, and after a fashion not uncommon at a period when, "in speaking of dangerous majesty," it was necessary to be guarded. The letter was brief and secret, partly in figures, and the Countess read it aloud to her friend:

"Let not 1500* gain sight of 1000 till anger subdueth, or the hot blood of 1000 will chafe at what may peradventure follow; 1500 is wrathful, and the enemies of 1000 have worked during absence; keep, therefore, valour and worth employed till matters cool. Not only hath the disobedience of 1000 offended in the expedition, but 1500 hath seen a printed volume† of *t—t's*, title to *a—a*, a device, doubtless, of some crafty knave and enemy; 50 hath been committed this day to the tower."

"I understand it not," said Clara. Albeit it is plain enough to the eye, the sense is mysterious."

"It speaks to me of danger to my gallant son," said the Countess with a sigh, "and is from a dear and true industrious friend. It means that the Queen is angry with my son, and we must, therefore, hold him here if possible. You must aid me in this Clara, and we must endeavour to make Kenilworth a pleasing prison to him for a brief space."

"Thou knowest," said Clara, "that I am thy guest under promise of strict incognito: thou knowest, dear Lettice, that I am strict in my resolve to remain unknown."

"I know thou art proud in spirit, Clara, as becomes one of the princely line of Plantagenet. But 'tis a mother who asks thee to aid her in keeping her darling son from danger. Heaven knows I have little heart for revelling just now, but something we must invent to detain Essex at Kenilworth till the danger blows over."

*Elizabeth was expressed in these letters by the figures 1500; Essex by 1000; *a—a* was the crown.

†A seditious Catholic publication, dedicated to Essex, to ruin him.

CHAPTER LX.

THE RETURN.

OUR readers must now again look upon the town of Stratford. whilst the bright mid-day sun shines upon its roof and chimneys, and glitters like innumerable diamonds upon its multitudinous windows.

With one of those sudden changes so common to our climate, the damp weather has cleared up, and turned to frost. The air is light and cheerful, and a hoary tinge is given to all around.

How sweetly rural are the quiet old towns of England, as the approaching winter begins to give us that cozy anticipation of the comforts and fire-side enjoyments to come with the snow and the bracing blast.

In Elizabeth's day, when the season was fraught with games and revels, each house in the quaint-looking street seemed to promise its hospitality. The citizens' wives, as they bustled through the street, appeared to experience this feeling. The native burghers seemed to accost each other with a more cordial greeting. The change, even in the open country, albeit it is sterile, and the "one red leaf" is all that dances on the tall tree, is so seasonable, that it is grateful. The human mortals love the coming winter. Its change seems to freshen up all around. Even the old crone, shivering in the ingle neuk, looks with a renewed feeling of pleasure upon the frosted pane, and listens to the sound of the wind without with a kind of enjoyable feeling as she turns her eye again upon the bright hearth-log. Its very crackle seems to chirp of Christmas festivities—"to tell of youthful prime," and those departed days of lusty bachelorship and maiden coyness, with all the romps and revels of the time. And then, with the changeful current of thought, as remembrance dwells upon the many departed, amidst the many known,—then comes the more sombre picture, the superstitions of the old age, the sheeted ghost, the evil genius, the witch, and the thrice-told tale of Gramarie—those cherished remembrances of the hallowed period

"Wherein the Saviour's birth was celebrated."

Stratford, so picturesque in its old-world look, so peculiarly English, is just now putting on its winter garb.

A couple of days subsequent to that on which Captain Fluellyn arrived at Clopton, whilst the inhabitants progressed the streets, they seemed once more filled with the import of recent news. Rumour, in the absence of all assured information, with all its exaggeration of circumstance, was afloat amongst them. The great difficulty amidst the variety of information was to gain the real story which had arrived.

Grasp, who had suddenly returned, had brought it; but then Grasp, who was hardly to be believed on his oath, had shut himself up the moment he arrived, and would see no one. Certain, however, it was (for everybody said it) that another desperate attempt had been made upon the life of the Queen. By some it was reported she had been stabbed; by others that she had been shot. Master Doubletongue went so far as to say that she was both dead and buried! But as such surmise amounted to treason, he was ordered by the head-bailiff to go about and deny all he had asserted, the drummer of the town being sent round with him, in order that he might proclaim himself a liar at every corner.

Those of our readers who have an eye for the picturesque can, we dare say, imagine the High Street of Stratford-upon-Avon at this season of the year, peopled thus with inhabitants clad in their quaint costume, their short cloaks, doublets, and high-crowned hats. Those respectable, dignified, and grave-looking men, progressing with an assured and stately step, cane in hand, not hurrying about, as at the present day, but greeting each other with something of ceremony in their deportment. Many of them stand in groups of three or four and discuss the news, whilst the good wives of the town, albeit they are few in number, for it was not considered over seemly for the sober sort of females to be much upon the tramp, are also to be observed in their wide-brimmed hats, mufflers and kirtles, passing and repassing along the highway.

The street altogether has, with the beetling stories on either hand, the clear frosty air, and the costumed figures, with here and there a red cloak amongst other sad-coloured suits, altogether the appearance of a winter view in an old Dutch painting.

The news is of import, and all seem impressed with it—for, in Elizabeth's day, so much importance was attached to the life of the Queen by her Protestant subjects, that men looked grave and anxious at such a rumour as the present. Public safety and the prosperity of the nation seemed to hang upon her life.

Grasp, albeit he was slightly regarded in the town, was called on several times, but no one could gain admittance at Grasp's. He seemed to have rammed up his doors against the world. He was sick, engaged, not within, not to be molested. Meanwhile, as the day passed and the evening approached, a light and gentle fall of snow seemed to herald the coming winter weather. And as light thickened, the sharp and rapid sound of an approaching horseman is heard at a distance on the Warwick road. Let us listen to the sound, as the sharp spur of that rider urges on his steed; now from a rapid trot to a gallop, and then again apparently he pulls up to a slower pace.

'Tis sweet to hear, in the still evening, the sound of hoofs on the hard road, mellowed by distance, now clattering along, loud and sharp, and now again so indistinct as to be almost lost to the ear.

One or two of the townsfolk have walked forth to meet that traveller and inquire the news, and at length he nears the suburb, spurs on his steed, and enters the inn ; an event in the annals of that place which, could the inhabitants have appreciated it, would have doubtless been sufficiently noted.

He came comparatively unknown amongst them, that horseman, unannounced even to his own family. He thought not of his own importance, he knew it not, yet not a building, could it have spoken and felt, but would, we think, have uttered a note of joy. The very bells of the old tower should have rung out a joyous peal, and the hollow steeple of the guild of the Holy Cross have cracked with the reverberation of the sound.

Nay, we can almost wonder that the inhabitants did not, one and all, go forth to greet the rider in the high-crowned hat, long boots, ample cloak, and the long petronels in his girdle, for, take him for all in all, Stratford will never look upon his like again. His capable eye glanced down the High Street, as he rode ; a tear glistened on his cheek as he beheld its well-known aspect, and then he spurred his steed, and rode up Henley Street. A few moments more and he was in the midst of his relatives. William Shakespeare had returned to Stratford-upon-Avon.

CHAPTER LXI.

THE DISCOMFITED SCRIVENER.

Grasp's return home was somewhat more sudden than he had intended. He returned indeed in an exceedingly discomfited and excited state.

His friend Dismal was the only person who had gained access to him, and that but for a few moments. During the interview, however, Dismal had gathered from Doubletongue, who also arrived in all haste, that great events had transpired in London, of one sort or other. But so extraordinary and so perturbed did both the lawyer and his friend seem, that except certain incoherent expressions about an attempt upon the Queen's life, a spectre he himself had beheld, and various allusions to poison, assassination, death, destruction, and utter ruin, Dismal completely failed in discovering the exact news the travellers had to tell, and hence the variety of reports circulated through the town. Something certainly seemed to have gone all wrong with the lawyer. His friend Doubletongue had never seen him so put out, and altogether he feared that his wits were going.

To explain the meaning of this agitated and nervous state of the worthy Stratford lawyer, we must go back a few paces in our history.

Grasp, then, it will be remembered, whilst in London, had considerably extended his practice. He had apparently involved Walter Arderne in ruin; he had even carried on his intrigues so as to make the dark Earl, he of Leicester, a party concerned in his plot. For Grasp had given the Earl a hint about certain abbey lands and a manor near Kenilworth, which would fall to the said Earl in the event of Arderne's decease. He had ferreted out the existence of a plot, by means of which he hoped to rise to great preferment; and he had succeeded in beguiling a simple-minded gentleman, resident in Warwickshire, that he was indeed the real and undisputed heir to the estates of the before-named Clara de Mowbray, and actually by bribery, and using all sorts of villany, got a verdict in such person's favour, and placed him in possession of some portion of the property.

Somehow or other, however, like the labours of the alchemist, which at the moment of projection are frequently overthrown by the bursting of some vessel containing the divine elixir, so all Grasp's schemes seemed unaccountably blown to the winds, and himself discomfited.

Acting upon wrong information, he had followed a female, who travelled in male disguise, as far as Oxford, where he lost all trace of her; and whilst he tarried at the City of Palaces, an express overtook him, with directions to hasten with all speed to Cornbury Park, where the Earl of Leicester was then lying sick, having arrived there by easy stages on the way to Kenilworth, a few days before.

Now, Grasp, since his first introduction to the Earl of Leicester, had made such considerable advances in that bad man's good graces, that the Earl had sent an express for him, in order to make some alterations in his will.

Grasp accordingly set forth, leaving directions that Sir Humphrey Graball, the gentleman who was disputing the succession of the Mowbray estates, and Master Quillett, the Temple lawyer, and with whom he had arranged a meeting at Oxford, should follow him to Cornbury. For Grasp argued very wisely, that both the matters of business apertaining to the Earl's claim, and the concoction of a new will, might be arranged at one and the same time.

The will of the sick and fallen favourite, had we space to dilate upon it, would perhaps be well worthy of contemplation. That part of it especially in which he bequeathed a costly legacy to his royal mistress —the bequest being wrapped up in a preamble of honeyed words, being not the least curious part of the document.

It was night when the Earl finished his business with Grasp, and the bleak winds of September sounded through the park of Cornbury, as the lawyer, after the interview, sat with the before-named client and the Templar, in a small apartment of the mansion. It was a dark hour, and a certain feeling of awe seemed to pervade that household.

The overgrown and fallen courtier lying helpless and hopeless, alike body and soul. His "ill-weaved ambition" shrunk to the smallest span—his parks, his walks, his manors forsaking him. His swollen body, a thing abhorrent even to himself. That beautiful Countess too, attending upon him without love; and whilst duty called her to the side of him who had so vilely used her, the selfish courtier even envying her the life and health she enjoyed.

Nothing however, could exceed the elation of Grasp. He beheld in prospect a glorious array of difficulties and litigation consequent upon the matters he was engaged in; and most of all the success of his machinations in favour of Sir Humphrey Graball, and his succession to the manors of Mowbray, promised him endless profits.

"Sir Humphrey is altogether an easy simpleton," he said, "a most weak and debile man, and can as easily be led by the nose as an ass. Ergo, I shall thrive."

Accordingly, as Grasp sat with his client discussing matters of moment, whilst they relieved their labours by occasional indulgence in the good wine of the house, amongst other papers called for, was the will of the Lady Clara de Mowbray—an instrument we have, on a former occasion seen in his possession. There is always a secret horror suitable to the time, when in some antique apartment, and, by night, men meet together to peruse the musty documents which speak the last wishes of those within the tomb, more especially when sickness and those signs which foretell the ending of mortality pervade the habitation. On this rough night

> "The owl shrieked, the fatal bellman
> Which gives the sternest good night."

Suddenly, as Grasp glanced upon that will, he became, as it were, transfixed. At the same moment a sort of hubbub seemed to pervade the house. In place of the silence which the sick Earl had commanded there was suddenly heard an opening and shutting of doors—a summons of persons in all haste, and something apparently of dreadful import in agitation.

Grasp, however, heeded it not. He seemed still engrossed with the parchment before him. He held it back at arm's length; he drew it close to his nose; he uttered an exclamation of astonishment, and the word "codicil" escaped, as one of the domestics rushed into the room to announce that the Earl was dying in fearful agony.

Without heeding the news, Grasp fled from the room, rushed to the stable, mounted his horse, and rode off for Oxford. With the will still in his hand, the excited lawyer dismounted from his steed, and strode into the tavern, where, heeding not the assembled guests, he threw himself into a vacant seat, with the air of one possessed by a demon. And, again, with fearful eye, regarded the instrument he held in his hand.

"Can such things be?" he said. "Can the dead return to life, or is it the evil one himself who thus palters with my sight and senses?'

The tavern was on this night tolerably well filled with guests. One of them, who was seated opposite to the lawyer, was a person of a most expressive and pleasant style of countenance. His conversation and wit had indeed been setting the whole assemblage, gentle and simple, in roars, during the entire evening—the host and hostess of the tavern being not the least amused.

The advent of Grasp in his perturbed state, his extraordinary grimaces, his abstracted demeanour, and his travel-stained appearance altogether, called forth from this person so many curious remarks, that the laughter which had for the moment been interrupted by his entrance was renewed tenfold at Grasp's expense, till, as on unfixing his gaze from the basilisk he seemed to hold in his hand, he looked round upon the assemblage, and then steadily regarded his tormentor, he beheld himself face to face with the old subject of his former enmity—Master William Shakespeare.

"There is no rest for the wicked," saith the old proverb; and the renewed roar which followed the expression of Grasp's countenance at this sudden recognition, was actually driving him from the room, when Doubletongue, who had followed his friend, suddenly entered, and whispered something in his ear.

"Poisoned say ye?" exclaimed Grasp, starting in surprise; my Lord of Leicester deceased — dead — defunct, and thus suddenly? Poisoned, say ye? Art sure 'tis the Countess you mean?"

"No, 'tis the Earl himself," said Doubletongue; "and your having been with him just before, together with your sudden departure, hath raised a suspicion among the household that——"

"'Fore heaven, what mean ye?" said Grasp. "They surely suspect not that I had ought to do with the poisoning of my Lord of Leicester? There must have been some dire mistake in the matter. 'Fore heaven, I shall be hanged through this mistake!" and Grasp immediately left the room, bribed the ostler to procure him a fresh horse, and set off with all speed towards Stratford-upon-Avon.

Scarce had he gained a dozen miles when he came up with a couple of riders progressing the same road as himself. Company was ever welcome in those days, and the horsemen gladly acceded to his request to be allowed to ride in their escort.

The habitual caution of the lawyer, however, caused him to cast certain searching glances at his companions as often as the moon's light gave him opportunity of doing so, and ere long he became almost confirmed in the belief that in one of the armed riders he was accompanying he had fallen in with the identical female in male apparel whom he had before been in search of. There was comfort, at all events, in this supposition, and as they emerged from the dark covert of a wood they had been progressing through, he managed to push his horse between them and gain a good look at their features. And here again Grasp apparently beheld that which renewed his former perturbation. The face of the rider he first encountered wore the actual expression of one he had reason to believe had long been dead, and as he turned his startled glance upon the other, he beheld the exact lineaments of Clara de Mowbray. Pale she looked, as if her features were of sculptured alabaster; but as she turned her countenance full upon him, he could not be mistaken in their identity.

Conscience had already made a coward of Grasp—his clear spirit was puddled. The deep sea had apparently cast up the dead to discomfort him, and clapping spurs to his steed, he fled onwards on his route towards Stratford-upon-Avon.

CHAPTER LXII.

OLD FRIENDS.

Our story now draws towards conclusion, and we once more return to the point from which we at first started. Clopton Hall, after so many years of gloom, may now be said to have quite resumed that appearance of hospitality and prosperity as when we first beheld it in the early passages of our story, and ere disease, death, and misery, had so prevailed there.

For the first time for many years its rooms and offices, its stalls, kennels, and falconries, were all tenanted. After so many vicissitudes and strange events, in which its inmates had been separated, and became wanderers in the world, such of them as were in being were again assembled within its old walls.

The coming Christmas, that season so ceremoniously observed at the period, promised again to be the harbinger of festive scenes and old world rites of hospitality.

The old knight, for the first time for many years, seemed really to hold up his head, and glance around him with feelings of pride and contentment. His dearly beloved nephew was again with him; he had just come from over sea with Essex, and having left the Earl on the road towards Kenilworth, had galloped forward to Clopton.

In addition to this, too, which seemed to give Sir Hugh as much content as astonishment, that tried old friend, the trusty and shrewd Martin, who had so long been mourned as dead there, had suddenly reappeared at Clopton.

The old knight could scarce contain himself within bounds as he looked upon the pair. 'Twas hardly to be thought of, so much of contentment, after having so long been a lonesome mourner; for one way or other, Sir Hugh had now been in trouble so many years, that his happiness almost alarmed him, lest something should turn up to mar it afresh.

It was on the evening of the day on which we have introduced our readers to the inmates of Kenilworth that Martin and Arderne, together with others connected with our story, were seated beneath the hospitable roof of Sir Hugh.

To describe the unmixed pleasure experienced by these good and amiable friends on that evening exceeds the power of our pen; albeit we may attempt to describe some portion of the conversation which took place. Few things, we opine, are more gratifying than to glance upon a circle of true friends, so bound together as the ones in question, and on this occasion the party consisted of some half-dozen individuals, for, besides those we have already named, the circle contained the worthy Captain Fluellyn, and, "though last, not least," William Shakespeare sat a guest beneath that old chimney.

'Twas indeed a goodly fellowship, and in which, though perhaps 'tis a rare thing to say, where six mortals quaffed a loving cup together, not a particle of envy, hatred, or uncharitableness, pervaded.

The divine expression of Shakespeare's face, as he sipped the ruby liquor, the noble countenance of Arderne, as he glanced first at one and then another of the friends around, the excitement of the old host, as he pushed the cup about, the quaint look of the shrewd Martin, and the bluff, jovial style of the sea captain, as he puffed away at his capacious pipe, our readers must imagine. They sat in a circle round the huge log upon the hearth, and each and all had something to relate or something to listen to of stirring interest, for as each spoke of his own adventures, 'twas as if some brother told the tale.

"Your story, good Martin," said Shakespeare, as Martin paused after telling some portion of his adventure and escape from the Spaniard, "on mine own authority I would hardly dare avouch. 'Tis like some of those events in real life which scarce pass even in fiction."

"I dare be sworn on't," said Martin. "'Tis an over credulous and yet unbelieving world this, an' I may so word it, a mad world, my masters, and yet, ha, ha, 'tis a pleasant world, too. Aye, and this not altogether so bad a way of passing the time in't. What says the song,

"'Tis merry in hall when beards wag all,
And welcome merry Christmas."

"I pr'ythee, good friend," said Arderne, "continue the narrative of this tragedy; for I must needs call that a tragedy which comprehends the loss of so exquisite a lady as Clara de Mowbray."

"Aye, truly so," said Martin; "that was a sigh, indeed, Master Walter. Sighing, however, is of little avail when the object is beyond reach. 'Tis too true an evil; the Lady Clara is lost to us."

"Thou did'st, however, aid her escape from that burning carrick?" said Fluellyn, "and in which, indeed, we all suffered with those we saw suffer. "Twas a fearful sight."

"I take some credit to say I did so," returned Martin, dallying with his glass, and looking at the red flame of the fire through the ruby liquor. "Ah, ah, methinks I see those overweening Dons grilling in their treasure ship at this moment. I did aid in the lady's escape by the same token, I myself caused the conflagration that aided our escape; I myself, in my immaculate valour, destroyed the enemy. as Drake hath it, I singed the Dons' whiskers with a vengeance. Ha, ha."

"Tell us the manner of the exploit," said Shakespeare, who, by the way, had heard it from other lips.

"In few, then," said Martin, "and to continue from where I left. You are to know that the commander of the carrick no sooner beheld us upon his deck than he was about to cast us off again, and into the roaring sea. As he seized, however, upon my companion in misfortune, lo! you, he discovered he had prisoner of a female. The stately Don upon this steadily regarded his prisoner, and became struck all on a heap with her beauty. He then transferred his gaze to me, and (albeit he saw nothing extremely feminine, or even beautiful in my outward form) he was pleased to extend his clemency to us both. In few the blood of the Castillian was inflamed at the sight of the exquisite Clara; and, whilst the two ships lay glaring upon each other, we were both hurried down below, there to remain till more leisure should enable the magnifico to pay personal attention to us. My fate, doubtless, was to have been the sea. My companion's, perhaps, even worse. Whatever fate, however, was in store for us at the hands of the Don, we determined in no wise to submit to it. The cabin in which we were confined had a window in rear of the carrick. Without that window hung a boat. My companion got into that boat, and after I myself had lighted a bonfire in the cabin, and placed several barrels of gunpowder in very dangerous proximity thereto, I managed to lower that boat after getting into it, and finally, to cut her adrift. The blow-up of the barrels, and the gloom of the coming night, effectually diverted attention from our frail craft, as we mounted upon the crest of wave after wave. As we did so, we were horrified spectators of the scene of terror we had caused. One moment the burning ship was lifted on high, like some huge beacon, and the next lost in the deep valley of waters. Thus did we escape, for that time, the death and dishonour that awaited us, and, weak and debile ministers, destroyed our foes at one and the same time. But oh," continued Martin, "conceive us, my masters all, wanderers upon that vast heaving world, in a rotten carcase of a boat—no knowledge where to steer for, no knowledge how to steer, if we knew where to steer—no expectation but death. Do I not seem to ye like one sitting here telling of things imagined in a dream? That heaving water, in which our boat could scarce live — those roaring winds, which almost stopped our very breathing in their violence—that lady, whose form every sea drenched, and who for two long nights endured this extremity of dire distress."

"And died she so?" inquired Arderne.

"Not a whit," said Martin. "Her's was a miserable strait to be reduced to; but her spirit was great. She had scarce time to die. She helped me to bale out the waters, as they continually washed into our boat. She shared my small portion of biscuit with me, and she drank from the flasket I filched from the cabin when we escaped from the ship; and so she lived, good sir, lived to be picked up in the dreary waste of waters. For, look ye, we had constructed a sort of sail, when the wind moderated, and that betrayed us to the companion of the carrick we had burned. Yes, we were descried and picked up by another Don, commanded by another courageous Captain of Compliments, and forthwith carried off to the country of the Spaniard."

"And that lady," said Arderne. "Pr'ythee, good Martin, follow out your story. Her fate I dread to ask, and yet would learn."

"Nay," said Martin, archly, "methinks mine own fate might in some sort interest my hearers. But truly I seem not to command much attention in this story of adventure: and yet I showed myself courageous, and aided the weaker vessel too."

Shakespeare smiled, and a look passed between him and Martin. "'Tis the duty of doublet and hose to show itself courageous to petticoat, he said." "We are naturally given to pity the young and beautiful, rather than the strong and sturdy. Besides, thou hast escaped, art here to avouch it thyself."

"And so may that lady, for aught I know to the contrary," said Martin.

"How!" exclaimed Arderne. "Escaped! Methought she died, died in Spain."

"It may be so," said Martin, "but I never said it. When we arrived in Spain, we were both clapped up as heretics between the walls of the Inquisition, where, doubtless, I for one should have died upon the rack, but that I was eventually made useful at the oar. My companion's fate I cannot further avouch. I myself was rescued whilst helping against my will, to invade my native land, amongst other galley slaves. The craft we worked in was captured by one of Frobisher's vessels, and in that vessel I was forthwith carried to the Indies after the fight, and in that vessel have I returned; and here I am once more at Clopton."

"Nay then," said Arderne, if such be the case, thou hast but momentarily raised my hope and dashed it again, good Martin. Had that lady lived, and were I of all kingdoms king, I would give all for but one scattered smile of one so excellent."

The narration of Martin caused a sudden check to the previous hilarity of the company, since it recalled to most there the loss of kindred or relatives in former days.

Shakespeare, as he glanced around, remembered former scenes of mingled grief and joy in that house; the melancholy of Arderne was a melancholy of his own, the sundry contemplation of his mishaps and misfortunes, founded, as he then thought, principally upon the loss of one, who when alive, was unappreciated; whilst the captain and Martin also, in pure melancholy and troubled brain puffed away at their pipes with double vigour.

"Come," said Sir Hugh, who observed this gloomy fit stealing over his party, "we trifle time when we sorrow for what is past and irrevocable. It draws toward supper time. Remember, neighbours and friends, this is the first time of our meeting together after long years and much misery. Gloom shall not hold sovereign sway over Clopton again, an I can drive it hence. "Music ho!" he said, rising and clapping his hands. "'Fore heaven, nephew, we will e'en be jovial to-night. Have we not Shakespeare here, and can'st forget those scenes he furnished forth at the Blackfriars? Come, let music play, and serve the supper, lads!"

The custom of the period permitted this in the halls of the great. Many of the nobles and even gentry of condition kept up a sort of orchestra or band composed of their own domestics or servitors, and which gave a degree of enjoyment to their entertainment unknown to modern times. The sweet tones of the instruments kept off that starched etiquette, that awkward stiffness oft-times felt during the intervals of conversation, that struggle for wit that came not when called for, it filled up the evening, and the soft strains of melody engendered bright thoughts, whilst they soothed the mind at the same time. Whatever of romance is in our character is called forth at such a time by music.

And so the party sat around the festive board in their quaint costume, old and young, poet and philosopher, whilst as the musicians puffed at the French horn, and drew forth dulcet sounds from those antiquated stringed instruments, serving-men hastened about, trencher in hand, and bearing liquor on their salvers. Topics of conversation were plentiful, for still flowed the tide of interest concerning each other's separate fortunes during their career, and the jest's propriety lay in the ears of those who listened, whilst Shakespeare was the speaker.

Sir Hugh promised his friends a merry Christmas at Clopton; a Christmas observed with all due observance of the time.

In Elizabeth's day, most people, even of the higher grade of society, kept comparatively early hours. Those who dined at eleven and twelve, necessarily supped at five or six. The supper too, was the most festive meal, and most enjoyed; and when the season of the year, or old custom, gave warranty, your old English host not unfrequently kept wassail all night long.

On the present occasion the old Knight felt inclined to drink deep and sit late. He seemed resolved for a carouse. Martin and Shakespeare banded about their quaint sayings, and Sir Hugh seemed to revel in the idea of a merry Christmas at Clopton, observed with all due observance of the time; an observance, which in Warwickshire at that day was looked upon by old and young, rich and poor, with a feeling of enjoyment and love amounting to a passion. Every sport was got up with religious fervour; every old-world custom regarded with a veneration unknown to our own squalid days.

Chistmas-Day was at hand, and the old Knight talked of it like a child talks of a new toy; but whilst he spoke of good cheer and wine and wassail to set before his guests, a reeking post arrived, inviting himself and all consorting him to a feast held during the Christmas week at Kenilworth. The Countess of Leicester greeting her friend Sir Hugh, bade him welcome to her poor house of Kenilworth, to come with hawk and hound, kith, kindred and friends presently consorting him.

The Countess of Leicester was one in whom Sir Hugh had much interest. She was the daughter of his old friend, Lettice, Lady Knolleys, sister to Carey, Lord Hundsdon.

The Knight pitied her for her misfortune in marrying the evil-minded Leicester, for he had indeed loved her with a paternal affection; albeit the troublous current of his own life had lately hindered him from seeing much of her.

Under these circumstances, Sir Hugh felt delighted with the invitation, and resolved, if his party agreed, to accept it.

"How say ye, lads," he said, "shall we to this feast? Methinks I should like hugely to visit Kenilworth, and my charming friend, after so many years of absence. How say ye, Walter, shall we dine once more beneath the towers of old John of Gaunt, and Geoffrey Clinton?"

The company, as a matter of course, left it to their entertainer to accept or refuse, as he thought best.

"I am for a revel and a brawl any how," said Martin, "now I have come once more to a Christian land. Be it at Clopton or Kenilworth, all's one to Martin."

And so the party resolved to join in the Christmas revels at Kenilworth.

CHAPTER LXIII.

WHICH ENDS THIS STRANGE EVENTFUL HISTORY.

The festival held at Kenilworth on occasion of Christmas-tide, was not on such an extended scale as on former occasions had been customary there, when Norman kings feasted and kept wassail, and when "kettle-drum and trumpet brayed out the triumph of their pledge."

In Elizabeth's reign, however, when a noble held a festival in his own halls, the entertainment was sufficiently magnificent, and conducted with all the observances of older times.

The late demise of the dark Earl, of necessity curtailed the hospitalities: yet, still the enjoined rites of the period gave the Countess an excuse for some circumstance, some little pageantry of the season. Her brilliant son, too, "the glass of fashion and the mould of form," was to be with her. And, albeit the party she invited to meet him was but small, still it was composed of some of the *élite* of the country round. Almost all entertainments of this period partook of the dramatic character, the taste for such was universal; and it seemed, indeed, as if he who was in reality to create the drama in England, had sprung up just at this period to supply the want of that which was so imperfect, to substitute his own brilliant conceptions for those heavy long-winded stupid exhibitions then in vogue.

With all her power of persuasion, the Countess had not been able to persuade her friend, Clara de Mowbray, to promise her presence and participation during the intended festivities. All she could obtain being a promise, that, as that lady's departure was fixed to take place in a few days, she would remain over Christmas-eve; as on that night the Countess had invited Shakespeare to be present.

The fair Clara had before taken leave of her friend the poet in Stratford; but still, to see him at Kenilworth, and during the gaieties enacted there, would, she felt, be a great treat.

The Countess resolved to receive her son in the great hall of the Castle, an apartment which, those who have carefully perused the building will doubtless remember,—eighty-six feet long by forty-five in width. It had, some few years before, beheld those fierce vanities, what time Leicester, "with pomp, with triumph, and with revelling," entertained the Queen and her followers for seventeen successive days; and now, all in that lighted hall was green with holly and winter ornaments. The large bow window was festooned with "rarest misletoe," the various arms and trophies were covered with green boughs, whilst the white-hall, the presence-chamber, and other rooms of which nothing now remains but the fragments of walls and the staircases which led to them, were lighted up and ornamented for the nonce. There is ever something cheering in the aspect of all around at this period of the year; something bright and joyous in the country, when old Hyems "with his icy crown," seems to wield his severe sceptre and pervade the scene; when cottage and castle, lake and forest,—all are bound down by the sharp and biting frost. The good fellowship of the world seems then more rife, and Christian feeling and brotherly love to prevail. Perhaps, the good cheer enjoyed, and expectation of more to be enjoyed, openeth the heart of men. At Kenilworth, all was hospitality. The Countess was soon to give up possession to Ambrose, Earl of Warwick, her late husband's brother; and she resolved to quit the neighbourhood in no niggardly fashion. Butts of ale were broached for the poor in the villages and hamlets around, and oxen and sheep were roasted. The young Earl was expected on the eve of Christmas-day, and his popularity was just then so great, especially in that neighbourhood, that the coming of royalty itself could scarce have made a greater sensation.

The day was one of excitement to the Countess. Dearly she loved that brilliant Noble, and well she knew the dizzy pinnacle on which he stood. Her fears even then anticipated that ruin which was to ensue. Conversant with "the art o' the Court," and the dangerous mood of Majesty, she saw already a dark cloud in perspective. Nay, that which she was now about to do, namely, to receive her son, and entertain him beneath the towers of Kenilworth, when it came to be known, would be attended with danger. The Queen liked not interference with her pleasures or her purposes. She was at that moment seeking to beguile the tedium of the favourite's absence by visiting the seats of her different nobles; and during which her irritability was but too apparent. He, the adored, the magnificent, should on his arrival in England, have bent the knee in all haste, and asked pardon for his truant disposition. But he was haughty and rash as his queenly relative. The day had been one of excitement to the fair Countess. There is ever something to be thought of and arranged, even by the great. The Earl was to dine *en route* with his array at Rugby, and afterwards ride forward to Kenilworth, so as to join the select friends invited to meet him. In Elizabeth's day nothing was more thought of than dancing and playing (says Rowland White), and the invitation given by Lady Leicester might have parodied that of Capulet to his friends. There came Sir John de Astley and his wife and daughters, the noble knight of Clopton and his friends consorting, the Lord de la Warde and his beauteous sisters, the Lady widow of Lord Falconberg, good Master Murdake and his neices, Sir Thomas Lucy and his lovely daughters, the Lady Wolvey, and the lively Throckmorton. These guests, for the most part, were in the castle, but more were expected as the evening advanced.

Mistress Bridges, the most beautiful of the Queen's maids of honour, she whom Essex loved, and of whom the Queen was so jealous that she is said to have publicly struck her; Blount, too, the lover of the Countess of Leicester, and the Lady Katharine Howard, all were expected to grace the assemblage. And, at length, as the Countess and her guests awaited the hour in the great hall, the trumpet from the gate-house announced the Earl's arrival.

It was a brilliant sight to behold;—that gallant youth amidst the associates he brought with him. The magnificent Essex, looking some paladin of romance, came forth from amidst the glittering band, and gracefully saluted his handsome mother. A something regal was in his look, which suited well with that magnificent hall.

Nay, 'twas almost the last occasion on which those buildings entertained so noble an assemblage: they seem to have afterwards fallen to decay, as though later times and fashions would be unsuited to their grandeur—as though their work was done—their hour passed away.

On this night, however, as Essex and his followers entered, there came one individual with a somewhat smaller party, whose presence was more worthy of note than even the Plantagenet Kings who had dwelt there—one whose name would live

"Spite of cormorant devouring time,
The heir to all eternity."

He passed on with Sir Hugh Clopton and others of lesser note; and after exchanging a few words with the noble hostess, he perused the assembled company at his leisure. As he did so, he entered the building called the White Hall, and stood for a moment to gaze upon all around, for such a scene was likely to make a deep impression upon his mind. Softly the sounds of music floated through those vast rooms, and where all he beheld spoke of the past, and conjured up scenes he has himself impressed upon us all. For when, indeed, doth sweet music in lordly chambers, or in solitude, steal upon the ear, but imagination bodies forth those scenes which Shakespeare, and Shakespeare alone, is identified with. All the poetry of life is associated in those charming ideas. The man himself seems to glide around us. At such hour—assembled amidst the lovely and the high-born, amidst minstrelsy and lighted halls, there doth his glorious spirit seem to pervade.

And so Shakespeare passed on amidst the company, and quietly took his way through the gorgeous rooms.

It was evident the poet had before visited those chambers, for he appeared familiar with the various passages he passed through, till at length he reached a room at the extremity of the buildings. Here he stopped, and quietly regarded the apartment, which in its magnificent style might well have furnished forth the description he has left us in his own Cymbeline, for Shakespeare adopted in many of his descriptions the costume of the time.

Whilst he stood, a small door opened, and a figure, lovely as his own Juliet, advanced towards him. It was Clara de Mowbray! She uttered an exclamation of joy when she beheld the poet, and in an instant was at his side. The poet took her hand and led her to a seat, and the pair held converse together for some time.

Whilst they did so, it was evident the tongue of that poor player made some impression on his fair hearer.

"Marriage is a matter of more worth, lady," he said, as he at length rose from his seat; "than to be dealt in by attorneyship. You consent to an interview with my friend."

Clara, whose eyes were bent upon the ground in deep thought, glanced quickly upon Shakespeare. There was no mistaking the expression of that face. He was gazing upon her with feelings of mingled admiration and regret. The next moment, as if unwilling again to meet her glance, he turned and hastily left the apartment.

A few minutes more, and the Countess of Leicester entered the room, accompanied by a tall cavalier, clad in mourning costume. The sad expression, however, which for many months had suited with his habit, now however gave place to surprise, joy and admiration; and Walter Arderne beheld the living original of the portrait his eyes had loved to dwell upon. He knelt at the feet of Clara de Mowbray.

Our story is now so far ended. The sequel may be gathered "by what went before." Time and space alloweth not of dilation upon the gay revel held that night in the halls of Kenilworth. Shakespeare, whose mind was but ill-fitted for revelry, soon afterwards left the castle.

For some reason, which we are unable to explain, he felt unfitted for society. He left the hall of Kenilworth, and in the free air gave vent to the feelings with which he was oppressed. In the woods of Stoneleigh, the dawn found him, despite the coldness of the season, laying along "under an oak, whose boughs were mossed with age," and "high top-bald with dry antiquity." And as his eye glanced from heaven to earth—from earth to heaven, whilst the deer swept by,* his imagination bodied forth the forms of Jaques and Rosalind in Arden.

About a fortnight subsequent to the revel at Kenilworth, a noble-looking cavalier, accompanied by a lady (both mounted and attended by a numerous retinue,) rode on to the green before old Hathaway's cottage at Shottery. The cavalier and the lady dismounted, and left their horses with the attendants, and as they approached the cottage, they conversed upon the subject of some dearly-loved friend.

* Amongst the few traditions concerning Shakespeare, in Warwickshire, there is one which was kindly communicated to me by a nobleman resident there, namely, that he wrote the character of Jaques, in the park of Stoneleigh.

"I offered him," said Walter Arderne, "in your name, dearest Clara, half of what we possess, so he would but remain with us here; but the spirit of the man is great, and he will pursue his fortunes after his own fashion. Listen to what himself says;" and Arderne produced a letter, which he read an extract from, worded somewhat thus:—

"The portion of time I have spent amongst my companions of the theatre has made me desire to continue in my vocation. The success I have already achieved gives warranty to my expectations. I have friends, to, as thou knowest, amongst the nobles of the Court; and the spirit of my father, which I think is within me, leads me to think I can yet go on towards even a higher fortune than this that I have reached. In few, I could not with contentment at this period of my life sit down here in Stratford. My residence will be at my old haunt, where I shall hope yet to see those I so dearly love."

"In London, then, we will see him, Walter," said the lady.

"We will so," returned Arderne. "After our marriage, Clara, we will yet hope to visit our friend."

And should our readers also wish to visit the poet, amidst his associates of the theatre in London, we will also follow him to his old haunt in Paul's.

THE END.

H. T. COOKE AND SON, PRINTERS, HIGH STREET, WARWICK.

www.ingramcontent.com/pod-product-compliance
Lightning Source LLC
LaVergne TN
LVHW010205110826
845151LV00002B/614

* 9 7 8 1 4 2 5 5 3 6 0 1 5 *